Spain 1833–2002
People and State

MARY VINCENT

OXFORD
UNIVERSITY PRESS

OXFORD
UNIVERSITY PRESS

Great Clarendon Street, Oxford OX2 6DP

Oxford University Press is a department of the University of Oxford.
It furthers the University's objective of excellence in research, scholarship,
and education by publishing worldwide in

Oxford New York

Auckland Cape Town Dar es Salaam Hong Kong Karachi
Kuala Lumpur Madrid Melbourne Mexico City Nairobi
New Delhi Shanghai Taipei Toronto

With offices in

Argentina Austria Brazil Chile Czech Republic France Greece
Guatemala Hungary Italy Japan Poland Portugal Singapore
South Korea Switzerland Thailand Turkey Ukraine Vietnam

Oxford is a registered trade mark of Oxford University Press
in the UK and in certain other countries

Published in the United States
by Oxford University Press Inc., New York

British Library Cataloguing in Publication Data
Data available

Library of Congress Cataloging in Publication Data
Data available

Typeset by Laserwords Private Limited, Chennai, India
Printed in Great Britain
on acid-free paper by
Biddles Ltd., King's Lynn, Norfolk

ISBN 978−0−19−873159−7

1 3 5 7 9 10 8 6 4 2

For Paul

Acknowledgements

In an age in which British academics seem condemned to writing ever denser monographic tomes to be read by ever decreasing numbers of people, it gives me great pleasure to acknowledge the financial support received from the Arts and Humanities Research Board for the writing up of this relatively short, interpretative book. I am also indebted to the staff and students of the Department of History at the University of Sheffield who have provided a consistently stimulating intellectual environment in which I could rehearse many of the ideas elaborated here. My interest in questions of state power and violence has been furthered during conversations and seminar discussion with many colleagues, among whom I should single out Mike Braddick, who has generously shared both ideas and his book collection, and Ian Kershaw, who has encouraged this project from its inception.

Earlier drafts of sections of this book have been read by Frances Lannon, Noel Valis, and Paul Heywood. I am immensely grateful not only for the generosity with which they gave their time but also for their critiques, which were invaluable in helping me to refine and develop the arguments presented here. The analysis of legitimacy developed in the following pages owes much to the European Science Foundation Project on Occupation in Europe: the Impact of National-Socialist and Fascist Rule and I would like to thank my fellow members of team 1, above all Peter Romijn and Martin Conway. Some of the arguments found in Chapter 5 were first presented in a paper given at a colloquium led by Carolyn Boyd and José Alvarez Junco at the Centro de Estudios Políticos y Constitucionales, Madrid, and I am grateful to all who participated. I would also like to thank Kate Ferris for her help in locating some of the images.

Finally, I would like to thank my family and friends who have always reminded me that life is about more than writing history. My husband, Paul Heywood, and our children, Jessica and Thomas, have also lived with this book and have all contributed to it, though in rather different ways. The balancing act faced by every working mother has been made much easier in my case by the practical support offered by our childminder, Anthea Meakin; the love and encouragement of my parents, John and Margaret Vincent; and the intellectual and emotional companionship of my husband Paul, to whom this book is dedicated.

Contents

List of Plates

List of Maps

List of Abbreviations

ACNP	Asocación Nacional-Católica de Propagandistas: National Catholic Association of Propagandists
AP	Acción Popular: Popular Action (1931–37)
AP	Alianza Popular: Popular Alliance (1976–1987)
CCOO	Comisiones Obreras: Workers' Commissions
CEDA	Confederación Española de Derechas Autonomas: Spanish Confederation of Autonomous Right-Wing Groups
CiU	Convergència i Unió: Convergence and Union
CNCA	Confederación Nacional-Católica Agraria: National Catholic Agrarian Confederation
CNT	Confederación Nacional de Trabajo: National Labour Confederation
EC	European Community
ETA	Euzkadi Ta Askatasuna: Basque Homeland and Freedom
EU	European Union
FAI	Federación Anarquista Ibérica: Iberian Anarchist Federation
FNTT	Federación Nactional de Trabajadores de la Tierra: National Landworkers' Federation
GAL	Grupo Antiterrorista de Liberación: Antiterrorist Liberation Group
GDP	Gross Domestic Product
HOAC	Hermandades Obreras de Acción Católica: Workers' Brotherhoods of Catholic Action
ILE	Institución Libre de Enseñanza: Free Institute of Education
JAP	Juventudes de Acción Popular: Popular Action Youth
JOC	Juventudes Obreras Cristianas: Young Christian Workers
JSU	Juventudes Socialistas Unificadas: Unified Socialist Youth
NATO	North Atlantic Treaty Organization
PCE	Partido Comunista Español: Spanish Communist Party
PNV	Partido Nacionalista Vasco: Basque Nationalist Party
POUM	Partido Obrero de Unificación Marxista: Workers' Party of Marxist Unification
PP	Partido Popular: People's Party

PSOE	Partido Socialista Obrero Español: Spanish Socialist Party
SF	Sección Femenina: Women's Section (of the Falange)
UCD	Unión de Centro Democrático: Union of the Democratic Centre
UGT	Unión General de Trabajadores: General Workers' Union
UP	Unión Patriótica: Patriotic Union

Introduction: *The Long Search for Legitimacy*

In 1833, the first in a succession of civil wars broke out in Spain, setting a pattern of internecine conflict that persisted for well over a hundred years. The last and most significant of these civil wars, that of 1936–9, was played out on a world stage and the cleavages it created were only finally resolved after the 1970s. Political violence became such a durable feature of Spanish history that scholars and commentators alike saw it as a structural problem, often depicted in terms of Spanish character. The ludicrously inadequate stereotypes afforded by Latin temperament always found most favour among foreigners. In contrast, Manuel Azaña, president of the Republic destroyed during the Civil War of 1936–9, saw the problem as one of state power. The liberal state created over the course of the nineteenth century had lacked resources and presence, failing to extend its reach through society or to impose its will on the people.[1] Yet, this did not mean that there was no authority in Spain. All these civil conflicts produced clear victors, just as the lesser regional and cantonal revolts that punctuated 'peace' in nineteenth and twentieth-century Spain were emphatically suppressed. The problem was not simply that, as Azaña identified, the modern Spanish state lacked strength, but that it lacked legitimacy.

Political violence became endemic in Spain because victory could not be converted into legitimacy. Only in the late twentieth century did a form of state power develop that was overwhelmingly recognized as having the right to rule. By 2002—the year Spain joined the Euro—the country had a legitimate, functioning, and effective state. But between 1833 and the late twentieth century, no regime, whether monarchical or republican, benign or repressive, dictatorial or even democratic, could claim to have had a hegemonic legitimacy. Any form of rule has to be situated with a context: the 'political' is embedded in a series of diverse social and cultural realities. The exercise of state power depends at least in part upon whether or not its actions are seen as legitimate, whether authority is exerted in ways deemed to be proper both by those who enact it and those upon whom it is enacted.

The values and beliefs that confer legitimacy upon a state are seldom formal and rarely articulated. They do not exist as a defined programme. In neither nineteenth-nor twentieth-century Spain was there a single definition of legitimate authority: the accrued weight of monarchical and catholic tradition as well as the challenges of egalitarianism and class consciousness made for a diverse and even fragmented political culture. But some understandings of legitimate power had more salience than others. Naked force or a simple imposition of will on the part of a ruler could never, by itself, create a legitimate power, though the mobilization of pre-existing notions such as 'strong government' could act as agglutinates of legitimacy, as could stability, predictability, and the existence of some kind of functioning bureaucratic order. For understandings of legitimacy were both abstract and fluid, and they existed above all in the intersections and connections between rulers and ruled.

An emphasis on legitimacy not only provides the analytical keys needed to unlock the conundrum of political violence in Spain but it also raises the question of how we should—and should not—conceptualize the Spanish state. Misconceptionalizing the state is not a problem unique to Spanish history. The modern state is widely characterized as an accumulation of coercive power: its remorseless reach over its people was consolidated as earlier traditions of local autonomy and collective identity were swept away in the name of modernity and bureaucratic rationalization. This insistence that 'power comes out of the barrel of a gun' has led to an emphasis on the state as coercive force that has profoundly marked the historiography of modern Spain.

Relatively few historical analyses focus on the development of the Spanish state.[2] Those that do assume not only that the state was weak—which it undoubtedly was—but that it represented an official centralism that sat ill with local 'reality'. Like the nationalizing project, the ship of state foundered on the rocks of poor communications, underdeveloped markets, and hostile topography. For an emphasis on the material sinews of power leads to another historiographical opposition, that between state and nation. The 'weak' nationalization of nineteenth-century Spain meant a failure to create an integrative nationalism, radiating out from central government and gradually incorporating all its citizens in a cohesive and patriotic identity.[3] Such a narrative again emphasizes the weakness of the central state, arguing that this incapacity allowed rival nationalisms—above all the Catalan and the Basque—to survive and flourish. Focus—and agency—shift from the centre to the periphery but the basic interpretative point remains.

Yet, as a territorial entity, Spain is one of the longest-established nations in Europe. For five hundred years, native and foreign observers have spoken of Spain, Spaniards, and the Spanish, and few early nineteenth-century Europeans would have failed to recognize Spain as a nation. Spain should have had considerable advantages in any nationalist project: the country's borders were not in dispute, its language was spoken by millions worldwide and its literature feted. Its inhabitants were Catholic almost without exception, so precluding the confessional divisions, tensions, and discriminations which characterized most northern European societies. Nor, in contrast to regions such as the Balkans, was there any uncertainty as to the identity—or even the location—of the nation. Rather, Spain's modern history was bloody and divisive *despite* the existence of national feeling. Acknowledging this, some historians point to the weakness of the centralizing vision and, in consequence, an incomplete process of nation-building.[4] The articulation of regional nationalisms becomes a reaction to central authority rather than the emergence of primordial ethnic identities through the cracks of the centralizing facade, but the sense of a national Spanish identity in tension with the regions persists.

Those who argue for the 'failure' of Spanish nationalism claim there was no modernizing moment when the construction of a new state coincided with the 'nationalization' of its citizens. Such a moment should have been when, to paraphrase Eugen Weber, peasants became Spaniards. The model of an imposed integrative nationalism radiating out from a centralized state comes from France and, more specifically, from Weber's often normative narrative, although it was not the only way in which to achieve a self-conscious sense of nationhood.[5] Admittedly, the French system was deliberately applied to Spain, which was divided into provinces in 1833. These provinces still define Spanish territory at both national and regional level. They are the basis on which statistical information is collected; they serve as units of local government, and provide electoral districts. The delineation of the provinces marked the beginning of a self-consciously modern state apparatus in Spain, though the national map diverged from the French model, retaining different-sized provinces and a clearer sense of regional differentiation. For even by the mid-nineteenth century, Spain had an emotional presence, that lived-in feeling of instant recognition, which any and every form of nationalism demanded. The nineteenth century saw a systematic search of national discovery: territories were mapped, landscapes reproduced, customs collected. These processes of collection and classification changed 'nation' from a reified abstraction to a felt, if equally abstract, entity. Spain may have been tardier in elaborating this sense of itself as a nation than, for example, Britain and France, but neither the nationalist agenda nor the nation-building project differed significantly.

The appetite for codification affected state- as well as nation-building. Anthropologists, statisticians, cartographers, and folklorists both gave a specific territorial and ethnographic content to the nation and made it readable by those in power.[6] State structures developed alongside ministries and government independent of the crown. The tax reform of the 1840s was perhaps the most important in a series of measures that introduced and developed an impersonal bureaucratic rule. Like other European powers, Spain reformed tax codes, established police forces, introduced census and postal services. The machinery, personnel, and institutions of the state developed and expanded, creating new professions, such as Civil Guards and factory inspectors, and bolstering old ones, such as customs inspectors and civil servants. The modern state became much more than an extractive power, existing for the purpose of collecting dues such as taxes or military service from its subjects. Paradoxically, as the state accumulated power to itself so it became less reliant on the brute assertion of that power in order to rule. As the state grew in reach and capacity, so it diversified, developing additional, usually benign, functions. This process may have been less speedy and complete in Spain than in north-western Europe or the USA but it still occurred. In Spain as elsewhere, a general and gradual development of those quotidian, unremarkable processes of rule came to characterize the modern state just as much as the capacity for unrestrained force.

The century between the 1830s and the 1930s saw the creation of modern state institutions in Spain—including a national capital—but, with the exception of the Civil Guard, these have received relatively little attention from historians who persist in depicting the state as organized violence. Indeed, it is this emphasis on coercive force that leads to the common but highly misleading idea that 'the state' collapsed in 1936. An army coup meant that the sinews of force disappeared and, therefore, so did the state. But, as has already been pointed out, the state has many relationships with its citizens and not all of them are directly coercive. A state penetrates society in various ways: at every level, it must be embodied and represented, both through official business and through those who carry it out. State power only exists within a context of real social relationships.[7] If a state is to be legitimate rather than imposed then this has to be the case: state power is exerted through social networks and local agents, both formal and informal.

The actual workings of state power, and in particular the way it was embedded in a series of social and political networks was vividly shown under the restored Bourbon monarchy (1875–1923). With the Restoration 'system', the Spanish state assumed its characteristic modern form, crystallizing in a way that incorporated regional elites, avoiding the disjuncture between the centre and the localities and making regional interests intrinsic to the state itself.[8] Such a pattern was also found in Portugal, Italy, and Greece, always placing intermediaries between the abstract authority of the state and the individual citizen. Influence and patronage—the standard practices of face-to-face politics—became the accepted way of conducting business. There was a practical side to this. From the 1840s, the Spanish state became chronically impoverished: the scarce and fragile resources of state power severely limited both its ambit and its capacity. Given the lack of money, ceding capacity and expense to pre-existing elites seemed a pragmatic compromise, particularly in an age of oligarchic politics. The parameters of liberal politics were everywhere narrowly drawn, but in Spain the narrowness of the political class made the relationship between citizens and the state—particularly the incorporation of ordinary men and, later, women—inherently problematic. Liberals won every constitutional conflict over the course of the nineteenth century, but the authority of the liberal state was always compromised.

In effect, successive central governments failed to convert a formidable state presence into effective and legitimate state power. Every history of modern Spain discusses the phenomenon of *caciquismo*, the survival of traditional provincial elites as an buffer between state and citizen. The logic of the Restoration system made the caciques essential to the working of the Spanish state: indeed, in many areas the caciques *were* the state, a fact that undoubtedly skewed the state's penetration of society but did not necessarily prevent it. For among the many things in the caciques' gift was 'official' business and they were also, of course, office-holders themselves.[9] The classic understanding of *caciquismo* is that it represented the *pays réel* against the *pays leal*. Yet, if state authority is conveyed through 'networks of social power' then such a distinction is artificial. The co-existence of informal and formal representatives was not rare in the late nineteenth century. The direct, official authority of the state was winning out, however, and the limits of state power in Spain do not mean that its history should be read as one of inertia, stasis, or arrested development.

The Restoration system was workable, and it attained sufficient social consent to last for over forty years. During this time, Spain had constitutional government, a free market in land and, by the turn of the twentieth century, universal manhood suffrage. But no ruling group broadened the basis of its rule sufficiently to guarantee its stability; the vested interests within the state were always too powerful for those looking either to reform the state from within or to challenge it from without. In this way, peripheral nationalisms—notably in Cataluña and the Basque provinces—grew out of political opposition to those who commanded the apparatus of the state. So long as their interests were met, they remained culturally distinct regions, but when the loss of Spain's few remaining colonies after the Spanish-American War meant that resources were too scarce, their grievances became political and 'nationalist'.

Challenges from outside the state—whether from regional nationalists or organized labour—met a repressive response. In a weak polity the threat of naked force was never far from the surface. The compromises and accommodations that had been made in order to govern had become entrenched within the state, and the elites had no answers to the challenge of the streets. The central authorities fell back on the army, defining political protest as public disorder and becoming increasingly reliant on soldiers. The army had never been the servant of the state in modern Spain, and its autonomy within that state was now greater than ever. In 1923, a military coup led, for the first time, to military dictatorship. The defining characteristic of the modern Spanish state appeared to be the use of violence against its own citizens. Certainly, this is how historians of twentieth-century Spain have depicted it, as an instrument for coercion and class repression. Studies of anarchism, in particular, present a counterpoint between the people and the state, through the numerous confrontations between soldiers and strikers. Rioters invariably lost their confrontations with authority, but the persistence of repressive government in Spain—which ran down to Franco's dictatorship of 1939–75—nevertheless reflected the precariousness of a weak state with few resources other than brute force.

Investigations of state power in modern Spain thus emphasize both coercion and fragility. Nowhere is this more apparent than in studies of the Second Republic with their routine assumption that state power 'collapsed' under the impact of the military coup that led to civil war.[10] But such an explanatory framework cannot account for the quick reassertion of central authority—a mere seven months after its putative collapse—or, more significantly, for the rapid accumulation of state power during the Civil War. The process of state-building ran through the nineteenth and twentieth centuries, and the relationship citizens had with the state changed rapidly in the decades after the First World War. At no time did these relationships remain fixed. Rather, as any exploration of state power and particularly one that emphasizes the embedded nature of that power must recognize, they remained fluid and dynamic, even under an apparently static and repressive regime.

In terms of violence against its own citizens, the Franco dictatorship that emerged victorious from the Civil War was the most repressive Spain had ever seen. The sinews of state power seemed more naked than ever before. To those who define the state as coercive force, Franco's repression was a stark imposition of central power, so fearsome that the dictatorship remained in place until 1975. Yet, when Franco died in his bed, nearly forty years had passed, most of them without serious challenge to his authority. By itself, repression seems a weak explanation for such longevity. From the 1920s, the Spanish state had accumulated more and more direct knowledge of its citizens and this process was accelerated by the mechanisms of repression. Once secure in power, the dictatorship could explore other avenues of negotiation between state and citizens, such as welfare policies and consumerism. The regime thus achieved a limited but real social consensus. With economic development in the 1960s, both industry and the market began to develop, a phase often identified with the final emergence of civil society in Spain.

For some, democratization was dependent on this moment, the emergence of civil society.[11] The story of the post-Franco transition, and the establishment of a recognizably modern, West European nation-state is thus one of bringing the state into line with civil society. This book has a different emphasis, for its focus is on the way state power radiates through society, how it is embedded and represented within society. Civil society, as a sphere autonomous from and, indeed, resistant to, the state is thus a rather foreign notion. My argument is that changes within the state itself affected the transition to democracy as the state machinery, and those who worked within and with it, became increasingly separate from the dictator and his old regime. Only under democracy, however, was the process of constructing a modern nation-state completed in Spain. Only now did the state have the authority and, crucially, the legitimacy to demonstrate the political will that instituted the 1978 constitution and later took Spain into the European Union. Throughout these negotiations, the relationship between the nation and the regions remained problematic, the legacy of the rigid and repressive centralism of the Franco regime. Yet, a compromise was reached that satisfied the majority of all Spaniards and that in itself testified to the new-found legitimacy of the state. Partly as a result of EU membership, the regions have accrued more devolved authority and assumed increasingly autonomous personas. But that is not the failing of Spain as a nation-state nor the reflection of a lack of legitimacy at either national or regional level. Rather, just as the Spanish state finally achieved consolidated, legitimate power, entry into a European system of supra-national governance changed the nature of that power forever.

1

Setting Up the State, 1833–75

THE CORK AND THE BEER BOTTLE

Before 1789 Spain had been both an imperial and a major European power. Less than three decades later, the American colonies were lost and the peninsula ravaged. Once a great presence on the world stage, Spain was reduced to a peripheral role on the edge of Europe, the subject of diplomatic concern and military interventions. The few remaining colonies—Cuba, Puerto Rico, and the Philippines—kept abject humiliation at bay, but these 'crumbs from the imperial banquet' could not sustain pretensions to world power status.[1] As Spain lagged further behind north-west Europe, its decline became visible, commented upon by Spaniard and foreigner alike. In terms of domestic policy, the transition from eighteenth to nineteenth century seemed equally acute. The Enlightenment monarchy had introduced reform partly in emulation of the ideas of rational modernity being pioneered throughout Europe but also in order to administer an empire. The loss of the American lands meant that the focus and dynamic of Spanish history turned inwards. After 1815, the immediate concerns were for the stability of the Crown and the prevention of civil conflict.

In 1833, Fernando VII, the last Spanish monarch with absolutist pretensions, died and the ancien regime in Spain finally came to an end. As the king had predicted, with his death, the cork came out of the beer bottle. With only an infant daughter, Isabel, to succeed him, Fernando's crown was immediately claimed by his brother Carlos, and the first Carlist War began. The end of the old order was not simply a question of succession. To the nineteenth century's greatest social theorist, Karl Marx, the transition from the ancien regime meant a change in the mode of production from feudalism to capitalism, accomplished by a dynamic social class, the bourgeoisie, fulfilling its political destiny. Few would now present such a determinist model so baldly, but that some far-reaching transformation of Spanish government and political life took place in the first half of the nineteenth century is undeniable. During the civil war that followed Fernando's death, the legal bases of the old order were overturned and the principles of liberal government established. Government became separate from the crown while the administration of the state assumed a new rational and bureaucratic form. Impersonal structures replaced personal service to the royal household, and the modern state began tentatively to assume a recognizable form.

The first Carlist War lasted from 1833 to 1840, though its origins lay in the vicissitudes of Fernando's reign. Running the gamut of political options from constitutional radicalism to repressive autocracy, had left the monarchy isolated, reduced, in the king's words, to 'beating the white donkey (the absolutists) and the black donkey (the liberals)'.[2] Dependence on a narrow governing elite meant that Fernando, like many who succeeded him, could not afford to alienate any source of support, even if reconciling the demands of all was impossible. By the time of his death, many ultra-absolutists were more than willing to follow Don Carlos, or indeed any sympathetic claimant to the throne. The struggle for power, which many, including Fernando, had anticipated, was shaped by their attempts to preclude any liberal solution to the crisis of government provoked by the monarch's death.

Carlos' objection to his niece Isabel II was thus not just that of her sex. Rather than a simple dynastic dispute the first Carlist War began a new era in Spanish history. The victory of Isabel's 'national' troops which established the liberal hegemony that characterized the rest of the nineteenth century as a parliamentary regime was established under her mother María Cristina, the queen regent. Yet, even at the time of liberalism's greatest victory, it existed in opposition and relation to a strongly reactionary and anti-liberal monarchical undercurrent. Carlism became Europe's most tenacious reactionary movement and the symbiotic development of reaction and conservatism—which was epitomized in the late nineteenth century by the 'integrist' espousal of the confessional state against 'atheist' liberalism—profoundly affected the development of conservative thought in Spain, which remained 'integrally' Catholic in all aspects of its thought.[3]

To Carlos' rebels, any acceptable form of government would be Catholic. The consubstantiability of throne and altar was axiomatic, a matter of divine will, not civic feeling; hence the importance of legitimacy in the royal succession. Throughout its history, Carlism was distinguished by loyalty both to a dynastic claim to the throne of Spain, and to ultramontane Catholicism. The Carlist 'army of the faith' was placed under the supreme command of the Virgin of Sorrows, while Don Carlos' political ideology seems to have consisted only of submission to the will of God. Such a lack of content ultimately meant that it was seldom, if ever, able to articulate political demands and make political gains. Nevertheless, the enthusiasm for theocracy was to the taste of much of the Spanish Church. The bishop of León, for example, formed part of the rebels' 'secret regency' as did the father general of the Jesuit order in Spain.

This Carlist War was the first of three, though the second—a guerrilla campaign, known as the Guerra dels Matiners, confined to the highlands of Cataluña from 1846 to 1849—was more regional revolt than full-scale civil war, developing from the brigandage which persisted locally even after war had officially ended.[4] Carlism's longevity was remarkable: another Carlist War was fought between 1870 and 1875, while Carlist red berets were also seen during the Civil War of 1936 to 1939. In part, this was because of its plasticity. As a social movement Carlism served as a protest vehicle for various discontented peasant groups while, in political terms, it was an amalgam for reactionary opposition to any liberal status quo.[5] The ideological appeal was thus to counter revolution, despite the association with rural social protest. In the movement's formative years, some sympathizers even seemed to dispute the very idea of government: a Carlist parish priest in remote Galicia, for example, claimed in 1838 that 'there is no law other than God and king'.[6] In northern rural areas, the Church provided more than ideological support: one monastery in Bilbao was rumoured to have made two million cartridges for the Carlist army. Such rumours fuelled liberal determination to suppress the male religious orders, which they duly did in 1835. But, while liberalism was the Carlist enemy, the movement's association with rural disorder, particularly brigandage, alienated many conservatives.

Carlism proved so tenacious because it became identified with the Pyrenean region of Navarre. Here, the loyalty of succeeding generations to 'the Cause' was nurtured within families and local communities in a close regional association that nevertheless brought insurmountable difficulties in waging a national campaign. All the Carlist wars were northern affairs, and that of 1870 to 1875 was firmly centred on its Navarrese heartlands. Only during the 1830s when Carlist forces marched on Madrid and threatened Bilbao, was central government seriously threatened. Despite the military intelligence displayed by the Carlist commander, Tomás de Zumalacárregui, the rebels never succeeded in taking anywhere larger than the Navarrese town of Estella. Fighting was often indecisive and the first Carlist War was protracted. The country was in administrative chaos, with the chief minister changing nineteen times between 1834 and 1843. During 1836, when popular agitation was uncontainable, five different men acted as Treasury secretary, while the remaining five cabinet posts changed hands seventeen times.

Civil war wrested control from the Crown. A weakened and impoverished regency—Isabel II's majority was announced in 1845, when she was barely thirteen—was hardly in a position to impose its will on the land, despite military victory. In addition the radical promises of liberalism—the prospect of

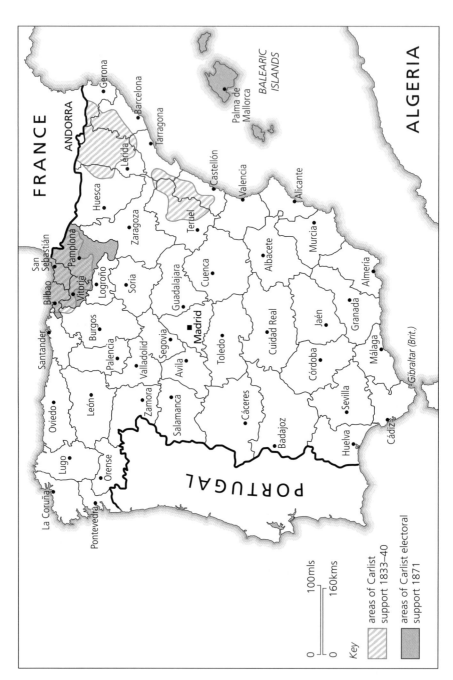

The Carlist Wars

national sovereignty and representative, meritocratic government—remained a latent challenge to the ruling order, for the parliamentary regime that emerged victorious from the war emphasized oligarchy and the autonomy of the Crown. The 1837 constitution established a two-chamber Cortes with a directly elected second chamber, but the franchise was restricted and the senate appointed by the monarch, albeit from nominees presented by the constituencies. Ministers were chosen by the Crown, which also retained the prerogative of summoning and dismissing parliament.[7] Like all constitutional settlements, 1837 was a compromise, initially accepted by all those on the side of parliamentary representation, both the oligarchic 'Moderates' and the more radical 'Progressives'. However, a reaction against the 1837 settlement came increasingly to define the 'Moderate' party, while many 'Progressives' stood out for further parliamentary gains against the Crown. This 'split in the trunk of liberalism' would determine the progress of Spanish politics, becoming still more apparent during the 1840s.[8]

At local level the picture was still more complex. Struggles between liberals and absolutists continued, while the radical emancipation promised by the discourse of representation and popular sovereignty attracted fervent support. The 1837 constitution allowed for popularly elected municipal governments and, in the cities and towns of Spain, a more radical vision of liberalism flourished among local men of substance who were nevertheless excluded from the great elites. In cities such as Valencia, radical liberal ideas spread fast among artisans, small businessmen, and smaller property-owners.[9] The Crown favoured the *moderados*, but the progressives had the support of the large towns. The 1837 constitution had also given them a weapon: the national militia was under the control of the municipalities. This was in part because the militia was an urban institution, open after 1836 to all householders and tradesmen who met with the authorities' approval to bear arms. Lower property qualifications made the municipal franchise broader than the parliamentary one and the call to arms could be a potent one. Throughout Spain during late 1835 and 1836, urban revolutionary juntas and their militias acted against Carlism, often tolerating violent reprisals. As in France, artisans' grievances fuelled urban revolutionary outbursts, and intense local radicalism in areas such as the Levante forced change at national level. The threat of genuinely revolutionary upheaval concentrated minds and was instrumental in creating consensus around the political settlement of 1837. The political agenda had thus been pushed forward by the radical urban juntas.

Subsequent constitutions tinkered with the form—the more conservative constitution promulgated in 1845 made the Senate a more elite body and (temporarily) suppressed the national militia—but they did not alter the 1837 model. The bicameral parliament remained and the crown became a constitutional monarchy, though its weakness as an institution of government—as well as the apparently congenital lack of political foresight on the part of those who wore it—meant that it never acted as arbiter in negotiating this new political settlement. Indeed, the architect of the 1837 constitution, Juan Alvarez Mendizábal, had been dismissed from office by the queen regent in May 1836 even though there was no receptive audience for absolutist solutions.

This was most apparent in the towns and cities which were liberalism's natural home. All over Spain, participants in these political struggles learnt to 'speak in liberal'.[10] This was the language which resounded through civic—that is urban—society in 1836, deciding Mendizábal's fate. Once the army had joined the agitation with a mutiny of the palace guard in August, the regent was forced to reinstate Mendizábal. At the same time, liberals—who were by definition men of means—were by now anxious to prevent a revolutionary situation becoming a red-blooded revolution. The spectre of social disorder had been raised by Carlism, but many liberal notables were not as convinced as they had been that 'the proletarian mob' was the natural preserve of Don Carlos. Revolutionary turmoil helped to reinstate Mendizábal, but it left many disillusioned by populism.

The political settlement which emerged by 1843 was oligarchic and, like nineteenth-century liberal systems throughout Europe, it was deliberately anti-democratic. Politics was still the preserve of those who knew how to govern, even if the political class was changing. But violence and revolution had played a vital role in forging the new power relationships which lay at the heart of government. This was not the end of the road for either reactionaries or revolutionaries: the persistence of civil conflict is one of the most striking features of Spain's modern history. The mob violence of June 1834 in Madrid led to the killing of some seventy-five monks, accused both of Carlist sympathies and of poisoning the water supply. The revolutionary turmoil of the decade before 1843 comprised both urban unrest and rural brigandage, as well as armed rebellion and the ensuing state-sponsored reprisals.[11] The recurrence of conflict—which persisted well beyond the 1840s—suggested that those who won the fight failed to impose their will in the following peace. In modern polities, hegemony is established as much by consent as by coercion; the problem in Spain was that such consent was granted only by very few. More were left outside the pale of settlement than were ever accommodated within it.

This is not to suggest that there were no victors in these civil wars. Liberalism faced its greatest danger between 1833 and 1839 and emerged the unquestioned victor. As one moderate Liberal politician put it, 'It was important to unite defenders of the cause of Isabel II by calling for the support of the classes who, by their birthright, their education, or their wealth, exercise most influence on the nation.'[12] That their solution had been imposed against opposition from the Crown seemed to underline the truth of these words. Spain's oligarchic liberalism was typical of nineteenth-century Europe but it had little reason to be grateful to the monarch. Nor were the people victorious. Suffrage was restricted and parliamentary government on the British model was introduced, for the first but not the last time. The intention was to provide representative government, no doubt measured by paternalism but untainted by populist democracy.

The victory of these governors by right, believers in progress and modernization, ensured a renovation of the apparatus of the state. This would turn Spain into a recognizably modern country, distinct from its northern European counterparts in many respects but with clear parallels with its Mediterranean neighbours. Coming from the face-to-face world of local notables, Liberals relied upon and emphasized local power networks, but they also believed in the nation, and in the community of the nation. This could seem paradoxical. Liberal notables would regularly seek to advance members of their own families even as they espoused the virtues of equality and the career open to talent. Madrid's first liberal mayor, Pedro Sáinz de Baranda, consistently denounced nepotism and privilege but used personal connections to establish his sons' careers, one in the Church, the other in the state bureaucracy.[13] The bureaucrat's career was distinguished, which would have come as no surprise to those who saw government as oligarchic, who believed merit resided in certain social groups, and who regarded democracy as a populist perversion. Family connections and face-to-face relationships were the social cement of nineteenth-century Europe, employed by monied liberals from Bristol to Bologna. This was not inimical to the construction of a modern state: on the contrary, the affluent and well-connected peopled the state in all its guises, holding office, serving the crown, or performing government functions.

A BOURGEOIS REVOLUTION?

According to Marx, class conflict is the motor of historical change. The transition from ancien regime to modern government was thus the work of the bourgeoisie, whose revolutionary task was to introduce private property, liberal government, and rational bureaucracy. In France, this was the result of a wider, tumultuous social upheaval which mobilized the peasantry and unleashed revolutionary violence on an unprecedented scale, but the revolutionary

upheavals that swept through Europe and America in the wake of the
French Revolution were essentially political phenomena and their tools were
legislative. The social effects, however, were profound.[14] The removal of
barriers to private property and a free market in land, equality before the
law, the end of the privilege of birth all contributed to, and in many ways
constituted, the transition from a pre-modern world based on status, office-
holding, and the (often devolved) authority of the crown, to a modern state
legitimated by popular sovereignty and administered by able men according
to impersonal rules. That such a transition occurred, often messily and never
completely, accounts, in part, for the persistence of the idea of the 'bourgeois
revolution'.

Historians of Britain, Germany, Spain, and even France have now con-
vincingly established that nowhere was the bourgeoisie—as a separate class,
conscious of its own distinct identity—strong enough to have challenged the
aristocracy for power over the state. This does not mean, though, that no new
class emerged. Some prominent individuals certainly conformed to the idea
of a new class. Mendizábal, the son of a moderately wealthy merchant family
in Cádiz, seemed to embody the idea of bourgeois ascent, though he never
flaunted his origins in a capital where many men basked in the comfort of
renowned and often noble lineage. Noble title became a very real aspiration
for men with wealth but no rank, facilitating the emerging of a hybrid group
who looked to the trappings as well as the exercise of power. José Canga
Argüelles, administrator of the Royal Estate in Valencia, and a convert to the
idea of a reforming liberal state, came from a family whose menfolk's careers
and wealth had been forged in government service. He gave his sons status and
education; they in turn added the title of counts of Canga Argüelles, though
they continued in administrative careers.[15] Nor were they unusual. Service to
the state, in either its military or administrative form, was regularly rewarded
with a title, a practice which took one of the oldest forms of political reward
and gave it a new meritocratic spin.

Societies are made up, in Michael Mann's words, of 'overlapping and intersecting power networks', and these are reproduced—though not necessarily
replicated—in the organized, institutional power systems which make up
what we call the state. The elites or 'class fractions' who inhabit the state and
compete to control resources and exercise power, are not necessarily cohesive,
nor is their co-existence necessarily coherent, particularly in periods when the
state was expanding, and in countries where the exercise of political power was
trammelled by the scarcity of resources.[16] In Isabelline Spain, there was a clear
need for state servants but limited funds with which to support them. Other
inducements—what later generations would call sweeteners—were needed,
and principal among these was noble status. Seventy-six of the 272 noble

senators who sat in the chamber between 1845 and 1868 held titles created after 1833. Aristocratic rank was no longer a prerequisite for ministerial office but aristocrats still accounted for just over half of all Isabel's ministers.[17] As government sought to make state servants dependent on the central administration, so dominant classes 'tried to ensure that bureaucracy was run by people like themselves'.[18]

Maintaining social status by emphasizing family connections, and pursuing marriage contracts likely to favour them, was a common preoccupation amongst the powerful in early nineteenth-century Madrid. The fortunes of individual families varied considerably, in Spain as throughout western Europe: some noble names became extinct, impoverished, or obscure while others adapted, preserving or enhancing their fortunes, which remained firmly embedded in land-holding. And family strategies were not the preserve of the aristocracy. Among bourgeois families such as that of the politician and diplomat Salustiano de Olózaga, matrimonial alliances were equally important. Olózagal's daughter was married to a fellow liberal politician, though paternal consent only came after more general approval by family and friends. Choosing a marriage partner was 'a social action'.[19] Family names marked out a certain social status and position. They were an asset, just like the family's estates, and in both cases, careful management allowed both bourgeois and aristocratic families to consolidate their positions. As an economic and political class, the aristocracy thus survived the nineteenth century, and this inescapable fact has led some to argue that, while the bourgeoisie ruled everywhere, nowhere did it do so alone. 'In effect a deal was struck: the nobility did not oppose the institution of liberalism and agreed to accept the loss of its jurisdictional rights in return for a recognition of its property rights.'[20] The bourgeois revolution is thus measured by its outcome—the legislative base of a recognizably modern state and, even more importantly, the enhanced legislative capacity of that state. The *desamortización* or sale of entailed lands created a free market in land and consolidated in law the notion of private property which persists to this day. This, together with some notion of representative government and the unassailability of the rule of law, was the crowning achievement of liberals throughout Europe. And without that achievement, the modern European state would not have existed.

As an ideology, liberalism was remarkably open. It took shape in local oligarchies, attracting adherents of all classes. It also gave expression to nation-states, even though liberal principles were universal rather than particular. When, in 1836, Mendizábal, initiated a programme for disentailing Church lands, he was not only raising money for the state, but also implementing ideas of merit, equality, and opportunity. The disentails were undertaken for urgent fiscal reasons in Spain, but they nevertheless continued a pattern seen everywhere since 1789. Spain may have been on Europe's periphery but that did not exclude it entirely from the mainstream. Land sales foregrounded the issue of property, which was in many respects the key to nineteenth-century liberalism. The local revolutionary juntas of 1836 had tolerated the seizure of Church property and, in radical cities like Valencia, had broken up entails, tithes, guilds, and other privileged relics of the ancien regime. However, the Barcelona junta had been deeply perturbed when the mob turned on the Bonaplata factory, an institution which may have represented the oppression of the workers, but had little connection to the old order. Property was the basis of the new political order, just as birth had been that of the old one. In 1836, Mendizábal's stated intention was to create 'a copious family of property owners' who would identify with the liberal cause.[21] The burning of the Bonaplata factory suggested that the allegiance of the workers was not guaranteed.

In an agrarian economy, landed property equalled wealth. Any system of free sales would inevitably favour those who had money to invest, and much of this money came either from other landholdings, including rents, or inheritance. Some land fell prey to speculators, both in 1836 and after the later, more extensive disentails of 1841 and 1855 which sold off municipal as well as ecclesiastical land. The 1855 law abolished entail, effectively making all land which did not belong to private individuals liable to expropriation and sale by the state. The sale of lands was not new—the alienation and sale by the crown of ecclesiastical lands had begun in the 1760s—but this far-reaching piece of legislation remained in force until the twentieth century. In effect, it cemented the creation of a free market in land: an essential precondition for the nineteenth century's ides of the state. In the new order, property conferred citizenship and, together with maleness, defined an individual as a citizen. Yet, liberal politics were also oligarchic and land purchases reinforced the importance of elites as both a socio-political reality and an idea of government. In complex, and sometimes contradictory ways, the ownership of land defined the relationship between society and the state, writing some into the apparatus of power and others out of it.

The amount of land that changed hands after 1836 dwarfed any earlier transfers: an estimated 30 per cent of the land area of Castile changed hands as a result of disentail. In the Carlist heartland of Navarre, most land offered for sale at public auction was bought by residents of local agrarian towns such as Pamplona and Estella—334 out of a total of 351 purchasers. The rising value of real estate meant that disentail was, as Gabriel Tortella puts it, 'good business for the wealthy'.[22] The laws were promulgated by liberal and conservative administrations alike, while many who were no friends to radical liberalism were to be found among the ranks of the buyers. Those purchasing land from early disentails in Salamanca, for example, included priests, aristocrats, and landowners—a few of whom were women—as well as members of the commercial and mercantile classes. The landowners looked to consolidate their estates, the *comerciantes* to make a shrewd investment; all wanted to make a profit. In Valladolid, just north of Salamanca, local residents purchased 51 per cent of the land put up for sale at auction, often paying a high price for it. They were predominantly farmers, or *labradores*, and ranged from tenants buying plots they already worked to agricultural landlords adding hundreds of arable plots to already substantial portfolios.[23]

It is hard to tell from the available evidence if the sales altered the structure of landholding in Spain. The case of Valladolid would seem to suggest that some modification of agrarian landholding did occur in certain areas, even though it is quite clear that, overall, land sales benefited those with money to spend. The poor and the landless lost out, not least through the loss of Church lands on which they might encroach for firewood and grazing and which financed the charity they depended on during hard times. Land sales were an elite matter and did nothing to alleviate the poverty and protest which came to characterize much of Spanish rural society, even if they did expand the elites, most notably at local level.

Nonetheless, in a society and economy based upon land, land reform left virtually no area of life unaffected. In the hierarchical conceptions of the ancien regime, property, authority, and status were intertwined and interdependent, in theory if not always in practice. Under the liberal reforms of the 1830s, 1840s, and 1850s, land became simply a commodity, a particularly valuable one, it is true, but something which could, nevertheless, be sold or disposed of as its owner saw fit. Similarly, despite the continued popularity of noble titles, they now carried no privileged legal status. Aristocrats might still be wealthy and powerful but they were no longer a feudal class, rather a group of subjects, equal before the law. And just as the bourgeoisie might aspire to noble title, so middle-class *mores* were adopted throughout society.

Joaquín Espalter's 1842 portrait of the Flaquer family (Plate 1) depicts a perfect bourgeois interior, carpeted and wall-papered, a portrait over the piano. Allusions to lineage are scattered throughout the picture: the portrait of a family forebear dominates the room; the *paterfamilias* is distinguished by the richness and colour of his clothing; his son and heir is the only person shown standing. There are few clues as to nationality: the earrings of the youngest daughter offer the only hint of Spanishness. Instead the portrait offers a composite of bourgeois family values. It is grouped so as to display both hierarchy and intimacy. Paternal authority is clear, but the family is sitting together amicably, in a comfortable domestic setting. Respectably dressed in 'Victorian' style, the women occupy the space as easily as the men, usefully occupied with music, needlework, and reading. The picture is of the bourgeois family as the bedrock of society, well-ordered and obedient, its members conscious of their place in society. They even display the virtues needed to maintain that society—duty, application, and the acquisition of knowledge—revealing the family as both a common good and a common enterprise, constructed by its various members in their different tasks and allotted ranks.[24]

For the bourgeois family was the microcosm of European liberal society, the fundamental constituent of the public good. Men earned their status as citizens as property-owners and heads of households. Child-rearing and education took place within the family; philanthropy brought its values to the wider world outside. As the Flaquer portrait suggests, family continued to be supremely important in Spanish society. Not all scholars, though, have seen this as evidence of increasing liberalism. Rather, the persistent importance of family networks, personal contacts, and the conduct of business through patronage has led some scholars to argue that the liberal legal edifice was undermined in the everyday practice of politics, which continued much as before. Thus, according to Jesús Cruz, 'Spanish society remained captive of a traditional Old Regime culture that impregnated essential aspects of the social practices of its elites and the rest of the social body'.[25] A political culture that utilized patronage and relied on political placemen to administer the liberal state, militated against the new legislative order, which encompassed not only a free market in property but also the codification of laws and the rationalization and centralization of the apparatus of the state.

According to this interpretation, the public discourse of liberalism always co-existed with the private discourse of family and patronage, in which connections, contacts, and personal favours were all important. The survival of patronage into the nineteenth and indeed the twentieth century is indisputable, but whether it remained the same closed elite system as under the ancien regime seems less certain. Private languages and codes of conduct may differ, often sharply, from those espoused by administrative elites in public. But the law is not merely a discourse. It has coercive force.

The legislative reforms of the first half of the nineteenth century established Spain as a society and a polity based on landed property. This was the case even if property-holders did not comprise an entirely new class and it remained the case despite the clear disparities in wealth and power that existed between them. The disentails worked against institutions and patterns of power which were seen as outmoded, even if they did few favours to the poor. The assets of the Church and the municipalities passed to those rich enough to buy them, and at local level at least, this proved to be a broad swathe of people. At the same time, some of their public functions which had depended on institutional landed wealth, passed to the only body theoretically capable of picking them up, the state.

ADMINISTERING THE COUNTRY

As the crown was at war with its own subjects, Mendizábal's 1836 disentail was undertaken for urgent fiscal reasons. But the fiscal crisis ran deep and could not be fully offset by the early land sales. Instead, a pattern had emerged of offsetting the crown's financial shortfall by 'American remittances'. These profits of empire had ended by 1824 with the definitive loss of all colonies on the American mainland, yet, every year, in a manner Gabriel Tortella describes as 'regular and almost habitual', state expenditure exceeded revenue by around 65 million pesetas.[26] Successive governments thus continued to act as if 'American remittances' were still an available income stream.

Attempts to get the country onto a sound financial footing were few and feeble, though there was a concerted attempt at tax reform in 1845. Even before then, an overwhelming need to obtain money from every available source had led to the eradication of archaic fiscal privileges. These were essentially taxes collected by bodies other than the state and their suppression was not always straightforward. During the 1840s, the Navarrese *pechas*, for example, were depicted as unjust obligations by those who paid them but as simple land rents by those who collected them. In a regime based on private property, this was a powerful defence.[27] Tithe was also a problem, and one only definitively resolved in the 1851 Concordat, which replaced it with state stipends for Catholic clergy. Before this, either local custom or sheer venality could take precedence over the law. In the 1830s, some clergy in Galicia—where the shortfall in stipends was unlikely to be made up in other ways—refused the sacraments to those who had not paid the amount the priest (rather than the law) thought owing to him.[28]

The reach of the law, though, increased throughout the 1840s. The 1845 tax laws introduced by the finance minister, Alejandro Mon, established an annual budget and a tax system on the French model.[29] The mixture of direct and indirect taxes lasted, albeit with considerable variation in the form of taxes, until the next major tax reform in 1977, a hundred and thirty-two years later. Though the most remarkable feature of the modern state would be its ability to penetrate both society and private life, in the 1840s no government knew enough about its citizens to tax income or personal wealth efficiently. In any case, such radical plans would have been politically unthinkable. For men such as Mendizábal, wealth was a private matter, and the state had no business prying into private affairs.

The originator of the reform, Ramón Santillán, therefore emphasized fiscal continuity and, like Mon, was pragmatic in what he set out to achieve, introducing a coherent and uniform tax system without altering the traditional structure of contributions. So, while quaint archaisms such as 'the codfish tax' were overturned, the *consumos* or taxes on certain purchased goods remained; regionally disparate tax burdens disappeared, replaced by a graded land tax which, together with taxes on urban rents and commercial profits, and stamp duty, formed the skeleton of the new system. Duplication, confusion, and fiscal privilege—all of which had led to the tax burden being higher in some regions than others—were eradicated. Yet, tax quotas—which left the responsibility for collecting land tax with the *ayuntamientos* (town halls) and that for industrial taxes with local guilds—survived, defended by Santillán. He believed that, in the absence of a land registry or cadastral map, local collective responsibility formed the only defence against concealed assets. In fact, the quotas left ample opportunities for fraud, and ensured that the tax burden fell most heavily upon the poor.

The constitutional mandate which had impelled the reformers towards general systematic taxation seemed to have been fulfilled. But the new regime also needed to generate sufficient taxes to cover state expenditure and this it never did. The way in which an essentially bureaucratic reform began with a legislative imperative illustrates how the machinery of state is never operated by a single hand. Reforms of this magnitude required technical expertise, as well as political will, and it is no coincidence that Santillán was a treasury civil servant. Despite the shortfall in revenue, the state was expanding in nineteenth-century Spain. Ministries and bureaucracies replaced positions attached to the royal household, and an era began in which, increasingly, the state would be seen as a provider of public services. In 1848, for example, three new government departments were created—commerce, education, and public works. Santillán thus belonged to the widening elites who inhabited the state, but the legislative capacity that this state now had made it an actor, as well as a place. The state made laws as well as enforcing them, 'speaking the law' in almost every aspect of its functioning.[30]

The accumulation of power on the part of the central state thus continued, but the failure to place government on a sound fiscal footing even in the 1840s—despite a genuine attempt to do so—meant a crippling, and accumulating, burden of national debt. The lack of any subsequent tax reform after 1845 had a directly determining effect on the development of the Spanish state, the nature of government, and even the growth of the economy. Not until the late twentieth century would the Spanish state be able to order social life with the 'purposefulness and intensity' Gianfranco Poggi discerned elsewhere. After 1845, the national debt accrued relentlessly, rising steeply after 1865, forcing a conversion as early as 1851 and another in 1882. These issued a new type of 'redeemable' debt, which speculators could use to some advantage but which caused such indignation in London in 1851 that Spanish securities were barred from the Stock Exchange.[31]

As states have external as well as internal forms, this did Spain no good whatsoever: during the remainder of the nineteenth century, the state had to pay an exorbitant price for credit. The effects on economic development were profound—not least in the high price of credit in Spanish money markets—as they were in Italy and other Mediterranean countries burdened with similarly persistent budgetary problems. But fiscal insecurity never foreclosed attempts to put the state on a more modern, centralized footing. In 1851, Bravo Murillo—a reactionary minister with an administrative sense of the state—reformed the prime minister's office, giving it a budget and its own ministry while the scope of its authority was defined by law. Like Mon, Bravo Murillo was part of the conservative Moderado faction, which dominated parliament in the 1840s. His 'frock-coated dictatorship' saw bureaucracy as an instrument through which to wield power and, while civil servants did achieve a certain independence of function, the narrow, oligarchic character of Spain's political class meant that bureaucrats were as likely to be a barrier to communication as a channel for it. In 1855, a mere three years after Bravo Murillo's great reform, he was accused of 'covering arbitrariness and governmental injustices with an impenetrable veil of useless formulae, enormous paragraphs and empty phraseology'.[32]

The Moderado belief in 'strong government' and the rule of law, meant they strengthened the executive over the legislature and championed bureaucratic efficiency (albeit somewhat unconvincingly). New administrative bodies were defined by the law to which they owed their existence and which could dispense with them if it were deemed necessary or expedient. The state 'spoke' the law and no longer were its functions justified in terms of tradition, natural law, or divine will. Henceforth, no institution would remain outside the ambit of the state or the arm of the law, not even the Church. The 1851 concordat had Catholicism as 'the only religion of the Spanish nation' but by ratifying the status quo, including disentail, the concordat itself represented an accommodation with the liberal state. The experience of disentail had, however, replaced the Church's assumption of privilege with a sense of uncertainty. Though it would be many years before it ceased to look to the state for protection and support—not least in denying freedom of worship to Spaniards until 1931—the Spanish Church now accepted the secular jurisdiction of the state and some idea of national sovereignty.

The nation was, however, an inherently ambiguous concept, particularly when a highly restricted suffrage made it clear that the term was not synonymous with 'the people'. The abstract nation legitimized constitutional documents, but the actual nation could not be trusted to exert its will directly. In Teror, Gran Canaria, for example, all male residents were entitled to vote after 1836 but only indirectly: voters returned fifteen representatives, who in turn elected members of the town council. In 1845, this system was replaced by direct council elections but now only substantial property owners and council appointees were allowed to vote.[33] At national level, after 1846, parliamentary suffrage encompassed a mere 1 per cent of the population. Restrictions in the franchise illustrate liberalism's essentially oligarchic conception of the political nation. For many Catholics, meanwhile, the nation was assuming a spiritual dimension as 'real' or 'true' Spain, unchanged by the vicissitudes of government or fashions in political thought.

After the unification of Italy and Pius IX's *Syllabus Errorum* of 1864, Catholic insistence on Spain's confessional nature set up an immediate opposition between the Catholic and the liberal nation. An authoritative external voice reinforced the internal tradition of conservatism which now spoke the language of nation but could only conceive of that nation in confessional terms.[34] Such sectarianism was compounded and aggravated not only by the growth of anticlerical working-class movements such as socialism and anarchism but also by liberalism's increasingly aggressive secularism. Despite the growing influence of freemasonry and French republicanism, the architects of Spain's liberal state were also Catholics, even though they believed that the state should regulate the Church's temporal affairs. Many Catholics, including clergy, identified with Carlism in the 1830s, integrism in the 1880s, and 'national-Catholicism' in the 1940s, but the Church itself had never been exclusively identified with the cause. Though not all Catholics would have agreed, there was an accommodation between Catholicism and liberalism in the nineteenth century. The constitutions of 1837 and 1845 protected Catholicism against other faiths while even Mendizábal never doubted that his own religion should also be that of the liberal state.

There was, therefore, always scope for the kind of accommodation which was eventually reached in the concordat. In 1869, legislation was put forward to redraw diocesan boundaries to make them co-terminus with provinces, as in France. Had this been put into effect—it only occurred, partially, in 1948—it would have strengthened the primacy of the state. Centralization was always symbolically powerful: the state was accruing power to itself, not least through the obviously rational, scientific process of acquiring, recording, and classifying information. Redrawing the national map in 1833 meant using legislation to organize the modern Spanish state, as well as to define the competence of its various constituent bodies. The old regional divisions were replaced with provinces modelled on the French *departements*. The map of Spain now visibly demonstrated the liberal principles of uniformity and equity: redrawing provincial boundaries along symmetrical lines suggested an almost bogus rationality as well as the principles of 'fair-dealing'. The 'realm' of Navarre, for example, was reconstituted as a *provincia foral* in 1841, becoming a simple province on the loss of its foral (that is, tax) privileges after 1876.

According to Julio Aróstegui, the administrative reforms of 1833 to 1856 represented the 'territorialization of the liberal state' and, certainly, they were rooted in liberal principle, as well as practical expediency.[35] Administrative reforms in 1845 articulated the role of municipal and provincial governing bodies (the *ayuntamientos* and *diputaciones*) and introduced centrally-appointed civil and military governors into each province. Centralization was thus both real and symbolic, representing the consolidation of political and bureaucratic power, and a heightened awareness of the need to penetrate society beyond. It also reflected the current state of geographical knowledge—which derived from Tomás López's 1810 general map of Spain—even if it then changed that information by requiring a redrawing of the map. Henceforth, information would be collected and recorded by the Spanish state on the basis of provinces. Presented as numerical orderings and classifications, and known as statistics, this kind of information was invented for the purpose of government.

The appointment of civil governors directly responsible to Madrid also increased political and bureaucratic knowledge of the country. A vision of a unitary state informed all these equalizing, centralizing reforms which in turn attempted to create one. But there is no such thing as a unitary state. Everywhere, and in every historical period, power takes different forms and its exercise is shared and competed for by diverse elites. Policy may be formulated centrally but it is implemented—or not—through the intersecting and overlapping networks of social power which exist at national and local level.[36] In the Basque Country and Navarre, for example, resistance to the centre ensured that the (deficient) statistical methods used to gain knowledge of taxable assets were not applied locally. A dislike of paying taxes was universal. In rural areas throughout Spain, quotas—that is the amount of tax to be paid—were decided by 'expert committees', made up of three members of the a*yuntamiento* and three Treasury nominees. As every pueblo in Spain had municipal status and, therefore, a town hall, the level of government was very local indeed; the central state was conspicuous by its absence. In Algeciras in 1858, the amount of tax due was negotiated rather than evaluated, being determined during discussions held over several days in the house

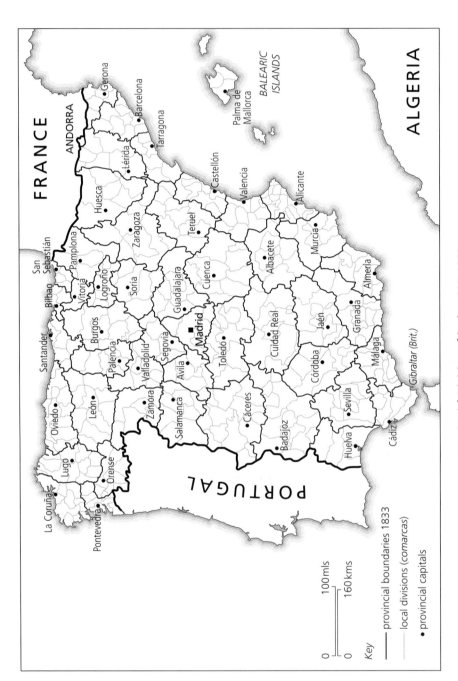

FRANCE

ANDORRA

ALGERIA

Gerona

Barcelona

Tarragona

Lérida

BALEARIC
ISLANDS

Palma de
Mallorca

Huesca

Castellón

Zaragoza

Teruel

Valencia

Pamplona

San
Sebastián

Alicante

Bilbao

Logroño

Vitoria

Soria

Cuenca

Guadalajara

Albacete

Santander

Murcia

Burgos

Madrid

Almería

Palencia

Segovia

Valladolid

Ávila

Toledo

Jaén

Ciudad Real

Granada

Oviedo

León

Córdoba

Málaga

Zamora

Salamanca

"Gibraltar (Brit.)

Cáceres

Sevilla

Lugo

Cádiz

Badajoz

Orense

Huelva

La Coruña

Pontevedra

PORTUGAL

100 mls

0

160 kms

0

Key

—— provincial boundaries 1833

—— local divisions (comarcas)

• provincial capitals

Territorial Division of Spain, 1833–1978

of a bureaucrat charged with resolving a complaint that the quota was too high. Inevitably the quota was reduced, the lone state functionary reduced to reporting events without being able to influence them.[37]

Such bartering also occurred in cities, though here at least the juntas were chaired by a representative of the central state, divorced from local interests. But this minimal safeguard against gross abuses could not disguise the lack of central authority in the system. Concealment was an enormous problem, the result both of local recalcitrance and a belief that private wealth was not a legitimate area for state intervention. Taxation remained a collective rather than an individual obligation, despite the ever-pressing need to increase state revenues. Yet, changing understandings of government were altering those very conceptions of public and private which many used to justify concealing taxable assets. The capacity of the state was increasing: property was, after all, part of the national, as well as individual, wealth.

Inevitably, resistance to land registries, declarations of income, and public knowledge of taxable assets continued and the deficiencies of the statistical base became a fundamental obstacle to revenue generation as well as to tax reform. A national statistical office was set up in 1846 but the project of a fiscal register was abandoned in 1850 for Bravo Murillo's system based on declarations of wealth. Forty per cent of taxable land disappeared overnight. In 1870, one newspaper declared, not as scandal but as simple knowledge, that most statistical returns were invented in provincial capitals by whoever was charged with drawing them up. So long as they produced the set quota of revenue, no one investigated. The concealment of assets was thus not simply a defect of the system but intrinsic to it.[38] The effect was to redistribute the tax burden so that smaller proprietors—particularly those smallholders who had bought or consolidated local landholdings during the disentail—paid more than large ones. The problem may have been less acute in areas with more equally distributed land holdings such as the fertile Levante but in areas dominated by the vast landed estates known as latifundia, the problem was immense. The *latifundista* area of Lower Andalucía, for example, had the highest concentration of fraudulently undervalued land. Calculations carried out for the Treasury in 1870 suggested that 64 per cent of the land in Huelva went undeclared as did 70 per cent of taxable wealth. Comparable figures for Córdoba were around 45 per cent for both types of asset and around 25 per cent in Seville.[39]

Even the figures for Seville represent an extraordinarily high level of tax fraud. Unsurprisingly, reformers continued to agitate for an efficient registration of tax assets, which might also have given an impetus towards modernizing Spanish agriculture. Reforming hopes centred on the idea of a cadastre, or public register of landed assets, proposals for which were

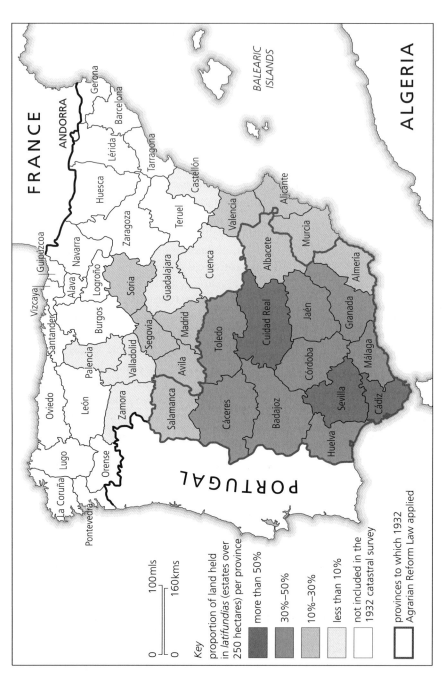

Key

proportion of land held
in *latifundias* (estates over
250 hectares) per province

more than 50%

30%–50%

10%–30%

less than 10%

not included in the
1932 catastral survey

provinces to which 1932
Agrarian Reform Law applied

0   100mls

0   160kms

Land Use and Agrarian Reform

repeatedly put forward, until surveying finally began in 1906. By then the idea of a cadastral map had assumed the status of a panacea, the final solution to Spain's tax problems. The experience of other European countries failed to dispel this idea. In France, for example, the *cadastre parcellaire* was almost complete by 1850, when it was already in need of updating.[40] The utopianism of nineteenth-century thinking about the cadastre in Spain also distracted from the lack of political will which was preventing its implementation. Part of this was the state's lack of penetration at local level. The energies of the land-owning classes went into concealing their wealth, a project in which successive governments were complicit.

When Napoleon Bonaparte introduced the idea of a state cadastre, he saw it as a tool of rational government, a complement to his legal code. As a soldier, he also understood the importance of good maps. Spain's General Narváez, took a similar view, establishing a permanent statistical commission in 1856 to fulfil cartographic, census, and fiscal functions. The commission worked on inconspicuously, modelling its methods on European ones and greatly increasing knowledge of the national territory. In 1865, the cartographic section became a separate department and produced accurately surveyed maps of Spain under another military man, Francisco Coello de Portugal y Quesada, who was already at work on his own national atlas. Coello's maps collected, systematized, and codified knowledge of the national territory. Atlases showed the territory and topography of Spain as a single unit defined by clearly differentiated boundaries, and so gave it symbolic as well as diagrammatic shape. Topographical features, administrative boundaries, and landholding patterns were set out in maps which presented a certain, top–down, understanding of the nation and presented it as complex, layered levels of information.[41]

As official information served official purposes, centralization was a clear theme, with maps elaborated from Madrid on the authority of central government. The many and varied mapping projects of the nineteenth century made society legible in a new way. Social reality—in all its messy complexity—was standardized into a series of maps and statistics which proclaimed equivalence and comparability.[42] Land was simply property, regardless of its fertility or location, and standard units of measurement allowed it to be presented as such. Nineteenth-century cartography celebrated the unitary state, just as cadastral maps reinforced the notion of a political system based on property rights, where ascertaining and safeguarding individual landholdings was a civic duty. State and public knowledge of the national territory was continuing apace and, as local and national authorities surveyed land, produced maps, and collected statistics on behalf of the Spanish state, so it became established as not only the arbiter but also the source of authoritative knowledge.

THE MAN ON HORSEBACK

A monopoly of legitimate force is the defining characteristic of the modern state, which is the sole source of the 'right' to use violence. Yet, while the ability to coerce lay at the heart of its power, most citizens' everyday encounters with the state had little to do with naked force: the defining quality was control over violence rather than frequent recourse to it.[43] This is often occluded in historical accounts, partly because of the tradition in Marxist thought of analysing the state as a tool of class domination. Marx's acute sociological observation of his own times lay at the heart of the analysis: law enforcement was a vital, and fast-increasing, area of state activity in the early nineteenth century. The London metropolitan police was established in 1829, the same year that Spain's customs and excise police (*carabineros*) were founded and coastguard patrols introduced. In a clear example of the changing nature of state function, the policing of national borders was no longer necessarily a military task.

As Marx observed, the routine assumption of law enforcement enhanced the capacity of the state and increased its penetration of society. This was the case even when, as in Spain, coastguards continued to collude with smugglers, or even act as privateers.[44] Such practices were fast being eradicated through-out Europe and, in Spain, the 'law and order' ticket adopted by successive governments in the 1840s made condoning them impossible: in 1846, a state-organized coastguard was established, with the boats, men, and political will to make determined inroads into the trade in contraband. A crucial weapon in this fight against brigandage was the Civil Guard, formed in 1844. The defence of property—that crucial component of the liberal revolution—had been the preserve of the local militias, those armed associations of urban property-owners that had become inextricably associated with the revolu-tionary juntas during the 1830s. Such groups could hinder law enforcement rather than uphold it: in the sherry-producing town of Jérez, for example, the local militia's own involvement in smuggling forced out the town's customs officers in 1841. As the Civil Guard took over the militias' role of defending property, the lines of state authority became clearer. Law enforcement was also now systematically extended to rural areas, where urban militias had little purchase.[45]

Under its original decree of 28 March 1844, the Civil Guard came under the ministry of the interior but was moved to the ministry of war as early as May of the same year. Officers were seconded from the army, guardsmen lived in segregated barracks, and the corps as a whole was subject to special (military) jurisdiction.[46] The original decree—while never repealed—had clearly been superseded. When the civil and military *reglamento* was published in October 1844, the latter simply ignored the Guards' supposed relationship with the minister of the interior. In 1878, the Civil Guard was made an integral part of the army and, though its name remained unchanged, any notion of a civil force was finally abandoned. It acted in response to a request from the civil authorities but was not controlled by them.

The first director of the Civil Guard, the duke of Ahumada, was instrumental in defining the military nature of the force. It was small in number, rising from a mere 5,500 men in 1844 to some 20,000 in 1900, but effective. The distinctive uniforms—including capes and patent leather hats—made it highly visible, while military discipline and codes of honour created reliable troops. The memoirs of one veteran, published in 1873, talked of injuries suffered and scars obtained for 'honour and the military Ordinances'.[47] Like other gendarmeries, the Guard used horses and military weaponry, policing the country through *puestos*—posts of as few as four men, established 'pueblo by pueblo, hamlet by hamlet, ravine by ravine' (Ahumada)—and patrolling in pairs. With relatively few men and resources, the Civil Guard succeeded in Ahumada's ambition of ensuring that 'there must be no sierra, no matter how hostile; there must be no scrubland, no matter how dense, without the three-cornered hat of the Civil Guard.'[48]

As these words suggest, Spain was difficult terrain. In western European terms, the country was inhospitable, exceeded in size only by France, in height only by Switzerland, and in aridity only by Greece. Nevertheless, the Civil Guard secured the national territory, eradicating brigands and safeguarding the highways through the lawless sierras of southern Spain. The deployment of a militarized gendarmerie was thus a practical response to an intractable problem and, as such, was seen as a success, in France, Italy, and the Habsburg lands as well as in Spain. In 1876, the Civil Guard was made responsible for maintaining law and order in the countryside, some twenty-two years after General O'Donnell had famously referred to 'a truly military occupation of the entire territory'.

The visibility of the Civil Guard, its quasi-military nature, and its deployment directly from Madrid, have led historians both to concur with O'Donnell and to talk of the 'arrival' of the state in the countryside.[49] As the Guerra dels Matiners had demonstrated, smuggling and brigandage were often linked to rebellion and distinctions between these activities were hard to draw. As the only agents of the state routinely empowered to use force against their fellow citizens, policemen easily came to symbolize the coercive power of the state. Yet, policing benefits citizens who are afraid of theft, assault, or criminal damage. Police forces also provided humanitarian assistance: the Civil Guard was deployed in cases of fire, flood, or natural disaster allowing police and people to work together, coordinating social life in a non-coercive way which nevertheless greatly increased the capacity of the central state. Gendarmes belonged to an array of government agents, whether employed full or part-time, who penetrated society establishing the infrastructure which, however deficient, connected state and society. The three-cornered hat was not, in and of itself, any more sinister than the peculiar helmet adopted by the British constabulary: both forms of headgear afforded the wearer some protection, stood out in a crowd, and may have had some deterrent effect when glimpsed by law-breakers. But the silhouette of the Civil Guardsman was never to attain the reassuring image of the British bobby.

Even military police forces originated in civil government, and were introduced and established via normal legislative and bureaucratic processes. Similarly, any armed force could be used in response to public order problems or even as a tool of political repression. The dichotomy between the civil and the military characterizes any gendarmerie, from the Civil Guard to the Royal Canadian Mounted Police, but militarization was to become a particularly pronounced feature of Spanish policing as urban insurrections continued the tradition of revolutionary juntas from the 'liberal revolution' of the 1830s. Even successful insurrections, such as those that returned the Progressive Party to power in 1854, damaged property and created opportunities for looting and riot. The persistence of civil conflict—notably through Carlism—meant that the fear of internal enemies persisted, while the beginnings of organized labour meant that the Civil Guard was used against strikers as well as against bandits.

Spain's military had an unusually strong presence in issues of public order. The absence of external threats to national borders meant that the army was rapidly losing any tradition of soldiering, becoming instead 'a great body of armed functionaries'.[50] As early as 1821, a decree had established that machinations against the constitution, the monarch, or the security of the state (whether internal or external), would be tried under military jurisdiction even if those accused were civilians. Numerous decrees and orders in council concerning public order were systematized after 1844 during a period of self-conscious 'strong' government. During the premiership of General Narváez, the Moderado Party enjoyed a period of hegemony, amending the constitution in 1845 to remove 'democratic' institutions such as the national militia and emphasizing the need for government in the name of order and progress. The introduction of the Civil Guard reflected the determination to eliminate the militias, centralize the administration, and impose order. By 1853, for example, the captain-general (military governor) of Barcelona could declare that any disorder in the textile factories would be met with martial law, even though declaring a state of emergency was actually the responsibility of the *jefe político* or civil governor. Crucially, though, no parliamentary authority was needed and, as many civil governors were former military men seeking state employment, this was a telling omission.

In 1867, the first law on public order was passed by parliament. Offences against public order were defined as 'any public demonstration offensive to religion, morality, the monarchy, the Constitution, the reigning dynasty, the legislature, and due respect for the law'. A 'state of alarm' could be declared by the civil governor if 'suspicion, news or facts', suggested that a public order disturbance was 'probable'. Should matters not calm down, a full 'state of war' would be implemented, with the civil authorities handing over command to the military, who then assumed 'administrative, judicial, political and civil powers'. All 'rebels', their 'accomplices, helpers, and accessories after the fact' became subject to courts-martial, and contact with them was presumed to have a criminal intent. Tellingly, the 'state of war' could also be imposed immediately, without the intermediary 'state of alarm'. In either case, the decision was taken locally, without parliamentary scrutiny. The 1867 law militarized Spain's public order 'problem' and so reinforced the inward trend of an army whose shortcomings as a defence force were all too apparent.

A confusion of military and civil power was the hallmark of the 'state of war', although this was perceptible in other areas of army life too. Civil Guardsmen figured in army lists, serving in Morocco in 1859, while soldiers guarded prisons. But the peculiarly Spanish tradition of the *pronunciamiento* took this confusion of military and civil power to the heart of the state. A *pronunciamiento* was a ritualized challenge for power on the part of the army, which became effectively institutionalized as a mechanism for changing the governing party. At some point, the leader of the *pronunciamiento*—always a professional military man and usually a general—would 'unsheathe his sword'. Less a direct threat than a token of assuming command, the drawn sword rallied support, demanding a change of government and political policy, invariably in the name of liberty. *Pronunciamientos* were calls to action rather than surprise attacks, initially at least simply a test of political opinion. If there was little response, the soldiers went back to barracks. If, on the other hand, additional supporters rallied to the call and neutral army units showed no propensity to intervene in favour of the ruling party, the *pronunciamiento* was successful and the government would change.[51]

Under these circumstances, the clusters of political factions and followings which made up the main 'parties' of Moderados and Progressives developed close military alliances. Each had its *espadón*, or 'broadsword', serving as a military protector: General Espartero was the arbiter of Progressive politics after the Carlist War; Narváez overthrew him in 1843 ushering in a period of Moderado rule. Neither man—nor the future *espadones*, Generals O'Donnell and Prim—emerged as a party arbiter because of any particular political talent. The Catholic thinker Jaime Balmes, for example, observed of Narváez: 'we see him today trying to act like a parliamentarian and tomorrow, sabre in hand, menacing the parliament. His instincts, his ideas, his sentiments, and his interests are in perpetual conflict'.[52] They were professional military men, whose code of honour was embedded in their very pronunciamientos. A failed attempt to displace Espartero in 1841, for example, led to the execution of the *pronunciados*, as was usual. The young Diego de León rode to the firing squad in full uniform and an open carriage, and distributed cigars to his executioners. These were later put on display in the army museum which Espartero established in Madrid, where they could be seen at least until the 1960s.[53]

General León's heroic end was not simply the stuff of Moderado legend. Rather, the story encapsulated quintessentially military values—resolve, courage, self-control—which, while they would have been widely recognized and admired among Spanish men more generally, also suggested a barracks culture which distinguished army officers from their fellow citizens. In 1843, the Spanish army had one officer for every five or six men—9,000 out of a total force of some 50,000—'the most grotesque disproportion' in any contemporary European force.[54] Military adventures were very few: only the Moroccan War of 1859–60 provided any significant military action outside mainland Spain or its colonies, notably Cuba. This left the Spanish army poised to acquire that 'explosive mixture of arrogance and boredom' which was a pre-condition for interfering in politics.[55] Professional grievances were legion—in 1842 the Guadalajara infantry had to sell their bread ration to buy soap—yet professional expertise was hard to acquire.

Isolated in barracks or resident in garrison towns, educated in military academies, informed by its own newspapers and periodicals, increasingly endogamous in terms of both marriage and career, the Spanish army became more separate from the society it supposedly protected. Similar patterns were instituted in the Civil Guard, whose agents never served in their native province. Unsurprisingly, watchfulness or the surveillance of the population, became one of its prime tasks, and its public order function encouraged a particular relationship with the landowning classes, allowing further inter-penetration of state and society, at least within elite groups. Yet, while the distinctiveness of Spain's armed forces was exaggerated, it was not unique. Armies everywhere were insulated from society. Governed by separate law codes—which in Spain also covered soldiers' families and dependents—and increasingly specialized in function and technical skills, their profession 'encouraged caste autonomy within the state'. Paradoxically, the modern state's monopoly of legitimate violence was wielded by an institution which retained a segmented authority within the state.[56]

For some scholars, notably Diego López Garrido, the nineteenth-century Spanish state was characterized by a dichotomy between its civil and military components, easily equated with progress and reaction. Others speak of the army 'colonizing' the state. From here it is a relatively short step to characterize the state as repressive, wielding military power against 'terrorized populations' who 'will not normally step beyond certain niceties of compliance but whose behaviour cannot be positively controlled'.[57] Such characterizations are more often applied to later periods of Spain's history, particularly the twentieth century, but the warped development which led to this supposedly militarized state clearly began in the 'age of pronunciamientos'.

But is it possible for an army to colonize a state in a real rather than a hyperbolic sense? The political power of the central state might ultimately rest upon coercive force, but it does not rely on this in its day-to-day operation. The 'strong' government of the Moderado hegemony in the 1840s modernized the court system and codified the criminal law as well as establishing the Civil Guard. The 1848 Penal Code abolished torture, for example, and while its implementation in military jurisdiction was delayed—the Military Penal Code was only implemented in 1884—the legislative impetus was clear.[58] Nor did any *pronunciamiento* lead to a military regime. Rather, military intervention replaced electoral or parliamentary decisions as the mechanism for political change. As Balmes put it in 1846, it 'is not that the civil power is weak because the military power is strong but rather that the military power is strong because the civil power is weak . . . . The political parties have alternated periods in power; but none has succeeded in building a civil power'.[59] In the last instance all turned to the military to resolve their political differences.

The reliance on bugle-blowing made for a very narrow conception of the political nation. This had profound effects, but its origins were relatively simple. The first Carlist War had both strengthened the army and depleted the administration. Espartero was the principal architect of the liberals' military victory and, like the other *espadones*, was promoted to the rank of general during the war. The queen regent's shaky hold on power left her mortgaged to the military and she abdicated in favour of Espartero in 1840. Contingent circumstances and political ineptness on the part of the queen, and later her daughter, led to the entry of the military into politics. But, once the soldiers were there, there was little real incentive to widen the basis of politics. The *pronunciamiento* institutionalized the relationship between generals and politicians and made it part of the working of the state. The narrowness of the political nation meant that government remained the preserve of a series of political cliques, a state of affairs which did nothing to undermine the army's position as the only apparently solid institution in the liberal state. There was no need to re-evaluate the pact between politicians and soldiers while it seemed to work, despite the damage done to representative government and the public sphere. Increasingly divorced from Spanish society, and more powerful than the parliamentarians, there were few to gainsay the army when it said, as one officer did in 1841: 'We cannot and we will not say—"We are the state"; but we do say: "We are the country", or if you prefer it, "the purest part of the country".'[60]

Even with this military reticence to claim possession of the state, the segmented authority of the army could only weaken that of the state. The shift to 'strong government' which had been a marked feature of Moderado government since the 1840s had brought real advances in modernizing the machinery of the state, yet successive Moderado administrations—which were openly favoured by the crown—became increasingly heavy-handed in dealing with political opposition. As the Progressive politician Carlos Rubio put it in 1865, Spain was divided into two peoples: 'one which says, "I have rights" and another which replies "I have cannon"'. As Rubio's words suggested, the Moderado hegemony had deepened 'the split in the trunk of liberalism'. The discourse of strong government—underpinned after 1845 by a more authoritarian constitution—had taken Spain's liberal revolution firmly to the right.

In response, the Progressive Party loudly reiterated the language of classical liberalism, while radical outriders like the Democratic Party (founded in 1849) elaborated a programme of citizens' rights. The Moderados' easy recourse to force made organization difficult, but both Progressives and Democrats continued to call on the 'people', in the name of their inalienable rights. Their populist programmes notwithstanding, neither party succeeded in dominating Spain's admittedly undeveloped public sphere. If the Progressives represented any society, it was that of the cafés and clubs: contemporary lithographs of committee meetings show tall-hatted men sitting around dining tables. The world of the radical committees merged seamlessly with that of the *tertulia*: committees were supposed to guide the citizenry to action, but they functioned erratically, and sometimes conspiratorially. Both Republicans and Democrats were active in secret societies, such as the 'Sons of the People' of the 1850s and 1860s, although these societies were even more prone to local fragmentation than were the Progressives' committees.[61] Though easily infiltrated by police spies, the secret societies penetrated southern rural society, as cafés echoed to theatrical passwords and secret oaths. The sense of solidarity the societies fostered attracted virtually the entire adult male population in some pueblos in the provinces of Málaga and Granada and seem to have contributed to the insurrections which broke out in rural Seville in 1857 and Loja (Granada) in 1861. Both revolts were easily, and forcibly, suppressed by the army, but not before hundreds of armed men had taken to the streets.

The secret societies drew on an urban insurrectionary tradition that had been maintained by those outside the political system, who found their points were most effective when made directly. The Progressive Party was briefly returned to power in 1854 by a combination of *pronunciamiento* and popular insurrection in Barcelona, Madrid, and several provincial capitals. Barricaded streets prevented the free circulation of people and traffic, in Madrid literally impeding access to the seat of power.[62] According to one observer, 'every house was a fortress, every resident a combatant'.[63] The insurrections were, as usual, principally the work of artisans and members of the petty bourgeoisie: when the national militia was re-established by the new government in an attempt to undo Moderado dominance, artisans made up 38.5 per cent of its Madrid membership. Unsurprisingly, the 1854 insurrections soon took on the character of a popular fiesta. As well as fighting, there was dancing, while barricades were festooned with garlands and flags. Commemorative lithographs showed Spain's red and yellow flag flying over the impromptu fortifications, sometimes adorned with slogans such as 'Long live the sovereign people'. Used by the navy since 1785 and the army since 1843, the national flag was now being used in a popular rather than a military idiom. The language of nationalism, like that of liberalism, could be used to justify events, as could that of popular justice. 'The death penalty for thieves' was one of the less progressive placards displayed on the barricades in 1854.

This period of military and popular urban unrest which briefly returned the Progressives to power lasted only until 1856. It ended as it had begun, with military intervention and bloodshed on the streets of Madrid. For insurrections invariably lacked national co-ordination, defined political programmes, and coherent leadership, and were easily suppressed. Those dancing on the barricades had always seemed unlikely comrades-in-arms for army generals, even liberal ones such as O'Donnell and Prim, even though both were some way from the top-hatted world of the political clubs. A strong bourgeois exclusiveness isolated the constitutional regime 'from above' and 'from below'. The mechanisms for change all seemed to come from outside the system. Yet this was, of course, itself part of the system. Such a pattern was written into the very structures of the state. The role of the army, the limited nature of the franchise, the local networks which modified and conditioned the implementation of policy, all reflected and, in turn, reproduced social conflicts and class relationships. And as such conflicts were institutionalized within the state, so they would condition future social struggles.

In Spain, changes of regime or even of government could not be accomplished by civilian politicians or electors; parliament was not capable of reproducing itself. It was not that the constitutional solutions of the mid-century were implemented 'from above'. This was hardly abnormal. Only revolutionary states are constructed from the bottom up, and even then this claim lies less with the proletariat than with its self-appointed vanguard. Rather, the narrowness of the regime in both social and institutional terms—with the army substituting for either electorate or political elite in determining when it was time for change—meant that governments were always vulnerable both to military intervention and to popular insurrection. Pressure from below could not in itself institute change, but it could be part of the process. Army rebels invoked change in the name of the people, and when soldiers joined the barricades—or at least refused to dismantle them—change was inevitable.

All political groups in Spain—even the most radical and conspiratorial—thus courted the army as an essential lever to power. Espartero, 'the people's general', was easily the most visible, as well as the most popular Progressive figure. His name went up on the barricades in 1854, while his portrait appeared everywhere, even on cigarette papers. Popularity could not, though, entirely substitute for political sense or a coherent programme. Like many of his comrades-in-arms, Espartero took refuge in generalities, promising to comply with the national will or to defend 'liberty, properly understood'. His great rival, Narváez, 'loved power for itself and for what it brought: luxury, display, ballerinas, stock-exchange tips'.[64] Such attitudes did not make for durable political solutions: the system Espartero and Narváez had done so much to shape could fashion expedient solutions but lacked the strength to resist real challenges.

THE FIRST REPUBLIC

The weakness of the governing system eventually led to a protracted political crisis which lasted from 1868 to 1874. In the dangerous year of 1868, another revolution repeated the pattern of 1854, combining military and popular action in an uneasy alliance of professional soldiers and urban radicals.[65] Popular pressure was so great that the crown's isolation became obvious and Isabel II—the principal architect of the monarchy's alliance with reaction—was forced into exile. Her military defenders, O'Donnell and Narváez, were both dead and, when General Prim and Admiral Topete landed at Cádiz on 18 September, there was no *espadón* to defend the queen. The naval revolt was marked by the cry 'Down with the Bourbons!': impatience with the ruling system had reached breaking point. Isabel left for France from her holiday villa in San Sebastián without even returning to Madrid. When, two years later, she renounced her claim to the throne in favour of her son, Alfonso, Spain's break with the past was revealed in that most potent of symbols, the removal of a reigning monarch.

Though the main players in the 'glorious' revolution were, as ever, the military, popular pressure had a role to play. Just as in 1854, the urban juntas used the revolutionary moment to push through a radical political agenda. When Prim arrived in Madrid, he found a junta already in place, and the city wasted no time in re-establishing its local militia, now as the 'Volunteers for Liberty'. The social basis of populist political action was now changing: by 1872, almost a third of Madrid's militiamen were workers. The petty bourgeoisie no longer spoke for the people, or at least the people could now answer back. The militias took workers to the heart of political change, and popular pressure brought about the introduction of universal male suffrage in 1868. Promises of freedom of worship, universal suffrage, the abolition of the death penalty, and trial by jury—in short, the full legal panoply of progressive constitutionalism—engendered great enthusiasm. The 1868 revolution thus earned its soubriquet, *la gloriosa*, in direct imitation of England's Glorious Revolution of 1688.

As in 1688, an unsatisfactory monarch was replaced by a more amenable one. Here, however, any superficial similarity to the robust English constitutional settlement ended abruptly. Isabel's place was briefly taken by Amadeo of Savoy, invited by Prim to take the throne of the Bourbons in the name of 'democratic monarchy'. The assassination of the king-making general in December 1870—on the very day his new king arrived in Madrid—left Amadeo isolated. The fragility of the post–1868 political order was by now all too apparent: even the revolutionary settlement proved to be shallow. At local level, reaction to a radical programme of democratic change quickly set in. Neither soldiers nor moderates viewed armed workers with enthusiasm: affluent *madrileños*, for example, showed their unease by establishing a counter-militia of 'honourable neighbours' in March 1873, 'Volunteers for Property', who stood face-to-face against the 'Volunteers for Liberty'. At national level, the new regime was coming under sustained pressure. Fear of unrest was growing: insurrection continued to be a danger in the towns; the Carlists were rearming in the north; Cuba, still ruled directly by a captain general, was in revolt. The Cuban war would last until 1878, stretching the Spanish state's resources well past the point they could comfortably reach.

Economic crisis was thus added to the new regime's difficulties, particularly after Carlist unrest turned into outright civil war.

Urban, Carlist, and colonial unrest continued, affecting the way in which the new regime was perceived as well as constraining its sphere of action. The state's indebtedness had become critical: between 1871 and 1874, 'debt interest payments fell precipitately because the treasury was completely unable to meet them.'[66] In the year before the effective suspension of payments, the amount spent servicing the national debt amounted to more than half the annual budget. Palliative solutions were sought in the sale of assets: the French Rothschilds, for example, bought railway concessions in 1855 and leased the Almadén mercury mines in 1870. But there was no serious attempt to resolve the underlying problem, which would have involved tax reform. State institutions did make some progress: a central bank was established in 1874, and granted a monopoly of note issue. This was another way of monetarizing the national debt: banknotes were printed at a higher volume than ever before and the public effectively accepted this debt by accepting the notes. In the 1880s, following yet another conversion, the debt stabilized, at least temporarily. But any lasting solution to the Spanish state's chronic lack of fiscal resources lay far beyond both the will and the capacity of contemporary governments.

Throughout the revolutionary period of 1868–74, the political classes were split over the issue of the Crown, party structures remained rudimentary, and electoral fraud was ubiquitous. In the elections of April and August 1872, the abstention rate approached 50 per cent; in May 1873, this had risen to 61 per cent. A 'democratic monarchy' brokered by a general and without strong support in the Cortes was never likely to be a popular or political success. Amadeo abdicated on 11 February 1873, the very day that parliament declared Spain to be a Republic. As Emilio Castelar, president of the Republic from September 1873, announced to the Cortes, 'nobody has destroyed the monarchy in Spain, it has died through internal decay.'

With Amadeo's tenuous hold on the throne visibly faltering, a republic was the only logical step. Spain's First Republic was voted into existence by an overwhelming parliamentary majority—despite the relatively small number of paid-up Republicans in the chamber. The Federal Republican Party never won more than between 10 and 15 per cent of the seats in the Cortes, though in 1868 they did provide the mayors for twenty provincial capitals, including Barcelona and Seville. Along the eastern seaboard, republicans were the heirs of a tradition of urban radicalism but, throughout the country, republican politicians favoured moderate, centralized republicanism on the French model, rather than a radical, federal version. Yet, it was the latter which, perhaps surprisingly, came to characterize their short-lived regime.[67]

Throughout the land, the structures of power were becoming decentred, testimony to the weakness of the central Spanish state. By 1874, the Carlists were able to organize an incipient state in the north, with its own government offices, post, and press. An alternative vision of devolved power was expressed through federal constitutionalism, which had been given a new impetus by the creation of a unified German Reich in 1871 and the north's victory in the US Civil War. In May 1873, Federal Republicans also formed the government in Spain, under Pi y Margall. Though their victory was due in large part to abstention and indifference, legalism was a defining characteristic of Pi's Federal republicanism. His party rejected the revolutionary justice of the barricades and any idea of implementing political change from below, even while insisting that the Federal Republic was genuinely the will of the nation. Believing that a *directed* federal revolution was still possible, Pi devoted much of his brief premiership to preparing a new federal constitution, even as the revolutionary impetus moved decisively to the localities.

The belief in constitutional solutions to public order problems—indeed in the constitution as a panacea for disorder—was commonplace among nineteenth-century liberals and would recur under the Second Spanish Republic of the 1930s. For Pi, resorting to force would lose the Republic its legitimacy. Yet, general agreement over changing the nature of the unitary state, brought no consensus over whether to retain the 1833 provinces or to return to the 'historic' regions. Locally, the matter was even murkier. As the minister of finance—admittedly not, himself, a federalist—put it in the Cortes in March 1873:

you have no federal republic because you do not know what your federal republic is. For the intransigent masses the federal republic is not even a feeling [. . .] for them the federal republic is here a farm to be divided, a wood to be partitioned, there the fixing of a minimum wage; in another province a battering ram opening a breach in the forces of law and order so that contraband may pass; poor against rich, the partition of property, tax payer against the exchequer, all these monetary interests, all these social utopias, deep yearnings, great needs, ardent appetites constitute the essence of the republic amongst the people, but you will never find among them [. . .] the germ of a programme for society.[68]

Such localism was amply demonstrated during the cantonalist revolts which spread through Andalucía and the Levante from the summer of 1873. Taking advantage of the deployment of soldiers to the north to fight the Carlist rebels, various towns and cities declared independent cantons. The cantons were politically radical, sometimes inspired by directives from radical federalism's central committee in Madrid, but essentially the work of local elements. Cantonalism continued the traditions of the municipal revolutionary juntas, being radical but not necessarily popular. The Cordoban leaders, for example, included a professor of canon law, notorious for preaching atheism in his lectures, while even radical deputies, like the Cádiz hothead José Paúl y Angulo opposed any redistribution of common land.

Central to the spirit of cantonalism were the declarations of municipal independence which characterized these short-lived, often ephemeral, revolts.[69] Yet, that in itself raised many questions about the canton's relationship, not only to the central state, but also to the surrounding towns. The cantonalists had no coherent political programme even at regional level. Both Seville and Cartagena, for example, encountered fierce resistance from towns in their hinterland: the former's attempt to incorporate Utrera was met with armed resistance while the latter's attempts to raise war-taxes caused smaller towns such as Lorca to look to Madrid for protection.

The Republican cantons were particularist, occasionally to a near-farcical extent. After minting its own coins and selling off state property, Cartagena declared that all the canton's debts would be charged to the Madrid government. But even this naive political trick shows that the cantonalists had no separatist ambitions. Indeed, the Murcia junta had already declared on 16 June that 'this Junta represents neither an insurrection nor a pronunciamiento against the institutions of the country.'[70] Democratic language reinvented these institutions in the cantonalist imagination. Whether in mountain pueblos or substantial cities, the language of Republicanism prevailed. Decrees and proclamations invariably used phrases such as 'the people's mayor', or the 'constitutional *ayuntamiento*', derived from the proclamations of the larger cantons. The proclamation of the canton in Cartagena, for instance, concluded with 'Long live the sovereignty of the people!'

As such language came from outside the pueblo, it has been seen as essentially empty, imposed from above rather than reflecting the convictions of those below. Yet, even mimetic language may have meaning to those using it, and the memory of the Federal Republic—soon intertwined with that of the repression which followed it—entered into the political imagination. The Federal Republic was claimed as the forebear of later revolutionary movements, particularly anarchism, as historic events passed into proletarian myth. In Andalucía, where a huge rural proletariat depended upon the harsh latifundia economy, federalism and anarchism proved hard to disentangle. Men such as Fermín Salvochea, who led Cádiz from insurrection in 1868 to cantonalism in 1873, ended their lives as committed anarchists. Introduced to the radicalism of Thomas Paine and the utopian socialism of Robert Owen as a young man in Liverpool and London, Salvochea spent much of the time between 1873 and his death in 1907 between prison and exile.

As the Progressive politician Fermín Caballero pointed out in a letter to the social reformer Concepción Arenal in 1868, the sheer desperation of the

Andalucian landworkers made desperate measures increasingly likely. 'The state of these villages is appalling', he wrote, '. . . if the government does not raise substantial funds, which it certainly won't, the hunger, misery, and misfortunes the winter will bring are incalculable.'[71] Events in Montilla (Córdoba) in 1873 demonstrated the prescience of his words. Here, local workers lost patience with the intransigent local reactionaries known as 'the party of the cudgel', and took to the streets crying 'the hour of vengeance is here'. Looting followed, as the rebels sacked the houses of the rich, drank their cellars, and torched their buildings. In a gesture that was to be seen again in the 1890s, the early 1920s, and 1936, the property register was burnt.[72] In 1873, notarial records were also burnt in Sanlúcar de Barrameda, the sherry-producing town in Cádiz. Here, though, the cry 'Long live the International' was also heard, as it was in the industrial town of Alcoy, near the Alicante coast.

In contrast to Montilla, where social protest took the traditional form of a Jacquerie, protestors in Sanlúcar and Alcoy looked to the future rather than the past. In Alcoy, international socialist organizers transformed a workers' strike into a municipal revolt that claimed several lives, including that of the mayor, and razed factories to the ground. Atrocity stories abounded: even liberal papers spoke of heads on pikes, human torches, and hanged priests. Shades of the Paris Commune were hanging over Alcoy: the spectacle of blazing property and murdered mayors combined with the spectre of socialism to terrify liberals as well as reactionaries. Even though the virtual absence of social revolution from the cantons testified to the weakness of the internationalists rather than their strength, in the images of Alcoy the communards' struggle seemed to have come to Spain.

Cannon were used against the cantons just as they had been against the Commune. In August 1873, the new president, Emilio Castelar, ordered the army to crush the cantons. This was easily achieved, at least as soon as troops had been deployed from the Carlist wars in the north. Many of the smaller cantons—such as those at Torrevieja, Algeciras, and Fuenteovejuna—collapsed at the mere threat of force; Seville and Valencia were quickly crushed. Only Cartagena held out, favoured by its position as a leading naval port: as Raymond Carr put it, 'any government would hesitate before it blew up its own navy'.[73] In January 1874, however, even Cartagena capitulated.

Like his French predecessors, Castelar believed that re-establishing order was the Republic's only hope. Bourgeois Republicanism found reactionary rebellion, socialist revolution, and peasant Jacqueries equally unappealing. Yet, the absence of any protracted resistance suggests that the threat was limited. The turbulence of 1873 occurred in a period of governmental crisis and civil war. The recourse, once again, to military might to restore order and impose the central authority of state reflected the weakness of that state rather than its strength. It also set a pattern for the future. Barcelona had played little part in the Federal Republic. Even though the city was one of very few in Spain with an industrial working class, it proved deaf to Internationalist calls for a general revolutionary strike. Similarly, although the Catalan deputies acted as a clear interest group during that turbulent summer, there was little popular appetite to sever links with Madrid while three Catalan provinces were directly threatened by Carlist rebels. The refounding of an oligarchic political system, would, however, only further the cause of Catalan nationalism. Similarly, the easy recourse to armed repression would severely dent proletarian organizations, but it would never break their resolve. As federalism waned, it was overtaken by international communism, in either its socialist or its anarchist forms. The challenges of class struggle were to be far sharper in the future.

2

Imagining the Nation, 1875–98

THE FUTURE AND THE PAST

What the eye is to the lover . . . language—whatever language history has made his or her mother tongue—is to the patriot. Through that language, encountered at mother's knee and parted with only at the grave, pasts are restored, fellowships are imagined, and futures are dreamed.

Benedict Anderson, *Imagined Communities*, 1983

Language has always been seen as an impediment to Spanish nationalism. The persistence of Basque, Catalan, and Galician signifies to many the failure to establish a Spanish nation-state. This is primarily understood as a peculiarly powerful kind of nationalism: for the nation-state to exist, Spanish citizens would identify themselves as such, would believe in the existence and historical identity of Spain, and would perceive this identity so strongly that they would be prepared even to die for it. Though Spain was hardly unique in having other languages spoken within its borders—it would be hard to think of a European country where that was not the case—their vitality demonstrated the shortcomings of Spanish integrative nationalism. Those who lived in Spain were loyal not the patria but to the *patria chica*, to the locality rather than to the nation.

Regional identities were vividly symbolized by a shared minority language particularly when, as in the case of Catalan, this was undergoing a cultural resurgence or, as with Basque, it was anciently established and linguistically unique. An estimated 54 per cent of Basques still spoke their ancient language in 1868, though, as in Cataluña and Galicia, the number of monolingual speakers was falling.[1] Yet, while bilingualism could have served as an equally potent national symbol, it tended to go unremarked. Many regional nationalists were highly suspicious of it and, as their political activities took off in the late nineteenth century, they emphasized the need for cultural, or even racial, purity. Even though he was not a native Basque speaker, the founding father of Basque Nationalism, Sabino Arana, wrote bitterly of immigrants 'bringing with them their bullfights, their flamenco songs and dances, their "refined" language so abundant in blasphemous and filthy expressions'.[2]

Arana's hostility to 'immigrants' was overtly racist, but he recognized that his Basque nationalist struggle was not only against Castilian words and syntax. The language of 'Spanishness' encompassed image and landscape, culture and history as well as grammar and vocabulary. Cheap reproductive techniques such as lithographing provided a new medium for this highly visual language. Its images, emblems, and symbols spread throughout the land, in a selection which was neither arbitrary nor surprising. Despite its supposed lack of integrative nationalism, nineteenth-century Spain had already achieved that 'lived in' sense of nationhood. In an era in which many of Garibaldi's southern Italian followers assumed that Italia was his mistress, Spain was an accepted reality.

This is not to say that all Spaniards fully understood their own relationship to their governing state, but then neither did the impoverished Londoners interviewed by Henry Mayhew in 1849. The idea of the nation was an ordinary and familiar one, composed of images and references which were immediately identifiable as Spanish. The Romantic movement of the early nineteenth century had led to a new interest in a shared, 'traditional', Spanish past. The carefully observed *costumbrista* novels of Fernán Caballero or the paintings of Valeriano Domínguez Bécquer depicted the costumes and customs of Andalucía as picturesque rather than impoverished. The suggestion of a timeless Spanish past, rather than an agonized present, was reinforced by *costumbrismo*'s connection with the great genre tradition of the Golden Age. At a country wedding depicted by Caballero for example, the *novios* dance a fandango—an 'eminently national dance'—moving graciously 'with an elegant swaying of the body'.[3]

Dancing, singing, the folk-culture of the pueblo contributed to the commercial spectacle of flamenco, whose gypsy traditions were then being rediscovered by the founder of the modern Spanish musical idiom, Felip Pedrell, and his pupils, Isaac Albéniz, Enrique Granados, and later Manuel de Falla. Despite the incorporation of distinctively Spanish folk idioms, classical music was an elite taste. In contrast, the popular display of bullfighting—which became Spain's principal cultural industry after 1880—was inextricably bound up with ideas of national identity. Of course, bullfighting had its critics. Fernán Caballero detested it, and made the hero of her 1849 novel *La gaviota* flee the Seville bullring, unable to watch the spectacle. But she was in the minority. The number of *corridas* fought each year went up from around 400 in the 1860s to over 700 in the 1880s as what had been either an aristocratic or a village spectacle became a national pastime. By 1880, Spain had at least

105 permanent *plazas de toros*, now a distinctive feature of the Spanish townscape.[4]

In commercial terms, bullfighting was highly profitable. For cities such as Valencia the bullfight was crucial to modernizing and commercializing the local *feria* in the 1870s. Special trains ran to the brand-new *plaza de toros* on bullfight days, often with attractively low-priced tickets. The commercial bullring was a new venue for a familiar sight, a place of popular assembly and shared spectacle. Although seats were divided by price, and therefore by class, attending a bullfight was a communal ritual. The performance of the matador demonstrated qualities which all those present would see as virtues: bravery, *orgullo*, the dominance of man over beast. These were the shared prerogatives of Spanish manhood, acted out under clear blue skies, before ladies in lace mantillas and to the applause of the common people.

The bullfight appeared everywhere, testimony both to its popularity and its undoubtedly Spanish nature. Even places without a permanent bullring would still see bull-running in the *plaza mayor* or *vaquillas* in some temporary structure. Over a hundred newspapers and journals dedicated to the *toros* were published during the 1880s and 1890s, and all the main Madrid dailies ran a bullfighting column. Numerous artists followed Goya's path to the bullring, painting portraits, action pictures, and sentimental genre scenes. But while Andalucía might have been regarded as bullfighting's spiritual home, its artists had no monopoly on the subject. When the Valencian novelist Vicente Blasco Ibáñez published his bullfighting tale, *Sangre y Arena*, in 1908 it became a best-seller. The Catalans Ramón Casas and Ricard Canals both painted the *corrida*, while the Basque Ignacio de Zuloaga painted matadors.[5] Famous bullfighters appeared on wine labels and cigarette papers, so bringing the bullfight into the local bar and the family home.

Identity, though, was not simply a question of familiarity. For individuals to become citizens, they had to write themselves into their surroundings, to perceive themselves as part of the traditions, history, and landscapes that made up Spain. For example, landscape painting—and the prints, etchings, and lithographs to which it gave rise—was not simply a kind of applied topography. Rather, it provided customers with familiar geographical scenes, 'framing' the countryside for national commercial consumption. As increasing numbers of Spaniards moved to the cities, landscape painting allowed for the urban consumption of nature. The locus of the nation might have been increasingly metropolitan, but its soul lay in the localities.

Advertising images were ubiquitous reminders of this. The olive oil company, Carbonell, established in 1866, chose a landscape as its label (Plate 10). The undulating olive groves of Andalucía decorated its containers, their contours framed by a decorative banner bearing the company legend, 'Spanish olive oil'. In the centre, a girl posed before an olive tree, a fringed shawl over her simple white dress, with a high comb, and a carnation behind one ear, her arms raised to gather olives, but in a gesture taken from flamenco. A particular landscape, part of a shared idea of Spain, was thus brought into the everyday landscape of the kitchen, the market, and the shop shelf. Ornate frames were used to display Spanish images on other forms of packaging, whether girls in Valencian dress on 'Sos' rice or Baroque religious images on Extremaduran paprika.

Similar echoes were found in advertising posters such as that designed by Ramón Casas for the local liquor Anis del Mono, which also used the figure of a woman in long, full skirts, a fringed shawl, and carnation. The Catalan artist's choice of what was in origin an Andalucian image, showed how the local was being reworked in a national context, to create a common idiom of Spanishness. The use of recognizably national images, and the framing of such images on packages so that they could be glimpsed, just as one espied countryside or parkland at the end of a city street, helped advertising to create a national gaze. High culture too increasingly allowed for the expression of personal or even poetic moods. The memories evoked by landscape paintings, for instance, were clearly part of the paintings' appeal.

Regionalism was a strong strand in landscape painting, shown in both the luminous Mediterranean coastal scenes of Joaquín Sorolla and the sombre Castilian townscapes of Ignacio de Zuloaga. But regionalism did not necessarily countermand a developing sense of the nation in Spain any more than in Germany. Rather, what Nicholas Green has referred to as 'a nascent rhetoric of nationalism' saw the nation as centred upon and located in the regions.[6] Landscape painting conveyed this in various ways. Romantic artists such as Fortuny or Villamil populated their landscapes, using obvious props such as women with fans or mantillas, often in a Goyaesque manner. But these were not the only means of conveying or signifying Spanishness. For observers to feel an emotional link with a landscape, they had to visualize themselves within it. One way for the viewer to enter the picture in this way was if it evoked personal experiences. Landscape artists, genre artists, and even internationally renowned artists such as Sorolla all painted life in the open air. The subjects were diverse, ranging from markets, dances, and processions, to picnics or *meriendas*. But all captured and reproduced that quotidian experience which is at the heart of identity. For Spanish life was, to a great extent, lived outside, whether through the formal *paseo* of the city streets or in the *romerías* and outdoor gatherings of life in the pueblo. Scenes of people strolling through open land or stopping to cook over wood fires evoked not only the scenery but also the smells and tastes of Spanish life. After all, a wood fire was the way to cook paella, a Valencian dish which outgrew its homeland as comprehensively as did England's Yorkshire pudding.

The repertoire of open-air scenes—which was continued and extended by later *plein-air* painters—not only made viewers more familiar with the countryside, but also idealized it. Long after Fernán Caballero, the countryside was implicitly presented as a repository of pure, Spanish values, against the decadence of the liberal town. Indeed, it was not only conservatives who idealized the Spanish peasantry. The liberal historian Rafael Altamira, for example, even while bemoaning the grievous problem of illiteracy, wrote of

the fact of a culture, in part self-taught, in part traditional, which finds expression in the proverbs, pithy sayings, and maxims which everybody knows and everybody applies with complete appositeness when occasion presents. That is the knowledge of life, the shrewd insight and deepheld wisdom . . . an inherent originality of the Spanish mind.[7]

The example Altamira used was Sancho Panza, an allusion which emphasized the timelessness of his observation, for this same 'inherent originality' had been observed in the sixteenth century by no less a master than Cervantes.

Traditional rural Spain thus provided a national landscape which was shaped by the past.[8] As Altamira's comments show, the regional present was offset by a shared historic past, one wrought by subjects of the Spanish Crown. In the century of Hegel and Marx, a new dialectic brought a change in people's sense of historical time. History was not simply a repository from which symbolic events might be selected for the edification of the present. Rather, both nations and individuals had to situate themselves within historical time, as only a sense of the past would reveal future destiny.

For this to be the case, knowledge of the past had to be scientific, its findings indisputable. Realism was the watchword of the nineteenth century, unsurprisingly given the pronounced sense of destiny which formed its zeitgeist. Narrative and history dominated both visual and written culture: according to Roland Barthes, narration was the 'privileged signifier of the real'.[9] And just as progress was real—both technological development and political liberties bore testimony to that—so it needed to be grounded in a real, factual sense of the past. For some, these facts were conveyed by the era's great historians, Macaulay, Michelet, or Ranke. But, while Portugal possessed a historian of stature in Alexandre Herculano, Spain did not. The politician, Antonio Cánovas del Castillo, edited a national history in 1890 which broke the monopoly of another politician, the ex-priest and Progressive deputy, Modesto Lafuente. His thirty-volume *Historia general de Espana* (1850–67) was reputed to be 'one of the most read books during the second half of the nineteenth century'.[10] The state of the national education system was such that this did not necessarily require a great number of readers, but Lafuente's was an influential project, not least among the history painters who were, at the time, the darlings of the academy.

History painting was as revered and as popular south of the Pyrenees as it was in the rest of Europe.[11] Its guiding light was France's Paul Delaroche, who was among the continent's most admired artists at the mid-century. The genre featured heavily in the national exhibitions held annually in Spain. Prize-winning canvases were invariably purchased by the state for the National Museum, intended as a temple both to art and to progress, and merged with the royal collections in the Prado after 1868. Provincial academies also organized exhibitions and bought pictures to display in public buildings, sharing their Madrid counterparts' taste for a genre of painting which aimed 'to teach, to make virtue desirable, to elevate the good, to moralize and perfect the nations [*pueblos*]'.[12] Celebrated history canvases, such as Francisco Pradilla Ortiz's *Lady Juana 'la loca'* (Plate 5), which bore an obvious debt to Delaroche and took the medal of honour at the 1878 national exhibition, reflected contemporary academic taste. Juana was a historic personage, who did indeed travel round the country with her dead husband's body. But her tale was romantic rather than important. The theatrical composition had been recommended to Pradilla by a leading art critic as both 'Spanish and dramatic' and the artist may also have been influenced by Teodora Lamadrid's acclaimed performance as the mad queen on the Madrid stage.[13] Composed as a grouped scene in a landscape, the painting played on the emotions rather than the intellect. The centrality of the isolated figure of Juana made the scene one of pathos: the viewer was invited to empathize with her plight and so develop a historical imagination.

Pradilla's technique was that of much contemporary devotional painting.[14] The emotions evoked by the picture of Juana were timeless and to that extent her representation was iconic. But the only factually specific information in the painting comes in the title, and the viewer is required to use his or her own knowledge in order to tell the story. A shared knowledge of the national past was thus a prerequisite for historical painting, though the observer was left with plenty of scope to weave additional stories around the canvas. Pradilla's picture of Juana, like Delaroche's of Joan of Arc, was a study in mood and an invitation to psychological speculation as to the character and state of mind of the principal character. As with much nineteenth-century devotional art, attention focused on the face and the demeanour; it is no coincidence that many history painters were accomplished portraitists.

As with devotional pictures or even, in some instances, portraiture, historical canvases were designed for meditation. The emotional and psychological 'truths' they depicted were conveyed via the emotions, now seen as a true vehicle for the transmission of meaning. Whether these truths were sacred and transcendental, as in religious art, or secular and worldly, they could be seen as the essence of the nation. Similarly, sacred and secular ambitions or destiny could either be seen as consubstantial or as separate or even as antithetical. Inviting the observer to engage with a picture in such an open way meant that many readings were available as they were, in a more general sense, around the idea of the nation itself.

Nowhere has the nation been an uncontested concept. In Spain, as in France or Germany, different groups bitterly contested the imaginative constructs of the nation. Catholics, monarchists, liberals, socialists, and anarchists compiled differing visions both of Spain's past and of its future. Covadonga (Asturias), the supposed site of the start of the *Reconquista*, was designated a national monument in 1884, its story one of heroism and resilience.[15] But, both Covadonga and the *Reconquista* were also associated with Christian myth, and a basilica was consecrated there in 1901. To those to whom Spanishness and Catholicism were synonymous, this made perfect sense. To others, however, the basilica was emblematic of a reactionary and repressive centralizing nationalism. As at Montmartre or Tibidabo, the assertion of sacred space through self-consciously monumental buildings seemed to defy the secular state. This counterpoint between Catholicism and liberalism was an even more marked feature of the French Third Republic—where it was eventually resolved in favour of the Republican state—than it was of Restoration Spain. However, as the nineteenth century gave way to the twentieth, the weakness of the Spanish state was increasingly obvious. It was this failure of government that led to Spain's 'disintegration' in the twentieth century, not any lack of national identity in the nineteenth.

RESTORATION

Revolutionary turmoil and constitutional upheaval had impeded the development of the modern nation-state in Spain. Achieving constitutional stability after 1875 meant the first period of continuous government since the Moderado hegemony of the mid-century, and attention turned to increasing the effectiveness of government, the reach of the law, and the primacy of the state. The restored Bourbon monarchs proved more prudent than their predecessors, keeping possession of the throne until 1931. The architect of the Restoration system, Cánovas del Castillo established a governing system which continued until 1923 and, at least until 1898, provided a functional and modernizing form of government. Day-to-day politics was no longer an exciting or unpredictable business. As a Conservative, Cánovas was preoccupied, like so many of his time and political persuasion, with checks and balances. The new constitution thus balanced power between Crown and Cortes, assigned sovereignty to both, and further trammelled legislative power by creating a bicameral Cortes on the British model. The entire system was encapsulated in article 18 of the 1876 constitution: 'The legislative power lies in the Cortes with the king.'

Under the Restored monarchy, and particularly in the years before 1898, the Spanish state assumed its modern form. The political system rested upon a certain notion of national sovereignty: the Crown both embodied and represented the nation, not least in its dealings with the executive. The British model to which Cánovas was so devoted was not simply a facade. Rather, his intention was to emulate that stable, smoothly functioning, broadly representative system of government that delivered, in Michael Bentley's words, 'politics without democracy'.[16] But the early transition to industrial society had profoundly changed Britain. The country was also unusual in having an elite political class which was firmly settled on the land. Victoria's court may have been rapidly gaining in pomp and circumstance, but her aristocratic advisors were estate-managers and politicians before they were courtiers. In Spain, absenteeism left grandees largely divorced from the land, even though their latifundia estates dominated southern Spain. A largely unreformed rentier class thus also dominated the political elites of the Restoration.

To use Michael Mann's term, only after 1875 did the modern Spanish state 'crystallize', establishing a certain set of relations between centre and periphery, and articulating a particular mode of exercizing power. It was, for instance, geographically exclusive: between 1833 and 1901, only twenty-four out of a total of 902 cabinet members were Catalans.[17] Spain's Restoration system assumed a more oligarchic form than its Victorian counterpart. The highly privileged position of the Crown within the new system inevitably made for a pyramidal power structure, but this was then reinforced by the overweening presence of the executive in the governing system. '[T]he executive controlled everything; among other things it controlled elections, that is, the legislature.'[18] At a symbolic level, the person of the monarch symbolized a class as well as a nation, and the enormous importance given to the royal prerogative in the Restoration system only emphasized the role of the elites. In the words of one scholar, the role of the monarch was not only emblematic of the exercise of power and of the emotional integration of the community, but it also legitimated the political elites' monopoly of power.[19]

The reinforcement of executive power depended, at least to some extent, on the efficiency of the bureaucratic apparatus through which decisions were transmitted, legislation implemented, and power exercised. The changing nature of state power was reflected in this apparatus. While some ministries, such as the Exchequer, developed naturally from crown offices, others represented a redefinition of the power of the state or a recognition of its expansion. The ministry of the interior was a nineteenth-century invention, as was the ministry of development (*fomento*). Indeed, their initial creation, as a single nucleus, in the 1830s, has been seen as crucial in articulating a modern form of politics in Spain, at least in an administrative sense. Other ministries expanded. The cabinet was given a proper ministerial office in 1875, despite having its own budget since 1852; the number of staff employed by the Treasury increased more than threefold between 1857 and 1878. The smooth and proper operation of government affairs was a vital part of political business, and under the Restoration a separation between government and state, between the temporary and the continuing finally became apparent. From 1851, when the ministry of development gave its name to the general areas of commerce, education, and public works, new areas of state activity became prominent, part of both a widening political agenda and a general impetus towards the modernization of Spain.[20] Throughout Europe, from around 1880, the number of people employed by central states in a full-time, permanent capacity at last allowed contemporaries to speak of the state as an entity separate from both wider society and the Crown.

In 1900, education, or public instruction as it was known in Spain, finally became a separate ministry. Forty-three years earlier, the *Ley Moyano* had introduced compulsory elementary education for all Spanish children, even though the economic resources needed to make this law effective were not available until over a hundred years later. Nevertheless, the law laid down minute regulations for the training, employment, payment, and promotion of teachers from elementary through to higher education.[21] A specialized *cuerpo* or corps of functionaries was thus created, following a model first elaborated in the 1830s for highly specialized areas such as mines or engineering. At least twelve of these corps predated the Restoration, and others followed: post, office and telegraphs was established in 1889, state lawyers (*Abogados del Estado*) between 1881 and 1886. As the scope of the state moved away from war, taxation, and the administration of law and order, so a crying need for professional personnel became apparent. The *cuerpos* could at least guarantee entry standards and appropriate qualifications, demonstrated by state examinations known as *oposiciones*. They were a response to the demands of modern society, coping with the state's imminent role as the provider of postal and health services, prison, school, factory, and customs inspectors, tax collectors, auditors, and public notaries. The corps increased the effectiveness of executive power within the body politic and facilitated the implementation of complex legislation. Yet, they also developed an increasingly overt sense of corporate privilege. The *Abogados del Estado*, in particular, soon won privileges for themselves vis-à-vis their own profession.

The evolving bureaucratic machinery widened the scope of the state, bringing more citizens into its orbit. While state service had long been a recognized means of preferment in Spain, its nature changed profoundly between the 1850s and the 1890s. Demand for civil service employment reached such a pitch that it was known as *empleomanía*: those in search of posts were *pretendientes*; those who had lost them owing to a change of ministry or loss of favour, were *cesantes*. The latter were numerous: in 1840 there were 3,636 applicants for thirty-three jobs in the post office; one character in Benito Pérez Galdós' 1898 historical novel, *Mendizábal*, had been employed by fourteen governments, losing his place seven times. Testimony to the underemployment of the Spanish middle classes, and to the lack of expansion and dynamism in the national economy, the *cesante* survived into the Restoration, his name serving as the title of a satirical magazine as late as the 1880s. But while he was still a stock figure, he no longer really existed. Reform of the bureaucracy meant that ministers no longer brought their retinues with them; permanent employment put an end to entire staffs being dismissed simply because a government had changed.

This did not mean, though, that patronage no longer had any role in the state bureaucracy. In a political system that depended on favours, placemen and the ability to provide places for them, were vital. The culture of *enchufismo* began even as the state attempted to create qualified, salaried officials who were appointed and promoted according to impersonal criteria. This process of bureaucratic modernization had begun with Bravo Murillo, whose cumbersome administrative machinery offered ample opportunity for political reward. This continued under Cánovas: the Restoration bureaucracy seemed small when compared to more developed countries, but it was large given Spain's GDP. The Restoration state curbed the worst excesses of Bravo Murillo's spoils system but, as José Alvarez Junco points out, this was a modernizing state but not yet a modern one. Nor was the pattern necessarily improved by the growth of the *cuerpos*, although admittedly the existence and function of these bodies were defined by laws which could dispense with them if it were deemed necessary or expedient. But the political will needed for such a step was always hard to find, and the increasing rigidity of the system militated against reform.

By the turn of the twentieth century, the machinery of the Spanish state pointed inexorably to its 'weak, yet heavy' nature. The image of 'a pen-wielding army' directing others towards endless form-filling and meeting every enquiry with an instruction to come back tomorrow, still resonated thirty, fifty, even a hundred years later. The *cuerpos* only reinforced the heaviness of the state, their segmented position serving increasingly to protect personal privilege rather than fulfil any functional purpose. Civil servants repatriated after the loss of Cuba in 1898 were simply reintegrated into the peninsular bureaucracy: they did not have to justify their employment, the mere fact of it was enough. Given the budgetary constraints which so trammelled the competence of the Spanish state, this corporative presence severely skewed its articulation of power. The emerging social areas of state action, notably education and welfare, remained woefully under-funded: under 2 per cent of public expenditure went on elementary education in 1900. In 1902, this amounted to under 1.5 pesetas per capita, as opposed to just over 1 peseta per person in 1860.[22] State indebtedness was acute—between 1880 and 1885, public debt was running at 168 per cent of public income—making it hard to justify the proportion of the budget that went on salaries. But, as chronic indebtedness made for chronic weakness, the problem became harder to address. The configuration of the state assumed its own logic and privileged urban bureaucrats protected their own position, profoundly affecting the way in which state power became embedded in society at large.

As the twentieth century would show, in times of crisis this left a weak state with little recourse other than armed force. Even so, in both administrative and legislative terms, the state was clearly modernizing. This was never a clean process: in France too, bureaucratic office remained persistently intertwined with political allegiance during the nineteenth century. Here, the meritocracy favoured by liberal Republicans gradually took over as their regimes became more robust. In Spain, however, the political system evolved in such a way as to confirm the elite and oligarchic nature of politics.

By the 1880s, political stability had become such an over-arching goal that nothing was to stand in its way, not sovereignty, not elections, not the popular will. Determined to keep soldiers in their barracks, Cánovas had looked to institute a 'more civilized, more reasonable, less crude and dangerous' mechanism for governmental change than the *pronunciamiento*.[23] Ensuring that political parties became less faction-ridden and unstable was part of the same process, and so coherent, unified parties were rewarded with power. Nearly four hundred deputies sat in the chamber, and some 20 per cent of their seats were determined at local level. But most were *disponibles*, that is at the disposal of the ministry of the interior, which decided who would be returned, and then employed a chain of command—which went from Madrid to the provincial civil governors and then to the municipal *alcaldes*—to ensure that they were. Essentially a spoils system, this elaborate form of state patronage was written into the very framework of the liberal state, just as it was in rotativist Portugal or Giolittian Italy. Articulated and manipulated by urban elites, who communicated by telegraph, the process depended on a multi-layered, complex series of negotiations which was designed to ensure that all those within the system were represented. Oligarchy was hardly open government but it was, in this form, liberal.

According to contemporaries, Spanish elections were not 'voted' but 'written'. As the Restoration system evolved, two stable political parties alternated in power, governing for as long as a majority could be commanded in parliament, and then ceding power to their rivals—a decision legitimated through general elections, the result of which was never in doubt. Rotativism or, as it was known in Spanish, the *turno pacífico*, appeared to date from the death of King Alfonso XII in 1885 when Cánovas, ever fearful of military intervention, advised Alfonso's pregnant widow, who was now regent, to call on his Liberal rival, Práxedes Sagasta, to form a government. Yet, the 'peaceful turn-around' was inherent in the very logic of the Restoration system. As early as 1881, Sagasta had formed a government even though the Conservatives still had a majority in the Cortes, and the rotativist system itself had first appeared in Portugal.

In the immediate term, the manifest dishonesty of the system may not have appeared to matter other than in an ethical sense. Governments of the time were representative rather than democratic and it could be argued that, although the channels of representation were informal rather than formal, the net result was more or less the same. Liberal gains were still possible: under Sagasta, trial by jury was reintroduced and universal male suffrage re-established. Two fundamental achievements of the First Republic were thus restored by the same regime that had abrogated them. In 1889, the Civil Code was put through by Alonso Martínez as part of the systematic application of what Villacorta Baños refers to as the 'codifying principle'. A hallmark of nineteenth-century liberalism, codification allowed for a general rationalization of the judicial process. The competencies of ecclesiastical and military tribunals were severely circumscribed as the administration of justice became a state monopoly. A recognizably modern judicial system, from the supreme court to ordinary magistrates, was defined by law, as was its administration by an independent judiciary. Henceforth, those appointed as judges should be 'not the apt but the most apt, not the worthy but the most worthy' and their aptitude should be demonstrated through *oposiciones*.[24] But, the implementation of these laws remained hedged about by custom, precedent, and procedure. For example, the injunction that trials were to be conducted orally, in public, and wherever possible by jury, proved impossible to implement, although real progress was made.

Liberalism thus left its mark on Spain's judicial system, and the pattern was repeated in the economic sphere. The Bank of Spain was given a monopoly of banknotes in 1874, so encouraging the widespread adoption of the peseta, not least because it printed notes at double the previously permitted rate of issue. A single national currency was a potent symbol of integrative nationalism: the public's acceptance of the notes affirmed their trust in a government which represented itself on those very banknotes. As they passed through so many hands, banknotes were also invaluable in establishing a national iconography. 1,600 million pesetas were circulating in paper form by the turn of the twentieth century, their pictures seen by more people than ever entered a museum or even picked up a newspaper. These 'portrait galleries in little', were, from the first year of issue in 1874, virtually monopolized by great men, Quevedo and Goya among them.[25] Ideas of national descent and national identity were thus stamped on the image of the state. The iconography was conventional, not least because it had to be both accessible and acceptable. Portraits took the form of busts, emphasizing the will and intellect which shaped the national character rather than the hands which created it. Classical busts also abounded, appropriately for a liberal regime. These posited a connection between the classical past and its present-day heirs, between liberal legislators and the citizens of Greece and Rome. Classical-style allegories, of commerce, agriculture, work, family, or justice decorated Spain's early banknotes. There was, though, more than a hint of Baroque in the decorative motifs of flowers and cherubs that adorned the notes, and in the borders and heraldic devices which framed them.

Paper money, unlike gold(-backed) coinage, has no intrinsic worth, and the value of the peseta fluctuated. While the wild fluctuations of the Republican parenthesis were avoided under the Restoration, the fiduciary policy of financing the national debt through the issue of paper money meant that its value was, to some extent, illusory. And the same was true of the Restoration system more generally. Ostensibly meritocratic but actually oligarchic, the regime came to depend on keeping established elites in power. Elections were held, but nothing depended on their outcome. Electors were enfranchized, but the governing parties continued to function as clientelist retinues. Newspapers were published, but political decision-making remained an internal, elite affair. The growth of publishing, journalism, and urban cafés led to the concomitant growth of a public sphere, but politically informed comment and debate simply existed alongside (and outside) the governments' accepted channels of communication.

The rule of law was also compromised, though it was neither flouted nor ignored. Rather, the state's crystallization as 'weak, yet heavy' meant that Spain developed into a heavily ruled society in which few people obeyed the rules, at least not at a petty, quotidian level.[26] This had a profound impact on Spain's development, but it could not disguise the universality of the language of liberalism. Oligarchic liberal regimes were not scarce in nineteenth-century Europe. Like the Restored monarchy, they excluded many, but their laws had the incipient power to include all, even groups, such as women, whom not even the most radical envisaged enfranchizing. Legal codification was originally implemented in favour of male property-owners, but its legacy, like that of the Restoration itself, was far wider.

CONSTRUCTING A CAPITAL

The relative stability and undoubted longevity of the Restoration system brought respite from the turbulence of civil war and rebellion. Day-to-day questions of government were no longer in constant dispute, and attention turned to other ways of enhancing the state's presence in the lives of its citizens. Foremost among these was the construction of a city which merited its designation as national capital. Madrid was the single, undisputed, centre of government and administration. Restructuring local government, collecting statistics, mapping the national territory had put the national capital at the heart of the nation-state, as well as at the centre of the country. Yet, in both architectural and economic terms, Madrid was little more than a provincial capital, marooned in the centre of the Castilian plain, confined by city walls.[27]

Madrid's position as Spain's foremost city never went unrivalled. It was more populous than Barcelona but, in European terms, neither was large: not until the 1930s did Madrid's population approach one million. Chosen by Philip II for its symbolic position in the centre of the peninsula, Madrid could never be an economic capital so long as wealth was generated by industry and commerce. The coastal cities of Barcelona and Bilbao had many more natural advantages. Madrid was a political capital and, under Alfonso XII, it was rebuilt as such. During his short reign, which lasted only from 1875 to 1885, Madrid saw ten times more construction than during the preceding three-quarters of a century. A guaranteed water supply was the key to expansion. In 1856, the water company known as the Canal de Isabel II brought fresh water to Madrid via the eponymous canal, storing it in huge tanks to the west of the city. The new railway system radiated out from the capital and so, during the mid-century, Madrid simultaneously escaped its twin topographical legacies of poor communications and drought.[28]

Expansion changed the character of the city as well as its size. Construction began outside the old city, which was widely perceived as overcrowded and insanitary. In 1857, with a population of 271,254 crammed into a mere

507 hectares, the old city was undoubtedly both, and the inauguration of a competition for a plan to extend the capital came as no surprise. But the social promiscuity of traditional city living also came under great suspicion. The new plans were all for a segregated city, with different neighbourhoods for the rich, for '*censualistas y cesantes*', and for 'the labouring classes'.[29] In some proposals, these were to be distinguished by style of building as well as by street, with individual gardens reserved for the upper classes but interior patios for the middling sort. Proper planning would ensure order as well as comfort, keeping the working classes close to their places of employment and the 'dangerous classes' away from the affluent. Social segregation was ubiquitous in nineteenth-century cities, characterizing Barcelona as well as Madrid, Milan as well as Manchester. The sharp critiques of radicals such as Frederick Engels did nothing to prevent the increasing subdivision of European cities, whose neighbourhoods offered distinct contrasts in both living standards and architectural style.

The high value of real estate, together with rising urban rents, provided great opportunities for speculators and, despite municipal government's increasing interest in planning, expansion did not necessarily follow agreed architectural plans. Madrid's *Ensanche* was built piecemeal: the Salamanca district, for example, took its name from the entrepreneur marquis who financed it. The city's haute bourgeoisie have lived in its elegant blocks ever since, though it cost Salamanca himself his fortune. Octagonal apartment buildings gave Barcelona's *Eixample* a distinctive architectural form but here too the demands of profit led to the interior patios, designed as gardens to give residents equal access to light and air, being lost to extra rooms and more apartments.

But freeing people from the fetid conditions of the old cities was a genuine reforming impulse, and one made urgent by cholera, which had ravaged Spain in 1855 and returned in 1865 and 1885. In the Madrid district of Chamberí—which grew exponentially from the mid-century, rising from around 500 inhabitants in 1853 to 2,478 in 1868 and 31,675 in 1895—construction was governed by the regulations laid down by the *ayuntamiento* in 1862. These were particularly concerned with air, insisting that a sixth of the overall floor space be used for 'patios de iluminación y ventilación'. Staircases, which were on no account to be spiral, had to receive direct light, with steps no more than 15 centimetres high. Bedrooms should contain at least twenty cubic meters of air, unless they were for servants, in which case fourteen cubic meters would suffice. Discriminatory though this undoubtedly was, the regulation did still address the issue of servants' accommodation which, in a single floor flat, was customarily situated off the kitchen, often in rooms with no windows.

Living conditions in Chamberí were unquestionably better than they had been in the slums which were cleared for the development. Originally, a workers' *barrio* but soon attracting more affluent residents, some of its buildings retained a multi-class character. Along Fuencarral, for example, identical facades concealed apartments that varied from 370 square meters to 70. Inevitably, the very modest homes had access only to an interior patio while the grander houses of the bourgeoisie contained servants' quarters and offices from which the men of the house could conduct business. By 1900, 56 per cent of the buildings in Chamberí had porters, a clear sign of middle-class occupation. Exterior decoration also varied as those fortunate enough to look onto the street, particularly on the lower floors, took advantage of balconies and windows embellished with ornamental ironwork. The demand for property continued, however, and by the turn of the twentieth century, Chamberí was rising in height as well as in population as extra floors were added to many buildings.[30]

Unlike old Madrid, dominated by the court and populated by convents, this new city's public spaces were cafés, restaurants, parks, theatres, and libraries. This was a liberal, bourgeois city. Pérez Galdós set nearly all his contemporary novels there, claiming that his 'inexhaustible source' was the middle class, which had 'taken on the sovereign role in all nations'. His novels, like the city itself, reflected nineteenth-century man's 'initiative and intelligence', holding a mirror up to the audience, that they might recognize their strengths and failings.[31] But the bourgeoisie's 'sovereign role' needed an established frame of reference and a suitably monumental architectural style. As befits all capitals, Madrid was fast developing a sense of its own monumentality. Its model was Haussmann's Paris. The wide boulevards and decorative facades of the Second Empire inspired urban reformers all over Europe. The demolition of the narrow, walled-in streets of medieval Paris and their replacement by avenues suited to horse-traffic not only improved circulation but also made the city impossible to barricade. In Spain—where cities were associated with radical politics and revolutionary insurrection—the attraction was clear. Sixteen provincial capitals doubled their populations between 1850 and 1880, including San Sebastián, Valencia, and Seville, which all lost their city walls in the 1860s. Barcelona's walls had been torn down in 1854, the first stage in the redevelopment of the city. Everywhere, urbanization meant the expansion of municipal government, which now assumed an increasing range of functions, from local policing to poor relief and urban planning.

As Restoration governments self-consciously abandoned their country's turbulent past, these new cities were to be models of prosperity and urban order. Madrid was pre-eminent among them, with magnificent and grandiose Second Empire-style buildings, such as the Ministerio de Fomento (1884–6), today the ministry of agriculture, that displayed Spain's resources, indicating a prosperous future. The men who had contributed to this pleasant—if largely illusory—state of affairs were commemorated in a new era of public monuments. That to Alfonso XII in the Retiro park which abutted the Ministerio del Fomento was erected in 1900 after a national competition. The park itself was a legacy of the 1868 revolution when it was effectively ceded by the Crown. Now it became the city's most cultured leisure space, with charming buildings, some of them, such as the Palacio de Velázquez and the Palacio de Cristal, erected for national exhibitions.

The style of architecture employed in late nineteenth-century Madrid is most commonly categorized as eclecticism. Contemporary allusions were common: politicians and generals bestowed their names on new streets and, after 1903, Metro stations, as well as contributing their equestrian statues to new squares and gardens. But a strong strand of classicism ran through the new Madrid, creating a city which 'spoke in liberal' by building in the architectural style of republicanism and, more broadly, representative democracy. The Cortes building was a fine example: a Graeco-Roman temple to liberty whose interior walls were decorated with paintings hymning the liberal heroes of Spanish history. Antonio Gisbert's *Los comuneros* hung in the Chamber of Deputies. Alongside historical figures were the allegorical ones which were found everywhere from banknotes to the roof of the Ministerio de Formento. In 1882, Cánovas himself had carried the classical imagery further when he defined the nation as a 'unique temple in which each could practice his cult'.[32] Classicism was universally recognizable, providing a link with the past as well as an aspiration for the future. Cánovas' classically liberal sentiment thus also implied an idea of civil society—John Stuart Mill's aspiration that no man should feel an alien in his own land.

More formal and conventional expression was given to Cánovas's ideal by an 1893 competition organized by Madrid's Royal Academy of Fine Arts (Real Academia de Bellas Artes de San Fernando) for a depiction of Spanish culture as represented by the 'great men' who had created it. This was not in itself contentious, as there was widespread agreement not only that such men had existed but also who they were. The winning entry, by José Garnelo y Alda, grouped men in a variety of historical costumes within a classical space. The composition is framed by Corinthian columns, while the open central space acts as a debating chamber, possibly the forum itself. The painting thus represents the national culture as ordered, masculine, and egalitarian. Isabel the Catholic is centrally placed, one hand on a globe, the other pointing upwards and outwards, a personification of the destiny of Spain. Otherwise, men of distinction are shown talking together in small groups; great masters such as Cervantes and Velázquez are distinguished, but no one is shown sitting at their feet.[33]

In 1890s Madrid, such a canvas would have had a clear appeal. Not only did it present a decorative and mythologized idea of Spanish culture, but it also represented it within an idealized public space. The picture was intended for display in the new national library—built in the classical style between 1865 and 1892—and so was always associated with the world of print, learning, and, increasingly, free discussion. Conventional and academic in aesthetics and technique, Garnelo y Alba's painting nevertheless employed the contemporary idiom of the public sphere. As Madrid developed, so did civil society. Newspapers flourished, the streets leading to and from the Cortes building housed cafés and restaurants, which in their turn were home to *tertulias*, regular informal discussion groups, some devoted to the bullfight, most to general political and cultural comment. One *tertulia* described in Galdós' 1887 novel, *Fortunata y Jacinta*, had members who were 'much given to politics, and discussing their country as if it were one of their personal possessions'.[34] In this convivial, masculine atmosphere, the debating traditions of the pre-Republican Progressive clubs developed into a wider, autonomous public sphere, attracting skilled working men and artisans. One such group formed around the typesetter, Pablo Iglesias Posse, who founded the Spanish Socialist Party (Partiolo Socialista Obrero Español: PSOE) in 1879, during a 'fraternal banquet' in a Madrid tavern.[35]

In combining classicism with a recognizably contemporary sense of public debate, Garnelo y Alda's picture suggested that the nation existed outside historical time. Despite the appeals to the past, Spain's real historic roots had been abandoned. Representing Spanish culture through an assembly of Visigoths—no matter how idealized—was simply unthinkable. Spain's great men, in the past, the present, and the future, were heirs to the public assemblies of Athens and Rome. As well as a certain political destiny, the classical idiom suggested an eternal Spain, a repository for the values of western civilization. This notion was also found among those who looked for the essence of the nation in churches rather than temples. The Christian story was one of eternal truths. These were demonstrated by past experience as well as by teaching and prophecy, for historical time was the arena in which the workings of Providence were displayed.

For all those involved in the rebuilding of Madrid, then, the capital city had to embody a sense of the nation's past as well as of its destiny. Many buildings contained clear historic references. Most conspicuous was the red-brick-and-tile style known as *neo-mudéjar*. This took the Mozarabic style of Spain's post-Islamic past as its cultural reference point, erecting buildings with patterned towers such as those on the Escuelas Aguirre (1884–7) or the Hospital del Niño Jesús (1879–85). *Neo-mudéjar* became the defining ecclesiastical style of the Restoration, the architecture of choice for the churches and convents which were being erected all over the expanding city. The style spread to the provinces as the Catholic revival which underpinned Restoration politics took architectural form. Legal restrictions on religious orders were lifted and burgeoning numbers, particularly of young women, flocked to religious houses.

New congregations of nuns founded schools and hospitals, orphanages and reformatories in towns and cities throughout Spain.[36] Paradoxically, even though the sisters now shared both physical and intellectual space with secular ideologies, Catholic proselytizers were more visible than ever before, released from the cloister to carry out their mission among the urban poor. Religious foundresses from Madrid were commemorated in the side-chapels of the city's new cathedral, which was begun in 1879 but completed only in 1992. The conspicuous lack of any effective state-coordinated alternative to Catholic philanthropy made the convents' presence indispensable. But this did not leave them unaffected by secular currents of thought. A vehement and uncompromising anti-liberal rhetoric camouflaged a slower and more gradual process of negotiation with liberalism which led to profound changes in both Catholic charity and Catholic politics. This was, perhaps, inevitable. The Church showed a clear predilection for urban spaces over rural ones, but it never again monopolized city life. Madrid's Plaza de Chamberí housed the first convent and dispensary of the Servants of Mary, but it was also the birthplace of the socialist union leader Francisco Largo Caballero.

Neo-mudéjar also had secular manifestations. The sense of 'Spanishness' it conveyed, together with the flexibility it offered to circular buildings by tile and brick, made *neo-mudéjar* the definitive style of the *plaza de toros*. The brick and tile of the Madrid bullring (1874; rebuilt 1934) was echoed in provincial towns throughout the country. As Madrid became a city of red tile and wrought ironwork, history was woven into its very fabric. The character of the city became established in other ways, through the novels of Pérez Galdós or the partly-spoken operettas known as *zarzuelas*. The *zarzuela* dominated theatrical entertainment in the later nineteenth century, establishing the stock characters of *majos y chulapas*, cocky streetwise types from the capital, distinguished by the traditional dress of the Madrid poor. Even Galdós' bourgeois characters, as little girls, dress up as *chulapas*, 'their hair combed in the *Maja* style with a backcomb and flowers', embroidered Manila shawls, 'as Spanish as tambourines and bulls' over their shoulder.[37]

The Madrid *Majas* were both local and national, part of an invented folkloric tradition which, like the hugely popular *zarzuelas*, made rich and varied regional traditions the pastime of a nation. The *zarzuela*, like the bullfight, was 'a truly popular Spanish nationalism'.[38] In this sense, *madrileñismo* was simply another local ingredient in the varied national dish, but Madrid's status as national capital was reinforced: Federico Chueca's 1886 *zarzuela* 'Gran Via' even took the city's urban planning as its topic. *Zarzuelas* had reinvented Madrid as a character in Spain's national drama but their *majas y chulos* could not disguise the profound changes in working-class life in the capital. Burgeoning construction offered burgeoning employment, and the city's industrial capacity expanded along with its size. With electrification, which transformed the capital after 1885, the city finally escaped the constraints a lack of water power had always placed upon it. In terms of both energy and industry, then, modernity appeared to offer the city opportunities which it had never had before.

Many of Madrid's new spatial symbols were self-consciously modern. The railway stations which now linked Madrid to all the other major cities in Spain, and thus to France and Portugal, were built of glass and iron. The curvilinear structure of Atocha station (1889–92) echoed the roofs and interiors of the Bank of Spain and the School of Mines (1884–93), while the crystal palace in the Retiro park was built in imitation of London's. The architectural possibilities offered by modern technology were also explored in the rebuilding of Barcelona, creating a city which consciously explored the possibilities of both a Catalan past and a European future. Liberalism, with its rationalism, its faith in science and progress, was, after all, an urban creed. Inevitably then, the urban project was not simply about architecture, or even living standards.

Late nineteenth-century municipalism was rather about responsibility and government. As the remit and competence of municipal councils expanded along with the cities they administered, so they looked to determine the nature of the public sphere over which they presided. The combination of a conservative restoration and a Catholic revival meant a resurgence in ecclesiastical self-confidence, at a time when liberal appetite for a secular public space had never been keener. Republicans, liberals, socialists, and even spiritualists all contested the Church's monopoly on certain kinds of urban space, certain areas of life. Campaigns for new cemeteries were mounted in all of Spain's cities, ostensibly on public-health grounds. But a fear of typhus was not the only reason that those who saw themselves as progressive wanted graves removed from churchyards. To many, the nineteenth-century city was a moral universe and it was the responsibility of the city fathers to ensure that the right, rational, and secular, morality prevailed. Such an ambition could only conflict with those of equal paternalism but a different, God-given, morality.

LA PATRIA CHICA

'Today, Spain is not so much a nation as a set of watertight compartments.'

(José Ortega y Gasset, 1917)

Ortega's eye-catching statement is characteristically hyperbolic. Even allowing for Spain's difficulty topography, it is hard to see anywhere in Europe as a 'watertight compartment' in an age of railways, post offices, and telegrams. Ortega's lament for Spain's apparent failure to put the country before the locality, the whole before the part turned lived experience on its head. Of what does a country consist if not of regions? These are not 'water-tight compartments' but interlocking and interrelated areas, whose citizens leave and return, making friends, finding marriage partners, and visiting relatives. A strong sense of the nation does not have to depend on homogenization. The journey of national self-discovery is achieved by contrasts: the passages from urban to rural, metropolitan to provincial, articulate the essence of the nation, which is both personal and impersonal, and composed of collective as well as individual identities.[39]

Mobility was boosted by the railways, which also encouraged the relatively new phenomenon of travel for its own sake. Neglected during the turbulent years after the deposition of Isabel II, work resumed on the railway network under the Restoration, facilitating the development of fashionable seaside resorts such as San Sebastián. The court decamped here every summer after 1885 swiftly followed by other ranks of the well-heeled, bent on enjoying the pleasures of the beaches and the newly-built casino. Serious-minded pilgrims also took advantage of the new forms of travel. The popularity of new shrines such as Lourdes in the French Pyrenees as well as old ones such as Montserrat in Cataluña, would have been impossible without modern transport. Indeed, as if in deference to the railway, advertisements for first-, second-, and third-class pilgrims were routine.

Although communications were not easy in Spain, the railways opened up the interior. By 1895, when Spain had over 10,000 kilometres of normal-gauge track, more of the country was accessible to more people than ever before. Regional contrasts, the passages from city to landscape, were now possible, the result of wider knowledge of the national territory and the ability to move through it. Military engineers and civil administrators mapped the physical territory of Spain; travellers, novelists, and folklorists recorded their observations of provincial life; historians, archaeologists, and anthropologists, codified and collected data. Madrid's Museum of Anthropology (today Ethnology) was inaugurated in 1875, with much of its permanent exhibit dedicated to provincial customs, material culture, and traditional dress. A society for the study of Andalucian folklore was established in 1881, 'to collect, to preserve and to publish'.[40] It was soon followed by many other regional folklore societies, all of which sent out questionnaires, publishing the findings as a form of local ethnographic survey. In 1901, the Madrid Athaeneum sent its own questionnaire around Spain, lodging copies of the replies in the ethnographic museum.

A similar process of cultural mapping was achieved in *España: sus monumentos y arte*, published in Barcelona between 1884 and 1892. Although produced in the Catalan capital, this multi-volume work was undoubtedly a Spanish enterprise. Appropriately, Pi y Margall, the former president of the First Republic, co-authored the volume on Cataluña (1884). A Catalan by birth and upbringing, Pi's belief in federalism never wavered, even under the unpropitious circumstances of the Restored monarchy. He was a Catalanist—learning the language in order to preside over the cultural festival known as the Jocs Florals in 1901—but never a separatist. Indeed, as well as writing on his native region, he contributed volumes on Andalucía and had also published a general history of painting in Spain in 1851.

Even to Catalan intellectuals such as Pi y Margall, the idea of Spain was essentially unproblematic, although the role of Cataluña within it was not. Catalan demands for greater political recognition and a more liberal tax regime found expression in a more combative sense of identity. Catalan history painters, for example, represented the region's independent medieval past rather than its dependent present. But the fundamental belief was still a 'gran Catalunya' in a 'gran Espanya'. Recognizing and even celebrating local differences was not inimical to Spanish nationalism but integral to it. Despite Ortega—and many like him—regionalism may serve an integrative function. For example, in Scandanavia by the end of the nineteenth century, regional identities were seen as training for a national one, and so were explicitly encouraged in schools.[41] Similarly, in the United Kingdom, Scottishness may well have been antagonistic to Englishness, but it was entirely compatible with a British identity, as numerous army regiments, crown servants, and imperial adventurers demonstrated. The experience of many European countries demonstrated that the homogenizing culture of French republicanism was not the only nationalist model to which others might aspire.

If the home region is understood as a constitutive part of the nation, then love of the *patria chica* is love of the patria. Oppositional regionalisms existed, and Carlism was easily the most intransigent example. But Carlism was defeated in 1876 and, while it kept hold of its Navarrese homeland, it remained quiescent for decades.[42] And, even in the Carlist case, the tension between nation and region did not mean the two were mutually exclusive. The *boinas rojas* took up arms against liberal Spain for monarchical Spain: even in Navarre, the existence of the nation was taken for granted. The rediscovery and promotion of regional languages, cultures, and histories—already well established in the Basque Country, thanks in part to the *fueros* tradition—was understood in Cataluña and Galicia as fostering a complementary identity, just as it was among the Basques. Region and nation thus overlapped, territorially, culturally, and in the minds of the individuals who inhabited both simultaneously.[43]

There was thus the potential to create a strongly integrative nationalism from a regional base in Restoration Spain. This was already occurring in a united German Reich and an imperial Great Britain, but these were—or were becoming—strong states, easily capable of using schooling and educational policy to foster national feeling, and institutions like the army to provide both a symbolic and an actual physical integration of different regional groups. In Spain, the state was both able and prepared to use symbolism and propaganda to encourage a national sense, but its fundamental weakness—not least its paltry education budget—meant that its active presence in the life of the nation was severely curtailed. Compulsory education was a prime tool of both nineteenth-century governments and nineteenth-century nationalism, taking the raw material of unschooled youth and turning it into model citizens. The state's determining role in education was recognized in Spain's 1857 *Ley Moyano*, which established education as a national project, though the provision of state schools was largely devolved down to local level. Pueblos of more than 500 inhabitants had to provide schooling for those aged between six and nine; cities and provincial capitals were required to make educational provision for those up to the age of thirteen, while the latter also had to provide secondary and pre-university teaching. This system devolved much of the cost and the administration of schooling down to the municipalities and provinces. These were separate administrative entities and the implementation of the law fell to local committees, made up of 'fathers of families' together with representatives of Church and government. '[A]t this level, local autonomy was nearly absolute.'[44]

A predictable effect was that the *Ley Moyano* was only ever patchily implemented, its provisions often ignored even in places where schools existed. In 1900, only 1.5 per cent of national spending went on education; in Germany the comparable figure was 12 per cent. In so far as the shortfall was made up, it was by religious congregations. In 1895, only just over 30 per cent of Spanish children attended any sort of school at all; five years later, nearly 20 per cent went to Church schools. The shortage of trained teachers was acute, not least because of the poor pay which, for those teaching in municipal schools, often arrived late in any case. But members of religious congregations were specifically exempted from the requirement to be qualified. The girls' school established by the Society of the Sacred Heart in Bilbao in 1875, for example, was freed from state inspection in everything except hygiene, and successfully resisted an attempt to impose inspection in 1902. Nor did its textbooks conform to the values of a liberal nation-state, but rather proclaimed the primacy of both the Catholic Church and its most conservative political teachings.[45]

As was common, the Sacred Heart sisters in Bilbao ran a poor school alongside their more exclusive academy. The two used adjacent buildings, the girls entering through separate doorways, wearing different uniforms. The charity pupils cleaned their own classrooms, and studied a more restricted curriculum, made up entirely, in 1895, of religion, needlework, and the three Rs. Church schools were hierarchical and paternalist. But, in urban areas, they did at least offer some basic education to children who would otherwise have had none. In rural areas, the supply of schooling was lacking, but so too was demand. In 1900, 19.1 per cent of the population of Spain lived in Andalucía. Three quarters of them were illiterate, the same proportion that worked on the land. In the world of the southern pueblo, where collective values were strong, leisure was a poorly defined activity, and a child in school meant less income for the family, there was often no great incentive towards education. Literacy rates were twenty to thirty points higher in the north than the south but, at the turn of the twentieth century, the level of illiteracy in Spain was still estimated at 60 per cent.

For those who valued education but who were either geographically or ideologically distant from the Catholic Church, the road was hard. Pablo Iglesias left school at nine after his father's death. With his mother and younger brother he walked from El Ferrol on the Galician coast to Madrid, where he completed some schooling in the orphanage where his mother was forced to place him before being apprenticed as a printer.[46] The self-improvement of the working man remained fundamental to socialist thinking, just as it did to anarchism. The anarcho-syndicalist leader, Angel Pestaña, born in a Leonese village in 1886, led an itinerant life with his 'entirely illiterate' father, a miner who worked blasting tunnels for the new railways through Spain's numerous sierras. Left with an uncle in a Basque village so that he could attend school, the young Angel was put to watch sheep while his uncle pocketed the money left for the boy's board and books. He started work in a mine at the age of eleven, but his father's ambition for him not to spend his working life as a 'beast of burden', led to this unlettered man making his son read out a few sentences each night, allowing two mistakes, but hitting him on the third. 'What did he, in his ignorance, know of letters or of words which are difficult to pronounce?' Others finally persuaded him not to teach his son with blows and when Pestaña learnt to read a newspaper aloud to itinerant miners hungry for news, his father's pride was clear.[47]

   This world of the autodidact, a sense of the community of the self-taught, was an integral part of the Spanish labour movement. To the followers of both Bakunin and Marx, knowledge and understanding were essential to emancipation. Dolores Ibarruri was quizzed by the Socialist secretary of the miners' union on her understanding of Marx's *Capital*, which she was studying by herself.[48] At a more elementary and emotionally deeper level, an anonymous villager who became a committed anarchist in the early twentieth century spoke movingly of his illiteracy:

I was already a man and I did not even know how to make a round O with a quill. And I was ashamed to be a man and not even know the letter A. I said 'This cannot be,' because not knowing how to read one cannot work with words. Nor can one converse with people, or anything like that. I had to learn, even if it was only a little . . .[49]

Self-improvement was not the only goal: anarchists also wanted to evangelize and to communicate between each other. Primers which both extolled the virtues of literacy and helped people learn to read were produced in pamphlet form: one had been through ten editions by 1907. Working-class associations—driven underground after the cantonalist revolts—were legalized in 1881, and an anarchist press developed, with at least seventy-five titles appearing before 1898. Similarly, *El Socialista* was established as the Socialist Party's mouthpiece in 1886, surviving as such until 1939. Located in Madrid, the paper was firmly under the control of Iglesias, and reflected his own pragmatism as well as the rather dour asceticism shared by so many of the lay saints of the European labour movement.[50]

   Many anarchist publications were ephemeral, appeared only occasionally, or reached only the most local of areas. But, together with ideological tracts, political memoirs, and simple, often didactic novels, poems, and plays, these papers and bulletins established an anarchist literary and publishing tradition that would flourish down to the 1930s. Publishing encouraged the transmission and exchange of libertarian ideas, experiences, and memories. Reading aloud—whether foreign news reports, translations of Tolstoy and Zola, or the political thought of William Morris and Peter Kropotkin—was central to anarchist meetings and activity. It helped to create an anarchist identity and, crucially, allowed it to survive, particularly during periods of clandestinity. By 1872, an estimated 56 per cent of anarchists in the sherry-producing town of Jérez de la Frontera were able to read although, four years earlier, the general level of literacy for this area of Cádiz province was only 29 per cent.[51]

Anarchist organizations created a vibrant subculture, even in illiterate Andalucía. When the early anarchist activist Anselmo Lorenzo visited Jérez de la Frontera he found that men of a like mind met in a bar called Paris. Situated across the street from a Republican café called Versailles, the anarchists had chosen to remind them of the brutal suppression of the Paris Commune by a repressive French state.[52] Egalitarianism was founded upon sociability: by 1872, the year of Lorenzo's visit, Jérez already had more than twenty-five anarchist sections, mostly organized by occupation. The visitor believed that these men would have been 'inclined towards truth and goodness if they had lived in a worthy and honourable society'; but in contemporary Jérez they reminded him of 'those slaves ordered by Nero to throw themselves into the tanks where eels were fattened for the imperial table'. For Lorenzo and his co-religionarists, human existence was perverted by the state, the exercise of power by some over others. Individualism was their guiding creed but, in Lorenzo's words, 'it is impossible for humans to separate the notion of collectivity from the notion of [the] individual. The individual needs the collectivity to attain his full being.'[53] Authority, not society, deformed people's innate freedom. A federation of autonomous, collective communities, freed from the shackles of Church and State, was the only acceptable form of political organization.

Such was the anarchist vision of the *patria chica*. Here, activists sought to implement their ideals, giving them real meaning in people's lives. Anarchist associational life encompassed night schools, cafés, libraries, museums, and women's organizations as well as trade unions. Ethical values and political principles were promoted collectively, to small communities looking to refound the world in their image. In Cádiz itself, Lorenzo found himself addressing a women's meeting at the local centre, testimony to the greater egalitarianism promoted by anarchists. Couples lived together in 'free union' eschewing the marriage rites of Church and State. Saints were abandoned when choosing names for (unbaptized) children. When José Olmos came to establish an anarchist syndicate in the pueblo of Casas Viejas, in Cádiz province, in 1914, he brought with him three children: Paz, Germinal, and Palmiro, called after the ancient city of Palmyra, idealized by anarchists as a free, collective settlement.

Popular cultural forms were used to convey political messages, both enhancing and changing established 'traditions'. Carnival traditions were strong throughout Cádiz, so labour struggles were commemorated by singing groups known as *murgas*. As with all carnival songs, these incorporated themes of inverted class relationships, sexual transgression, and popular justice. One, collected in Casas Viejas, described how the fiancée of a blackleg worker was set upon by her girlfriends and given a beating that 'left her with a swollen belly'.[54]

In its principled, proselytizing disapproval of many aspects of pueblo culture, anarchism set itself up as an alternative local subculture. It was aggressively secular, rejecting all forms of religious ritual alongside belief in God, the idea of whom was seen as entirely incompatible with human freedom. In Bakunin's words: 'if God existed we would have to destroy him'. Nor did committed anarchists respect other kinds of popular custom. Drinking to excess, visiting brothels, gambling, and playing cards were all condemned as degrading, while belief in natural law and, in particular, the harmony of nature, led anarchists to eschew bullfights. Some also avoided eating meat, others even cooked food. But, anarchism did not simply set itself up in opposition to the workers' culture of the pueblo. Its struggle for justice and the emancipation of the workers found a powerful resonance in subversive cultural traditions such as those of carnival—long condemned by the Catholic Church—not least because they echoed a much older tradition of village communality. Anarchism may have provided an alternative to local culture, but it was also embedded within it. The aspiration to transform the pueblo in a way consonant with social justice and a fairer distribution of wealth was a popular egalitarian demand as well as an anarchist ambition.

The *patria chica* was the locus of Spanish anarchism, the place where it took form, and turned abstract ideals into some kind of lived reality. As with many chiliastic creeds, revolutionary anarchism also gave the pueblo a utopian existance. This was the place where the world would be turned upside down and changed forever. In his novella, *La nueva utopía* (1889), the anarchist thinker Ricardo Mella fictionalized a small fishing community transformed by revolution. A downtrodden, enslaved, impoverished community was now home to 'great buildings perfectly aligned, separated by gardens where the neighbourhood children happily play'. Poverty was consigned to the past, eliminated by 'iron and electrical power applied prodigiously to all of the combinations of the marvellous machine.[55] Such a vision clearly owed as much if not more to contemporary visons of the United States than to the communal traditions of the pueblo. Anarchists had an appetite for foreign news, celebrating the anniversary of the Paris Commune as a workers' holiday and commemorating the execution of the Chicago anarchists held repsonsible for the Haymarket bombing in 1886.

Ceremonies such as those held to commemmorate the 'Chicago martyrs' showed anarchist loyalties to be both local and international. Their allegiances were to the community and to the proletariat; the revolution would be achieved within the *patria chica* but it would lead to the emancipation of the international working class. Anarchism was utopian but it was not irrational. Its bedrock was the local community, which it both idealized and rejected. Adherence to an anarchist creed brought new visions, both of the future and of international solidarity. But it also rejected the state as an instrument of repression, made national identities irrelevant, and engendered a deep suspicion of political life as a tool of class control. Embedded in the *patria chica*, anarchism rejected both the idea of the nation and the reality of the state.

A COUNTRY OF CACIQUES

Anarchism is perhaps the prime example of an anti-statist ideology and it achieved a greater presence in Spain than in any other west European country. France and Italy both saw indigenous anarchist movements develop in the late nineteenth century, only to dispel in the twentieth. In Spain, however, anarchism proved persistent, lasting through the Civil War of 1936–9. Its appeal lay partly in its anticlericalism, partly in the vision of a new, egalitarian society it offered to the desperately poor *braceros* who worked the latifundia estates of southern Spain and Italy. But anarchism was also successful in urban societies, among artisans such as the coopers of Jérez and in the small textile workshops of Barcelona. Anti-statist dogma struck a chord among those to whom the state offered no redress. The *turno pacífico* ensured that power alternated between conservatives and liberals, both representing landed interests, marginalizing the opposition politics of republicanism or socialism. Electoral politics were a sham; the opposition was effectively disenfranchised. To the stern moralists of the anarchist cells, Spain's governing system confirmed all their suppositions about government, authority, and the repressive nature of state power.

There were others, though, who looked to capture the state rather than destroy it. The socialist party established Spain's first national trade union the Unión General de Trabajadores (UGT: General Workers' Union) in 1888. In order to maximize its recruiting appeal, it dispensed with any doctrinaire ideological creed and emphasized its organizational centralism. This, along with its location in Madrid, allowed the UGT to proclaim its national aspirations: the connection between unitary centralism and a national presence was again made explicit, even outside the organization of the state. But organizational centralism made for rigid structures and the UGT proved to be an unresponsive and inflexible organization, making little headway before the turn of the century. When it did begin to gain ground—notably with the affiliation of the Asturian miners in 1901—the pattern that emerged was far from national. The UGT became a major presence in the heavy industrial regions along the Atlantic coast as well as its native Madrid, but only in the

1930s, with the foundation of a landworkers' union, did it achieve a truly national presence.[56]

The experience of elections, local militias, and local juntas during the mid-century had, in some senses, established a representative form of government, if not a democratic one. This should have opened up the possibility of national political parties, as well as of achieving some redress under the existing system. Yet, under the Restoration, the networks of social power, that is the connections between governers and governed, were further defined. Laws governing municipalities (1899) and provinces (1882) confirmed a certain articulation of territorial government from the centre, in which the locality became central to political identities. The right cherished municipal autonomy as a means of maintaining its own political and social power, while those on the radical left did so as a means of articulating their own ideological autonomy in resistance to state/class power. Republicans still used local committees as their defining organizational form, still met in cafés, and conducted politics in an explicitly urban way. Yet, even after the great hopes engendered by universal manhood suffrage in 1890, few Republican deputies were returned to the Cortes. Alicante, for example, had Republican representation for a mere three years between 1876 and 1923, despite the city's political complexion. It did, however, fare better than the Atlantic port of Santander, where Republicans were equally strong but never elected. All this militated against the prospect of national political parties. Despite being virtually the only party with a real language of nation, the Socialists fared worst of all: no Socialist deputy was returned to the Cortes until Pablo Iglesias was elected in Madrid in 1916, twenty-six years after the supposed introduction of 'one man, one vote'.

This disjuncture between appearance and reality, the *pays leyal* and the *pays réel*, meant the effective exclusion of political opposition in all its forms. Civil governors, the state's agents and representives, concentrated on achieving the political control which was essential to the survival of the rotativist system. As a consequence, the representative function passed to the *fuerzas vivas* of the area, and the connections established were those between local and national elites. The integration of the poor into this system was, at best, only nominal, a problem which was compounded by the scanty provision of state schooling. Unsurprisingly, the façade politics of the Restoration system—in particular the rigged elections—were widely perceived as corrupt. Corruption undermined the moral health of the nation, but it was also emblematic of this moral health, testimony to the way in which the wealthy and powerful, at every level of the state, reproduced themselves within it.

In this way, the Restoration system was heavy because it was everywhere, but weak because the articulation of power was so fragmented. The 'networks of social power' which made the state a reality consisted of patronage chains, and the intricacy of these clientelist networks meant that, in Adrian Shubert's words, the liberal state never succeeded in 'touching all its citizens directly'.[57] Complying with the demands of the state, even obeying the law, became a matter for negotiation, arranged not with the acknowledged agents of the state but with its informal representatives, the caciques. José Varela has made the point that most of the Restoration bosses, or *jefes*, were actually political appointees or bureaucrats.[58] The liberal state radiated out from Madrid and allowed officials (or those with access to them) to distribute permissions, authorizations, exemptions from military service, and judicial sentences in such a way as to maintain their clienteles.

Although 'cacique' would become a generic term for all political bosses and patrons, strictly speaking they were local big-wigs, the *fuerzas vivas* of a locality. Some were great men: Juan de la Cierva was first returned as parliamentary deputy for Mula (Murcia) in 1896 and represented the area in an unbroken run from 1899 to 1923, becoming notorious as the province's 'cacique de caciques'. But few caciques were this conspicuous. Most were obscure individuals, persons of status and influence, rather than of great wealth, who held sway only in the most local of areas. Nevertheless, the caciques underwrote the outcomes of elections by ensuring that local results followed the script already written in Madrid. Another of the Murcia caciques, Mariano Zabálburu y Basabé, took his seat in the Cortes in 1875 and left the chamber only in 1887. A member of the national political elite, he lived in Madrid, exerting influence at provincial level through his manager. The desired outcome was achieved by trading favours, reminding those below them of the debt they owed to their patron, while demonstrating to those above them how useful a dutiful client could be. Juan de la Cierva maintained his control of Murcia even though he lived in Madrid, by keeping his brother Isidro, who lived in the province, aware of his wishes. Isidro would then deal with the lesser men who acted as patrons in the different parts of the province. Politics thus became a huge patronage chain, and the pork barrel the most familiar way of conducting official business. Both Mariano Zabálburu and Juan de la Cierva then became intermediaries between Murcia and Madrid, 'between provincial institutions and national institutions, between the private interests of the provincial elite and the interests of the national elite'.[59]

Caciquismo was, in some respects, simply a means of conducting business. If the central state had neither the economic resources nor the democratic legitimacy to ensure the impersonal operation of government and the rule of law, it nevertheless had to find a way of ruling. Co-opting established local elites by a process of reward and then making them integral to the way government functioned, confirmed its oligarchic nature. The caciques constrained the actions of 'elected' deputies, ensuring that parliament would not pass unwanted legislation and that any reform measures that did get through the system would not hurt the dominant elites. The Murcia example showed the dyadic nature of patron/client systems: the hierarchical relationship between the superior patron and the supplicant client reproduced a certain set of class relationships within the machinery of state power. *Caciquismo* thus meant that class interests and dominant identities persisted even as the state broadened its social base. For the caciques formed a network of social power which connected centre and periphery, state and society, capital and locality. And, for the final quarter of the nineteenth century, the identity of interest between central government and the caciques made for a relatively efficient, if not a just, rule.

The caciques' influence was usually based upon landed wealth, at least in some respect. This did not, though, mean that all caciques were predominately landowners nor that those that were represented the grandees of Spain. Virtually every province had rural areas controlled by a single local hand, such as the *comarcas* of Ciudad Rodrigo and Ledesma in the province of Salamanca, respectively dominated by the Sánchez-Arjona family and the duke of Tamames. An agrarian economy meant that those with money invested in land, which provided an identity, as well as a source of wealth. Estates gave the caciques specific, territorial spheres of influence. Outside Salamanca, few had heard of the Sánchez-Arjona, but in Ciudad Rodrigo, theirs was a truly impressive name.

Cacique estates did not have to be used for farming or related agricultural activities such as the bull-breeding which characterized provinces as distant as Seville and Salamanca. Even in rural areas, politics was an urban activity while the Restoration system which the caciques, quite literally, supported was liberal. Backwaters such as Ciudad Rodrigo were the preserve of those who simply had land. More important places were influenced by those who, like the Ybarra in Seville were involved in a range of economic activities. Much of their wealth was based on shipping, but they had diversified into financial and agricultural activity. Similarly, in Málaga, the Larios family, whose wealth came from sugar-refining, gin-distilling, and wine-trading, were the undisputed *dueños* of the coast to the east of the city, where they had estates. But their influence reached further along the coast, into Granada province and down to the Campo de Gibraltar.[60] These local elites moved in both the urban and rural worlds, establishing networks of influence which stretched into commerce, finance, retail, and transport, as well as agriculture. Such families created entrenched interests, the defence of which depended upon an ability to control politics at local level and so negotiate with other entrenched interests at national level.

Although patronage is perhaps the oldest form of conducting political business, caciques such as the Larios defended their interests in a managerial fashion. Trading favours is part of face-to-face politics, and depends upon personal knowledge: patron and client have to know and, to a certain extent, trust each other. *Caciquismo* was no simple process of manipulation, still less of electoral fraud. Quotidian transactions may have been extra-legal, but they were not normally illegal and nor was the process always or uniformly resented. The benefits conferred were not equal, however, and nor were they intended to be so. Managerial experience in family businesses made for a corporate understanding of family interests. In Málaga, the Larios family, together with their agents and dependents who conducted the ordinary, everyday transactions of *caciquismo*, used patronage where possible and coercion where necessary. Recourse to electoral fraud around Torrox, just east of the city of Málaga, was frequent, while outright force could be used against working-class voters, particularly if they were also employed by one of the family enterprises.

A similar pattern was seen in the province of Huelva, where British-owned mining companies had bought up copper-rich land from 1873. Companies such as Río Tinto were active worldwide, moving into the mineral-fields of southern Africa, and looked to create a docile workforce by a combination of vigorous policing and welfare schemes. In 1898, protests by miners' wives at the price of bread led to thirty-three women being arrested, but the parent company in London immediately lowered prices in company-run food shops and shipped in flour.[61] Paternalism and clientelism was thus echoed in the business ethos of company managers. Indeed, the mining companies assumed the role of caciques, dominating both the locality and the lives of those that worked there.

While the system ran smoothly, it did at least work, but it lacked any means of brokering widespread dissatisfaction, collective grievances or, in particular, class demands. A face-to-face system in which much was done informally or privately could only resolve individual grievances. And many caciques, whether landowners, commercial family elites, or the managers of industrial enterprises, still aspired to social control. This could be done overtly, particularly in latifundia areas with a permanent surplus of agricultural labour. Giving a nod to one or a wink to another, including or removing certain names on employment lists, or instructing farm managers to ignore some of those assembling in the town square in hope of work could end someone's chances of employment, whether for a month or for a season. As social protest and public disorder were inextricably linked, particularly when complicated by political radicalism, the Civil Guard could also be brought to bear. This was a national police force and, as such, a tool of the central state, but the caciques were embedded in that state, which depended on local elites being able to control their own areas. As Clive Emsley argued for Italy, the gendarmerie 'could not help but find itself used to defend the interests of these regional and local elites against popular protest and economic unrest'.[62]

Such circumstances could only result in sporadic surges of rural violence. Gerald Brenan even claimed that 'every Civil Guard became a recruiting officer for anarchism'.[63] During the 1880s, rumours of a libertarian secret society, the Mano Negra, which was dedicated to assassinations, surfaced after a series of murders in Jérez de la Frontera. Although the relationship of the Mano Negra to the wider anarchist movement has never been demonstrated—it may even never have existed—fear of it indicated the state of rural social relations in southern Spain. Belief in such occult organizations—which had, after all, existed in radical, republican, and anarchist guises—provided a clear rationale for repressive force. On 8 January 1892 several hundred workers marched into Jérez, wielding makeshift weapons and crying 'Long live anarchy!' The 'revolt' was easily suppressed, but an attempt to lay siege to the town gaol and proven contact with the imprisoned radical, Fermín Salvochea, in Cádiz was enough for it to be seen as sedition. Sentences were passed down by a military court: on 10 February, a mere five weeks after the rising, four men were garrotted.

The political system of the Restoration depended upon 'social passivity' and what Borja de Riquer has called 'the inhibition of citizenship'.[64] *Caciquismo* ensured that individuals acted not as citizens but as clients, pursuing their own interests via vertical contacts rather than going to law, running for office, or joining pressure groups such as trade unions. Similarly, José Varela has argued that the worst of the system was not *caciquismo* but the 'inert masses' and the cultivation of rural apathy, not least through the application of the infamous Article 29 of the electoral law, which provided a mechanism for candidates to be returned unopposed.[65] In countless rural areas, the well-oiled wheels of influence ensured that there were no overt electoral abuses, but neither was there debate, campaigning, political parties, agents, hustings, voters or even, in any real sense, candidates. Such inertia was not a consequence of the politics of patronage, it was the purpose of the system. Inertia was how politics was meant to be conducted; the state could not respond to any form of dissent. Operating on the assumption that 'every man has his price', caciques met opposition by expanding their client circles to incorporate the dissenter. But while this operated reasonably well in small communities, it was not a sufficient mechanism for dealing with extended or ideological opposition. Then the weakness of the state became evident, and the only recourse was to armed force.

Even by 1898, urban areas were becoming much more difficult to control. Isolated rebellions such as that in Jérez were easy to quell. But in the great cities and sizeable towns, local bosses were only able to achieve the electoral results they wanted at the cost of coercion, fraud, and outright illegality. Everyone knew of occasions when the dead turned out to vote, when voters were confronted with glass ballot-boxes, or votes were simply bought. By 1893 the going rate paid by the Liberals for a vote in the Madrid plaza of Cuatro Caminos was 3 pesetas. Yet these abuses only occurred because the caciques' will was contested, because newspapers, *tertulias*, and political organizations had created a public sphere in which discussion and debate could take place. Life was made difficult for the caciques in the most developed and economically vibrant areas of the country. Here there was an incipient idea of civil society, an autonomous public sphere. But in the country as a whole, the emergence of any kind of civil society was fatally trammelled by the Restoration system.

3

Nationalizing the Masses, 1898–1931

1898 AND THE MAKING OF BLACK SPAIN

In 1898, Spain went to war with the United States of America. At issue were Spain's colonial possessions: Cuba had again been in revolt since 1895 and, for all Cánovas' intransigence, huge numbers of Spanish troops had been unable to quell the island rebellion. By the time Cánovas was assassinated by an anarchist in August 1897, the Philippines were also in revolt and it was clear that US intervention in the Caribbean was only a matter of time. The two countries squared up to each other the following April, with Spain deploying more soldiers than the USA had in its standing army. Rapidly, though, the US troops gained the advantage, particularly at sea. On the morning of 1 May, at Cavite naval station in Manila Bay, Commodore Dewey battered the Spanish Pacific squadron so badly that all surviving ships had to be scuttled. Two months later, Spain's Atlantic squadron was destroyed. For a once great maritime power, the extent of defeat was clear. At the very start of the nineteenth century, Spain had seen its fleet destroyed at Trafalgar; now, at the close of that same century, the navy had been obliterated for a second time. After a mere six weeks, the Spanish–American War was at an end.

In arranging peace terms, Spain accepted the loss of all overseas territories outside Morocco and confirmed the rise to power of a parvenu, Protestant nation. The United States dominated the Caribbean and increased its reach into the Pacific with the annexation of the Philippines and other Spanish Pacific possessions. Spain no longer had any claim to be an imperial power, or even a first-rate one: the Caroline Islands were simply sold to Germany. National humiliation seemed complete. The defeat, soon rechristened the 'Disaster', turned attention to the 'problem' of Spain. A distinct psychological mood of cultural introspection affected the nation, voiced primarily by its elites—notably the literary 'generation of 98'—but echoed in *tertulias*, public meetings, and private letters the length and breadth of the land. Such a mood was not invented; rather it marked the culmination of trends of thought which had developed through the century: concern at internal decadence on the one hand, and external incomprehension on the other.[1]

Proof of this incomprehension had come in 1892, the commemoration of Columbus' 'discovery' of the Americas. Statues of Columbus stood in Madrid and in Barcelona, both atop pillars. Jerónimo Suñol's Madrid statue looked heavenwards, holding a flag surmounted by a cross; the staff rested on a globe, which in turn stood on a capstan. The conflation of national destiny, religious identity, and historical event was intrinsic to the statue's imagery, which was erected in 1885, lauding the civilizing achievements of a great imperial power as part of the rebuilding of a modern capital.[2] In similar vein, Spain sent a prize-winning history painting to the World's Columbian Exposition in Chicago in 1893, as did its former colony, Mexico. The first was received, according to the exhibition literature, as a 'commonplace' and 'entirely conventional' depiction of Columbus' greeting by supplicant, primitive peoples; in contrast, Mexico's dramatic rendition of the last Aztec king dying under Spanish torture went on to win a prize in Philadelphia later that year.[3]

Spain's exhibit at the Chicago Exposition was intended as a showcase of the nation. Housed in a replica of Valencia's merchants' exchange, La Lonja, paintings and photographs presented a canvass of Spain's past and present achievements. In the 1890s, the language of nation held sway and, after 1898, few doubted that Spain was experiencing a national crisis. In an age of social Darwinism, it was widely accepted that nations had destinies. In the United States, the experience of 1898 seemed simply to confirm this fact, returning Spain to the bottom of the Great Powers' evolutionary food chain. Spain was, as Lord Salisbury had informed the House of Lords in May 1898, a dying nation; the national destiny appeared to have been stopped in its tracks. Even Spanish culture seemed moribund: as the Chicago exhibition showed, its artists were unappreciated, its vision of the past contested. To the outside world, Spain's glorious imperial past was a dark and obscurantist story, 'the black legend'. The loss of Spain's last American colonies also put paid to the imperial idea of Hispanidad. The vision of a commonwealth of Spanish-speaking nations, tied together by immigration, culture, and religion had been fatally undermined by Cuba's bitter struggle for independence. It now seemed that, in Borja de Riquer's words, the 'official Spanish identity [was] obviously obsolete.'[4]

This meant that, in Spain, the 'nationalization of the masses'—as George Mosse put it—was fraught with difficulty.[5] After 1898 Spain had no possibility of the imperial adventuring and successful colonial wars which served as crucibles of patriotic feeling in Britain and France. 'Juan Español' never became the equivalent of Britain's Tommie Atkins serving both as an epitome of the nation and a means for ordinary working men to identify with it. Yet, even in Spain, the 'people', in the guise of the ordinary working man, were becoming central to national identity. Universal manhood suffrage meant that political leaders had to take account of working men, even if they were not yet entrusted with determining the outcome of elections. The vote gave them a voice—at least potentially—while military service wrote ordinary men in to the fabric of the state. There were also echoes of the jingoism that had become a potent force for a new kind of popular conservatism, which lauded military achievement, often against colonial populations, and a national spirit exemplified by the stoicism and sacrifice of fighting men.

This had been shown in Spain during the lead-up to the Spanish–American war which, up until the moment of defeat, had seemed to be a truly nationalizing endeavour.[6] The 1898 war 'touched the lives of almost all Spaniards'—not least because nearly a quarter of a million soldiers had served in Cuba or the Philippines between 1895 and 1898. War was also immensely popular, and a marked initial enthusiasm for confrontation led to 'most of Spanish society' being mobilized. American eagles were torn down from the walls and doors of US consulates while popular songs, café entertainments, and *zarzuelas* celebrated the military virtues of Spaniards and poured scorn on their opponents, who were stigmatized as porkers.

> If the war lasts a long time
> The price of ham will fall
> Because of the many Yankees
> That the Spaniard will kill.[7]

Bullfights were dedicated to the patriotic cause, with matadors dressed in the colours of the Spanish flag and, in one case, the sand in the ring dyed red and gold. Even Republicans competed in these demonstrations of patriotism, with *El Progreso* declaring in 1897 that, 'before all else, we are Spaniards [and] lovers of the patria'.[8] The Spanish–American War was a genuinely nationalizing moment in Spain's history but, as its aftermath showed, it is much easier to build a nation in victory than it is in defeat.

The government that loses a war is stigmatized by failure. A crisis of authority is the inevitable result. Yet, surprisingly, the governing system in Spain soon recovered sufficiently to remain functioning until 1917. Crucially, the loss of Cuba and the Philippines did not entail a general economic crisis, partly because of the 'repatriation' of significant amounts of capital but also because much trade was already done with Europe and a fall in the value of the peseta generally boosted exports. But the Restoration state also suffered a messier, less obvious, but ultimately far more damaging crisis of legitimacy. The regime could still function but, even in a time of national crisis, it had no national solutions to offer. Embedded in a series of localist, territorial *caciquismos*, the relationship between state and nation became fractured, while that between state and citizen was only defined via intermediaries. The events of 1898 dealt the Restoration system a fatal blow. Pork barrel politics cannot operate without a barrel of pork and the loss of the colonies had, in effect, killed the fatted pig. Virtually every part of these once stable relationships came under challenge: the relationship between centre and periphery, the role of the people as opposed to their elite representatives. The absence of national representative structures—above all of national political parties—made it hard to address these questions. Faith in the Restoration system ebbed away and, as it did so, the legitimacy of the entire governing system came into question, for the Spanish state was peopled by the very same caciques who were increasingly blamed for Spain's ills.

At the heart of this crisis of legitimacy lay the identification of Spain as a 'problem'. Cultural introspection compounded the problem: far more attention was paid to diagnosing Spain's ills than to remedying them. Putative solutions often turned out to be simply a search for scapegoats, while the division between clerical and liberal, right and left, ran through many of them. The material legacy of 1898—the loss of colonial markets and industrial income—also posed specific problems for an already impoverished state. The capacity of the central state was thus curtailed just as it came under its greatest challenge. But few contemporaries paid much attention to fiscal questions: the mood of the nation was closer to an examination of conscience, exploring the historical roots and persistent realities of the 'problem' of Spain.

In 1888, the Spanish landscape artist Darío de Regoyos had travelled around Spain with the Belgian poet Emile Verhaeren, publishing an account of their travels in 1899, under the title *España Negra*.[9] The book hit a public mood, for Verhaeren and Regoyos' voyage had been moral as well as geographic. As Regoyos put it in his introduction, while 'most foreigners . . . see us through blue skies and the joyfulness of the bull-ring, Verhaeren perceived a Spain which was morally black'. The notion of Black Spain was an attempt to identify the 'problem' of Spain: according to Verhaeren and Regoyos, there was something at the heart of its cultural and, indeed, national identity that was backward and twisted. Their depiction of rural Spain stood in stark contrast to the men's own urbane, European worldview: Regoyos had studied in Belgium and shared studio space with his friend James McNeill Whistler in London. Unsentimental, almost brutal in both effect and style, Regoyos' Spain offered a landscape of sombre hues, empty spaces, and static figures *España Negra* depicted Castile in elemental terms: the pueblos and *tipos* who populated the landscapes were a natural part of them.

'To live in the ruined cities of Castile is to live in what's dead, albeit under a blue sky.' Those who inhabited such places assumed similar characteristics.

Women, in particular old women, became part of this eternal landscape, naturalized by their sex and religious sensibilities into the essence of Castile and then objectified by the male travellers' sophisticated metropolitan gaze. 'Oh such old women of Spain, many of whom seemed to have been there during Christ's agony!' One was heard humming a strange song, motionless, with the tremor of old age: 'She seemed to remember some sadness that no-one else could recollect.' The themes of age, decay, and sadness were repeated in the descriptions of the pueblos, with their church interiors 'in ruinous state and as dark as a mine', their once proud houses with the heraldic shields of former occupants now ruined or covered with black cloths. Though the weight of tradition, as represented by the now defunct coats of arms, hung heavy over these once civilized streets, animals and dirt now held sway there. Women fed their babies in the street as feral cats roamed the doorways in search of discarded fish bones.

Even the music and dance of the village fiestas failed to change the mood. The bonfires and processions of St John's Eve were solemn affairs, which took place among 'fallen palaces and ruined towers'. The observers discerned a 'funereal' character, even in the fiestas, in a land where death was ever present. Coffins were displayed in carpenters' shops, bones lay open to view in graveyards, crudely-hewn but mesmeric statues of Christ in his passion transfixed a population patrolled by priests who resembled nothing so much as birds of prey. Flagellants in Holy Week processions allowed the visitor a glimpse of the middle ages even if he also had access to electric light and the railway (Plate 6). Tradition and religion stifled the land, creating a silent landscape in which nature, history, and material creation merged. There was, though, beauty in this sadness. Regoyos' illustrations turned even the cities into elemental landscapes. His paintings of Burgos cathedral—at dawn and at dusk—created an unchanging image. The church's spires weigh down both scenes, while the emptiness of the plaza in the foreground accentuates the preponderance of the cathedral and connects the city to the depopulated landscapes of rural Spain.

Verhaeren's description of funeral prayers in a Basque village was later staged, almost exactly, by Luis Buñuel in his film about the Extremaduran region of Las Hurdes, *Terre sans Pain* (1932). This impoverished, isolated mountain region, ravaged by goitre, malaria, and malnutrition, became a cause célébre in early twentieth-century Spain, the subject of both a royal visit in 1922 and a Royal Commission. Buñuel filled it with shadows, contrasting the church façade with the stunted, wrinkled people who lived under its weight. Verhaeren wrote of kneeling women with candles whose 'crude light . . . threw into relief those lined faces, the shining faces with wisps of grey hair, and clasped hands holding rosaries'. It was, in his eyes, 'an impotent devotion', a view Buñuel seemed to share. Black-and-white film offered an unrivalled opportunity for depicting shadow and candlelight, though it lost the sombre hues of the landscape. Photography also presented an apparently truthful account of the harsh realities of rural life in Spain, again using women to represent its eternal, elemental, character. An aged crone was shown walking the steep streets of the mountain pueblo of La Alberca (Salamanca), tolling a bell for the souls in purgatory as she went. Women were closer to nature, divorced from the rational, scientific world: at the end of the film another old woman reflected on the need to think constantly of death, 'to say a Hail Mary for the souls of the dead'. But death was not depicted solely in terms of the consolation—or obfuscation—of religion. Rather, it was a constant emphasis in a film which heaped image upon image of misery, poverty, dirt, and superstition.

Despite Buñuel's mannered Surrealist cinematography, his film purported to be 'a filmed essay in human geography'. *Terre sans pain* captured the lives of real people even as it textualized them, reworking a notion of Black Spain which had been part of the country's visual imagination since Goya. The themes of *España Negra* were taken up by several major and numerous minor artists, portraying a world of austere landscapes, harsh lines, and muted tones. Ignacio de Zuloaga's *El enano Gregorio el Botero*—the subject of a 1911 essay by José Ortega y Gasset—showed a blind dwarf against the background of a Segovian hill town. Ortega saw Gregorio as a symbol of the Spanish race in its resistance to modern European culture and certainly the figure retains the dignity of the 'noble savage' while the pueblo behind him, despite the painter's murky palette, remains picturesque, even down to the bullring nestling among cypress trees at the foot of the mountain. Zuloaga was among the most famous Spanish painters of his generation but his sentimentalism contrasted with the realism of Regoyos or other painters who wished to show everyday life as they thought it was. José Gutiérrez Solana, for example, also produced a book under the title *España Negra*, which was planned in 1905 but not published until 1920. His themes were those of Zuloaga but his treatment far sharper. In one depiction of village life he lined up the stock characters of rural life—the priest, *beata*, hen-wife, landowner, smallholder—in front of their pueblo, and gave it the bitter title *The Automatons* (1907).[10]

The difference of view was, to some extent political. Zuloaga, who later painted Franco, rejected any idea that Spain should become more European. But to others, traditional Spain was a strange and unpleasant place. The *tipos* staring out of Solana's canvas seemed capable of anything, including the cruelty which was a recurrent theme in depictions of Black Spain. Verhaeren, Regoyos, Solana, and Buñuel all showed cruelty to Christ in the images of the crucifixion, to the human body in the flagellants who still accompanied some Holy Week processions, and, above all, to animals. Bulls were tortured, chickens had their heads ripped off in village fiestas, domestic beasts laboured under the weight of their burdens. Such cruelty signified primitiveness, a rural condition which stood in clear opposition to metropolitan civilization. Arturo Barea, who was born in 1898, recalled spending his childhood summers in 'a boring village' where the only 'amusements' were torturing bats—which were believed to drink children's blood—and the inept butchery of improvised bullfights, which showed the villagers as 'the kind of brutes they were'.[11]

For the Republican Barea, cruelty was the consequence of ignorance and so had a remedy, education. The savagery and superstition of Black Spain could be corrected, despite their persistence. This was essential: those who wished to modernize Spain had to find a course which would cleanse and change the country but would not destroy it. The philosopher Miguel de Unamuno, for example, claimed that bullfights were not brutalizing but did make people 'more stupid'. Such ambivalence towards the lower classes was not uncommon, either in or outside Spain. The people may have been the backbone of the nation, but they were also still the 'masses', the 'dangerous classes', the 'mob'. Guidance, education, paternalistic social reform was essential if they were to escape the 'natural' stupor of centuries—as depicted by Regoyos and Verhaeren—without releasing the barbarism inherent in the natural human condition. The people played a passive role, feminized, infantilized, and in need of paternalistic attention. The place of the people—known in Spanish as the *pueblo*—within the modern nation-state was thus inherently problematic.

The notion of Black Spain was not uncontested. National pride was a potent force even in an impotent nation. Even in his preface to the 1909 edition of Verhaeren's work, the novelist Pío Baroja recalled how he had tartly told the poet that 'We do not find Spain as black as you do.' To other Spaniards, Black Spain was simply a reworking of the Black Legend. Foreign observers—particularly those from northern Europe—had long depicted Spain as rotten, a land of 'beggars, *toreros* and friars lighting the auto-da-fe' as 'the smell of incense mixes with that of burning human bones'.[12] To Catholic observers, this was an impertinent and entirely false retelling of national history. Any foreign gaze was inappropriate, any scheme to 'Europeanize' Spain, erroneous. Spain, the *Patria*, was indeed a moral as well as territorial unity but one in which past and present came together as a single essence. National glory thus lay precisely in a stubborn and unwavering Catholicism. According to one Jesuit apologist, the *Patria* was the product of a history that was itself determined by Providence. The shape and composition of countries was ordained by God and loving that country was therefore a sacred duty. The '*Historia patria*' was a 'physical and moral unity, but more moral than physical'.[13]

Father Ruíz's analysis was similar to Regoyos and Verhaeren's in that they all accepted the moral dimension of Spain. His conclusions were, however, very different. Citizens or, for monarchists, subjects could reform the condition of their country but not 'renege upon its past'. Admitting that Spain was a moral entity simply confirmed that it was also a religious one. The diagnosis of Spain's ills thus posited a diametrically opposite understanding of Spain and had a very different view of its future. Indeed, for some Catholics Spain's future lay in its past.

Whether Spain's past was seen as a burden on the present or an inspiration for the future, after 1898 there was general agreement that the country's current state was deeply troubling. The diagnosis was often that of degeneration, reflecting the organicism which so profoundly affected turn-of-the-century political thinking. As a mode of thought, degenerationism was underpinned by Darwinism. Spain was imagined as both a moral and a biological entity, epitomized in Costa's famous call for an 'iron surgeon' to cauterize 'the gangrene of his country'. Yet, this was only one putative solution, and many were offered. Indeed, the lack of any lasting consensus as to what should be done or of any suggested solution on the part of the government led to a clear if ill-defined sense that 'Spain' had been betrayed. Acres of political commentaries and cartoons placed the blame squarely with those who ruled, but even the sharpest critique offered explanations rather than solutions. Blaming 'politicians' or 'caciques'—in ways which made it clear the terms were synonyms—found ready acceptance but offered no way forward. Contemporary 'explanations' served as ritual laments rather than real analysis. The writer Ramiro de Maeztu identified 'frivolity' as the culprit for 1898, insisting that the blame lay with 'Our idleness, our laziness . . . the bullfight, the national chickpea, the ground we tread and the water we drink.'[14] But banning chickpeas was no more a solution to Spain's ills than was the extirpation of all politicians. Even the discrediting of *caciquismo* was more complex than it at first appeared.

The most famous statement against *caciquismo* was Joaquín Costa's *Oligarquía y caciquismo*, published in 1902, which served as a founding text to the 'generation of 98', a small group of writers, philosophers, and artists, who included Maeztu, Zuloaga, and Miguel de Unamuno. All gave literary expression to the general mood. Costa, for example, gave moral solutions to the problem of Spain as much prominence as practical ones: in his last political speech in 1906, he declared that the first task was 'to renew internally all that is man . . . to create men, to make men'.[15] Other writers, notably Unamuno, talked of renewing or regenerating Spain but few coincided in just how this was to be achieved. A concern with the moral health of the nation led to numerous intellectual investigations, searching for *lo esencial*, the identifiable character of Spain, and so cementing the idea of Spain as a problem. This was particularly true in the case of those who found *lo esencial* either in the past or in an idea of national character or 'race'. But the would-be political reformers read the problem of Spain as political, a solvable crisis of legitimacy. The circles around Costa developed a pyramidal view of the Spanish state, seeing power radiating out from Madrid to the subordinate localities. The caciques were the cogs in a machine kept oiled by the grease of corruption: removing them would restore the moral health of the nation.

Such an analysis greatly underplayed the autonomy of the localities even though this helped explain the Restoration system's surprising resilience. Indeed, none of the proffered solutions recognized the reality of *caciquismo*. It was presented as characteristic of backwardness, the product of a parliamentary system for which Spain was not ready. But few recognized it as testimony to Spain's partial modernization, to a disjuncture between a small political class and a relatively extensive bureaucratic apparatus; or that its strength, and the reason why the Restoration system was able to withstand the immediate crisis of 1898 was that it was genuinely representative of those within the system. The problem came when those outside the system began to outnumber, or to surpass in strength, those within it. This process was not determined by the 'generation of 98' or the 'tortured introspection' which, in Alvarez Junco's words replaced 'the pompous rhetoric of patriotism' after the Disaster.[16] But it was profoundly affected, in the early twentieth century, by the regime's failure to incorporate or to satisfy 'the people' in the sense of broader and increasingly diverse constituencies. The actions of successive governments suggested that Spain had become an entity, the work of God or of nature, instead of a political community. Rather than participating in a social contract, Spanish citizens were to safeguard an inheritance, and so preserve a state system which they now appeared to have no power to shape or to transform.

REGENERATION

We are a poor country, is it strange that we have been beaten?

Práxedes Sagasta, 1903

Few explanations of the Spanish condition after 1898 were as prosaic, or as true, as Sagasta's explanation. Its very matter-of-factness contrasted with the hand-wringing of those looking for the 'problem' of Spain: a simple explanation for military defeat suggested that Spain had no particular 'problem' or, at least, that it was not profound. Many were determined to keep the existing show on the road: there was no political will for wide-ranging change. This lack of political determination was demonstrated by the absence of any sustained programme of reform after 1898. There was a much-needed attempt at budgetary stabilization in 1899 by Raimundo Fernandez Villaverde, but even this talented finance minister shied away from reforming Spain's increasingly archaic tax system though he successfully balanced the budget, creating a series of surpluses.[17] Again the intention was to ensure that the established system continued to function, rather than to envisage ways in which it might be reformed.

Spain was acknowledged to be a poor country, even if the acute impoverishment of the state attracted much less notice. An obvious solution was thus economic development, although Spain lacked the entrepreneurial classes and established markets that had created British or Dutch prosperity. Nor was there a strong central state capable of fostering industrial development from the top down, as in Germany. Rather, Spain's weak but heavy state was in almost the worst position to foster economic development. As the state was heavily peopled, incentives to reform were few; as it was intrinsically bound up with established local elites, resources were invariably already allocated. The need for development, for modernization, was clear but how to achieve it was not. As ever, practical solutions were few, and those that were voiced invariably ran into the buffers of vested interest. Rather, another discourse emerged, that of 'regeneration', lauded by everyone as the way through Spain's difficulties, but actually symptomatic of those difficulties. It was as if the impediments to reform embedded within the Restoration state were so great that developing another discourse was all that could be done.

The idea of 'regeneration' was introduced in Angel Ganivet's *Idearium Español* (1897), where he called for spiritual renewal to compensate for crippling lack of will, or *aboulia*. His version of renewal was heavily influenced by Hegelian notions of *Volksgeist* and he saw his role as being to address a national audience, stimulating the lower classes into civic action and the middle classes into responsibility.[18] His work—a founding text for the 'generation of 98'—illustrates how regeneration has been seen as a project for nationalization.[19] The model was France: a modern nation-state posited on an integrative and centralizing nationalism that created equal citizens who identified exclusively with the *Patria*. This particular version of the nation-state was as unlikely in Spain as it was in Germany, but the nationalist content of regeneration was in any case incidental. It was essentially a synonym for modernization, which many believed necessarily involved nationalization but did not actually have to do so.

Regenerationist language did, though, show how the question of modernization was inextricably bound up with the nature of Spain. For—whether couched in terms of regeneration, Europeanization, or modernization—the project was to change Spain. It never achieved consensus, precisely because it involved renouncing, abandoning, even despizing national characteristics. And as, in an every-day, lived-in sense, Spanish identity was well-established, to some such characteristics were precisely what they valued, what, to them, constituted Spain. It was not hard to identify Spain, or what was Spanish; the problem lay in articulating a political programme of reform, a vision of a future Spain. For the nature of the state militated against such a vision: the Restoration system had recognized diversity—the variety of political positions, regional identities, the embedded nature of power—and had thereby institutionalized it.[20] As the state crystallized around the caciques, so it acquired the ability to replicate these power structures and protect the system for those within it. The political class' overriding concern to preserve the state system left it with little interest in developing integrative or consensual politics. Instead, politics fractured into competing manifestos. Regenerationism was distilled into a series of discrete initiatives: most conspicuously those dominated by secular, republican liberalism and by the Catholic Church

Most influential in defining the progressive, liberal project was Francisco Giner de los Ríos, founder of the Institución Libre de Enseñanza (ILE). From 1876, the ILE aimed to provide the rational humanist education a modernizing elite would need to 'Europeanize' Spain, attracting other like-minded intellectuals, including Joaquín Costa. The guiding philosophy of the ILE was Krausism, derived from the work of the relatively obscure German Romantic, Karl Christian Friedrich Krause (1781–1832), whose organic thought rejected Hegel's (and later Marx's) dialectics in favour of 'harmonic rationalism'. This stress on unity and harmony accorded with contemporary Catholic thinking, but the ILE fiercely opposed the rigidity, hierarchy, and cultural hegemony of the Spanish Church. Yet, this same hegemony had left its own mark on the ILE. In Paul Heywood's words, 'it would be remarkable if even [the Church's] most bitter opponents did not bear the mark of Abel as well as that of Cain.'[21]

The appetite for regeneration led to a new prominence for the ILE. A generation of politicians was educated under its auspices: Manuel Azaña, Fernando de los Ríos, and Julián Besteiro were all to come to prominence in the Second Republic. In the twilight of the Restoration system, they battled its corrupt politics, hoping, in true regenerationist style, to inject a new morality into the conduct of public business and thereby bring the people into politics. For Giner, education was the key to revitalizing the nation, whose greatest impediments were illiteracy and ignorance. The character and essence of a nation, its 'internal history' was to be found in its literature: Golden Age drama showed Spain's history 'most truthfully in its fullest spirit'. How could a nation flourish if so many of it citizens could not read this history and thereby discover their identity?

Civic feeling, as well as opposition to 'obscurantist' Catholicism, thus underlay the ILE's creation of a liberal intellectual elite. A university residence, akin to an Oxbridge college, was founded in 1910. The Residencia de Estudiantes was to attract some glittering pupils: Federico García Lorca, Salvador Dalí, and Luis Buñuel met there in the 1920s. Less conspicuous but more radical was the 1915 Residencia de Señoritas, the first in Spain to be dedicated to the higher education of women. In response, and spearheaded by the Society of Jesus, the Catholic Church led an assault upon lay education. Mixed schools of all sorts were condemned: for the hierarchical Church, all education must be religious. Far from emancipating young people, liberal education made the child a 'slave of his own blind pride'. Such 'pedagogic naturalism' was 'false' and 'unsound', symptom and symbol of a wider trend towards the separation of Church and State. The Jesuit catechist Peter Canisius was held up 'as a model to all who fight for Christ in the Church's army' and his brothers in the order took up the call to arms with enthusiasm.[22] Noted for intellectual rigour, as well as zealotry and casuistry, the Jesuits had established Spain's first private Catholic university at Deusto, Bilbao, in 1886, explicitly to provide an education which was both modern and Catholic; a technical university was added in 1916. The bankers, engineers, journalists, and politicians who passed through Deusto's doors would be both fully prepared for modern life, and 'fully armed against all modern errors'.[23]

In explicit contradistinction to the ILE, Deusto was dedicated to the formation of a Catholic elite. Like the *institucionalistas*, these men were educated for leadership: either group's success would be the other's failure, for their ideas were seen as antithetical and each was openly looking to counteract the 'pernicious' influence of the other. Yet, both projects were successfully established: the ILE proved extraordinarily influential in the constrained world of state education policy, training university professors, school teachers and Republican politicians; similarly, the Jesuits educated a new generation of Catholic men in public life. One such man, the Deusto alumnus Angel Herrera Oria, was instrumental in establishing the Asociación Nacional-Católica de Propagandistas (National Catholic Association of Propagandists: ACNP) in 1908. This 'very select minority' operated discreetly but soon became prominent in political life, publishing, and social Catholic initiatives such as the network of rural syndicates established in the Confederación Nacional-Católica-Agraria (National Catholic Agrarian Confederation: CNCA) from 1917. The ACNP's prevailing self-image was that of a Catholic fifth-column, influencing society from within. As with the ILE, its principal aim was for the regeneration of the nation, here understood as the restoration of Catholic morals and renewed religious faith.[24]

Though both the secular and the Catholic projects of elite formation experienced considerable success, neither became hegemonic. The struggle to regenerate the nation soon became a struggle for the control of the state—admittedly the only instrument capable of realizing such a project—while the competition between the ILE and the ACNP only emphasized how regeneration fragmented into exclusionary projects. Increasingly, plans for reform or renewal were framed either for the right or for the left: conspicuously few politicians translated regeneration into an integrative programme of national reform. Among the most potent was the Conservative Party's idea of 'revolution from above', associated with the premiership of Antonio Maura (1907–9). Though any proposed social reform was extremely modest, Maura spoke the language of anti-*caciquismo* and made a sustained attempt to broaden the basis of the conservative vote in an attempt to create 'sincere' elections.

Maura's vehicle for reform was local government. A storm of legislative proposals centred on eliminating electoral fraud and reforming municipal administration, creating 'honest' elections by breaking the power of the caciques. This could have been a moment when the masses were nationalized, creating a citizenry able to participate fully in political life. But Maura's attitude to the people was ambivalent. His proposals were intended to broaden the political class to include more bourgeois elements but not to democratize local government, still less Spanish politics. He gave no credence to republicanism and described street politics as a 'sewer'. The fundamental problem was again that of accommodating the masses within a still-functioning system predicated on narrow participation and elite control, particularly when the structures of *caciquismo* still served some kind of representative function. It was not just the great caciques who opposed Maura's 'revolution'. Many politicians were only too aware that electoral transparency usually meant defeat for the established parties, both Conservative and Liberal. Indeed, the liberal leader, Segismundo Moret—who also declared his faith in electoral 'honesty'—saw Maura's attempt to nationalize the masses as treason. Quite simply, Maura was breaking the established rules of the political game. Real elections would destroy the *turno pacífico*, ending any guarantee of a peaceful exchange of power between the parties. Should one party be elected with an absolute majority, then the old system of power-sharing would be gone for good.[25]

Moret's reasoning was undoubtedly correct. Surprisingly, though, a grubby exercise in defending established elites became a moral crusade. During 1908 and 1909, the Liberal and Republican press thundered to the call 'Maura No!'. Many Liberals regarded Maura as a parliamentary dictator: he ruthlessly suppressed social unrest and regarded the press with contempt. But this was not the only explanation. Essentially, enough of the political class remained embedded in the Restoration system for Moret to hold sway. In private, Maura excoriated his opponents as venal hypocrites: 'greedy bastards who seek their own profit like myopic pigs that dig up potatoes instead of truffles'.[26] State structures were too entrenched and the prospect of renewal too uncertain for those within the cacique system to dismantle it willingly. Maura was effectively dismissed by the Crown and, under the less colourful but adept Eduardo Dato, politics regained some normality.

Few would now claim, as the Nobel Prize-winning neurologist, Santiago Ramón y Cajal, had done, that *caciquismo* was 'an indispensable organ of national life'. Indeed, the agitation around Maura had thrown into relief the troubled relationship between those within the state and those outside it. The 'Maura No!' campaign had brought new cohorts into politics. Maura's own intention had been to use these male voters as the basis of popular conservatism; the campaign against him had the unanticipated side effect of boosting republicanism. Even opposition politicans, though, played by the rules of the game. Republicans gained a foothold in urban centres, from the great cities of Madrid and Barcelona to provincial capitals such as Málaga and Santander and small industrial enclaves such as the textile town of Béjar (Salamanca), which returned a republican doctor, Filiberto Villalobos, after 1918. These were often personal votes. The followers of the Republican novelist, Vicente Blasco Ibáñez, were even known as *blasquistas*. They won control of Valencia in 1898 and retained it until 1923, losing only two elections in the interim. Their particular brand of republican populism mobilized the petite bourgeoisie and large sections of the working classes, effectively creating a new electoral constituency. Even the only socialist elected for the city, in 1918, stood on a *blasquista* ticket.

In organizational terms, Blasco's populist experiment remained entirely local, inextricably bound up with the personality of its leader. 'We are', he boasted, 'the masters of Valencia.'[27] And although his party identified and occupied political space in a recognizably modern fashion, mobilizing, campaigning, and electioneering, Blasco Ibáñez, by his own admission, functioned as another grand cacique. The same was true of Melquiades Alvarez in Gijón (Asturias), whose Republicans had taken over the town hall in 1909.[28] In both cities, votes were cast for men, or their retinues, rather than parties, or their representatives. Face-to-face politics was still an effective way of conducting business, and there was also a persistent difference between those looking to establish democracy and those who saw the upsurge in opposition politics as an opportunity to join the ranks of the political oligarchs by establishing a new clientele.

Republicanism took different local forms: the shape of the state not only reinforced such localism but also facilitated what was in effect the substitution of new caciques for old ones. Elite liberals throughout Europe believed the masses to be incapable of citizenship, a belief the rise of socialism did nothing to dispel. A diverse political elite should be entrusted with government and the pact-based politics of the *turno pacífico* could allow periodic access to power. In this way, the system was broadened after 1898 but with no discernible effect. Republican demagogues—men like Blasco Ibáñez and, above all, Alejandro Lerroux—typically began with extravagant denouncements of the corruption of the system, only to establish a local hegemony and so be incorporated into the system itself. Access to power required an accommodation with *caciquismo*; such was the nature of the state. And the increasingly complex negotiations over the allocation of resources within that state left room for elite dissidents, if not for their proletarian counterparts.

In this way, Lerroux's spectacular success in Barcelona brought a new social group into politics without challenging elite privilege. Barcelona was Spain's greatest commercial city and, despite its fame as a proletarian stronghold, it was dominated by the 'middling' sort. Unrepresented under the Restoration—between 1876 and 1918, the city's electorate never amounted to even 40 per cent of those registered to vote—they made their presence felt from the 1890s.[29] In contrast to most of Spain, the social and associational substructure of mass politics already existed in Barcelona, and Lerroux took full advantage of it. An outspoken Republican journalist much given to challenging his opponents to duels, Lerroux had a taste for theatre. He invigorated the city's politics with an intoxicating mixture of populist demagoguery, revolutionary rhetoric, and dramatic rallies. His personal vote rose from 5,000 votes in 1901 to 35,000 two years later and, while he had a genuinely working-class following, his 'natural' supporters came from the 'middling sort'. Forty-six new daily papers were established in the city between 1892 and 1910; several of these were short-lived, but the mere number indicates a literate, politicized public. Lerroux's main weapon was always his oratory, and his anticlerical rhetoric borrowed the language of violence, albeit uncomfortably. For the main character in Lerroux's demagogic oratory was Lerroux himself: much of the content of his rhetoric depended on one man's vision of honour, masculinity, the cleansing power of violence, and the moral force of republicanism.[30]

Lerroux served as a deputy for Barcelona from 1901 to 1923, breaking out of his Catalan stronghold in 1910 when he redefined his party as a national one. He became a powerful politician, but his new style remained idiosyncratic. Together with other Republicans, Lerroux had been fully behind the prospect of war with the United States—a stance which hampered any prospect of regime change in its aftermath. His populism helped to make Barcelona a dangerous place, not least for the Madrid government but, as with the Republican caciques, his personality-driven politics contributed more to a general fracturing of the Restoration system, than to any direct challenge to it. However, populism has, by definition, an interclass appeal, and Lerroux's sense of the power of the masses illuminated early twentieth-century Spanish politics. It also helped to transform Barcelona into a political epicentre, as was confirmed by the eruption of Catalanism as an electoral option.

As befitted Spain's greatest commercial city, Barcelona had been rebuilt after 1856 in an Art Nouveau style appropriately known as *modernisme*.[31] The new city rested on industry and technology, but its architectural language was floriferous, presenting the city as an organic expression of the Catalan nation, its character rooted in the soil of the region. The rebuilding of Barcelona was central to the Catalan cultural revival of the late nineteenth century. Steel and glass were formed and twisted into fluid shapes to form buildings that were then adorned with images of flowers, trees, water, and the natural world. Alongside the eccentric elegance of Barcelona's showpiece boulevards lay other cities, inhabited by the proletariat and the petite bourgeoisie. The streets around the Paral·lel developed as a popular, modern urban space, where journalists, union leaders, and industrial workers frequented the cafés, tango bars, and jazz clubs which developed there after 1914. The Paral·lel provided the public space for Barcelona's defining social class, the petite bourgeoisie. For Barcelona not only fuelled the Catalan cultural revival, but it also provided the economic base which made it possible.

As the Catalan middle classes rediscovered a distinct cultural persona so, after 1898, they developed a discrete political one. Some sectors of the Spanish economy had been badly hit by the loss of Cuba, among them Catalan textiles and the Atlantic ports, including Bilbao. As Catalan companies went under—thirty of them by 1900, according to one contemporary estimate—so the Catalan elites looked to forge a political path which was increasingly independent of Madrid. New markets had to be found and, in the medium to long-term, this could best be done by raising domestic demand to a level consonant with that of a modern European country. Yet, Catalan and Basque commercial interests found few sympathetic ears among the Madrid oligarchy, whose social base was still the landed elites of central and southern Spain. In a state perennially short of funds, there was little in the way of surplus with which to ameliorate the hardship suffered by the Catalan textile industry. The rediscovery of Catalan culture during the second half of the nineteenth century contributed towards a renewed sense of Catalan identity, but the movement found no sharp—and certainly no separatist—political voice until after 1898.

Only then, amidst a general resurgence of anticlerical and Republican politics, did Basque and Catalan nationalism emerge as organized party-based, political movements.

Neither Catalanism nor its Basque counterpart originated in ethnic or cultural feeling, though these were obvious preconditions for their success. Rather, they were reactive: a protest at the failure of the central state to respond to their needs. The peripheral economies had long outstripped the agrarian centre but central government was doing less and less to reward or even accommodate these thriving regions. Fluency in the local vernacular reflected a constituent identity rather than a competing one, though attitudes varied even within these regions themselves. Basque elites were predominately Spanish-speaking, seeing Euzkera as a peasant tongue. Miguel de Unamuno—the most famous Basque of his generation—believed the language to be a 'relic' from the Middle Ages and an impediment to progress.[32] Unlike their Catalan counterparts, Basque elites played almost no role in the emergence of regionalism and regarded the movement with suspicion. Those interested in regional privileges also had an alternative political choice in Carlism, which was still vibrant in the rural Basque Country. But the economic development of both the Basque Country and Cataluña made it clear that modernization—or regeneration—could be achieved through finance, industry, and trade. The work ethic that underpinned commercial success was commonly understood to reflect local character, the aptitude of the Catalans or the Basques. Prosperity was the token of moral virtue and this vision of regeneration thus contributed to the *fet diferencial* that distinguished these regions from the centre. In Spain's northern periphery, regeneration meant regional resurgence, and that was increasingly regarded and referred to as 'nationalism'.

Newly-founded political parties served as the principal vehicles of regional nationalism: Cataluña's Lliga Regionalista and the Partido Nacionalista Vasco (Basque Nationalist Party: PNV) articulated regional nationalisms as political programmes for the first time. Both were socially conservative movements, created in response to the deficiencies of the central system. Essentially, if the central state could not provide solutions, then the region should do so. In Cataluña, this was quite clearly an elite project: the Lliga enjoyed the support of significant sections of the local industrial and financial elites, although its electoral roots reached considerably further down the social scale.[33] The PNV also achieved electoral success, though primarily in small towns: the industrial proletariat of Bilbao proved a fertile recruiting ground for socialism while business elites only began to see the PNV as an attractive proposition at the end of the First World War. Nevertheless, like Lerroux's Radicals, the regionalist parties broke the electoral mould and created a new kind of mass politics, appealing directly to artisans and white-collar workers.

The Lliga attempted to forge even wider interclass, Catalanist alliances through Solidaridad Catalana, a broad coalition that swept the board in Barcelona in the 1907 elections. The Lliga's Conservatives dominated the leadership of the coalition, creating tensions with more progressive, democratic elements. Beset by differences of both policy and tactics, Solidaridad Catalana finally collapsed over Maura's 'revolution from above'. The proposals to reform local government made provision for corporate representation in the *ayuntamientos*, supposedly to prevent town halls stuffed with placemen. The idea was well received by the Lliga but excoriated by progressives. Hopelessly divided between right and left, Solidaridad Catalana collapsed.

The PNV had more success in forging interclass alliances but was constrained by the limited context of its electoral gains. The party could not compete with the UGT for the votes of the industrial proletariat while, at the other end of the spectrum, Carlism was still deeply entrenched in some rural communities. Nor did the PNV have much purchase amongst those who spoke Spanish. Typically, the party's first town hall majority was returned in the small fishing port of Bermeo, where the PNV could build on Basque cultural and sporting associations to mobilize young people and draw on its Catholic identity to bring women into the Nationalist fold. In this way—unlike the Lliga—the PNV also succeeded in mobilizing those whose social position had seen them entirely excluded from political life. In Bermeo, the youth movement attracted good numbers of fishermen and seamen, who were among the poorest sectors of the town. Even a regional party with a relatively small and well defined constituency could not have achieved such a wide social base under *caciquismo*, when local political identities were simply defined by an individual's or group's relationship to the cacique and business was conducted through his brokerage. The emergence of a genuine interclass political option in the Basque Country suggested that here, at least, the machinery of the state was cracking.[34]

The PNV's success in small towns and rural communities reflected their greater social cohesiveness. The party could not replicate the Lliga's success in Barcelona: Bilbao remained a daunting prospect for the PNV. Even in Barcelona, though, social cleavages were replicated within political parties, including the Catalanist ones. Yet, despite the Lliga's class identity, the emergence of a regionalist option meant that, for the first time in Spain, votes were cast for parties, rather than for individuals. Both the PNV and the Lliga created recognizably modern party political machines though the latter, centred as it was on Barcelona, retained an essentially municipal focus. It received its reward in 1914, when the Mancommunitat was established, scarcely a year after legislation permitting a degree of autonomous government for the regions. This inevitably reinforced the local focus of regionalist politics and, while this was hardly a problem for those looking to mobilize, and so regenerate, their local nation, it reduced their presence in the central state.

The call to regenerate the local nation created a new political language and brought about a new political mobilization. Nationalist networks, first cultural and then political, created an 'open space' in which all social groups could participate. In 1898, the founding father of Basque Nationalism, Sabino Arana had published an article entitled 'Regeneration' that called upon his fellow countrymen to: 'join under the same flag, found purely Basque societies, write Basque newspapers, open Basque schools and even Basque charitable institutions. Let everything seen by our eyes, spoken by our mouths, written by our hands, thought by our intelligences and felt by our hearts to be Basque.'[35] The nationalist project was thus exclusive even when it was not elitist, appealing to a defined ethnic group, whether understood in terms of lineage or of residence. In Cataluña, a broad, essentially cultural understanding of Catalan identity developed, although tensions between 'native' Catalans and 'immigrant' Spanish workers persisted, notably in the working-class districts of Barcelona. In the case of the Basques, however, racial exclusiveness was made explicit. This strand of thought distinguished the PNV sharply from the Lliga Regionalista, despite the conservative social and religious attitudes which they shared. Both parties were confessional, seeing Catholicism as the bed-rock of moral and social virtues. Arana went further, arguing that Basque identity was only available to those who were both racially Basque and personally Catholic. In both cases, though, Catholicism still provided a strong link with contemporary notions of Spanishness, particularly as patterns of Catholic practice in urban Cataluña meant that confessionality would increasingly identify the Lliga with the right rather than the left, the affluent rather than the poor. Even in the Basque Country, where Catholic practice was widespread, the PNV's profound and sincere religiosity found little purchase amongst the dockers and steel-workers of Bilbao. Many of these men came from outside the Basque Country and so, often, did their families. Rejected by nationalism, they found a political voice in socialism, as the Socialist Party established its first real base outside Madrid among the industrial workers of the Atlantic coast.

Against this, the followers of Arana posited the 'modernity' of racist thought. Immigrant workers, derogatorily known as *maketos*, were morally and racially inferior to the Basques. Races were scientifically understood to be separate: national characteristics were determined by physiognomy and so could be decoded by a proper understanding of craniology, finger-printing, or any of the other physical 'mappings' so popular in intellectual circles at the turn of the twentieth century. Basque identity held the key to the regeneration of the Basque Country. It was not simply that the Basques were superior; other 'races' were inferior, both physically and morally degenerate. Regenerating the region and, presumably, the wider nation meant curing the body social of a threatening disease. This would be achieved partly by quarantine as migrant workers were effectively corralled into poor urban areas and excluded from the burgeoning Basque cultural networks. But, in the absence of an ethnically cleansed, homogenously Basque independent state, a longer term solution required a different remedy.

REVOLUTION

The cacique state preserved and replicated a certain set of class interests, making these normative for the machinery of the state. It also institutionalized a certain mode of political operation—essentially that of face-to-face negotiation—as the usual way of conducting business. The Restoration state system's resilience after the impact of 1898 showed that it could respond to political challenge; there was sufficient flexibility within the system to incorporate opposition politics and, more precisely, opposition politicians. For the limits of this responsiveness were shown by the state's failure to incorporate, or nationalize, the masses. Bourgeois Republican opposition was accommodated by incorporating its leaders into the patronage structures of the state and thereby turning it into a series of vested interests. Just as in the 1840s, an oligarchic understanding of politics determined who could and who could not be included within the governing system.

As the nineteenth century turned into the twentieth, however, the politics of oligarchy became increasingly untenable. Universal suffrage had led inexorably to the rise of mass politics in Britain and France and even where the suffrage was still limited, as in Italy, or deceptive, as in Spain, the proletariat was knocking at parliament's door. The social situation became precarious: the Basque Country, for example, was rocked by miners' strikes in 1903, 1906, and 1910 as Socialism established itself as the representative ideology of the industrial working class. From 1898, the PSOE vote rose to around 30 per cent in Bilbao, with the proletarian suburbs providing about 60 per cent of those voters. Significantly, in 1900, around 62 per cent of residents in those areas had been born outside the Basque Country.[36] The Socialist–Nationalist rivalry, which came to characterize Basque political life after 1910, reflected and, in some senses, recreated the social and ethnic divisions of life in the region itself.

The inscription of local hierarchies within the Spanish state meant that political pluralism, like the nation itself, was understood in regional terms. The most successful attempts to forge representative, interclass political grouping—Valencia's *blasquistas* or the PNV—thus tended to have a regional identity. But, as the rise of Socialism in the Basque Country showed, this was seldom sufficiently robust to withstand the challenge of organized labour. The PNV never incorporated a predominately Socialist proletariat, despite the efforts of a local priest, Policarpo de Larrañaga, who tried to implement the Christian 'third way' between Liberalism and Socialism by establishing a Basque trade union in 1911. The STV (Sociedad de Trabajadores Vascos: Basque Workers' Society) was helped enormously by the robust religious identity shared by most Basques, and it fared much better than other Catholic unions, which were invariably—and justifiably—stigmatized as blacklegs. Even so, the STV had little real strength before the 1930s. Its foundation was testimony to the fear, and increasing strength, of socialism in the Basque Country, a fear which was compounded as small numbers of highly committed Anarcho-Syndicalist and Communist union organizers made inroads into the heavy industrial areas after 1919.

The situation was even more acute in Barcelona, where a tax boycott organized by shopkeepers and small businessmen between October 1899 and March 1901 had led to Barcelona being put under a 'state of war'. This was a Catalanist cause: the aggrieved party was the petite bourgeoisie and the villain central government, which had raised the hated *consumos*. These indirect taxes were essential to the fund-raising capacity of a state incapable of taxing either land or income, but they were widely perceived as unfair, a punitive tax on the productive classes whose industry was being squeezed to keep the landed elites in comfort. The *consumos* fell heaviest upon the poor, and the female-led bread riots which greeted the rise in taxes rang to shouts of 'Death to the rich', 'Long live the workers' party' and 'Death to the bourgeoisie'.[37] The rhetoric of Catalanism did not disguise the sharpness of class divides in the city.

A Catalanist political option had thus neither removed the threat of class conflict nor curtailed the expansion of trade unions. In Barcelona, unionized workers numbered 88,000 in 1918, as opposed to 42,000 in 1903, while the number of days lost through strike action increased at least eight times between 1905 and 1919.[38] Organized labour's most effective tactic was the general strike, such as the one which paralyzed Barcelona in 1902. To anarchists, the general strike was a revolutionary weapon, to socialists, a means of political protest, but blurring the distinction between strike and riot conflated a problem of industrial relations with one of public order. This was crucial, for the response to a difficulty in collective bargaining was potentially very different from that to a public order crisis. However intractable, the former should be resolved sectionally, by those involved in the particular dispute. A threat to public order, however, threatened the entire locality, automatically involved the civil and military authorities, and was genuinely frightening, particularly—and regardless of what language they spoke—to the bourgeoisie.

Urban insurrection and the general strike were the weapons of revolutionary labour throughout continental Europe, their iconography set by the 1870 Paris Commune, commemorated every 18 March by workers' associations throughout Spain. The symbolism of the Commune was more useful to the Spanish labour movement than the highly ambivalent legacy of the First Republic: the socialist miners of Gallarta (Vizcaya), for example, pledged themselves annually to the memory of the communards:

> Let is sing to the memory
> Of those who raised the red flag . . .
> Beloved Commune, we revere you
> And when another Commune arises,
> Your defenders will be avenged.[39]

The legend of the general strike emphasized the internationalism of the working-class movement, although its praxis depended on mobilizing those local communities where the movement was most embedded.

Riot was a time-honoured way of mobilizing the poor. Waves of food riots occurred in 1898 and 1918, when women protested publicly at 'unfair' prices and so demonstrated the failure of a supposedly paternalistic government to provide for its people. Male and female rioters acted both as 'private' individuals and as 'public' worker-citizens mobilizing entire communities. This was an archetypal form of protest, creating the spectacle of the mob and redefining protest as violence. The immediate threat to property and the established order meant that, inevitably, a 'state of war' was declared. When workers squared up to soldiers, the result was never in doubt, even if the presence of women complicated the use of force. Two women were killed by a cavalry charge in Málaga in 1918: a five-day general strike was the immediate result.[40] Public disorder led to a veritable battle for control of the streets, but while the outcome of the skirmish was rarely in doubt, it was often less clear who had won the war.

Riots were further testimony to the segregated nature of city life, the division of urban space between the comfortable and the impoverished. Class conflict was enacted on city streets, obviously so in Cataluña, where strikers were met, not only by troops, but also by the local citizens' militia, the Somatén.[41] In its failure to incorporate the working classes, the Spanish state was revealing its own weakness. With no representative channels within the state system, the labouring classes protested against it; if the parliamentary door would not be opened to them, they would burn it down. And with every violent demonstration, the authorities fell back on confrontation and the language of public order, mobilizing troops in response to social and political process. The central power became increasingly reliant on coercive force, which made its weakness increasingly obvious, not least by augmenting the segmented autonomy of the army within the state.

In 1905 the Barcelona garrison took exception to a satirical cartoon published in a local paper. Always sensitive to affairs of honour, and with no love for Catalan nationalism, the soldiers ransacked the paper's offices. The *¡CuCut!* incident, as it was known, led to the 1906 Law of Jurisdictions under which insults to the honour of the army were tried by military courts.[42] Though the new law confirmed a legal privilege which already existed in practice, recognizing this as a judicial norm suggested that the army could rewrite civil law and so was effectively outside its reach. Courts-martial were given jurisdiction over civilians, the judicial apparatus of the state eroded, and the function of the army as servant of the state impossibly confused. The Law of Jurisdictions pandered to both military vanity and the army's overweening position within the state. And both seemed confirmed on each occasion soldiers and Civil Guardsmen were deployed against the people. As if in protest, Ramón Casas retitled his 1899 picture *The Charge*—which shows a Guardsman, sword drawn, riding down an unarmed protester who sprawls under the flailing hooves—*Barcelona, 1903*.

The exaggerated position of the army was justified in the officers' mess-rooms by the belief that soldiers were 'guardians of the nation'. Outside the barracks, conservatives spoke of public danger, the protection of property, and the social order. The city was being defined as a place of deviance that required surveillance and control. Rioters were transgressors; like anarchists and gypsies—with whom they may well have overlapped—they defied the established bourgeois order. The Catalan artist Santiago Rusinyol sketched portraits of anarchists with prominent noses, beetling brows, and deep-set eyes. In contrast, his friend Isidre Nonell painted beautiful, unsentimental portraits of gypsy girls, which attracted attention because of their human treatment of this entirely marginal social group.[43] The 'dangerous classes' were increasingly seen as morally degenerate and depicted in racialized terms.

Part of the difficulty was that, in police terms, much of Barcelona was still 'illegible'.[44] Rebuilding the city had created wide boulevards along which carriages and cannon could travel easily. But these areas were inhabited by the middle and upper classes; the poor lived in the crowded narrow streets of the medieval city or the run-down port area. In effect, two separate cities co-existed, each on occasion living in fear of the other. Protests and demonstration were one of very few ways in which many ordinary people could engage in politics and this demotic mode introduced new complexities and dynamics to Spanish life. Liberals had long staked a claim to public space, monopolized for generations by the confessional state. Tussles broke out between Republicans and Catholics over monuments, street-names, and, especially, cemeteries. Dolores Ibarruri—later Spain's most prominent communist—recalled how one man's insistence that he give his daughter a civil burial in the municipal graveyard of Gallarta—a mining town in Vizcaya—led to the pall-bearers being arrested by the Civil Guard. Two years earlier, in 1901, a local Republican received a religious burial in Gijón, despite his well-known wishes to the contrary. [45] As Catholics and liberals fought for control of the street, so the determination grew to extirpate the other's vision of the nation. The introduction of French-inspired legislation against the religious orders created a genuine mobilization, a nationalization of Catholics which brought a new visibility to religion. Public demonstrations to 'enthrone' the Sacred Heart in public buildings, encourage the cult of Mary or foster devotion to Christ the King made the deep association between Catholicism and the monarchist right in Spain quite explicit.[46]

Anticlerical struggles were not necessarily expressions of class conflict; nor was every battle between right and left couched in confessional terms. The PNV and the Lliga Regionalista tried to forge interclass identities around shared religious as well as cultural and ethnic identities. But, for many, secularism was a fundamental tenet of republicanism, as well as of anarchism and socialism, and the rise of populist political options in cities as diverse as Barcelona, Valencia, and Gijón, made the rhetoric of anticlericalism ever more prominent. As Blasco Ibáñez put it, 'we applaud what is anticlerical and fight what is monarchist'—a statement that showed the battle-lines had been drawn up.[47] In many cities, anticlerical demonstrations became a running battle for control of the streets. Anticlericalism was a good vehicle for protest, being more flexible than food riots, and more provocative.[48] In 1901 anticlerical riots spread quickly through Spain's cities; they needed no social flashpoint and seemed unrelated to prevailing economic conditions. Sacrilege, parody, blasphemy, and sexual vulgarity were their stock-in-trade, although republican intellectuals often found this as distasteful as the conservative right did shocking. Yet, the class differences within this interclass phenomenon remained disguised, largely because of the increasing confidence of their Catholic opponents. Once order was restored, retaliatory processions, enthronings of the Sacred Heart, and open-air masses would be held in 'expiation' of such public sins. And that was only possible because the Church, like the army, enjoyed the legal protection of the Restoration state.

The complexities of street politics were revealed in the Tragic Week that gripped Barcelona and the surrounding industrial towns in July 1909. The flashpoint was conscription, which was well known to be avoidable for those with influence and money. Apparently oblivious to the changed political climate in the city, a party of conscripts boarded ships owned by the marques de Comillas, a noted Catholic industrialist, en route for an unpopular colonial war in Morocco. The soldiers were accompanied by patriotic addresses, the Royal March, and religious medals distributed by pious, well-dressed ladies. The narrow social construction of the Spanish state was thus on display for all to see, an affluent Catholic oligarchy impervious to the rise of secular mass politics. As the crowd jeered and whistled, emblems of the Sacred Heart were thrown into the sea.

A week of antiwar protests followed, bringing all shades of anti-establishment opinion into the streets. On 26 July, the city's metalworkers declared a strike against the war, and their example was quickly copied. Women roused the neighbours; businesses closed or had their windows broken; barricades went up in the streets. A fluid violence characterized the Tragic Week, leaving over a hundred dead. Men replaced women on the streets as barricades went up, rioting escalated, and anarchists attempted to realize the rhetorical violence which characterized their press. Lerrouxists *de base* torched convents, apparently following their leader's exhortation to 'lift the veil of novices and raise them into mothers'. Fifty-two churches and thirty convents went up in flames, including hospitals and soup kitchens. Working-class men and women burlesqued liturgical forms, defacing religious statues and disinterring nuns' corpses, even, in a famous incident, dancing with them down the street. As the civil governor, Angel Ossorio y Gallardo, said: 'In Barcelona a revolution *does not have to be prepared*, for the simple reason that it is *always prepared*.'[49]

For some, the Tragic Week was the beginning of a spiral of violent class conflict that was to take Spain to civil war.[50] Certainly, it was the moment that 'Red Barcelona' came into being. One of the two most developed cities in Spain, proletarian Barcelona was in many respects abandoned by both local and national government. The only policy enacted upon it was that of control, for violence was a real problem in the city. Anarchist groups created the 'city of bombs'—82 of which were detonated in the city between 1883 and 1900—turning Barcelona into the 'rose of fire'. The violence of the Tragic Week, was, as González Calleja points out, the protest of a society in transition.[51] As the state had shown itself unwilling—or incapable—to aid that transition, the object of the rioters' ire was the coercive power of the state, identified in their eyes with the ruling classes. During the week beginning 26 July, Barcelona was divided into two camps: '[a]narchists, socialists, radicals, a few militants . . . strikers, deserting conscripts, sectors of the lumpen-proletariat and of the city's underworld—and, against them, the army, security forces who had not abandoned their units, some Carlists and the Civil Guard'. Yet the real ruling classes of Barcelona stood aside. During that week respectable folk remained inside their houses, without light, gas, or transport; the local bourgeoisie, both great and small, who voted for the Lliga Regionalista, were merely spectators.[52]

For these 'spectators', class interest was to win out. After 1909, the Lliga became the voice of the Catalan bourgeoisie, abandoning all nationalist interclass pretensions. The logic of the state system had required the Lliga to act for Barcelona, to be its very own representative and cacique. The Tragic Week demonstrated the impossibility of that; there were no national political parties or other vehicle for representation to act when the local system broke down. The only resources those who governed Barcelona had to call on were the military reserves of a debilitated central state and they thus reduced the legitimacy of the governing system even further. One hundred and four civilians died during the Tragic Week but only nine policemen and soldiers. An endemic public order problem seemed confirmed by the foundation of the anarcho-syndicalist CNT (Confederación Nacional de Trabajo) in 1912, which soon came to dominate organized labour in the city. By the summer of 1918, the CNT represented half of all the city's trade unionists, and could mobilize several times that number for protests, strikes, or direct action.

In response, a belief in the need for 'strong' government became engrained among Spanish conservatives. This was not simply the result of respect for the army, still less of fear of it. Rather, it reflected the presence, even the perceived omnipresence, of an identifiable enemy. The CNT brought a violent, anti-state ideology into politics, if not into the governing system. Anarchist terrorists—who had paralysed Barcelona, assassinated Cánovas, Dato, and, in 1923, the cardinal archbishop of Zaragoza, and lobbed a bomb at Alfonso XIII's wedding procession—suggested that invisible enemies could wreak havoc at any time. Anticlerical rioters threatened the very basis of social order. And the outbreak of Bolshevik revolution in Russia in 1917 both gave a new impetus to anti-system movements, and also internationalized them.

In the wake of 1917, the struggle changed all over Europe. Underlaid by the seismic shifts of the First World War, the political cleavages of the Russian Revolution reshaped a continent already convulsed by the mass mobilization of troops and the experience of prolonged warfare. A 'visceral' understanding of Spain's weakness on the part of its rulers led to neutrality in the Great War[53] and the population remained largely indifferent—the goring of the famous matador Joselito was a matter of far greater interest than the assassination of Archduke Ferdinand. Yet the war created an artificial boom in the economy and a corresponding expansion of the urban proletariat. Nor was this group unaffected by international events. Both Socialists and anarchists were profoundly affected by the Soviet struggle, as they were by Mexico, in revolution from 1911. The world appeared to be throwing off its chains: anticlerical proletarian revolution was uniting workers everywhere.

The Bolshevik revolution lit the blue touchpaper for a new, more urgent kind of proletarian politics. 'Across blood-drenched Europe, I salute you . . . oh noble Russian revolutionaries' wrote one young Socialist in 1918. By 1920, the executive committee of the Socialists' youth wing had reconstituted itself as the Communist Party of Spain (PCE: Partido Comunista Español). The foundation of the Comintern in 1919 was met with enormous enthusiasm. Indeed, the Bolsheviks' actions had received their first, and most enthusiastic, welcome from Spain's 'pure' anarchists, convinced, as one Barcelona paper put it, that 'The world is being swept away by the revitalizing breath of the advancing social revolution.' 'Anarchist ideas', they claimed, have triumphed.[54] Although some syndicalists were more ambivalent, the Russian revolution sharply enhanced the sense of ideological urgency among the ranks of the CNT, which sent Angel Pestaña to Moscow in April 1920 to see for himself.

In 1917, Spain was rocked by events that seemed to presage a revolutionary outcome. Discontent began among junior officers, who were troubled by the (unrealized) prospect of military reform and conscious of their poor rates of pay. In defence of their own professional interests, they established juntas and defied government orders to disband them. For a short while, the stand-off 'deprived the Spanish state of its praetorian shield' and the Catalanist Lliga called a constituent assembly—essentially an alternative parliament—in Barcelona.[55] As soldiers, Catalans, and striking workers joined the protests, Spain appeared to be on the brink of a general revolt. But, once the soldiers had been bought off—and the Dato government was quick to placate them—the only direct threat was posed by a general strike. Called jointly, but hastily, by the UGT and CNT, this failed utterly in Madrid and was soon over in Barcelona. Only in the northern mining districts did the strike prove durable, so demonstrating the shallowness of the movement elsewhere in Spain. The events of 1917 served to show how far Spain was from revolution, rather than how close. Yet this did not prevent swift and harsh repression, implemented by the same army that had sparked off the trouble. Around eighty people died as a result of the disorder, nearly all of them at the hands of the forces of law and order.

'1917 produced in Spain a crisis of authority—a crisis, one may say, of the state and not of the people.'[56] It highlighted the moral and political bankruptcy of the ruling system: Barcelona was now not alone in being 'ungovernable'. An outbreak of 'Russian fever' in the predominately anarchist southern countryside led to the *trienio bolchevique* or 'the Bolshevik years' of 1918 to 1920. Strikes, land invasions, crop burning and arson became familiar as peasant unrest spread from its heartland of Córdoba through Andalucía, Murcia, Valencia, and even as far north as Aragón. A member of the Institute of Social Reforms professed himself astonished that news of peasant land seizures spread so quickly from the Russian steppes to the Andalucian sierras. This was testimony both to the imaginative power of the Bolshevik model and to the efficiency with which that model had been disseminated through the left-wing press. Between 1918 and 1919 over a hundred anarchist syndicates were founded or re-established in Córdoba. In May 1919, martial law was declared there and the army sent in to crush a general strike. By the following month there were fourteen infantry and six cavalry companies in the district, in addition to the Civil Guard.[57] Trotsky's referring to Spain as 'the Russia of the West' had done nothing to reassure the comfortable classes.

Dangerous times made for dangerous solutions, and there was an increasing tendency to disregard the rule-book in the name of 'order' or 'strong' government. Declaring martial law literally, a 'state of war' provided a legal mechanism for suspending constitutional guarantees but, in Barcelona, even this proved insufficient. In November 1920, General Severiano Martínez Anido, was appointed civil governor of Barcelona in a move which seemed to prove that 'strong' government could only be posited on a weak state. He ruled the city virtually as a personal fiefdom. In blatant disregard of the rule of law, he financed gunmen from the 'yellow' Sindicatos Libres to fight against those of the CNT and, in January 1921, he reactivated the 'Ley de Fugas'. Those 'trying to escape' could now be shot to death without fear of penalty. Though the CNT was eventually driven underground, police terrorism escalated the violence in the city. Martínez Anido left office in 1922, but Barcelona was still effectively under military occupation.

THE IRON SURGEON

By 1923, Spain had come to 'a constitutional dead-end'.[58] Thirty-four governments between 1902 and 1923 had left the parliamentary system fragile, widely mistrusted, and patently unable to put an end to spiralling social unrest. When General Miguel Primo de Rivera, marqués de Estella and capitan-general of Barcelona, staged a coup d'état on 13 September, it was opposed by almost no one and welcomed by many. Exhausted and broken, the CNT declared a general strike but the action seemed merely nominal. Primo de Rivera left Barcelona to the cheers of the Lliga and the Somatén: stock market values rose, as did the peseta; bishops welcomed the new regime as 'a resurrection';

conservatives throughout the land praised the general's 'brave and patriotic action'.[59]

While the left was despondent and the right enthusiastic, many were neutral. One observer commented on the 'absolute indifference' of people in Madrid. This makes it hard to interpret the coup, as Ben-Ami does, as a last-ditch defence of the established interest, finally threatened with a true mass democracy.[60] Parliament was enjoying a putative resurgence in 1923, but it is hard to extrapolate from this to a full renaissance of political and civic life. Rather, as the old system was clearly worn out, opposition figures seized upon events and used them as sticks with which to beat an incompetent administration. The Moroccan War—never a popular cause—was going badly. In 1921, military collapse in eastern Morocco—with the loss of at least 8,000 lives at Annual—caused widespread recrimination. Amid accusations of incompetence and imprudence, two parliamentary commissions were set up and eventually agreed that the commanding officer, General Berenguer, should stand trial. Sixteen days later, Primo de Rivera's *pronunciamiento* established the first military regime in Spain's history. No longer was the army the arbiter of politics. In 1923, the army was politics.

Ostensibly, the new military directory was to respect the constitution; in practice military rule abrogated it. Primo disbanded the directory in favour of a civilian equivalent in 1925 but, while both forms may have disguised the general's personal dictatorship, neither superseded it. Indeed, during the coup itself, though he could rely on a reluctance to take up arms against a brother officer, Primo lacked the active support of most of the army. The events of 1923 were not a crisis of the state. Until the moment of resignation, the out-going regime remained in full control of the bureaucratic machinery. Measures to secure public order and the supply of food were put in train immediately. Primo's *pronunciamiento* did not challenge the government's effectiveness but its legitimacy. In essence, the general claimed that the civilians no longer had the right to rule. Given the current debates as to who was responsible for the Moroccan debacle, the crux of the problem seemed to be the right of civilians to rule over soldiers. Yet, Primo's small-scale coup, far from being dismissed as special pleading, changed Spanish politics for good. Belief in 'the problem' of Spain was engrained, and civilian government appeared to have run out of options. The king used his privileged constitutional position to underwrite an entirely illegal military action. Primo was commanded to form a government and, in his own words, 'throw the ministers out of the window'.[61]

As Alfonso XIII was commander-in-chief of the armed forces, no coup could succeed without his sanction. Like his father, the king had been educated at Sandhurst and regularly appeared in uniform, not least in portraiture. During his reign the relationship between Crown and army had gradually tightened:

the king's 'military audiences' meant he communicated with his chiefs of staff independently of the prime minister. The crisis of 1917 had seen Alfonso mediating between the army and the government as the only institution which represented both these bodies. As the government now depended on armed force, these interventions only strengthened the bonds between the army and the 'soldier-king', increased their separation from civilian government, and reinforced their segmented power within the Spanish state. The figure of the soldier-king had been created 'to impede military adventures not to lead them', but now it was serving an opposite function.[62]

The coup of 1923 was, therefore, more than the opportunistic manoeu-vrings of privileged actors. Primo's self-appointed role was that of Costa's iron surgeon 'come to cure the maladies of his country', but it soon became clear that applying military principles—honour, discipline, duty—to Spain's civic life would be a considerable task. Ideologically, Primo's regime was one of mixed metaphors. The language of regenerationism was used only in so far as it suggested curative excision, tutelage, and paternalism. Joaquín Costa's early writings, which had referred to dictatorship as a 'therapeutic', 'medicinal' solution to the ills of Spain, were useful but his substantial democratic legacy was not. The language of progress was also employed, particularly when it came to building roads, establishing public works projects and supposedly kick-starting the economy. Catholic paternalism was another influence: unemployment would be solved by the economic programmes, while other social problems would be met with Christian charity. Underlying many of these discourses was a sense that dictatorial regimes—'strong governments'—could serve as periods of tutelage for politically immature nations, such as Spain. Yet, overlying them all was a straightforward allegiance to the values of the officer corps and the culture of the military academy.

Under Primo, education for boys was reformed along military lines, with an emphasis on physical education, pre-military training, and drill. This emphasis on creating 'the men of tomorrow' also led to a rise in the budget for elementary education. Much of this was devolved down to the municipalities, in part because of rising local demand, though regional variations persisted. Although access to education varied by locality and girls were still less likely to attend lessons than their brothers, the provision of schooling rose. Just under 8,000 elementary schools were built under the dictatorship; the number of teachers rose by nearly 20 per cent and the number of enrolled pupils by 22.9 per cent. Literacy rates accelerated sharply: for girls they rose almost ten points over ten years but, none the less, by 1930, still only a fraction over two in every three Spanish adults could read and write.[63] The rise in schooling was not—and nor was it seen as—a purely technical achievement. Expanding state education was essential for national regeneration, which depended on an active, patriotic citizenry. An expanded presence for the central state was the inevitable effect: schools were built where none had existed before, more teachers moved into state employment, and the content of the syllabus was actively scrutinized.

As early as October 1923, teachers were ordered to use only Castilian in schools, even those where children were more fluent in Catalan or Basque. On 12 February 1924, school inspectors were instructed to close schools and dismiss teachers who imparted 'doctrines opposed to the unity of the patria, offensive to religion or of a dissolvent character'; three days later the prohibition on 'antisocial doctrines or those contrary to the unity of the patria' was reiterated for university teachers.[64] The history of Spain occupied a particularly important place in this educational project, being the culmination of secondary level studies and continuing through university. Text books were monitored for secular and 'dissolvent' ideas, though there was far less agreement as to any official history text that might ensure sound knowledge and imbue children with a patriotic love for Spain. Yet, on the conservative right there was both an emerging sense of a glorious national past and a belief that the young people of Spain could and should be mobilized in its defence. Such was the logic of regeneration.

This led to a new, visible emphasis on youth. Local children were now often incorporated into public events, as in Molledo in the province of Santander in 1927, when, complete with flags, they marched back to their school after a public address by the mayor. This espousal of military values did not only effect education; on a national level it meant that alternative visions of Spain were to be expunged, or at lest repressed. As educational policy showed, regional separatism was to be quashed. By 1928, one Barcelona paper could declare that 'Cataluña is not a nation, nor has it ever been one, except in an imperfect and embryonic sense.'[65] The emphasis was, in the general's own words, on both 'national unity and uniformity'. A single nation demanded a single, centralist state. As the ban on vernacular languages in schools showed, regional identities were to be confined to private life. Political parties were banned and the Mancomunitat disbanded; fines and beatings awaited those who spoke Catalan in public, and the Church was sternly discouraged from preaching or catechizing in vernacular languages. In Cataluña, this last injunction was stoutly resisted, not least by the cardinal archbishop of Tarragona, but it had more effect in the Basque Country, where the Burgos-born local bishop was an enthusiastic centralizer.

Regionalism divided the Church as well as the nation, but ecclesiastical dissent was no more palatable to the regime than was political opposition. Spain was a confessional state and Primo was quite prepared to use religion for emotional display, as well as pomp and circumstance. But militarism was a secular tradition, which recognized and respected Catholicism as essential to Spanish identity, but gave it no primacy within that. In consequence, under Primo an 'official' nationalism finally achieved centre stage. The *Día de la Hispanidad*, which commemorated Columbus's landing in the Americas, was established in 1918. Other official celebrations, including the declaration and celebration of Spain's patron saints, were definitively established under the dictatorship. The shrine to the Virgin of the Pillar at Zaragoza became feted both regionally and nationally while regional pilgrimages to shrines such as Salamanca's Peña de Francia or Santander's Bien-Aparecida experienced a noted revival during this period.[66] Great showcase events such as the International Exposition in Barcelona in 1929 or the Ibero-American Exposition in Seville in the same year also demonstrated the relationship between region and nation. Aníbal González's semi-circular Plaza de España was the centrepiece of the Seville exhibition. Representing Spain's 'embrace' of the Americas, the plaza's colonnade was divided into sections depicting, in alphabetical order, Spain's provinces, each of which had a map and a historical scene laid out in painted tiles and topped by a ceramic coat of arms.

Given González's own fame as a regional architect, the Plaza de España was an unambiguous assertion of regionalism within the context of a state-sponsored, conservative nationalism. Visitors could search out their 'own' province—as they still do today—but the use of space in the plaza, its creation of an apparently seamless whole through its semicircular 'embrace', was a constant reminder of both Spain's unity and its imperial mission. The Catalan exhibition was yet more complex. Here, the construction of a miniature, walled, Pueblo Español both reaffirmed the importance of the Spanish regions and simultaneously denied it. Such villages had been a great hit at the Paris Expo of 1900; the Barcelona version employed Catalan architects and, along with the rest of the Exposition, brought a considerable economic boost to the city, not least in construction. But this compendium of vernacular styles from all over Spain was imposed on a city with an architectural style of its own and one which, increasingly during the 1920s, looked out towards Europe, a contrast which was starkly represented by the location of Mies van der Rohe's German Pavilion next to the central exhibition hall.

Visitors entered the Pueblo Español through the gates of Avila, passing by careful reproductions of identifiable buildings, which together created a townscape of narrow streets, overhanging buildings and steep stairways. The contrast to the *modernisme* of the surrounding city was sharp. As one of the advertising leaflets put it, 'each corner evokes the old and noble Spain of the Golden Age', so depicting Spain in a way which both coincided with and differed utterly from Black Spain. Nor were buildings the only display. Regional characters or *tipos*, wearing folk dress and demonstrating traditional, artisan crafts, inhabited the Pueblo Español in a living ethnographic exhibition which also produced goods for sale. Though Spain's manufacturing exports were actually produced in the factories of Bilbao and Barcelona, in the 1929 exposition 'old and noble' Spain was not only on show, it was also up for sale.

King Alfonso XIII opened both expositions, saying that, in Barcelona, the world could see 'what is, in reality our nation' as well as 'the feelings of a people for their king'. The Primo regime projected the king, just as Antonio Maura had done, as the representative of a monarchy that served the nation for centuries, a monarchy that was 'above classes and in the heart of citizens'.[67] Monarchism was, of course, a useful tool for an aristocratic military dictator, particularly one who had good reason to be grateful to the king. It symbolized a certain, hierarchical vision of the social order, in which social peace was intertwined with social status. Much was made of the public persona of the king: commemorative medals were struck, and acts of homage staged that created some sense of connection between the monarch and his subjects.

The king's head also appeared on all coins, though rarely on the banknotes that were reissued during Primo's rule. Every note was redesigned, using common themes of architecture, portraiture, and Spain's Golden Age. Titian's portrait of Philip II graced the 100 peseta note, inserted over a vista of his monastery-palace at El Escorial. On the verso, was Alvárez's historical canvass of the king surveying the building of his palace from a mountain vantage point known, like the painting, as 'la silla de Felipe II'. Both sides were framed by decorative borders, inviting the user to gaze upon the face, or the essence, of Spain. Cervantes received similar treatment on another 100 peseta note, Veláquez on the 50. Another king, St Ferdinand III, was on the 1,000 peseta note, alongside the magnificence of Seville cathedral; the verso reproduced Ferrant y Fischermans's picture of the royal saint receiving holy communion.

Under Primo de Rivera, history was everywhere and everything. Every banknote encapsulated a certain vision of Spain's past; every tiled scene in Seville's Plaza de España harked back to a 'Golden Age'. Granada was shown being 'freed' from the 'Moors'; Huelva was illustrated by the embarkation of Columbus. Each scene thus tied the province being represented back into the history of Spain. Spain was established as *the* nation, the repository of past glories, the compendium of regional variety, the sum of individual heroism, virtue, and adventure. The overwhelming tenor was conservative and historicist. The only modern scene represented in the Plaza de España was the 2 May uprising against Napoleonic occupation in Madrid, while Alfonso XIII was the only contemporary figure depicted on a banknote, his collar and tie oddly juxtaposed against Madrid's eighteenth-century Royal Palace.

Primo's new regime thus appropriated a particular understanding of Spain's past, using history to represent one vision of Spain against another.[68] In a military dictatorship, this translated into a victory of one Spain over another: by accepting the coup Spain's conservative classes had 'signed an implicit pact of collaboration in favour of 'social order'.[69] The army was now free from parliamentary checks or any kind of state surveillance or civilian sovereignty. Confirmed as the 'guardians of order', so internal routes to promotion became defined in these terms: the military's segmentation within the state seemed almost complete. The regime was not particularly bloody, but the abrogation of legal norms combined with a process of militarization to make it genuinely repressive. The number and nature of offences subject to trial under military law became progressively wider; in April 1924 a royal decree included armed robbery in this category, with equal penalties for foiled attempts as for actual ones, for conspirators as for perpetrators. Civil governors were initially substituted, then placed under overall military control, with delegates at every level, right down to that of the *comarca*.

Such intervention at the local administrative level clearly increased the reach of the regime, not least in terms of policing local strikes and other forms of political and social protest. But it also increased the reach of the state, regardless of the nature or purpose of the regime. This was to affect both left and right but the dictatorship fostered a particular understanding of the state among its own supporters. Civilian participation in government increased after 1924, when Primo also established a single party, the Unión Patriótica (Patriotic Union: UP). As the heir to the regenerationist mantle, the UP signified an assertion of the *Patria* against politics, replacing the atomized politics of liberalism with the unity of the nation. It was supplemented by the Somatén, reconfigured as a national militia on 17 September 1923. Organized locally, under military command, the Somatén quickly developed a public ceremonial life, with flags, dedications, medals, and acts of homage. In regions such as Valencia, the Somatén soon came to play a leading role in the public life of the pueblos and country towns. Military values, as well as a quasi-military mobilization, thus spread down into Spanish society. The militarization of the nation was, though, far from complete. One sardonic commentator described the Somatén turning out to welcome the king and queen back from a visit to Italy: 'It was made up of several excellent burgesses, all of them over forty, heads of families, undoubtedly, with more resemblance to peaceful day-trippers than to heroic guardians of the social order. Their appearance and height were heterogeneous; their suits and hats were too.'[70] If this account is to be believed—and it is far from unique—the Somatén amounted to little more than a pantomime of national force, a fitting testimony to a dictator described as 'a glorified café politician'.[71]

However, the Somatén's role in the defence of the nation was always and unambiguously understood as the protection of the social order. It could be employed repressively, most commonly against local strikes, as befitted a 'civic union', mobilizing 'men of order' against the threat of bolshevism. For this threat was both external and internal, mounted by both the Soviet Union and the indigenous proletariat. In effect, the regime had reworked Maura's project of mobilizing the 'citizenry' or 'neutral masses'—originally seen as a means of eliminating the venal politics of *caciquismo*—in a new, ideological way. This mobilization was then continued through the Somatén's 'little brother', the UP, which took civil defence into civilian life, implicitly contrasting social peace and social conflict, hierarchical order and populist disorder. And if this opposition was maintained by force, then there is some substance to Eduardo González Calleja's hyperbolic depiction of the dictatorship as 'institutionalized violence'.[72]

But mobilization was the key to understanding the regime. New institutions and civic movements contributed to a new definition of citizenship. The rhetoric of the Primo regime was, in party terms, apolitical: responsible adult male Spaniards were invited to join its institutions simply because of who they were. There was no need for a title; membership or command was not restricted by social status. The caveat came with the social, moral, and in a broad sense, political views which would make an individual predisposed to join the UP. Bolsheviks and anticlericals were not welcome. Women, however, were welcomed into the official embrace, first as a ceremonial presence in the dinners, displays, and demonstrations of loyalty that punctuated civic life in the 1920s. Once the militia became a national institution, for example, no self-respecting branch was complete without a flag, a blessing, and a 'godmother', whose 'participation . . . with her beauty, love and virtue, induces heroism'.[73]

The development of corporatism as the defining ideology of the regime, provided a suitable idiom for those women looking to develop a more active presence. Single and widowed women could take full part in public life, voting in local and plebiscitary elections, running for municipal office and, from 1927, serving in the dictator's consultative National Assembly.[74] The thirteen women who took up seats in the Assembly thus represented their sex within the body of the nation. However, they also exercised various professional functions: María de Maeztu, for example, was a university teacher and head of the Residencia de Señoritas. Josefina Olóriz Arcelus, trained teachers in San Sebastián where she was also a municipal councillor.[75] National Assembly delegates were, by legal requirement, either unmarried or widows: married women remained unenfranchised. Even so, by 1929, Spanish women had accessed the public sphere. Political activists were still a small and legally-circumscribed minority, but women participated in the 1926 plebiscite which ratified the National Assembly both as voters and as campaigners; female delegates to the Assembly had real public status while the ceremonial public platform occupied by the more numerous *madrinas* and benefactresses also gave women a presence in civic life.

The logic of corporatism gave the regime even less likely collaborators. Most conspicuously—and despite Primo's antipathy to 'Bolsheviks'—the Socialist Party collaborated quite happily with the regime for some years. The dictator's project of resolving class conflict along fashionably corporatist lines was, in this respect, a genuine one, while the Socialists' policy of '*hay que estar dentro*' brought them considerable benefits. As both party and union were able to operate legally, they maintained their organization and membership while Primo's determination to smash the CNT also indirectly benefited the Socialists. The UGT became Spain's largest trade union, providing labour representation on the regime's arbitration committees. Socialist deputies participated in municipal *ayuntamientos* and provincial *Diputaciones*, and Largo Caballero was made a councillor of state in 1924. Wage disputes were now officially mediated, taking the state into new areas of Spanish life. But the curtailing of party politics under Primo gave the PSOE, as distinct from the UGT, only a limited role: the number of Socialist deputies in local government totalled only forty-six. In Oviedo (Asturias) for example, the *Diputación* comprised 'one socialist, five independents, all people of prestige, with all others being from the UP'; similarly in Vigo, the town council included twelve *upetistas*, two Socialists, 'two *señoritas*', and an independent.[76]

Everywhere, the UP predominated; its members 'peopled' the regime. The endless acts of loyalty presented a microcosm of the desired corporate social order. Military, ecclesiastical, and civil authorities—the last inevitably members of the UP—held the stage; women and children played auxiliary roles. The 'nation' was assembled, to the exclusion, of course, of 'the mob'. In this way, under Primo, conservative nationalism was finally untrammelled. As this protected and, to some extent, coincided with Catholicism, it was greatly to the taste of the Spanish Church. Though there was some wariness as to the essentially secular nature of Primo's state project—a scheme to reform rural labour relations caused disquiet for 'the increasing role of the state, even a theoretically Catholic one, over social groups'—the protection and privilege this afforded was enthusiastically received.[77]

Nowhere was this more apparent then among the ranks of the UP. In so far as the party—or, as it liked to be known, 'anti-party'—had a coherent political ideology, it owed much to the thinking of Popes Leo XIII and Pius XI. Paternalism, hierarchy, a stress on 'organic' social harmony, and a profound distaste for the 'atomized' politics of liberal democracy provided the common currency of (Catholic) conservatism. There was also an emphasis on 'experts', appropriately enough in a regime which built roads and resevoirs, and inaugurated Spain's first reliable radio station. In an agrarian country, this modernizing conservatism suggested a new breed of agricultural technocrats, found most easily among Angel Herrera's Propagandists and their Catholic agrarian syndicates. Herrera's national newspaper, *El Debate*, became an organ for the UP, working tirelessly for the mobilization of citizens behind the regime. The young Propagandist, José María Gil Robles, used his position as secretary of the CNCA (Confederación Nacional-Católica Agraria: National Catholic Agrarian Confederation) to foment the UP, speaking at founding meetings all over Castile. At local level too, those who were prominent in the CNCA also turned up as *upetistas*: in Valladolid, for example, the first directive members of the UP also had interests in the CNCA, the Catholic Railwaymen's Syndicate, and the diocesan Casa Social-Católica.

In this way, both a new generation and a new class became politically active under Primo. Great aristocratic landowners were not commonly found in the UP, nor were the 'old' figures of dynastic politics. The mantle had passed to the local elites, the *fuerzas vivas*, typically a mixture of substantial landowners—possibly titled but resident in the locality—and the rural bourgeoisie. These 'new men' of the dictatorship were epitomized by Gil Robles, a Salamancan lawyer still in his twenties. As Herrera's protégé, he was at the centre of that generation of Catholic activists who did, in a sense, regenerate the state. They modernized the right under Primo, taking full advantage of the regime's attempt to establish an integrative nationalism, based on ideology rather than on class. Yet, the 'nationalization' of Spain's citizens under Primo was always exclusive as well as inclusive. The regime's civic mobilization remained dependent on other associational currents, notably the Catholic, and ultimately existed in parallel to them. Nor did the Socialists—always divided over the issue of collaboration with a military dictator—provide a simple means of incorporating the working classes into the regime.

To a Church which anathematized Socialism as much as liberalism and many of whose adherents were far more fearful of the former than of the latter, Primo's dalliance with the UGT had always been distasteful. And there was also a fear of extending the power of the state, even if this was done along corporatist lines. Extending state arbitration to the countryside, for example, would have destroyed the power of the CNCA. Modernizing Catholics would mobilize in support of the regime, but they would not sacrifice an organizational subculture to it.

By 1928 the gloss had worn off the regime. The following year, the world economy delivered the hammer blow that would destroy it. In the wake of the Wall Street Crash far fewer visitors than expected visited the International Expositions in Seville and Barcelona. The grandiose re-creation of the Spanish nation went largely unseen. No amount of creative accounting could now produce money for other public works schemes. The boom which had fuelled the tentative modernization of Spain was over. Dissent grew, the Republican opposition began to mobilize, and the number of Socialist affiliates grew exponentially, rising by over a thousand per cent in some areas between 1928 and 1931. In January 1930, Primo resigned; in August of the same year the Socialists signed a pact with all the republican parties to work together for the installation of a democratic republic in Spain.

Looking Spanish: An Essay in Pictures

A. People

1. *The Family of D. Jorge Flaquer*, Joaquín Espalter y Rull, 1842. Credit: Museo Romántico, Madrid

2. Café Society. Credit: Photograph by Chris Heywood

3. Republican Civil War poster *Salud, heroico combatiente de la libertad.* Credit: Universitat de València

4. Members of the Sección Femenina performing local dances, Málaga 1940

B. Landscape

5. *Lady Juana 'la loca'*, Francisco Pradilla Ortiz, 1877. Credit: Museo del Prado, Madrid

La procesión de San Vicente (boj).

6. *St Vincent's Procession*, from Emile Verhaeren and Darío de Regoyos, España Negra (1899). Credit: British Library

7. *The Republic is defended with discipline*, Parilla. Credit: Imperial War Museum

8. Spanish pavillion, Expo 92, Sevilla. Credit: Photograph by Paul Heywood

9. Paseo de la Castellana, Madrid. Credit: Photograph by Chris Heywood

C. Products

10. Advertising image for Carbonell olive oil. Credit: Photograph by Jessica Heywood; image reproduced by permission of Grupo SOS

11. The Osborne bull, on the N-III motorway, Spain. Credit: Photograph by Jorge Tutor http://www.jorgetutor.com

12. Bullfighting festival, Pamplona 1982. © Harry Gruyaert/Magnum Photos. With thanks to Iñaki Nebreda Artieda

13. Spain's leading department store, El corte ingles. Credit: Photograph by Chris Heywood

4

Fighting for Spain, 1931–43

THE REPUBLIC'S 'NEW DEAL'

After 14 April, we shall all be something other than we are.

(José Ortega y Gasset)

The sudden appearance of a Republic in Spain suggested to many that the country had finally broken with its past. At a time when much of Europe was rejecting parliamentary government, Spain embraced constitutional democracy. Primo was gone, his fall discrediting the king as a collaborator and so offering little prospect of a return to the *status quo ante*. Using what remained of his royal prerogative, Alfonso charged General Berenguer and other senior military men with the uncomfortable and ultimately impossible task of re-establishing 'normality' as defined by the 1876 constitution. Both monarchists and republicans admitted that the municipal elections called for 12 April 1931 would be a plebiscite on the constitutional future of Spain.

The results were shattering. The Republican alliance took forty-five of Spain's fifty-two provincial capitals; on the mainland, they lost only Avila and Burgos in Old Castile, Lugo in Galicia, and the Andalucian port of Cádiz, the last quite possibly by fraud. The Republican councillors elected in 1931 remained in post until the Civil War, setting the tenor of local administration through various changes in national government. No one disputed the Republican victory, even though Spain was still predominantly rural and rural Spain had voted overwhelmingly for the monarchist cause. But the strongest monarchist results were in the smallest, poorest, pueblos. In Andalucía, for example, the Republican collation won seven out of eight provincial capitals, taking every single electoral district in each one, and had challenged hard in towns of over 6,000 inhabitants. As everyone knew, the larger the town, the weaker the caciques: set against the demonstration of popular will in the cities, the village results were meaningless. It did not matter whether they had been achieved by habit, manipulation, or outright falsification: the rural vote was not a free one. No one bothered to publish, or even collect the final results; these were an administrative matter: the political point had been decided.

The break with the past was immediate and profound. The results from the cities made it clear that the governing authorities had completely lost their ability to 'make' elections. The dynastic parties were dead, their place as representatives of the right usurped by Catholics, agrarians, and other erstwhile *upetistas*. As Berenguer said of the king, 'unfortunately, political control had escaped from his hands'.[1] Alfonso admitted as much in his final speech to the nation: the elections 'clearly showed' that he had lost the love of his people. Though he did not abdicate—'I do not renounce any of my rights, for . . . they have been deposited in me by History'—the king left Spain on 14 April. The change of regime was achieved without a shot being fired.

Alfonso's fall was not due to any shortage of monarchists: the right had mounted a robust monarchist campaign in the run-up to the elections, proclaiming hierarchy, religion, and social order as the basis of the realm. But there were few left to defend this particular king. By the evening of 12 April, a sense of unstoppable change was manifest in the streets of Madrid. Berenguer later recalled that the 'multitude' around the Puerta del Sol 'made no secret of their sense of triumph'. Even the army's role had been reduced to that of a sullen onlooker. 'The forces of Public Order seemed dumbfounded, passive, before the avalanche of enthusiasm.' As for the old elites, they 'observed the fall of the monarch as they might have watched a bad film'.[2]

Yet, the popular fiesta Berenguer observed in the centre of Madrid was not, as he thought, the work of the 'mob' but rather a celebration, a performance even, of popular sovereignty. Welcoming the Republic on the streets, or participating in the 1 May celebrations which followed a fortnight later, connected politics and people, transforming acts of government carried out in the name of the people into the actions of the people themselves. This kind of 'social magic', to use Santos Juliá's phrase, had a powerful legitimizing effect, particularly in a country entirely unaccustomed to the exercise of popular sovereignty.[3] On 14 April, similar celebrations were taking place simultaneously in every city in Spain: in Gijón, for example, the Republic was proclaimed, to tumultuous enthusiasm, even before word had arrived from the capital. Throughout the country, a few men stood on town hall balconies to proclaim the Republic while many more men in the squares below threw their hats into the air.

The festivities of April and May 1931 were a *national* performance: the revellers were demonstrating the existence of the Republican nation. From Asturias to Andalucía the proclamation of the Republic was met with the 'Marseillaise', the Spanish Republican anthem, the 'Himno de Riego' and the

'Internationale'. The second of these replaced the 'Royal March' as Spain's national anthem on 10 May; the first and third demonstrated the new regime's historical antecedents as they were understood by the people on the streets. They were creating the new regime, establishing its calendar, its festivities, its identity, even its place in history as defined by its relationship to other Republican states. A new iconography, elaborated by the citizens themselves, would characterize the new regime, cementing its position in the hearts of the people. The moral high ground belonged to the Republic and the change of regime sparked off a spontaneous municipal fiesta the length and breadth of the land.

Finally, Spain seemed to have a legitimate government, a regime under which '*everything* was possible, including "peace" '.[4] In April 1931 the fate of the Second Republic was neither predetermined nor a foregone conclusion. But, while the idea of popular sovereignty went unchallenged, it could be understood in various ways. Insurrection was as strong a tradition on the left as the *pronunicamiento* was on the right, as a failed attempt to impose a Republic by force in 1930 had shown. Republicans of every persuasion had a Jacobin faith in the 'republican moment', when 'the people', acting as a *deus ex machina*, would institute a new regime. Being voted into power may have been a bonus, but it was not a prerequisite. Republicans had to accept the will of the people but, as they were convinced they understood the popular will, how this was manifested became almost incidental.

For those further to the left, proletarian solidarity—demonstrated most clearly in the 1 May celebrations—demanded an international understanding of the Second Republic, as a stage towards the inexorable victory of the working class. Neither anarchists nor Communists had much truck with nation-states, and the exile which many had experienced during Primo's time in office had only accentuated their revolutionary internationalism. The experience of a right-wing military dictatorship made it unthinkable for moderate Socialists and Republicans to abandon the victims of repression, no matter how uncomfortable their alliance was. So long as the Republican–Socialist alliance held, the left would stand together against the right. Already though, the Italian anarchist Enrico Malatesta was warning his Spanish co-religionists not to put their faith in a parliamentary regime where 'the people will lose impetus and [their] revolutionary aspirations, and will adapt to the social status quo, based on reforms and class collaboration, because it is easier, and less effort'.[5]

This was undoubtedly the ambition of many in the Republican provisional government, notably the prime minister and future president, Manuel Azaña. The architect of collaboration with the Socialists in the pact of San Sebastián, Azaña was political heir to the regenerationist dreams of Giner de los Ríos and the ILE. Convinced that the people were 'the only source of authority, which must always be exercised by the delegation of the majority', he saw implementing the popular will as an elite task.[6] The Republican moment was a revolutionary one—the constitution would restore the dignity of the citizen and introduce a new order, based on social reform, which would redress the ills done to the Spanish people during decades of oligarchic rule—but it was not necessarily a proletarian one.

Republicanism had for so long in Spain been a repository for opposition to the established order, that its victory could only be understood as a confrontation with all that had gone before. And it was often combative. In August 1931 in Málaga, for example, the usual celebrations in honour of Our Lady of Victory, under whose patronage the Spanish Crown had driven out the 'Moors' in 1497, were replaced by a beauty pageant to find the city's 'Miss Republic'.[7] Although all proceeds went to unemployed workers, it would have been hard to devise a celebration more calculated to offend the Catholic right. To convinced monarchists, the Republic was not merely distasteful, it was an anathema. The Carlist militias, long confined to their Navarrese heartlands, were training in the mountains as early as 1931. Armed opposition to the new regime was extremely rare but antipathy and mistrust were not. In the minds of the comfortable, conservative classes, a Republic had for many years been synonymous with chaos, the association between Republicanism and disorder engrained in common culture. The conservative Republican Angel Ossorio y Gallardo recollected how mothers would reprimand their children's untidiness with the words, 'This looks like a Republic!'[8] The right's defeat left it temporarily rudderless but it was never a neutral mass, ripe for conversion to a Republican consensus. Some were prepared to give the new regime a chance, but many more, particularly those in the ex-*upetista* circles around Angel Herrera and José María Gil Robles, accepted the rules of the democratic game only as a means to destroy the 1931 Republic.

The definition of the Republic was always ambiguous. Never a single movement, Republicanism had historically been defined by doctrinal pluralism, encompassing liberals, radicals, federalists, and even early anarchists. By the early twentieth century the movement had become 'a hybrid of traditions'.[9] The Socialist Party was of course Republican, but only as part of a wider political programme. For socialists, the Republic was a means to an end; for some Republicans it was an end in itself. Under a democratic parliamentary regime, legislation would become the true expression of the popular will, the embodiment of the aspirations of responsible citizens. Hence, the decision to create a unicamaral legislature: the chamber of deputies would embody and represent the national will, with no fear of elite interference from a senate or second chamber.

But the attempt to elaborate a programme of social reform revealed the divisions which beset the Republican–Socialist coalition. Even the first article of the new constitution, which defined Spain as a 'republic of all workers' seemed a compromise between those whose Republic would be shaped around the ideas of 1789 and those who followed the torch lit in 1917. The Republic came into existence freighted with expectations, a universal panacea for an apparently endless list of competing claims. The Socialists were the only party in the new government to have a genuine mass basis. In 1930, they had finally established an agrarian section, the Federación Nacional de Trabajadores de la Tierra (National Landworkers' Federation: FNTT), which vastly increased the UGT's membership but brought a large, poor, and increasingly radical constituency into the movement. All were agreed as to the imperative necessity for social reform, particularly land reform, but there was no consensus as to the precise form this should take, even among socialists.

The crux of the difficulty lay with the issue of private property. Some in the governing coalition believed it to be an absolute right; others thought this should be qualified by social function; a few were committed to collective ownership and socialization. Passionate and prolonged debates in the Cortes—lengthened further by a determined if ultimately futile filibuster by the agrarian right—eventually led to a compromise agreement, enshrined in article 44 of the constitution, which allowed for land to be expropriated for reasons of social utility. A full agrarian reform law followed in 1932, together with a raft of labour legislation designed to protect workers, both urban and rural, against ill-treatment and unemployment. Other areas ripe for reform were tackled at the same time, notably the religious question. No fewer than six constitutional articles were used to define the new, subordinate, place of the Catholic Church, many of them modelled directly on the Portuguese Constitution of 1911.

The 'children of Erasmus', those 'whose dissident conscience was strangled for centuries' ensured the separation of Church and State.[10] Freedom of worship became a fundamental civic right; civil marriage and divorce were introduced; schools and cemeteries were secularized. Religious rituals ceased to have any official function, and even Catholic marriages had to be sanctioned by a registrar before being blessed by a priest. Catholic schools continued, but outside the state system, and in 1933 further legislation banned all monks and nuns from teaching. In what was a compromise move, the Jesuits were expelled from Spain: the only alternative had seemed to be banning all religious communities, as had happened under the Portuguese Republic. Establishing a secular state was a fundamental tenet of Republicanism but there was less unanimity as to other anti-religious policies, as the parliamentary debates over these clauses revealed. Yet, there was no doubt that the religious question was a burning political issue or that it would be resolved by parliament. There was also much sympathy for those on the left who argued that their politics were simply a response to the 'clericalism' of the Restoration establishment. For decades, they had been calling for an 'urgent clerical disinfection' and now, finally, the opportunity had arrived.[11]

The new Republican nation was, in a sense, to be legislated into existence. But it was also to be created through a system of state education, which would be secular, obligatory, free of charge, and available to all. Cataluña, the Basque Country, and Galicia were allowed to seek devolution; they could preserve local institutions, foster regional culture, and teach in their own languages. After Cataluña attained autonomous status in 1932, the Republican nation clearly had a regional base. But some local traditions were viewed less favourably. Under the Constitution, religious worship was confined to religious buildings and the Socialist minister of justice, Fernando de los Ríos, argued in vain that deputies had no right to deprive communities of their traditional festivities. Can you not see, he asked, that processions—Holy Week in Seville or Corpus Christi in Toledo—do not have a purely religious significance? But his words made no impression. Religion was to be confined to the private sphere, forcibly if need be; the public world of the Republic was resolutely secular.

The religious clauses of the Constitution suggest that this new Republican public sphere was expected to spring into existence simply as a result of the legislation. Such naive regenerationism beset many Republican projects, but it did not mean that there was no attempt to construct a Republican nation. The new regime's education policy was valiant and its results impressive. Though some, such as the Socialist Rodolfo Llopis, who felt that the real Republican project lay with labour reform, believed the regime 'took refuge in pedagogy', under Marcelino Domingo the ministry of public instruction adopted its most active role ever.[12] Teacher training was reformed and all teachers, including those in private schools, were required to be qualified, to degree standard in the case of secondary-school teachers. More spectacularly, budget allocations were changed to favour elementary schooling. By 1935, public spending per head of population was running at 5.41 pesetas per person, as opposed to 3.26 in 1931 and 2.51 in 1923 and 80 per cent of the education budget now went on elementary schooling. The number of teachers also rose—from 36,680 in 1931 to 51,593 in 1935—and in its first year of existence, the Republic built 7,000 schools. By the time the Republican–Socialist coalition lost the general elections of November 1933, Spain had 13,570 new schools, all modelled on the *escuela única*, in which education was secular, co-educational, egalitarian, and free.[13]

The Republican vision of education did not end in the schoolroom, however. Cultural 'missionaries' were created in the Misiones Pedagógicas—modelled on revolutionary Mexico's Misiones Culturales—who took literary and visual culture to outlying pueblos.[14] Between 1931 and 1934, the missions visited 495 villages, mainly in inaccessible mountain areas. The decree establishing the project spoke of bringing progress to the people and allowing the remotest villages to share in 'the advantages and noble pleasures' of the city centres. Federico García Lorca's theatre company, La Barraca, was the most famous example of this cultural endeavour but the cinema was probably the most popular, a living embodiment of scientific progress. Convinced of the educative power of film, the missions made great use of documentary films, particularly geographic ones. Films such as *Spanish Airmail Lines*, shot from a plane, showed remote communities the size and variety of the land to which they belonged, as well as the advantages brought by both technology and modern government. Wind-up gramophones were taken to pueblos with no electricity so that villagers could hear classical music, contemporary Spanish composers such as Manuel de Falla, as well as Beethoven and Schubert. Regional folk-tunes—incorporated into the classical repertoire by Albéniz and de Falla—were consistently the most popular. At the end of the visit, the missions established a library, again with Spanish and European works, for both adults and children, and left behind some reproductions of great paintings from Madrid museums.

As the missions consciously chose to visit isolated communities, their visits provided a striking contrast between urban and rural life, creating an epiphany of Republican values in traditional Spain, which was then captured by the photographers travelling with them. In Pombiego (León), the villagers initially hid from the visitors, were astounded by the gramophone, and cried out in fright when a train appeared on the cinema screen, apparently careering towards them. But fright gave way to wonder: pictures of gap-toothed peasants in headscarves and battered hats, eyes shining, captivated by the silver screen became as emblematic of the Republic as its three-coloured flag. Republicanism was an urban creed, politics an urban activity. But the Republic was now bringing enlightenment to Black Spain, dispelling the fog of superstition and ignorance. Such a project was, of course, in the best traditions of the ILE. The cultural vision peddled by the missions was unashamedly improving, driven by a sense both of Spanish culture and of Republican citizenship. Urban commercial culture was excluded from this vision: the missions had no desire to promote *cuplé* or cabaret. But they did show Hollywood films and, in the long run, the universal appeal of Charlie Chaplin may have been among the lasting legacies of the Misiones Pedagógicas.

While it was not without commercial competitors, notably the cinema, the Republic's educational and cultural policy had the explicit aim of creating citizens—the active, engaged, informed citizens of the Republican imagination—and so to make a nation. This could not be achieved overnight. In the political sphere, the policies enacted by the new Republican government had an immediate effect; the education policy did not. School-building did not come cheap and, despite the Republican new dawn, the resource base of the Spanish state remained as limited as ever. The Great Depression did not affect agrarian economies as early as it did industrial ones, but it was still a great constraint. The change of regime also created political imperatives that left little room for economic policy. In all the Republican programme of social reform there was no talk of tax. No income tax was elaborated, nor were fiscal measures used as instruments in the struggle for agrarian reform. The Republican government did establish an Inventory of Expropriable Property in1933, principally to redress the absence of a complete cadastral map of Spain. As an agrarian reform measure this was too late, and too legalistic, to assuage the proletarian hunger for land, yet more gradual solutions—based, for example, on a graduated income tax or a penal tax on rents from land—were never considered. The desire for redress, for confronting the injustices of yesterday and obliterating them in one fell swoop, was simply too strong.

The Republican 'New Deal' was thus essentially a legislative project. This is not surprising—what other weapon do legislators have?—but its aim was the transformation of Spanish society rather than of the institutions of the state. Some of these, notably the army, were addressed. But the shape and function of the state—its crystallization—remained, invisible, yet impervious. Republican legislators believed that democracy and education—in a word, progress—would transform Spain. In the sense that they believed that the 'true' Spain of the people would now be revealed then they too were heirs to the regenerationist myth. Attempts were made to secure the loyalty of the forces of coercion with the establishment of the Assault Guards and Azaña's military reform. An extensive and ambitious legislative programme also meant that the bureaucracy expanded, yet it remained organized into *cuerpos* and its personnel was neither purged nor retrained. Restoration figures could still don Republican shirts and so maintain their local clientelist networks.

Caciquismo had been curtailed at local level during the 1920s and early 1930s, but it was not obliterated. To some extent, the old habits of deference, patronage, and personal contacts benefited those new *dueños* of the northern countryside, the Catholic agrarian right. But other, Republican, politicians were even more reliant upon the old politics. Among the parliamentary parties, only the Socialists and the newly-reinvented Catholic right possessed the mass support and administrative structures needed to create modern political parties although Azaña's 'new' Republicans—born in the moral conviction of opposition during the 1920s—also offered a clear contrast to the pragmatism of the 'historic' Republican parties led by Lerroux or Melquíades Alvarez.

These 'centre' parties—who were in fact drifting to the right throughout the Republic—relied on the workings of 'old' politics. As minister of the interior, Miguel Maura received their petitions, heard rehearsed accounts of their (or their fathers') Republican credentials, and privately categorized many of them as 'calamities'. As civil governors, these men would be the only direct representative of the Republic at provincial level, yet one requested placement in Segovia, because he'd always found it a pleasant place to spend the summer.[15] The interventionist role traditionally played by provincial civil governors, remained strong. The hastily-convened re-run electoral contests of May 1931 were proof of that. They resulted in an overwhelming victory for the Republican–Socialist coalition—the new polls in Seville province did not return a single monarchist candidate—but few doubted the role played by official 'influence'.

This was not simply a question of transition. Having weathered regime change once before, the older Republican parties had become primarily concerned with maintaining political networks and controlling local institutions, a process which crystallized 'into different models of *caciquismo*'.[16] In 1931, for example, the ranks of Lerroux's Radicals were inflated by fugitive caciques whose former political affiliations had simply disappeared: Juan de la Cierva's entourage in Murcia was one example among many. Though this process sat ill with the urban populist demagoguery which had given birth to these parties, it fitted the municipal character of both Spanish Republicanism and the Spanish state. For example, in Asturias Melquíades Alvarez was a notable Republican cacique, while the following his co-religionary, Filiberto Villalobos, had in Salamanca was entirely personal. It had to be. Not only did Alvarez's party have no real national machinery, but also in Salamanca Villalobos was virtually its only member. Like Alvarez's Gijón, Valencia also retained a distinct Republican character down to 1936. Blasco Ibáñez died in exile before the Republic was proclaimed, but his city remained *blasquista*. This was testimony to the party's established influence rather than Valencia's sentimental loyalty to the great man, but it neatly showed the continuing importance of the politics of personality as well as the way in which national and municipal politics could diverge.

To some historians, the flag of convenience that 'old' Republican parties provided for 'old' caciques was, at least potentially, a necessary and prudent way of establishing a social basis for the new Republic.[17] No fledgling democracy can hope to survive without the support of its citizens and the broader a regime's social base, the greater its chances of success. But the desire of monarchist sheep to enter a Republican fold did not come about because of their wish to strengthen the regime. Rather, as they had survived the Primo regime with their local networks more or less intact, they saw no immediate prospect of surrendering them to a republic. Despite Primo de Rivera's regenerationist initiatives, many conservative local caciques had found refuge in the UP, while some branches of the Radical party simply went over to it, or the *Somatén* en masse. Because it relied on face-to-face dealings and local knowledge, *caciquismo* was both adaptable and durable. At local level, it still oiled the wheels of the system, even if it was no longer the system itself.

The hope of local influence-peddlers—whether 'old' Republicans or 'new' agrarians—was that the *pays réel* would weather changes in the *pays leal.* In 1931, established and accepted ways of conducting political business imme-diately begin to shape—and some might say pervert—the Republican state. The clientelist networks of the 'old' Republican parties became increasingly bourgeois, composed of those concerned with the defence of private prop-erty and public order. Lerroux's position as minister of foreign affairs in the Republic's provisional government initially favoured those retinues, as it held out the prospect of ample rewards for placemen. But the minister's increasing estrangement from Azaña and his eventual abandonment of the Republican–Socialist coalition, reflected his new constituency as well as his own political preferences.

As the right regrouped, and particularly as the reforming legislation of the first *bienio* began to bite, it became clear that 'old' and 'new' politics was now being combined in the tactics of Spain's first mass conservative party, the Confederación Española de Derechas Autonomas (Spanish Confederation of Autonomous Right-Wing Groups: CEDA). Its self-definition as a coalition of 'autonomous right-wing groups' reflected not only the right's distaste for the language of party but also the reality of rural politics in 1930s Spain. The local groups differed sharply in composition and political complexion, but all employed local influence, whether wielded by landowning families or agrarian syndicates. But the CEDA also drew on its leaders' experience of the UP, emphasizing propaganda, publicity, and organization. It was a modern party with traditional roots and, as such, mounted a challenge to the Republic which the founding fathers had never envisaged.

BALLOTS AND ARMBANDS

The foundation of the CEDA in February 1933 consolidated the suprema-cy of Angel Herrera, his discreet political elite, the ACNP, his protégé, José María Gil Robles, and his newspaper, *El Debate*, the same circles that had orchestrated the right's instinctive response to the 1931 Constitution. A campaign for its revision had begun the moment the final document passed the Cortes, despite an overwhelming majority in the chamber, and this campaign provided the momentum Acción Popular (Popular Action: AP, later the CEDA) needed to establish an electoral machine. Equally opposed to the Republican programme—particularly agrarian reform, which entrenched landed opposition—AP/CEDA formulated a modern political programme for the right. And, as agrarian reform notably failed to do anything for the northern peasantry—or indeed much for the southern proletariat—they found a new constituency among the Catholic smallholders of Castile.

The campaign against the constitution began in these Castilian heartlands. The church-burnings which broke out in Madrid, Barcelona, Málaga and other cities on 11 May 1931 led to a wave of anti-Republican feeling, and a series of rallies against a constitution Gil Robles claimed was 'born dead' culminated in a crowd of over 20,000 in Palencia on 8 November 1931. On 29 October, however, the Cortes had passed the Law of the Defence of the Republic, and the campaign was promptly banned as anti-Republican. The new law gave the Government extraordinary police powers to last the length of the Constituent Cortes, even though the 1931 constitution itself allowed for the suspension of 'constitutional guarantees'—freedom of expression and association, habeas corpus, and civil rights in general. Spain's recent history had given all governments good reason to fear popular unrest and this one had little desire to assuage the Catholic right, some of whom would never regard the Republic as legitimate.

From the late nineteenth century, the Spanish Church's response to anticlericalism had been primarily political. 'Social Catholicism'—establishing labour unions, savings banks, insurance schemes, workers' associations, agrarian federations to function alongside traditional forms of beneficence—was part of this drive to mobilize the faithful in the political defence of the Church. The campaign against the constitution was thus part of an existing pattern. Fernando de los Ríos had warned Catholics 'not to beat the drums of war' during the constitutional debates on the religious articles, but it can have come as no surprise when they did.[18] To the left the religious question posed no difficulty—though it would have done if treated too leniently—but the extraordinary powers the government assumed in order to deal with it were a different matter.

Almost from the first moment of its existence, the legitimacy of the new regime began to decay. The Republic had never included all Spaniards, and those looking to defend the Church were now mobilizing against it. In time-honoured fashion, the state response was to define this as a public order problem, which allowed the government to assume extraordinary powers. But the effect of the Law for the Defence of the Republic was to strengthen the executive, as well as to employ an increasingly overt reliance upon coercive power. The law was also a reaction: the Republic's enemies, rather than its government, were setting the political parameters. There were thus harsh echoes of both the Restoration and the dictatorship in this entrenched response to disorder. These were the habits of a weak state, reliant on suppressing dangerous ideas and preventing their free expression. When this was directed against the right, the left could live with it. But when the Republic also appeared to be resorting to the violent means of its predecessors, then legitimacy leeched away.

This did not happen overnight. The Republic had abolished the death penalty, introduced penal reform along with Spain's first ever female director of prisons, Victoria Kent, and refused to deploy troops against civilians. But the Civil Guard provided an unsettling continuity, particularly after Guardsmen fired into a group of striking workers in Palacios Rubios (Salamanca) in September 1931, leaving two dead and two fatally injured. When local Socialists tried to organize a—technically illegal—strike in response, they found themselves under arrest by order of the civil governor. Four months later, in January 1932, during a strike called by the FNTT, four Civil Guards were stabbed and beaten to death in Castilblanco (Badajoz), an outrage which, unlike Palacios Rubios, became a cause célèbre. Less than a week after Castilblanco, Civil Guardsmen again shot into a crowd of striking workers, killing eleven, this time in Arnedo (La Rioja). Public order was, again, a serious issue in Spain, occupying public attention, journalistic as well as political. Victoria Kent was dismissed as 'too humanitarian' as Azaña conceded that 'the state of the prisons is alarming'.[19]

For the public, the events at Casas Viejas (Cádiz) in April 1933 were far more unnerving. This naive revolutionary insurrection was called in response to an armed rising instigated by the Regional Defence Committee of Cataluña, dominated by the hard-line Federación Anarquista Ibérica (Iberian Anarchist Federation: FAI). There was a highly formulaic quality to such declarations: in response, some strikes were declared by some workers in some towns in some regions, principally along the Catalan-speaking eastern seaboard. There was no possibility of success and the events posed no serious challenge to the government. Yet, such calls could always have an effect in pueblos with an engrained anarchist culture. In January 1933, the cry to arms led the small agrarian community of Casas Viejas to declare libertarian communism. Subsequent events indicated just how deeply patterned popular political responses were in these pueblos: for generations popular involvement in politics had meant riot, and the habits of generations did not change overnight. A group of men laid siege to the local Civil Guard barracks; reinforcements arrived and gun battles followed. Nineteen men, two women, and a child lost their lives after Civil and Assault Guards—three of whom also died—burnt out a house full of people in 'an authentic massacre'.[20]

The anarcho-syndicalist paper, *CNT* met the news of the deaths with a call to arms. 'Workers! Those shot in Casas Viejas were our brothers: our protest must be shown through a general strike.' For 'pure' anarchists such as those in the FAI, the spilling of proletarian blood—particularly by a government which included Socialists—was ample justification for mobilizing against the Republic. The presence of Assault Guards—the police force established by the new Republic as a loyal, modern force to replace the Civil Guard on the streets of Spain—at Casas Viejas seemed particularly significant. Distrustful of legal forms, contemptuous of bourgeois parliaments, and now convinced that state power was the same whoever wielded it, many anarchists returned to the basic tenets of their creed, proclaiming themselves victims of the Republican–Socialist 'dictatorship'. This was not true of all libertarians: a significant moderate faction in the CNT issued a manifesto emphasizing syndicalism over anarchism. One of its signatories, the talented and capable Angel Pestaña, would eventually abandon the CNT in favour of pure syndicalism.

The tensions the *trientistas*' manifesto unleashed in the wider movement were never resolved. But running battles between anarchist-inspired workers and the forces of law and order were threatening to become as marked a feature of the Second Republic as of previous regimes. The proletarian villagers in Casas Viejas attacked the Civil Guard as it represented the authority of the state, was associated with the upper classes, and was responsible for innumerable acts of brutality they had experienced over generations. No matter that Azaña had reformed and streamlined the Civil Guard: the unfounded accusations that he had given the order to 'shoot them in the guts' in Casas Viejas counted for far more. At the same time, however, property-owning, 'respectable' folk feared that the country was at the mercy of gun-toting anarchist hit-men and furious proletarian mobs.

Nowhere was this division clearer than in Barcelona. With the coming of the Republic, Catalanism had reappeared on the national stage. The Primo years had caused the movement to look outwards to Europe and not inwards to Spain. The experience of cultural repression also ensured that a distinct, Catalan, political option would be offered under the Republic and that it would hold sway. The Esquerra Republicana (Republican Left) achieved a crushing victory in the 1931 elections and maintained its electoral hegemony throughout the Republic. In this, the Esquerra was undoubtedly helped by the regional strength of the CNT and concomitant weakness of the Socialists. The Catalan Republicans had few parliamentary rivals on the left. But this also made the clash between the bourgeois, property-owning supporters of the Esquerra and the anarcho-syndicalist poor even starker, particularly after the establishment of an autonomous regional government, the Generalitat, in 1932.

The Depression hit hard in Barcelona. Neither central nor regional resources were sufficient to ameliorate its effects in any systematic fashion. Even in a period of rising unemployment, welfarist solutions barely figured on the political agenda, and could not possibly have been afforded even if they had. Many were desperate for social and economic change and yet, despite the hopes invested first in the Republic and then in the Generalitat, change did not seem to come. Under these circumstances, the militant FAI established a power base in Barcelona. The violence inherent in anarchist ideology, together with the FAI's propensity to raise funds through protection rackets and bank-heists, led to a clearly political use of force. When a jewellers' merchants laid off warehousemen in 1933, for example, it was raided by masked men, who removed merchandise as compensatory insurance payments.[21] As this was just one of over sixty armed robberies in Barcelona that year, the 'respectable' classes' suspicion that radical politics were simply a form of criminality seemed confirmed.

The establishment of the Generalitat made little difference. Neither national nor regional government could be seen to condone violence—which in any case they were never inclined to do—but nor could they offer any real solutions to it. Ameliorating economic conditions appeared to be outside the scope of the government, both because of the weakness of the state's resources and because of the political imperatives of a new regime. But public order was a real problem. A Republic which defined itself through the rule of law had seen its enforcing of that law challenged both at Casas Viejas and on the streets of Barcelona. As disenchantment with the Republic's constitutional project became more pronounced among the supporters of the left, politics moved outside the legislature, to be enacted, and legitimated, on the street.

Throughout the 1930s, shirted movements took to the streets of Europe, competing with the Italian Fascist standard of political spectacle by staging rallies, march-pasts, and all manner of mass meetings. Such theatrical events needed an audience, in part provided by photographers and pressmen. But the principal audience was the participants; ritualized mass rallies forged a collectivity out of disparate individuals. Spain's indigenous fascist party, the Falange Española y de las JONS, was established in October 1933, dedicated to new 'dialectics of fists and pistols' and the camaraderie of comrades in arms.[22] In March 1934 the party filled a theatre in the Castilian city of Valladolid with the full panoply of blue shirts, banners, insignia, and Roman salutes. Finding the socialist youth of the city awaiting their exit, the fascists threw themselves into a brawl that led to the death of one of their members. Henceforth, announced their leader, José Antonio Primo de Rivera, son of the late dictator, Falangists would address each other informally as *tu*: 'brotherhood in the face of danger demanded it.'[23]

Street fights between youths wearing different coloured armbands were becoming part of the European political scene, both emblem and symptom of a new kind of politics. For left and right, street politics provided legitimation, a demonstration of the popular will *in action*. The Falangists' blue shirts eliminated social and class differences, rendering invisible the unreliable ego of the individual and facilitating displays which emphasized discipline, order, and hierarchy. Proletarian parties paraded their social class rather than disguising it, encouraging informal uniforms, often simply a kerchief. But they too were well aware of the politics of display, and the lexicon of political action. The radicalization of the Socialist Youth—which merged with the Communist youth wing to form the Juventudes Socialistas Unificadas (JSU: Unified Socialist Youth) in March 1936—was ample testimony to this.

It was on the right, however, that the change in political style made most impact. The Falange fought the 1933 elections, though with no success, remaining a small, closely-knit but predominately upper-class party until 1936. A propensity for street-fighting and noisy display gave it a prominence out of all proportion to its importance, and the Falange was a continual irritant to the conservative right, whose own youth movement, the Juventudes de Acción Popular (JAP: Popular Action Youth) was fast becoming intoxicated by the new fascist style. This suited a leader—or *jefe* as the JAP preferred—seduced by modern technology if not by modern values. José María Gil Robles claimed the CEDA introduced a style of campaigning 'previously unknown in Spain' during the elections of November 1933. Queues of would-be donors formed outside the party headquarters in Madrid at the start of the campaign and remained there until the end. Ten million leaflets were distributed, alongside 200,000 coloured posters; party broadcasts were shown in all the major cities on screens mounted on large lorries. In the final half-hour of the campaign, Gil Robles broadcast from his own office 'to the whole of Spain'.[24]

During the 1933 campaign, the right was finally engaged in a dialogue with all Spaniards. Despite the resurgence of regional nationalisms after 1931, political discourse was nationalized under the Second Republic with a rapid development of genuinely national political parties. Yet, on the right this modernizing impulse could not disguise the real crisis of conservatism which was affecting Spain, itself a reflection of the wider European response to the rise of fascism. The genuine mass politics of fascism perturbed a political ideology based upon hierarchy and deference, albeit mitigated by paternalism. By 1933, it was clear that the 'nationalization of the masses' could not be undone: Spanish conservatism had to develop a mass base. The CEDA did this, rapidly and effectively, and not simply in response to the similar process of radicalization on the proletarian left which was undercutting liberal republicanism. But while they adopted the techniques of mass politics in order to defeat the Republic, the essential weakness of the conservative position meant that it careered rapidly to the right, imprisoned by a new political dynamic which it only partly understood and could not control.

An example is the fleeting prominence women attained within the CEDA. The development of a modern party of the right had seemed to open up new possibilities for newly enfranchised Conservative women. An army of female labour volunteered for party work, registering voters, staffing offices, establishing women's branches, and, above all, speaking at rallies. Their work paid off: in 1933 the left fared badly, the CEDA became the largest party, and the new government was formed by the Radicals. Nevertheless, four Socialist women were elected to parliament and only one CEDA member, Francisca Bohigas, the only female deputy returned for the right under the Republic. The discrepancy is surprising: both right and left were convinced that women would vote disproportionately for Catholic parties. The Basque Nationalists, the Carlists, and most significantly the CEDA, were the first to mobilize women, drawing on established church networks of pious sodalities and charity groups. These women achieved a formidable public presence and several ran for office in 1933. Yet, even though the right fully accepted the need to canvass women's votes, they never fully accepted female political agency. Both conservative and Catholic thought insisted on gender hierarchies as a fundamental constituent of social hierarchies. Women could no longer be excluded from definitions of the nation, or the people, but the rhetoric of domesticity could keep them in their place. Their votes were instrumentalized, their agency denied even as their public role became greater than ever. As one CEDA ideologue put it, the party 'had to create men, had to educate youth, had to capture the female vote'.[25]

Despite her pioneering achievement, Bohigas merits only a sentence in her leader's 850-page memoirs.[26] The women's moment proved to be the 1933 election campaign: once the initial mobilization had been achieved, the party's interest moved on. The rapid radicalization of politics under the Republic also had an effect. Adult women—most of them married and middle-class—were unlikely candidates for street politics or paramilitary spectacle, both the preserve of the the khaki-shirted JAP. Convinced of women's loyal discipline at the ballot box, the party leadership lost interest in the very constituency which might have anchored them most firmly to a tradition of bourgeois conservatism. The youth movement, on the other hand, was veering fast towards the radical right.

Despite the sneers of the Falange, who jeered at the 'venerable elderly' of a youth movement open to those in their thirties, this radicalism became most apparent under the right-wing coalition which governed Spain from 1933 to 1936. The impetus was provided by the most serious attempt at insurrection yet seen from the left: the Asturias revolt of October 1934. The defeat of the left in the November 1933 elections meant the abandonment of Republican reforms—de facto if not de jure—even before the CEDA entered the government in the autumn of 1934. For many in the labour movement—already radicalized by the grassroots pressure of the FNTT and the dashing of the reformist dream of 1931—the new government was simply the thin end of the fascist wedge.

Throughout Europe the left was being defeated at every turn. Hitler, ushered into power by the conservative elites in Germany, had destroyed organized labour, liquidating Europe's strongest communist party. In Austria, the Catholic corporatist Dolfuss, so admired by the CEDA, had used paramilitary forces to crush the Viennese working class. Convinced that they were acting within the spirit of the Republic—if not the letter of the law—the Socialist leadership turned to insurrection. Preparations were made throughout 1934, even though Socialist *casas del pueblo* were regularly being searched for arms. That in the Asturian mining town of Sama was searched three times in seven months, albeit fruitlessly, while the mineworkers' union's newspaper, *Avance*, was banned an astounding ninety-three times during a mere six-month period in the same year.[27]

When the Socialists called an insurrectionary general strike in October, the Asturian miners responded wholeheartedly. Elsewhere, the putative revolution was a disaster: a 'Catalan republic' lasted a mere ten hours and, despite an attempt at a general stoppage in Madrid, other strikes collapsed rapidly, leaving Asturias to fight alone. CNT and UGT fought together in the 'Asturian Commune', with a prominent role also being taken by the young radicals of the JSU. The fight was bitter, the outcome never in doubt. Miners' unions, even in unity, were no match for the coercive power of the state, particularly not under a government prepared to call in colonial troops to repress the revolt. General Franco, entrusted with the 'pacification of Asturias', ordered artillery attacks on the miners' strongholds. In the wake of the revolt, 4,000 were injured, 1,000 of them fatally, while 30,000 were imprisoned and many tortured.

After Asturias, the UGT leadership was imprisoned, Socialist newspapers silenced, and all the *casas del pueblo* shut down. Trials for sedition were conducted by military tribunals: when the death sentences passed by one such body on two Socialist deputies were commuted, CEDA ministers resigned from the cabinet in protest. With the return of open and direct state repression,

Republicans of all persuasions agreed with the moderate Socialist Juan Simeón Vidarte when he wrote in March 1935 that 'It is not the working class who have found themselves outside the law, for it is they who, with most vigour, have defended the spirit, the soul of the fundamental law of the State.'[28] In the 1930s this was a fashionable doctrine: legitimacy, the popular will, could be demonstrated, on the streets rather than in the polling booth. But it was also dangerous, and the response of several leading figures on the centre left—notably Manuel Azaña and Indalecio Prieto—suggested that it was seen as such.

To the right, Asturias was hard evidence of the revolutionary left's nefarious plans for Spain. The rebels had killed those they saw as class enemies, including thirty-four priests and seminarians—the most clerical blood spilt in Spain for over a hundred years. The CEDA paper, *El Debate*, talked of 'the passions of the beast'; the monarchist *ABC* of the 'perverse instinct of destruction'. There were stories of 'chekas', of prototype militiawomen, 'young and beautiful, though moral perversion showed in their faces, a mixture of shamelessness and cruelty'.[29] Against these dehumanized forces of the international revolution—believed to be manipulated by the shadowy figures of Soviet Communists, freemasons, and Jews—the army had stood firm. 'Acts of homage' were organized by the right throughout Spain, while *ABC* declared that 'The army always saves us, because it is unity . . . because it is hierarchy . . . because it is discipline . . . In short, because it is civilization . . . Because the Army is Spain.'[30] Paradoxically, the right's response to Asturias shows both how much, ideologically, remained the same and how much had changed. Once again, social and political unrest was redefined as a public order problem and so the solution was military repression, no matter what the underlying cause. But the spread of social Darwinist ideas of 'degeneration', the crystallizing of a class identity for racial decline, was now both defined and visible. Asturias was nothing less than the first manifestation of 'anti-Spain'.

Civilians as well as soldiers had to resist the 'anti-Spain'. During the October strike, *japistas* throughout the country had put themselves at the service of the authorities, driving buses, unloading lorries, and manning railway stations. In some areas, such as the city of Salamanca, the JAP also provided vigilante patrols which the local CEDA paper argued should be expanded into a full civilian militia, ready to defend 'true' Spain against Marxist 'tyranny'. The mobilization of youth thus continued apace on the right. For the left, this process was interrupted by the post-Asturias repression, but it never stopped, nor was it fully tamed. The street war of arm-bands and neckerchiefs continued, even though the government had taken the first steps towards banning paramilitary uniforms in June 1934, made it illegal for minors to join political parties in August 1934, and banned all 'unauthorized' mass displays and 'subversive' political emblems and uniforms in July 1935. Yet, the JAP continued to recruit, playing a highly visible and, to the left, highly sinister role in the electoral campaign of February 1936, when it was given control of national propaganda. A three-storey-high poster dominated Madrid's Puerta del Sol, with Gil Robles' head in the foreground, ranks of marching militiamen behind. 'Estos son mis poderes' proclaimed the poster, the very words used by Cardinal Cisneros in introducing his civilian militia during the historic power struggle for the throne of Spain. The provocation was clear. Surely now even hardened *faístas* would see that not all bourgeois governments were the same?

At its most fundamental, the left/right distinction was between those who supported the Republican project and those who sought to dismantle it. Manuel Azaña—whose attempt to reform the fragmented Republican option had begun immediately after the 1933 elections—made the case explicitly. He was heard by the moderate sectors of the PSOE, epitomized by Indalecio Prieto, but not by Largo Caballero's UGT nor the Socialist Youth, who were convinced the solution lay with wholehearted rather than half-hearted revolution. The split within the Socialist movement was now uncontainable. In December 1935, Largo resigned from the PSOE executive, turning his union into what was, in effect, a separate political party. Even so, the executives of the Socialist party, union, and youth movement all agreed to an electoral pact with the Republicans. Azaña's initiative was gathering pace: a series of open-air rallies took Spanish Republicanism from its 'natural habitat [of] *tertulias* and coteries' and transplanted it into popular soil.[31] On 20 October 1935, he spoke to nearly 500,000 on the outskirts of Madrid—the largest gathering ever voluntarily assembled to hear a European politician. Under his leadership, and with Prieto's support, the Spanish Popular Front took shape as a reassertion of the reformist impulse of the Republic. The aim of the alliance was to unseat the Radical–CEDA government, nothing more. If they succeeded in this, the Republicans would govern alone. Such was the price of UGT cooperation.

In 1936, as in 1931, the polls served both to assert the popular will and to demonstrate the Republican nature of that will. But this apparent continuity was illusory, undermined by the division in the socialist movement and a jealous concern for party autonomy. No joint meetings were held, even during the campaign. The radicalization of the UGT meant its increasing alienation from parliamentary politics and so the campaign was negotiated and run by Liberal politicians, looking to capture the votes of the labouring masses. There was no doubt that they would do this. The promise of an amnesty for all political prisoners—made by men who, like Azaña and Prieto, had been either in gaol or in exile—guaranteed that even the CNT would vote in February. But their further commitment to participation in a Popular Front programme of Republican reform was extremely uncertain.

In the wake of the elections, under a cabinet hand-picked by Azaña—but only by him—the legislative bases of the Republic were reasserted. Companys made a triumphal return to Barcelona and the Generalitat was reinstated. Agrarian reform began in earnest. In Salamanca, for example, nearly 50,000 hectares were legally expropriated between March and June. Further south, the situation was more confusing. Jaén offered a typical example: workers occupied latifundia estates; denunciations by the owners led to the Civil Guard requesting that the workers leave, but nothing more. In pueblos with Socialist *alcaldes*, the occupations were officially sanctioned, even being led by the local authorities. Legally, the situation was far from clear: the FNTT told its members to 'forget the red tape' and the occupations were invariably ratified retrospectively under the terms of the agrarian reform law.[32]

Severing the umbilical link between the UGT and the PSOE profoundly changed the nature of political action under the Republic. Even as the election results were announced, the Popular Front dissolved and the unions seized the political impetus. Only in the industrial enclaves of the northern Atlantic coast did the *Prietistas* hold sway. Elsewhere, as in the Jaén pueblos, the Socialists were the UGT/FNTT, not the Madrid-based PSOE. Church-burnings began again, and on a far larger scale than in May 1931. On 17 March Azaña wrote in tones of bitter irony: 'Today they have burnt Yecla for us: seven churches, six houses, all the right's political centres and the Property Registry.' His mood, he noted, was one of 'black despair'.[33]

As the soon-to-be president of the Republic observed, the agrarian proletariat—the radical base of the Republic—was now determined to take charge of its own destiny. Yet, the crisis of the Republic, which was apparent even before civil war broke out in July, remained a *political* crisis rather than a crisis of the state. This is suggested by the actions of the Civil Guardsmen when facing the land invasions in Jaén. Their response was uncomfortable, reflecting the difficulty of their position, but it was that of a state police force. At no point did the Civil Guard act as a private army at the service of the landed elites.

The sense of political crisis was compounded by government action—or the lack of it—at national level. The Popular Front's electoral victory was, in terms of votes, a narrow one but the composition of the new Cortes sealed the fate of the old 'centre' parties—the Radicals were virtually obliterated—and sounded the death knell for the parliamentary right. Just as, on the left, political impetus passed from parliament to the unions, so on the right, it passed to those who believed the Republic should be defeated by force. The Falange finally began to recruit on a wide scale; the JAP, in contrast, imploded. The government was faced with ever-increasing levels of violence, both urban and rural, and the prospect of a military coup. Some generals and many right-wing leaders were working increasingly openly towards an armed rising; in June, a redundant Gil Robles passed CEDA funds over to the conspirators. Warnings of the coming coup were now echoing through the corridors of power. The government ignored them.

A PEOPLE'S WAR

When, on 17 July 1936, a military rising began in Morocco, the depth of the crisis facing the Republic was starkly revealed. The following day, as garrisons rose in every city in Spain, the government issued a series of contradictory telegrams asserting 'complete tranquility' even as crowds gathered in Madrid's Puerta del Sol, clamouring for arms. By nightfall, the prime minister had resigned; by 20 July, a second attempt at a new cabinet had failed and José Giral took office. The Republic had had three governments within thirty-six hours. In what was already a retrospective measure, Giral authorized the distribution of arms to the people. Loyal artillery officers had been handing out rifles on Madrid's Calle Atocha on the day of the rising: 'I handed them out to anyone who showed me a left-wing membership card. I didn't know who they were—they might have been bandits and assassins—but at that moment the people had to be armed.'[34] In Barcelona too—though Companys resisted distributing arms—they were handed out piecemeal until CNT militants stormed the arsenals, fighting alongside Civil and Assault Guards to crush the rising in the city.

By 20 July, Spain was divided, its fault line running roughly between those areas which had voted for the Popular Front in February and those which had not. The eastern seaboard, the Atlantic coast, the latifundia south, and virtually all of Spain's major cities remained with the Republic. Loyal police forces were essential to the rebel defeat in these cities: over 50 per cent of the Civil Guard are estimated to have remained with the regime together with 70 per cent of Assault Guards.[35] Their stand could not, though, wipe out the suspicion in which the armed forces were held by many in the Republic after 18 July, a suspicion exacerbated by the fear of fifth columnists. Nor did the presence of loyal police disguise the extent to which political power, and a revolutionary initiative, now lay on the streets.

As the frantic cabinet manoeuvrings of the first hours of the Civil War suggested, the Republican regime had collapsed. Lack of central authority and co-ordination created the political space for a revolution, which Republican Spain experienced during the 'hot summer' of 1936. Spain was now mobilized into two opposing, class-based camps. This was shown most clearly at village level, where the only division which mattered by July 1936 was that between

Civil War, 1936

FRANCE

ANDORRA

ALGERIA

PORTUGAL

BALEARIC
ISLANDS

Gerona
Barcelona
Tarragona
Lérida
Huesca
Castellón
Valencia
Alicante
Zaragoza
Teruel
Guipúzcoa
Navarra
Álava
Logroño
Soria
Cuenca
Albacete
Murcia
Almería
Vizcaya
Burgos
Guadalajara
Santander
Palencia
Segovia
Madrid
Toledo
Cuidad Real
Jaén
Granada
León
Valladolid
Ávila
Málaga
Zamora
Salamanca
Córdoba
Oviedo
Cáceres
Badajoz
Sevilla
Lugo
Orense
Huelva
Cádiz
La Coruña
Pontevedra

Key

⊙ provinces returning
a Popular Front
majority in February

Nationalist-held territory, 20 July

Republican-held territory, 20 July

0   100mls
0   160kms

left and right. Whether the first was Socialist, anarchist, or Republican, the second monarchist, *cedista*, or fascist depended much on the character and affiliation of the local *jefe*. At this level, inter-party divisions were immaterial: everyone knew which side they were on. The popular violence which marked the beginning of the Civil War in the Republican zone was thus ideologically driven, but it did not 'belong' to any particular left-wing creed.

In patterns of violence which were deeply embedded in the community, landlords, military men, and right-wing activists were imprisoned, humiliated, or killed. Itinerant militia columns brought the revolution to the pueblos but, while militiamen acted as the agents of violence, they could not identify their victims without the active co-operation of at least some villagers.[36] Neighbours betrayed neighbours, identifying local rightists or betraying the whereabouts of the parish priest. Many were targeted for their office. In Higuera de Arjona (Jaén) the Civil Guard were burlesqued by revolutionaries who dressed up in their uniforms and three-cornered hats while army officers were often at risk. Yet many victims were lesser figures: in Churriana, where Gerald Brenan lived, the local baker was denounced as a rightist, apparently by someone who owed him money. A pious man, he had acted as local agent for the CEDA and, although he had not even voted in the 1936 elections, he was shot.[37] As the story of Juan the baker shows, religion could be the prime determinant in selecting victims. The experience of the Republic had 'fixed' the Church as the ideological enemy of the left. Even though the Church was not involved in the coup, few doubted its guilt. Churches and priests became conspicuous targets as the parish clergy was singled out for attack: 4,184 died as did 2,365 monks and brothers.

This was genuine persecution: anticlericalism had attained a central importance in the revolutionary imagination. Father Lorenzo Moreno Nicolás, for example, went into hiding in his native town of Lorca (Murcia). He wore lay clothes and, as practising Catholicism was banned, said mass clandestinely in his mother's house without vestments or liturgical objects. He was arrested there on 3 November and taken to some local mines where, after much ill-treatment, he was shot and his body thrown down a shaft.[38] The Brothers of St John of God cared for the mentally infirm in asylums throughout central Spain. They had no political involvement but as several were taken out to be shot in Madrid a voice was heard to claim that 'only they' were responsible for the military coup. Ninety-seven of the brothers were killed, despite their work and the vulnerability of their charges. Religion was to be expunged from Republican Spain, as the church-burnings and destruction of images made clear.[39] The rituals of religion, particularly where they coincided with those of the pueblo, were reinvented by the mob. In Almería, a statue of St Joseph was paraded around the streets with a spittoon on its head; in Murcia, a priest's body was dragged through the city and hoisted upon the bell tower of his own church; throughout Spain, churches were emptied, religious objects and jewellery removed from private houses, and the shrines of patron saints were singled out for attack.

This revolutionary reinvention of the *patria chica* was immediate and spontaneous, neither rational nor rationalized. As one CNT paper put it, violence could be 'a dark night between a bloody sunset and the creative joy of dawn'.[40] This meant more than a settling of scores: the purging effects of violence were acknowledged by anarchist and socialist alike. Landlords' houses were attacked alongside presbyteries; goods, valuables, and furniture were forcibly 'expropriated' and seized or destroyed; archives, and parochial and notarial records were burnt. Purgative violence was to recreate the local community, severing the shackles of superstition and deference and creating a spontaneous egalitarian freedom. All too often, however, people were forced to be free just as they were forced to be secular. Many pueblos were transformed, not least by their reinvention as collectives. Villages became agrarian cooperatives; industrial collectives sprang up in the cities, above all in Barcelona, organized by unions in factories, by residents' committees in neighbourhoods. All collectives were rooted in the Marxian aspiration to take 'from each according to his abilities' and give 'to each according to his needs' but some were production based while others looked to organize and re-model daily life, distributing goods and services more fairly or instituting an anarchist-inspired ethic of the liberating power of work.

The subject matter of the collectives was the fabric of everyday life. Many abolished money, though some introduced fixed wage scales; all emphasized communal exchange, often to the detriment of 'individualists' who wished to remain outside. Some collectives were highly utopian, others far more pragmatic. Establishing an equitable rationing system, for example, was important both on the ground and in terms of Republican policy. In the pueblos, collectivists could build on established communal traditions, such as *vecinos*' meetings of heads of households. The prevalence of subsistence agriculture meant that mechanisms for the production and exchange of foodstuffs could be established fairly easily but, while collectives such as that in the Aragonese pueblo of Tamarite de Litera claimed they also assured 'medical and pharmaceutical services and everything concerning collective needs and development', this was much harder to deliver.[41] The problems were foreseeable—Spanish pueblos could produce grain and cooking oil, but not coffee or petroleum; the villages could be fed but not the cities—but not necessarily immediate. In 1936, the proletarian traditions of the *patria chica*, with its utopian aspirations and egalitarian dreams, meant a resurgence of revolutionary aspirations, an attempt to recreate the world as it was lived, to establish new modes of being in the pueblo and so, in turn, transform the wider world.

Collectivization occurred in all Republican-held territory except for the Basque Country, yet the dislocation of central authority confirmed it as a highly localized phenomenon. The key players were the local 'committees', which varied in both composition and authority. Even the Council of Aragón—established by the CNT in October 1936 as governing council for that eastern part of the region which remained Republican after July—remained essentially 'a localism "writ large"'.[42] Despite the urgent need for economic co-ordination and the acknowledged military imperatives, spending priorities often reflected parochial concerns, purchasing tractors for example rather than vehicles for the front. Untrammelled CNT power made Aragón anomalous: elsewhere the political complexion of collectives reflected local social conditions.[43] Some collectives affiliated to the UGT while others were run by the two unions in collaboration: in Castilla la Mancha, for example, there were 45 UGT collectives and 35 UGT-CNT ones for the CNT's 174. Jaén—where the UGT outnumbered other workers' organizations by ten to one—was the only province where socialist collectives outnumbered anarchist ones. Here, as in Cataluña, some collectives eschewed the major trade unions to affiliate to Republican parties, the agrarian reform institute, peasant unions, or the Communist Party, all of which provided some defence for small farmers looking to defend their position—and their lands—from collectivist encroachments.

As these nonconformist Republican collectives demonstrated, reactions to the revolution were often ambivalent. The formation of the Council of Aragón was, in part, a response to fears that militia columns were leaving the villages 'in ruins'.[44] The Durruti column was directly involved in the forcible collectivization of some Aragonese villages while the Iron Column—which had recruited heavily among ex-prisoners from Valencia's San Miguel de los Reyes gaol—developed a savagely implemented, lumpenproletariat agenda that caused division even within anarchist ranks. Local committees also varied in nature, ranging from constituted Popular Front committees to hastily-convened ad hoc bodies, and this in itself affected the opportunities for revolutionary violence. For the collapse of central authority did not mean the same in every area of Spain. In the Basque Country—admittedly cut off from most of Republican Spain—the collapse was almost imperceptible. The Republican, but Catholic and socially conservative, Basque Nationalist Party, maintained continuity and control, ruling as an autonomous government and keeping revolutionary activity to a minimum. In other places too, some measures had been put in place before the outbreak of war.

Jaén, for example, had a properly constituted Popular Front committee, which included the general secretary of the FNTT.[45] Heeding Communist warnings of the impending coup, the provincial committee took up residence in the civil governor's office on 14 July, sending delegates into the localities to take precautionary measures even before the army had risen. Even as the initiative passed away from central government, a continuity of authority was maintained on the ground. This affected the nature, and the level, of political violence within the province. Levels of incarceration were very high, particularly in the provincial capital, as prisoners were sent there from smaller towns. With the gaols heaving and thousands of prisoners housed in appalling conditions in the cathedral, an arrangement was made in August to send two trainloads of detainees to prisons in Madrid. Few reached their destination: the second train was stopped on the outskirts of the capital and its passengers massacred. In the province itself, prisoners were removed from gaol and shot in the reprisals for Nationalist bombardments known as *sacas*. Such actions, like the detentions, were often the work of local militias or village committees. But by December, they had virtually ceased.

The situation in neighbouring Almería was very different. Here, the civil governor was a member of Izquierda Republicana (IR), who took up his post after the February elections, describing himself as a 'businessman (*comerciante*), industrialist, landowner. A bourgeois of the middle class.'[46] His position remained intact, but his authority was usurped by the parallel revolutionary committees which sprang up as soon as civil war was engaged. Pre-existing tensions between IR and the Socialist Party worsened the position and on 31 August the governor left for Madrid to petition the prime minister. He never returned. During August and September, Almería experienced more violent deaths than at any other time during the Civil War, as the Comité de Presos took the fate of prisoners more or less into its own hands. Only the appointment of a Socialist civil governor by a Socialist prime minister in October 1936 reintegrated local and central authority. In January 1937, the Comité de Presos ceased to function and its competence passed to the civil governor.

In this way, while the revolution occurred in the interstices of state power and, in particular, the space left by the temporary absence of central authority, it was also conditioned by local circumstances. The bishop of Jaén was murdered on the 'train of death' along with over two hundred others; in contrast, his counterpart in Almería was shot in the night along a roadside after being removed suddenly from a prison ship in a *saca* led by the Comité de Presos.[47] As the situation in Almería showed, the collapse of the Republican regime as constituted on 18 July was an accomplished fact. This is commonly, and erroneously, represented as the collapse of the state. Yet, at no point can the events of 1936 be seen as state collapse—the revolutionary moment was too brief and the reconstruction of central authority too rapid. In the aftermath of 18 July, the government lost both authority and direction and, as a consequence, state power faltered but its institutions did not collapse. Republican Spain never approached the levels of decentralized violence that characterize true state collapse—the competing war lords of post-Imperial China, for example, or the prolonged implosion of some post-colonial African states in a 'metamorphosis of societies into a battlefield of all against all'.[48] The reassertion of central control was also accomplished relatively quickly. The vacuum was political: once that was filled, then those who represented the state within Republican society resumed their role. The Popular Front authorities in Jaén took measures against pillage as early as August 1936 while all three provincial Popular Front committees—none of which had existed prior to the military rising—in the crucial citrus-producing region of Valencia collaborated with central government's Agrarian Reform Institute from early August.[49] Here moderate sectors of the Popular Front, including the CNT, quickly condemned the 'plague of committees' and uncontrolled militia columns which terrorized communities and dislocated the local economy.

The problem the Republic faced was thus that of re-establishing order rather than of defeating significant rivals to power. With a speed impossible under a true state collapse, this was achieved by May 1937 but the scale of the problem should not be underestimated. Rebel troops were cutting through swathes of territory in the south and advancing quickly towards Madrid. The Giral government survived until September, but none could claim that its writ was law. The end of the liberal Republican regime de jure as well as de facto came on 4 September when Largo Caballero became prime minister. The new government—which would be Spain's widest incarnation of the Popular Front—recognized the power of the unions, which came into government, most significantly in the person of the prime minister. On 26 September, the Catalan Generalitat was reconstituted, incorporating all anti-fascist political parties and trade unions; on 4 November, the power of the revolutionary unions appeared to reach its apogee, when the CNT accepted national ministerial posts in trade, industry, justice, and health. This highly paradoxical move was explained more by the exigencies of war than by tensions within the CNT itself: the new ministers did not represent a victory of 'moderate' syndicalism over 'pure' anarchism; two of them belonged to the FAI. Civil war had brutally revealed the practical poverty of the anarchist position. Despite its theoretical anti-statism, the Iron Column on the Teruel front defended the CNT's entry into government, arguing that 'the current situation demands immediately a work of national synthesis, not fractions'. Anarchists were already collaborating in the Generalitat as well as governing innumerable villages and collectives. As one *cenetista* put it, 'why differentiate between a regional and a national government . . . Exercising authority in a village was neither more nor less anti-anarchist than exercising it in a nation.'[50]

The CNT's influence should, in theory, have been enhanced when a mere two days later, on 6 November, the government of Spain left the beleaguered capital for safe haven in Valencia. Socialist-dominated Madrid offered less grass-roots support than the—admittedly moderate—CNT strongholds of the Levante, and what did anarchists care for capital cities or the symbolism of the nation-state? But fleeing Madrid left an indelible impression of cowardice, which tainted the CNT alongside the other parties. The point was forcibly made when several ministers, including two from the CNT, were stopped at a checkpoint run by anarchosyndicalist militiamen, manhandled and told that 'the Government should return to their posts'.[51] Though retorting that 'the Government took orders from no-one', the ministers turned back, reaching Valencia by the back roads.

The detentions on the road illustrated the continuing problem of 'dual power'. It was not just that the unions had real authority on the streets, parallel to the constituted government's. For the control the unions exerted over their own members was by no means certain. This was particularly a problem for the CNT whose lack of hierarchies and central command structures, as well as of agreed political programmes, left the organization, in Helen Graham's words, 'invertebrate'. The anarchosyndicalists failed to take power in Cataluña in July, when the Generalitat's survival was due only to Companys' virtuoso act of brinkmanship in offering control of the region to the CNT. As the government no longer existed, the union's refusal reflected only its own weakness rather than the collapse of the state in both its national and regional guises. The CNT were undoubtedly instrumental in the defeat of the military coup in Barcelona, but so too were the Civil and Assault Guards, whose commanding officers had been vetted for loyalty after the February elections, and they owed their allegiance to the Generalitat.

Regime collapse, revolution, and the dislocation of central authority con-ditioned the first months of war on the Republican side, but attitudes towards the exercise of state power were always more ambivalent than circumstances might suggest. Before they came into government, Largo Caballero had reportedly told the CNT that 'the existence of the legal government of the Republic, proclaimed and legitimized by the people in various elections' was its 'trump card'.[52] The CNT-FAI minister of health, Federica Montse-ny, returned regularly from Valencia to Madrid to imbue the defence of the capital with an anarchist presence—a stance which cannot entirely be attributed to rivalry with the communists who were spearheading the city's defence. The exercise of *legitimate* power was widely agreed to be the key to successful resistance. Even in 'Red' Barcelona, those who argue for the 'collapse' of the state agree that this 'had not entirely dislodged the principle of its legitimacy'.[53]

The hardline Council of Aragón—which was forcibly dissolved in August 1937—thus proclaimed its 'absolute identification with the Republican government' and intention of implanting all legal directives.[54] Legitimacy was indeed the government's most important—if intangible—asset. By the end of 1936, however, the structures of power had been altered by additional, intermediary layers of government. 'Dual' or decentralized power led to competing demands for resources as the war effort demanded efficiency, direction, and centralized command. The problems the collectives faced in forging a new, spontaneous, local social order while simultaneously providing resources with which to fight a modern war proved to be entirely insurmountable. The Valencian collectives introduced technical courses and accounting systems, establishing a reputation for efficiency which they shared with Socialist-dominated Jaén. But even though other regions faced worse problems of recording who had what and to what end, the Valencian coordinating committee still had to struggle against an ingrained culture of concealment, the product not only of anarchism but also of illiteracy and a tax system run on quotas which benefited caciques over the poor. Inventories were drawn up throughout 1937 in an economic modernization intended, above all else, to increase agricultural production and save the orange harvest.

This drive coincided with the demise of the collectivist dream. Many 'individualist' peasant smallholders withdrew from the collectives in Jaén and Valencia; in Aragón and Cataluña, collectives were forcibly dismantled by central government forces. Both trends were bolstered by the active ambition of the Communist Party, in both its Spanish and Catalan forms. Valencia remained free from violent clashes, but attempts to collectivize citrus exports had proved unsuccessful, not least because of the acute need to maximize the financial return.[55] The unions established an intermediary council (CLUEA) to regulate exports, but repeated appeals to local producers not to evade its control went ignored: citrus-exporters sent their own representatives abroad, let down customers, and failed to pay producers. As exports fell, the socialist union broke ranks and wrote to Largo demanding government intervention. In September 1937, under the premiership of Juan Negrín, citrus exports became the direct responsibility of the Treasury. CLUEA, like the Council of Aragón and the local committees, had emerged after July 1936 in a spontaneous modification of state structures. Over the course of 1937, the Council of Aragón was forcibly suppressed, CLUEA was replaced by a government initiative, and the municipal councils substituted for the Popular Front committees. The exercise of state power was centralized once again; intermediate levels of communication were reconstructed and where necessary the central authority lent its weight to those who would emerge victorious in local struggles.

The clearest example of this came in Cataluña, where a dissident Marxist group, the POUM (Partido Obrero de Unificación Marxista: Workers' Party of Marxist Unification)—which was both revolutionary and highly suspicious of the Communist Party—offered the only concerted opposition to the reassertion of the central state. The repression of the POUM—which involved handing over its leader, Trotsky's former secretary, Andreu Nin, to the Soviet secret police—was famously witnessed by George Orwell. *Homage to Catalonia* gave the POUM a renown out of all proportion to its importance. Although the Republican government resisted Soviet demands for show trials, the Stalinist methods involved in suppressing the POUM—ludicrous, trumped-up charges of fascist collaboration, Nin's disappearance, hundreds detained in Barcelona's gaols—were neither liberal, legal, nor constitutional. Rather than demonstrating Soviet control of a puppet regime, however, they were the time-honoured responses of a weak Spanish state, compelled to demonstrate force when it could not otherwise assert authority. When the POUM and local CNT threw up barricades in Barcelona in May 1937, the government response was inevitable. Armed police brought the Catalan capital back into line as they had done so many times before.

Control of public order was the key to the reassertion of authority and the arguments in favour of centralized command in war time were, in most people's eyes, overwhelming. Assault guards came up from Valencia to suppress the 'May Days', but Catalan police under the command of the Generalitat were already in the front line. The price Companys paid for this emphatic underlining of his authority vis-à-vis the POUM and the CNT was national control of Catalan streets. Workers' patrols had already been deprived of public order functions in other Republican cities. Extending such control to Barcelona was the precondition for ending dual power in this most autonomous of regions. *Cenetistas* were detained and harassed; their premises were attacked, their union cards destroyed. The sheer strength of anarcho-syndicalism in Barcelona, however, prevented a full-scale confrontation between the state and the CNT. The brunt of the repression was borne by the POUM.

Though the process of reasserting central control came to a head in May 1937, it had begun much earlier. Disquiet, even horror, at the spontaneous violence of the 'hot summer' of 1936 led the Republican government to establish legal mechanisms for the summary trial of those accused of sedition. People's courts were gradually established throughout Republican territory, reaching Aragón in January 1937. Soon afterwards twenty-four people accused of aiding the military coup stood trial in Caspe. Four acquittals were handed down alongside sixteen terms of imprisonment in labour camps and four death sentences, all later commuted. Tellingly, none of the defendants were killed even though in terms of political sympathies, social status, and supposed crimes they were identical to those who had died at Republican hands during the previous summer.[56]

The attention paid to due legal process—albeit of an abbreviated kind—shows how the legislative culture of the Second Republic persisted, even in extremis. But it now had a harder edge. The Caspe death sentences may have been commuted but the 1931 constitution had renounced capital punishment. Other judicial bodies, such as those created in June 1937 to hear cases of espionage and treason, used the death penalty more frequently as the military situation worsened and the fear of fifth columnists grew. Such a context helps to explain the scapegoating of the POUM, though the judicial hard line was not taken under Largo Caballero but by his successor Juan Negrín. As Barcelona was brought back under central control, so the arguments for centralization, efficiency, and strength gained more purchase. This was the position put forward by Communists, Republicans, and the moderate Socialists around Prieto, and these were the parties which made up Negrín's new cabinet after the crisis which deposed Largo in mid-May.

This government ruled Spain until defeat at Franco's hands in 1939. According to the Communist leader, Pasionaria (Dolores Ibarruri), Negrín's premiership marked the beginning of sustained resistance. Such a view was, at one level, mere chauvinism: the PCE had now attained a presence, influence, and membership that would previously have been unimaginable. The plight of the Republic had, however, made for some very unlikely fellow-travellers. The PCE became a mass party through an avowed and public policy of shoring up the Popular Front, emphasizing the legal basis of the Republic, and defending private property, particularly in the countryside. The new sternness in Republican policy also favoured the Communists. The minister of justice Manuel de Irujo, a Basque Nationalist and the only practising Catholic in the cabinet, resigned over the introduction of special courts for cases of treason and 'defeatism'. Like Prieto, Irujo consistently voted against applying death sentences, but such liberal scruples were seen by most as out of place during such a bitter war.

In other respects, though, the Republic appeared to be returning to its liberal roots. Radical social experimentation was rolled back, but there was no ideological vacuum. The Republic turned instead to the ideas of popular sovereignty which underpinned all left-wing political philosophies, from twentieth-century parliamentary liberalism to Marxism in both its communist and libertarian forms. The right to exercise authority, whether that was to provide good government or safeguard innate freedoms, was conferred by the people. It was not just that the Popular Front had an electoral mandate; the spontaneous popular resistance of July 1936 had created a people's war. Such an understanding lay behind the remarkable cultural output of the Republic at war. The young photographers who made their names in Spain—Robert Capa, 'Chim' Seymour, Gerda Taro, Agustí Centelles—captured the moment of popular resistance. Repeated images—men in shirtsleeves fighting behind sandbags, assault guards firing over the bodies of dead horses, overalled militiawomen, people of all ages, both sexes, and various dress giving the clenched fist salute—texualized 'the people's war' for both foreign audiences and future generations.

This was the people in arms, a visible demonstration of an active citizenry. Public space was filled with Republican culture, from the posters which wallpapered urban streets to radio broadcasts and documentary films. The fragmentation of authority at the beginning of the war meant that Republican posters jostled with UGT ones, while the CNT produced films on the success of the revolutionary movement. As central authority was reasserted, however, and Valencia emerged as the Republic's cultural capital, ideas of popular sovereignty were reproduced in an idiom which emphasized solidarity, heroism, and resistant. 'The Republic is defended with discipline', proclaimed the posters, or 'they shall not pass' (Plates 3 and 7). Physical strength as represented by the male musculature was consistently used to symbolize the Republic. Constructivist imagery emphasized the importance of the collectivity over the individual, often with deliberate allusions to Soviet poster art. 'Man as machine' simultaneously depicted the international proletariat and the Spanish Republic. Regional references persisted—posters were still produced in Catalan or with local images such as Valencian *falleras*—but the Republican nation was now the principal reference point. Centralized government was actively looking to empower its citizens, though along national rather than revolutionary lines. The contrast with the fluidity of the first stage of the war was sharp. Now, discipline was the watchword, presided over by the Communist Party members, Jesús Hernández, education minister after September 1936, and the poster artist Josep Renau, Director of Fine Arts.

PCE machinations were not the only force at work, however. Renau strove for a 'new culture' which would serve the people and, at the same time, safeguard their culture by resisting fascism. Popular culture, like popular sovereignty, became common currency among the Republican ranks for the war offered Republicans a unique opportunity to forge a nation through education and common understanding. Evacuated children needed schooling as well as care and accommodation. Militiamen would be transformed into citizen-soldiers, simultaneously liberated and controlled by education. Various agencies worked to this end, among them the Milicias de la Cultura, which ran literacy campaigns at the front. 'Illiteracy blinds the spirit' read one poster, 'soldier, teach yourself'. The purposes of this campaign were not simply practical, though admittedly illiterate soldiers were little use at map-reading. Rather, the Milicias de la Cultura were a direct heir of the Misiones Pedagógicas, a continuation of the Republican project of educating, and so transforming, Spain. '[W]ith arms we will attain the destruction of the old world, but . . . with Culture a new world will be built' proclaimed the cultural militias, 'the *miliciano* should never abandon his rifle, but neither should he abandon his book'.[57]

The liberating power of education had long been a fundamental constituent of Spanish Republicanism which had always conceived of itself as an intellectual project. Now, however, this project was being implemented in a way reminiscent of the Red Army. Soldiers were taught to read through model sentences: 'obedience to the legitimate government', 'the land for those who work it'. Yet, despite the crude, Bolshevik-inspired, political message, the educational initiatives of the Republic revealed a significant process of state-building. In recovering its fractured authority after July 1936, the Republic was rebuilt. This was far from being a complete process—political fault lines ran deep, time was short and the enemy strong. Negrín's Communist-backed government was viewed with suspicion by many, including the liberal constituency headed by an increasingly disenfranchized Companys. But challenges to state power, if successfully resisted, lead not simply to a recuperation of that power but to its increase. During the final, difficult, hungry eighteen months of war, the Republican state came to touch more of its citizens' lives more directly than it had ever done before. In the aftermath of the 'May Days', the Spanish state assumed a new authority. Centralization in the economy, a unified army, conscription, rationing, the movement of women into the workforce and above all the civil defence measures needed to evacuate cities and protect them from bombardment brought the Republic into the daily life of every man, woman, and child in Spain. In this way the Republic was rebuilt for resistance. But, though it held out against the Nationalists' war of attrition until April 1939, the Republican regime could never achieve victory.

The reasons for this lay largely outside Spain. The Popular Front was rebuilt partly in order to attract international aid, but too many of those seeking peace in Europe were prepared to pay any price for it. Non-intervention allowed Fascist Italy and Nazi Germany to aid Franco in covert, though highly effective, ways. At the same time, the Republic was starved of help: Texaco supplied oil on credit to the Nationalists while Spain's legal government struggled to find sources of energy. Only Mexico and the Soviet Union came to the aid of the beleagured Republic and, after 1938, Stalin's attention turned elsewhere. The

Nationalist assault on Cataluña coincided with the Munich crisis and Negrín's policy was reduced to holding out until war broke out in Europe.

Despite the heroic example of Madrid in autumn 1936, the Republic resisted few advances. It took no significant territory, though there were some temporary, and meaningless, gains in Aragón and, while the rate of loss slowed down considerably after May 1937, the Republic had already ceded as much territory as it retained. For Republicans, the experience of civil war was that of slow defeat. Photographers sympathetic to the anti-fascist cause captured this suffering: the people of Spain were now represented to a global audience as the victims of fascist aggression. Spain's struggle became universal. As the Nazi Condor Legion bombed Spanish cities, dead children and terrified mothers—their fear captured and frozen by the camera—were shown on posters which promised 'If you tolerate this your children will be next.' Capa photographed women standing protectively in the rubble of their homes, Seymour photographed children with fractured limbs racked on hospital beds, their vulnerability testifying to the victimhood of Republican Spain. Pictures of bombed-out buildings showed the destruction of the private in the ruins of Spain's cities: missing walls revealed wall-paper, furniture, a domestic life now brutally displayed to all. Martha Gellhorn wrote of her visit to 'a room where half the floor hung in space'. The women who lived there 'were picking up what they could save: a cup that had no saucer left, a sofa pillow, two pictures with the glass broken. They were chatty and glad to be alive and they said everything was quite all right—look, the whole back of the apartment could still be lived in . . .'[58]

The blurring of boundaries between public and private was not only the work of the bombings. Ration cards, identity cards, conscription—whether of women sent into the Basque munitions factories or men sent to the front—and evacuation also breached the barriers around home and family. Urban populations were particularly transient, as refuges flooded in, replacing the men at the front and evacuated families. The fall of Málaga in February 1937 led to a massive refugee exodus, moving both east and north. In response, the city of Jaén—where evacuation had begun on 29 September 1936—required refugees to move to the province's eastern *comarcas*, an order repeated in February 1938. Localities struggled to cope: the pueblo of Torredonjimeno registered 2,700 refugees in mid-1938, and the figure had risen to 3,200 by the end of the year. In Ubeda, it was announced that refugees without work would be enlisted in the labour battalions working on roads and highways.[59]

As the example of Jaén suggests, the life of a refugee was uncertain and precarious. Local communities, already struggling to feed and shelter their own residents, buckled under the weight of this massive, disorganized movement. The incomers often encountered resentment, and no one could envy their living conditions. The levels of privation and dislocation, experienced even in the first months of the war foreshadowed the final exodus of Republican Spain.

SILENCE FALLS

In 1939, 450,000 people trudged across the Pyrenees to an uncertain future which began in concentration camps in the south of France and ended, for some, either in the *maquis* or the Nazi punishment labour camp at Mauthausen. Whether fleeing to Jaén in 1937, or across to France in 1939, all these refugees were escaping the brutality of Nationalist victory. That so many would abandon all they had and, often, all they had ever known for fear of rebel soldiers speaks eloquently to the nature of the conquest. After the initial rising, the Army of Africa was airlifted from Morocco by German planes, moving swiftly up towards Madrid. Spain's only battled-hardened, professional troops advanced north rapidly, more than outmatching the hastily convened militias and instilling terror in the local population. The Army of Africa imported colonial war, 'pacifying' newly conquered territories in ways long familiar to colonized peoples but new to the European mainland. Its commander, General Franco, became commander-in-chief in September 1936, a preliminary step towards becoming head of state, an office he assumed the following month. As both the chain of command and the dictatorial nature of the insurgent regime became more defined, so did the Nationalist assault. To the intense irritation of his German and Italian advisers, Franco insisted on a slow war of conquest. His troops would secure the rearguard just as they had 'secured' the military protectorate of Morocco.

Punishment columns were sent into the pueblos to flush out 'internal enemies' while reports of military operations in the south spoke of *limpieza* or 'cleansing' as the 'punishment' of civilians was routinely incorporated into 'pacifying' conquered territory.[60] In the pueblo of Fuente de Cantos, twelve people had died in revolutionary violence on 19 July when the church was burnt with detainees inside it; the military repression which followed took twenty-five lives for each of those killed on the 19th. The troops pushed on to Badajóz; when the city was taken on 14 August, the massacres which followed left blood 'palm deep' outside the bullring where they occurred.[61] The commanding officer, General Yagüe, never denied, nor even dissembled the reprisals. 'Of course we shot them. What did you expect? . . . Was I expected to turn them loose in my rear and let them make Badajoz Red again?'[62] The violence was massive: during the civil war and the first years of the Franco regime an estimated 6,610 people were killed in repressive violence in Badajóz, 482 of them women. In Fuente del Maestre, villagers remember over 300 being shot, twenty or so of them women. Other women were raped, beaten, or forced to drink castor oil and taken 'soiled and ridiculed' to midday mass.

The same logic of terror was at work in other areas of Spain. In Castile—where the rebels could rely on genuine popular support—there was no large-scale resistance, no need to secure hostile territory. But even in the absence of a military imperative, the same process of purging and purification was seen. Well behind the lines, in cities such as Valladolid and Salamanca, known 'Reds' were easily picked off by loosely configured death squads. Access to a few trucks allowed a small number of Falangists, usually located in the provincial capital, to become a highly mobile police force. Acting spontaneously, under their own agency, these impromptu militias—whose main asset was knowledge of their local enemies—travelled out to pueblos 'where their presence was needed to guarantee order'. The violence of their actions was thus occluded by the mantle of social order, the actions themselves justified by the popular will. In Valora la Buena, north of Valladolid on the Burgos road, where 'subversive elements' were ready to support 'the Marxist movement', they were foiled by 'the entire pueblo, which took to the streets and kept watch, preventing any incidents'. The outcome of such actions was 'tranquillity'. On 19 July, the local newspaper reported that 'order and tranquillity in the city was total'; in the fields people 'worked tranquilly at their summer tasks'.[63]

As this example makes clear, peaceful order was the product of excision. High levels of popular support for the rebel cause in Castile allowed these squads to act with relative impunity. The selection of victims was highly contingent: many were 'guilty' only by association, while others were—by the rebels' own moral and judicial standards—not 'guilty' at all. In Zamora, Amparo Badayón, wife of the writer Ramón J. Sender, was shot in October, although she had a child at the breast and no party political affiliations. She had, however, contracted a civil marriage, and was both wife and sister to known 'Reds'. In marked contrast to the victims of Republican violence, whose bodies were reburied and whose lives were commemorated after the war, Badayón's fate was passed over. When Sender first wrote of his wife's death, he recounted what he knew, briefly and without elaboration. 'Even if I wished' he wrote, 'I could not write more about it.' Years later, their son pieced together his mother's story, finally breaking his father's silence and putting together the letters and photographs kept by the family in Spain through the long years of Francoism.[64]

Throughout Spain, the brutal dislocations of repression were met with distance and silence. This was, in part, a *silencing*, brutally imposed on the vanquished by the victors. But it was also simply silence, the silence of evasion, of averted eyes, of people not wanting—or fearing—to know too much; or the silence of acceptance, of quiet relief that the war was over or even that the Republic was no longer in charge. For how do we ascribe meaning to silence? In a riven society such as Civil War Spain, it could denote moral courage as well as cowardice. Those in hiding needed the protection of silence, and their lives were in danger if it was broken. In Granada—a city which had fallen to the rebels through audacity and subterfuge and as a result was marooned in a sea of Republican territory—the right-wing Rosales family sheltered political opponents. The whereabouts of the most famous of their guests, Federico García Lorca, was revealed to the authorities on 16 August 1936: he was shot three days later, in the olive groves of Viznar, outside the city. Hundreds of others were killed there during the early weeks of the war, their executioners identified by nickname, or by reputation, but only rarely by name. Their victims were buried in unmarked *pozos*, which left the land 'pitted with low hollows and mounds', still clearly visible when Gerald Brenan visited them 'with speed and secrecy', searching for the poet's grave, in 1949. He began to count the burial places but 'gave it up when I saw the number ran into hundreds'. The story of Lorca's death was pieced together from the muttered hints, asides, and evasions which greeted Brenan's questions. 'Among ourselves' he was told, 'we don't talk of these things, but we haven't forgotten them.'[65]

Lorca's body remained missing. A death certificate claiming that he died of 'war wounds' was issued only in 1940, its fraudulence providing the only public record until another foreigner, Ian Gibson, investigated Lorca's death in the 1970s. For generations of Spaniards, silence surrounded the circumstances of the poet's execution and occluded its fact. Euphemisms were ubiquitous. Two thousand people were shot in the Granada cemetery: those killed early in the war were 'killed by detonation of firearm'; others died later by 'order of military tribunal'. Gerald Brenan had seen some of these remains in the common ossuary, noticing that all the skulls had been shattered by bullets. Bloodstains on the walls spoke against the sanitizing language of the cemetery records.[66] The killings had scarred the cemetery, leaving physical reminders of the violence unleashed by civil war and the terror wielded by those fighting in the name of order.

For in contrast to Republican Spain, the killing did not stop once central authority had been established. The incipient Nationalist state was to be a military regime: the loosely-formed death squads had to be brought under military control. As early as August 1936, the military governor of Valladolid issued 'reminders' that only police and security forces should be involved in 'detentions, searches, investigations and anything related to public order'. The mere fact that such a reminder had to be issued showed how, in the chaotic aftermath of the coup, 'rigid discipline' was easier to assert than to implement. But the army always had the upper hand: even the most recalcitrant Falangist knew that, without the army, there would have been no rising. The Nationalist militias were under military discipline from the start of the war: the code of military justice was applied in the very declarations of a 'state of war' which heralded the rebellion.

Nevertheless, in September 1939, Falangists in Madrid were again reminded that they had no authority to search or carry out detentions.[67] The imposition of military authority was in theory absolute, in practice less certain. Civil law had been suspended under the state of war: on 28 July 1936 the rebels bombastically declared martial law to apply to all the national territory, defining resistance to the Nationalists as 'military rebellion'. Declaring a 'state of war' was part of the established tradition of *pronunciamiento*. It had allowed Martínez Anido to rule Barcelona and Miguel Primo de Rivera to stage a coup d'état, placing civilians under military jurisdiction. The law *as established* thus allowed the 'crimes' of rebellion, sedition, sabotage, disrespect to the military, strikes, public meetings and demonstrations to be subject to summary trial. But, among the first to be shot in 1936 were those brother officers and men who had remained loyal to the Republic. For all the rebel generals' patriotic rhetoric, and despite their assumption that theirs was the cause of Spain, the army was divided; had it not been, there would have been no Civil War.

As if to underline this fact, those officers who commanded the Civil Guard in Barcelona—which had stayed loyal in July 1936 and fought with the Republic through the Civil War—and who presented themselves to their new superiors the day after the city fell in January 1939, were taken before military tribunals, and found guilty of 'military rebellion'. The death sentences were, as was usual, confirmed by Franco himself.[68] For all the rumblings of discontent among the Falange—forcibly merged with the Carlists in April 1937 to become the single party, or *Movimiento*, of the new Francoist state—its cooperation was essential to the workings of both military justice and the new regime. By 1940, the Madrid Falange had 529,875 names on their files; in 1941 they forwarded 4,168 reports to the military tribunals. Collaboration on this scale can only have come about willingly and, while some Falangists bitterly resented their party's emasculation, most were more than content. The Falange was no longer the small, tightly-woven ideological community it had been under the Republic. Those 'new' members who had flocked to the Falangist militias from the JAP and the Catholic right, made for a more conservative, less radical, movement, which was easily channelled into loyalty to Franco. The party was now at the heart of the New State, its blue shirts, fascist insignia, mass displays, and patriotic watchwords providing the style and symbols of the regime, 'key points of reference which distinguished friends from foe'.[69] Such a position was unimaginable before the war: the Falange owed its pre-eminence to the force of Franco's arms.

According to the rhetoric of the incipient regime, these were the men who had saved the 'true' Spain. In an extraordinary reversal of logic, loyal army and police officers became the ones guilty of sedition. This inversion became institutionalized and systematized in a process known as *justicia al revés,* which allowed those faithful to their oaths and to the legal government to be executed for 'rebellion'. The tribunals which administered summary justice were the main agents implementing the 'official' repression. Many were purely military; others were more representative of the range of Francoist support. Those established to hear cases brought under the 1939 Law of Political Responsibility, for example, included magistrates and Falangists from the *Movimiento* as well as soldiers. These tribunals were 'charged with imposing sanctions', a formulation which made clear that, in post-Civil War Spain, justice was a mechanism for administering punishment, while peace was a euphemism for victory.

Justicia al revés continued, its fundamental premise—that the Republic was 'anti-Spanish' and so responsible for the Civil War—reiterated in law and supported by grandiose ideological institutions. Towards the end of 1938, a commission was set up to demonstrate the legitimacy of the rising against the 'illegal' Republic. In April 1940, the 'New State' began an 'informative' lawsuit, the *Causa General,* which compiled evidence of 'criminal activities on the part of the subversive elements who in 1936 openly attacked the very existence and the essential principles of their country'.[70] Prosecutors were sent into all the provinces that had formed part of the Republican zone, with authority to collect documents, conduct interviews and compile witness statements. Questionnaires elicited information from municipal and village authorities, the Civil Guard and the Church. Over 1,500 files were compiled to complement the military and political repression carried out in Spain before 1943/5.[71] The archive of their findings was, in effect, a prosecution of the Second Republic for crimes against Spain. Legally, as well as culturally, the Franco regime equated the Second Republic with 'red terror'. The Republican rearguard was represented as a desperate and dangerous place where barbarity and torment ruled. The language of the *Causa General,* like that of Falangist novelists, created a Manichean duality. As one such novelist, Tomás Borrás, put it, the war pitted 'Europe against anti-Europe, Christianity and classical Mediterranean civilizations, order, geometry and law, against Semitism and chaos, fable, instinct, schizophrenia, and utopia.'[72]

Appropriately, then, the Law of Political Responsibilities—which was promulgated after the fall of Barcelona—applied the Catholic concept of sin by both commission and omission to political life. Those who 'with actions or serious omissions' had hindered or opposed the Nationalist war effort were guilty of political responsibility (that is, resistance). As in the subsequent 1940 Law for the Repression of Freemasonry and Communism, the legislation was retrospective, making illegal actions, such as membership of a leftist political party, which had been entirely legal at the time. The Popular Front was criminalized: holding office under the Popular Front either before or after the war made a person liable to punishment as did occupying 'a position of leadership' or even simply belonging to any of the parties and trade unions which made up the left-wing alliance. The New State thus 'redrew the boundaries of criminality so widely as to make imprecise that which actually constituted a crime'.[73]

Clearly, *justicia al revés* meant purging, the excision from the new nation of all that was associated with the old. Even before the war began, General Molá had proclaimed that 'Whoever is, openly or secretly, a supporter of the Popular Front, must be shot . . . we must sow terror . . . eliminating without scruple or hesitation those who do not think as we do.'[74] Yet, the process of purging was also inextricably bound up with the definition and establishment of the incipient Francoist state. The purges continued the military idiom of discipline and authority, while imposing a centralized, hierarchical authority. This conception of 'social order' was, to an extent, defined in the Rif and the military academies of Zaragoza and Toledo, but it drew in more people than were found in the army (even in wartime), while the purge commissions helped to fill the gap left by the forcible destitution of civil government.

The process of purging was also adaptable. As the fate of the loyal Civil Guard in Barcelona shows, Republican soldiers and those prominent in the Popular Front could expect no mercy. Companys was shot for 'military rebellion' in 1940 after being returned to Spain by the German authorities from occupied France; the CNT leader Joan Peiró suffered the same fate in 1942. Both were condemned to death even before the trials began. No Republican figurehead would remain in Spain; opportunities for dissent would be closed down. Similarly, the physical elimination of Republican elements in the army left Franco with a tighter, more cohesive military, a united body, which owed allegiance only to the Caudillo. Whatever Franco's fate, it would not be the same as Primo's. The army and its auxiliaries in the 'patriotic militias', civil governors' offices, and magistrature drew closer in this 'pact of blood'.

Death is not the only form—or tool—of repression. There was never any intention to exterminate all Republicans—Francoist Spain had no genocidal plans—but the nation was to be purged of Republicanism. Both the civil service and the teaching profession were systematically 'purified'. The latter began as early as August 1938: the 'revolutionary hordes' were 'the spiritual children of the university professors and teachers who . . . shaped unbelieving and anarchic generations'. The moral responsibility of teachers was great, and the purge commissions, though woefully under-funded, gathered information on matters such as church-going, political beliefs, and union membership by sending questionnaires to parish priests, local authorities (including the Civil Guard), and Catholic parents' associations. The commissions themselves were generally composed of laymen chosen for their respectability and competence. These were bureaucratic bodies, intended to deliberate and deliver their verdicts—which could include permanent dismissal as well as demotion, temporary suspension, or removal to another part of the country—as efficiently as possible. The influence of the Church was enormous; in the New State, both morals and education were to be Catholic.

The process of repression was, then, one of exclusion and punishment. Those judged to be guilty made reparation for their sins against Spain. The inmates of the concentration camps set up in 1937 were forced, by the logic of *justicia al revés*, to labour for the 'reconstruction' of Spain, building roads, churches, and most notoriously, Franco's future mausoleum, the Valley of the Fallen at Cuelgamuros outside Madrid.[75] Around half a million people had passed through the camps by 1940; 50,000 were executed in the ten years after the end of the Civil War in April 1939; 100,000 had been massacred or executed by the Nationalists during the war itself.[76] The scale and the ubiquity of the repression had a paralysing effect; republicanism was expunged from public life, and those who had lost the war were excluded from the national community. As Manuel Azaña had written, the Nationalists' principle of authority was 'based on blind obedience and on suppression of free opinion'. Such power 'arrogates to itself the power of disposing of the lives of its subjects, and they act as if they measure authority by the number of people they kill'.[77]

The Francoist regime was born in violence and depended on violence. Killing was essential to its initial display of power. But as the gaols filled, and the administrative problems associated with running them became ever greater, the intensity of repression, and particularly the pace of killing, eased. Parole decrees were issued in 1941, 1942, and 1943 and, in 1945, there was a general pardon for Civil War 'crimes'. Those convicted of 'blood crimes' were excluded from all these decrees but tens of thousands of prisoners were released on licence.[78] In March 1944, the Documento National de Identidad (DNI: National Identity Document) was introduced, issued to ex-prisoners to facilitate surveillance. Its use was gradually extended: first to men who had to move around to exercise their profession or find work, then to men resident in large cities. In 1951, identity cards were made compulsory for all Spaniards, providing details of family, provenance, and, until 1981, socio-economic status. The process of introduction revealed the regime's insecurities but its accomplishment indicated its strength. For while violence may provide an easy and brutal display of force, real power lay in the 'disposing of the lives of its subjects'. Knowing the actions, histories, and sympathies of individual citizens, being able to bring them before tribunals, assessing their employment, place of residence, contact with family, even survival represented an exponential increase in power on the part of the Francoist state.

This level of surveillance was only made possible by the *denunicas* the police authorities and purge commissions received on a daily basis. The established legal custom of 'denouncing' individuals—including persons unknown—to the authorities as the means of reporting a crime had been encouraged by the circumstances of war and was easily adapted to those of repression. *Denuncias* implicated the community in its own repression, as did the reports and character references (particularly by clergy) which were a prominent feature of daily life during the early Franco years.[79] Neighbours informed on neighbours as affirmations of good character played an ever greater part in official life, so making society more 'legible', in James Scott's formulation. Those in power knew more and more about the people over whom they ruled and the information they garnered was filed and codified in accessible and systematic ways. With the introduction of the DNI, the state confirmed its interest in the individual.[80] Direct tax burdens were still expressed collectively, through quotas, and the regime's rhetoric spoke of communities, but the interest it took in its citizens showed that for perhaps the first time in Spain, rule was exerted directly over individuals.

Despite the ravages of war, the loss of productive labour, the physical damage to both cities and countryside, and the meagre financial resources of the new regime, the Civil War had dramatically enhanced the presence of the state in people's lives and therefore its capacity for social control. Individual citizens were now mapped just as the landscape had been; the state had achieved 'legibility'. Both Republican and Nationalist authorities had been forced by the exigencies of war to direct their citizens' employment, accommodation, food supply, and even leisure activities to an unprecedented degree. The capacity of the state, as well as its efficiency, had inexorably increased. And when this capacity was put to a repressive purpose, when centralized state power was turned upon (some of) its own citizens, there was little escape. Francoist Spain was defined by the victors against the victims. *Justicia al revés* even made these victims scapegoats for the crimes of the regime. As one Civil Guardsman put it in 1949, 'The times are bad. We are living among people any one of whom may have murdered our father or our brother and yet we have to treat them as if they were our friends.'[81]

Few expected friendly treatment. For proclaimed Republicans, silence offered the only protection, and that could be broken, usually by denounce-ment. As hundreds of thousands went into exile others disappeared within

Spain, some to the mountains with anti-Francoist guerrilla fighters, others into hiding. Manuel Cortes, Republican mayor of Mijas (Málaga) lived hidden for thirty years in his native pueblo; in Béjar (Salamanca), Angel Blázquez began hiding in his mother's attic in 1936, emerging only in 1955.[82] For these men, as for many others, the war did not end in 1939. The silence of their families protected them; they could trust no one else. But, in Spain more generally, the silence of repression mingled with the silence of privation; exhaustion kept some mute while others were silenced through fear. And, as open conflict faded, resignation, acceptance, and passive acquiescence brought their own silence. Historians talk much of the silence of the early Franco years, but it is as well to remember that, in discerning silence, all that can actually be heard is the absence of speech.

5

Governing Spaniards, 1943–73

During the 1940s the Franco regime consolidated its military victory. The nature of this victory made it clear that the power of the 'New State' rested on violence and death, yet the completeness of that victory paradoxically created the possibility of later consolidating the regime. For the regime's longevity cannot be explained by repression: wholesale killing had been abandoned by 1943 and the Falange was a junior partner well before the war in Europe was concluded. Axis defeat left the New State in need of a new identity. The lucky stroke of 'non-belligerence' in the Second World War meant that the dictatorship survived the 1940s. Spain was ostracized, punished for Franco's association with the Axis powers, but tolerated. No international attempts were made to remove the dictator. In what felt to many Republicans like a final betrayal, the Allied troops stopped at the Pyrenees after the Liberation of France. The Spanish maquisards who had fought against the Nazis in occupied France crossed the border in 1944 to continue the anti-fascist fight as a vanguard of liberation. But they found themselves alone, picked off as outlaws by the armed forces of a police state.

The defeat of the guerrillas by the end of the decade was a stark demonstration of the sinews of material power now commanded by the Francoist state. In 1947, the decree-law against crimes of brigandage and terrorism enabled the regime to attack those whom repression and defeat had forced into the mountains. Rather than simply contain the guerrillas—who often worked in their native regions, seemingly disappearing into the landscape at will—the Civil Guard now targeted those who helped the maquis, often because they had known them since childhood. After 1947, the armed presence of the state increased massively: the national reintroduction of the *Somatén* in 1945 led to around 100,000 men in smaller pueblos being given police powers and arms, while the number of Civil Guardsmen rose by around 20 per cent between 1936 and 1941.[1] Loyal citizens were now openly involved in directly policing their communities: the *Somatén* lined up with the forces of the state to eliminate the armed remnants of the Republic.

In June 1948, for example, reprisals in Villanueva de Córdoba, left six people dead in a single night, including the wife of El Ratón, a local maquis, who left seven children. All were killed under the *ley de fugas*, reinstated in 1947 and interpreted simply as summary execution; men were found beaten to death, though no one could plausibly be killed this way while trying to escape. The illegality of such actions was immaterial; they inflicted mortal wounds on the maquis. Any guerrilla group must control its locality, either by consent or by fear and, as the Nazis had found in occupied France, reprisals against the community severed the very links those in the mountains needed to survive. The imperative need to maintain the community's protection (or at least silence) led to reprisals by the maquis themselves in a spiralling dynamic of attack and counter-attack. Violence conditioned their daily lives. In Córdoba the number of informers killed rose after 1947: on 18 March that year one man was lynched in response to the massacre of six maquis in Cerro Cascoho; a further ten men were hanged in the same year while another had his throat cut. All were accused of passing information to the Civil Guard.[2]

Everywhere, the maquis suffered most when it was betrayed. The Civil Guard had posts in every sizeable pueblo in Spain and was well placed to oversee and register the comings and goings of the local population, aided immeasurably by *denuncias* from local people. For, as the maquis' struggle showed, the fight against the Francoist state was not simply against its uniformed representatives. The guerrillas' failure demonstrated the purchase of the New State, the control it wielded, and most importantly, the way in which it penetrated every pueblo. The nature of state power changed in the decade after the Civil War, and the authorities did not now rely solely upon military force. Opponents of the regime were brutally cowed while loyal supporters submitted willingly to a reasserted principle of authority. But while this division between victors and vanquished was the political mainstay of the regime, it did not translate into a simple social reality. There were many who clearly belonged to neither side, whose loyalties, like many families, were divided or who felt little affinity with politics. For them, the 1940s were a time of gradual accommodation with the New State. In the years of hunger, people 'preferred eating to freedom-fighting'.[3] The failure of the guerrilla demonstrated the completeness of Franco's military victory; the maquis never came close to their aim of fomenting a general, popular rebellion against the regime.

By 1949, mute acceptance of the status quo characterized much of the population, a passivity which did nothing to help the Republican cause but which was essential to establishing Francoism as a regime rather than simply a military victory. Over the following decade, a working social consensus formed around the regime, keeping it in place (if not in full command) until the 1970s. There was now no prospect of the New State's removal by some deus ex machina, such as invasion or spontaneous rebellion. The pace of repression slackened, and economic conditions eased; families were still poor but no longer starving. Ordinary people 'began to be able to breath' and, as one worker in Puerto de Sagunto (Valencia) put it, they started to 'swallow the bitter pill of Franco', helped in part by the development of a rudimentary welfarism. Among the better-off, the postwar resurgence of Catholicism did much to cement a new social consensus, helped by the muting of bourgeois republicanism. For the dual experience of revolutionary wartime violence and the brutal dictatorship left some liberals silent, dumb in response to their children's assimilation within the regime.[4]

By 1959, generational change and the ability to live some kind of ordinary life, had contributed to a silent accommodation with the regime which nevertheless re-established it with some kind of legitimacy. The Falange continued as Franco's single party and 'ideological ornament', but while it had served a crucial purpose in mobilizing military volunteers during the Civil War, it had no such mobilizing role after its end. As the *Movimiento*, the party was allowed to provide the regime's theatrical aesthetics, with an inevitable mimesis of Mussolinian spectacle, but not to mobilize the masses or establish the regime on an active, popular dynamic. Unlike its Fascist progenitor, the Falange administered and policed the population—providing the great majority of recruits to the *Somatén* for example—but did not agitate it. The politics of the Franco regime, for all its rhetoric, was in many respects the politics of elites. In the words of one man who held office in Yecla (Murcia), the driving force of the regime on the ground was 'the "establishment" . . . of that time . . . there were many people who weren't Falangist . . . a conglomeration of the surviving *fuerzas vivas*'.[5]

In some places, such as nearby Lorca, those who held local power were the traditional caciques: here, for example, little happened without the authority of the Condesa de San Julián, mother-in-law to the education minister, José Ibáñez Martín. But, while the term (and concept) of cacique survived as shorthand for influence-peddling and the failure of liberal democracy, the caciques were an anachronism, their power tempered by the enhanced capacity and power of the state.[6] The caciques' survived by incorporation; their re-emergence at local level was part of a wider process of peopling the New State. For those who aspired to wield influence were now functionaries as well as notables. Their interactions, like most administrative business, still took place face-to-face but increasingly Spaniards had to deal with officials who, even if they were personally known to the applicant, presented themselves in terms of their position, as the formal representatives of the state. Only functionaries could perform the 'state magic' of asserting reality in an official record, issuing identity documents or recognizing entitlement. This was a performance, carried out on behalf of the state and in representation of it. The proper conduct of business conveyed both the social fitness of those in positions of power and the abstract qualities of efficiency and good government. When those officials were in uniform, the contrast between the reach and unity of the New State and its lax, cacique-ridden Restoration predecessor was sharp.

For even though the new regime had to come to an accommodation with local elites, they, in turn, had to cede ground to the *Movimiento*. The purpose of the single party was now to reconstruct the social basis of the Francoist alliance and so bring people within the state. All the various institutions and mechanisms of state power established on a contingent basis during the military victory—purge commissions, party offices, loyal *ayuntamientos*—had to be brought within a single orbit. Forming an official party had created 'a new power-allocating system' and though local rivalries—such as those between radical 'old shirts' and conservative 'new shirts' or between Falangists and Carlists—were common, they are easily overstated.[7] All local councillors donned the Falangist blue shirt; all rival groups were ultimately loyal to the regime. As the single party expanded, fascist credentials became relatively unimportant. A 'more stable, greyer, and less turbulent' political class coalesced within the New State.[8] In Aragón, for example, party members filled more and more government posts—including governorships—and local councils, creating co-ordinated charitable institutions and a state-run system of labour representation. The numbers of state personnel thus increased exponentially: none doubted the primacy of state authority and the Falange functioned simply as the instrument of that state. Members of established, elite families joined the party, looking for influence and preferment. The caciques were now inside the New State; no longer could they act as intermediaries between government and people.

Rather, both politics and ideology were interpreted as 'loyalty' to the Caudillo. The regime's values were inculcated by an education system that may still have relied heavily on private Catholic schools but within which both teaching and textbooks were now regulated by the state—a prerogative established in 1857 but which was only now becoming a reality.[9] Throughout Spain, conservative elements regrouped within the single party, discarding earlier beliefs in favour of strong government and internal order. The class basis was clear to see: in the small Carlist village of Cirauqui, for example, those who held office during the postwar years came from affluent families; in Almería, Franco's first civil governor was the son of one of the Restoration's leading caciques and had been mayor of the provincial capital under Primo.

This continuity of established families was unsurprising in an agrarian society, where owning land provided the basic distinction between left and right. And the regime had to bring the established conservative right into the Movement; the 'forces of order' were the basis of the 'internal harmony' for which the party strove and they could provide the popular support the regime needed.

Creating a stable, workable, social consensus around the New State required different ideological tools from mobilizing for war. A determination not to relinquish power meant that Francoism needed to build interclass support, though it had little truck with the dangerous and ultimately uncontrollable dynamic of fascism. The ideological watchwords of the New State—unity, destiny, hierarchy—coincided with fascism but they were not defined by it. Organicist political language had as great a purchase in Catholicism as in fascism; discipline was as much a virtue for the army as for the militias. The purpose of government was, according to Catholic teaching, the assurance of internal peace, an injunction that was easily related to 'the peace of Franco'. In the New State, peace, order, and authority were inextricable: unity represented centralism which was, in turn, equated with hierarchy, both of which were understood as order. And this order was mandated by the past, whether history—as in Franco's claim that 'Spain was never greater than when she was one, and in this tradition lies our strength'[10]—or custom. In clear contra-distinction to other fascist movements, the Women's Section of the Falange referred in its statutes to the 'National-Syndicalist concept of returning each nucleus to its proper order, and each individual to their category of life'.

Social standing and hierarchy were thus a given, already set out in the established social order. And this was, in turn, represented in the person of the dictator, Francisco Franco, Caudillo of Spain 'by the grace of God'. This monarchical formulation was inscribed on the dictator's coins—his head on the verso from 1947–8—just as it had been on Alfonso XIII's and Isabel II's. All were sovereign, though the monarchs' claim to rule was tempered by liberalism: Isabel was 'queen of Spain by the grace of God and the constitution'. Franco's power was less trammelled. The iconography of his victory was inscribed on the reverse of his coinage, with the eagle, coat of arms, and the legend 'one, great and free'. Trial by combat had confirmed his position and, as conquest was only possible if God willed it, his position was divinely-sanctioned. Like Spain's kings, he would answer only 'to God and history'.

In July 1947, Spain was formally declared to be a monarchy, albeit one without a king. The law of succession defined 'a Catholic, social and repres- entative state which, in keeping with her tradition, declares herself constituted into a kingdom'. Fittingly, the dictator's self-presentation was increasingly regal, drawing on an established visual tradition of the 'soldier-king' and reasserting the formality and deference of a royal court. Establishing a court at his home of El Pardo—which also housed a notorious political clique—meant that Franco became a more distant figure, cut off from day-to-day politics by his isolation, and increasingly frequent hunting trips.[11] Such distance was, though, part of his regalism, a persona which developed as the trappings of fascism were discarded and which embodied older, conservative values such as deference, hierarchy, and social order. A world in which everyone knew their place had an appeal outside the Pardo palace. Regal images of the Caudillo were mechanically reproduced for a mass audience, 'conspicuously displayed' in every 'shop, garage, public building, restaurant, café, or pension'.[12] Cheaply reproduced portraits made the Caudillo omnipresent, Spain's representative as well as its ruler. His uniforms became increasingly ceremonial, less connected to the military history of the civil war, and he gazed out of the picture, beyond the viewer, in a timeless pose. Franco even tried to capture the romance of monarchy in set piece events such as the ball held for his only daughter's debut in 1944. She married in 1950—the year in which Spain's prison population again approached normal levels but when per capita meat consumption was still half that of 1926—before 800 guests.

Franco's royal masquerade found a ready audience through a press hungry for celebrity. Launched in 1944, *¡Hola!* presented the life and leisure of monarchy and aristocracy as a product for mass consumption. Glossy photography commodified the lifestyle of this anachronistic—and, in the case of the Francos, parvenu—class even as unctuous commentaries preserved a proper respect for birth, wealth, and status. Trivial though they may appear, the society news, family snapshots, and pictures of Franco out hunting which graced the pages of *¡Hola!* were part of a conscious strategy of legitimation. The aristocracies of Europe were repackaged in a way that combined social respect with the glamour of Hollywood. A new kind of princely celebrity was born. For the language of *¡Hola!* was deference, and in such circles, those with genuine royal blood in their veins had real charisma. Both the young prince, Juan Carlos, educated in Spain from 1949, and his cousin, Carlos Hugo, the Carlist pretender, were presented as exemplary modern royals. Their travels, sporting achievements, romances and, eventually, marriage to European princesses—Sofia of Greece and Irene of the House of Orange—made for excellent copy.

The young princes enjoyed the celebrity of monarchy, but the less photogenic Caudillo both claimed its dignity and enjoyed its power. Legislation was enacted only by his will, as represented in his signature; his was the right of turning legislative 'norms' into statute. Hence, perhaps his faith in legal promulgation as an instrument of change; like Primo, Franco used reform of 'fundamental laws' as a way to 'regenerate' Spain. His exercise of power was not unlimited—prudence, convention, and the advice of counsellors all acted to condition it—but power remained, in Franco's own words, 'a personal fiat'.[13] His right to rule represented the monarchical ideal of unity between sovereign and subject, with a wise sovereign governing in order to create harmony. According to Catholic teaching, the 'essence of peace' was a 'tranquil living together in order', where 'justice' was 'the proper working' of a monarchical social order. Under Franco, such an order was understood in a highly conservative, essentially static way. This was the 'peace of Franco' and it drew on an understanding of social order that had been made available in an outpouring of Catholic print culture which dated from the late nineteenth century and reached its zenith in reaction to the progressive, secularizing Second Republic. Sentiment and nostalgia characterized this work just as much as theological conservatism, influencing the depiction of natural order, social peace, and proper behaviour, often through appeals to a romanticized, pre-modern past. And across the border in Portugal, Dr Salazar kept alive the idea of Christian corporatism in his Estado Novo, which survived for decades after the fall of Mussolini.

The corporate project was reproduced in Spain as well as in Portugal. Vertical syndicates were to be the agents for order and harmony in the economy, integrating the productive process into a common effort of capital and labour. Introduced within the context of national self-sufficiency, Francoist corporatism was fascist-inspired, part of an autarkic project intended to discipline and modernize Spain. The potential scope of this project was immense. The state both claimed and achieved an absolute authority. The 'spatial confinement' of the early 1940s was imposed from above, by a resurgent authority which had the entire nation at its disposal. The New State 'would, above all else, be a strong, purifying, well-defined authority, within a well-defined space, able to orientate society'.[14] This was the moment of 'seeing like a state', when those who commanded power in Spain did so unambiguously. National resources—land, property, business, citizenry—were now mapped and so within the ambit of government control. Franco's rule was brutal, and always relied on coercive force, but it was direct. Many remained unconvinced by it, but none doubted that it held sway.

The Civil War had been essential to this modernizing of the Spanish state, and not simply because of the ruthless imposition of victory. The experience of war had shown the necessity of central coordination while the defeat of republicanism—and, more specifically, the eclipse of anarchism—ended the long anti-state tradition of significant parts of the Spanish left. With the defeat of the maquis, anarcho-syndicalism passed into history. There were now few who would declare with Proudhon that 'To be ruled is to be kept an eye on, inspected, spied on, regulated, indoctrinated, sermonized, listed and checked off, estimated, censured, appraised, ordered about . . .', even though this was now more true than at any previous time in Spain's history. But neither socialist nor republican left would oppose state power in itself, even though they dissented fiercely from Franco's regime, and bitterly opposed its use of such power.

Modern states accrue power to themselves: they have the potential both to improve the lives of their citizens and to destroy them. State-sponsored transformations aspire to an administrative social ordering, seeking to apply the new insights of technological development throughout the nation. The traditional discourse and historicist rhetoric of the Franco regime made little difference to this project. The regime looked to the idealized past of Catholic Spain but was determined to extirpate the immediate past of constitutional liberalism. It was also quite prepared to used the full panoply of state power to implement its plans: the sheer number of deaths shows that there was no lack of political will to restrain these large-scale ambitions. The stage seemed to be set for the kind of disciplined, hierarchical, 'high modernist', project which characterized not only the regimes of Hitler, Stalin, and Mao but also pettier dictatorships such as that of Ceaucescu as well as better-intentioned projects of agrarian resettlement in undeveloped economies.[15]

Yet, the ideological ambitions of the Franco regime seemed to stop with the repression of the early 1940s. Once Spain was rendered safe, the regime's appetite for grandiose planning dwindled, eventually amounting to little more than retaining power. The New State's corporatist ambitions coincided with the zenith of the Falange's influence, and were themselves evidence of a genuine fascist project in Spain. But this project was not abandoned simply because fascism became an embarrassing hindrance on the international stage after 1945. The Falange's fall from grace began as early as 1941, yet autarky was abandoned only in 1959 and the archaeological remnants of the corporate economy survived until after the dictator's death. Nor can the failure to develop any genuine transformative totalitarian project be attributed to popular resistance. Republican Spain had been flattened by the cumulative effects of war and repression. A cowed population could never have resisted Francoist plans for socio-economic transformation any more than it could resist purging and repression.

Autarky was, in part, defeated by the absurdity of its own internal logic. Even as an aspiration, self-sufficiency was not attainable in postwar Europe, particularly for a country which had no oil. But autarky took cultural as well as economic forms: it not only allowed for but also represented the imposition of absolutism. Its rationale was national well-being, a peaceful, ordered, co-existence for the good of Spain. Corporatism would recognize and reinforce the 'organic' nature of social and economic life while autarky would preserve this organic society from dissolvent foreign influences, both socialist and capitalist. Corporatism had achieved great sway on the right wing of European politics during the 1920s and 1930s, not least because of its endorsement by Pope Pius XI. Schemes to provide a 'third way', a path between the Scylla of socialism and the Charybdis of capitalism thus had as many Catholic and conservative variants as fascist ones. Order, hierarchy, social peace were key constituents of conservatism that—unlike mobilization, brotherhood, and direct action—were left intact by the fall of fascism. As well as paying lip service to a new fascist order, such language also incorporated both a reactionary order of landed elites and social privilege and a bourgeois order, understood in terms of authority, respectability, and paternalism.

As the Franco state moved from consolidating its victory to consolidating itself as a regime, so the plasticity of these ideas became more important. Catholic appeals to social order were potentially inclusive. In uncertain times, appeals to a natural order had great resonance, not least because they mobilized an idea of 'normality', acting as a metaphor for the reconstruction of society, an end to conflict, and the return of peace and prosperity. The key institution was the family, which served as both the foundation of wider society and its microcosm, acting as the support without which social structure would collapse. Observance of a 'natural' order made 'the lives of husbands and wives . . . better and happier'. Authority was essentially paternal, running through all institutions, the cornerstone of harmonious social order. The family had to be 'hierarchically constructed in a hierarchical society',[16] a vision asserted and promulgated in Francoist legislation. Marriage was indissoluble, with domestic society based on 'the primacy of the husband . . . the ready subjection of the wife and her willing obedience'.[17]

The social project of the Franco regime may best be defined as paternalism, an extraordinarily pervasive and long-lasting ideology which is hard to tie to any specific political creed. In terms of consolidating the regime, such a strategy had many advantages. The prospect of domesticity, a belief in paternal authority, appeals to a 'natural' order, these acted as agglutinates of legitimacy, allowing the unconvinced and the uncommitted some kind of accommodation with the regime. Family allowances were introduced, for example, and paid directly to the male head of household as part of the state's obligation to provide a 'family wage'. The notion of the family wage built on deep-seated ideas of domesticity and the dignity of work as well as of masculine authority. Like the general reassertion of family life, or the return of women to the home, such strategies resonated outside the relatively narrow circles of the faithful. The amorphousness of paternalism—its lack of any ideological specificity—was vital to the successful establishment of Francoism as a durable regime. But this lack of ideological sharpness, Francoism's dependence on older, conservative norms and values, militated against a state project of unrestrained social control and transformative change.

Ultimately, the social project of the New State was simply to impose victory and then to consolidate control. The political system was intended, above all, to depoliticize. The exclusion and punishment of those outside the regime was vital to its strategy of pacification, but life had to become bearable for those who stayed within it, so that it could become at least a 'lesser evil', in conditions which were, for all their shortcomings, better than the social and political conflict which preceded it. The welfarist measures put in place by the New State were effective, if far from comprehensive, and were seen as such even by industrial workers who had little ideological affiliation with the regime but who recognized the benefits of social housing, better retirement conditions, and social security.[18]

For this to happen, the reassertion of the family had also to mean a recovery of domesticity. According to Catholic teaching, the family was both a divine and a natural institution and so preceded the state. The family's autonomy was recognized by law, notably the Fuero de Trabajo (1938 and 1967) which defined it as 'the natural nucleus and foundation of society, and at the same time, the moral institution endowed with inalienable rights and superior to all positive law'. The ideological malleability of Francoism, and its symbiotic relationship with Catholicism, thus protected both the family and the space in which it existed. A sense of inviolable, private space—as at least attainable, if not actually realized—allowed the prospect of escape, endurance, survival. For there were spaces, both psychic and physical, which the regime never penetrated, for all the undoubted capacity of the state. And first among these was the home, where family members retained autonomy over their own lives, in a space governed by affective bonds. Like the family itself, music groups, folklore societies, rambling groups and sporting clubs could create non-politicized spaces for sociability and cultural exploration (which was particularly important in Basque and Catalan areas). The same was also theoretically true of religious associations, particularly youth groups, though here the ideological identification with the regime weighed heavy. Such private spaces, fostered in part by the regime's own paternalism, helped to ensure the regime's survival by allowing the establishment of some kind of functioning legitimacy behind it. They also, inevitably limited the totalitarian scope of the New State, and would eventually allow the emergence of the kind of anti-hierarchical opposition which the regime strived so hard to eradicate.

HOW FRANCOISM RULED WOMEN

The private sphere was understood to be the preserve of women, who were charged with running orderly households and dedicating themselves to family affairs. Conservative ideology saw women as little interested in politics—they had voted in the 1930s but only in response to dire threat. Once the danger was past and the Republic had been defeated, they should—and would—return to their 'natural' role. Women were apolitical beings, both connected to and representative of the 'natural' order that Francoist Spain had supposedly reasserted, and they thus became crucial for legitimizing the New State. Women could demonstrate the regime's compatibility with the essence of traditional Spain and, as they were far less associated than men with the violence of war, their participation in the New State suggested a stable future, the 'peace of Franco'. For this to be achieved, women had to be visibly incorporated into the New State; their adherence to the regime had to be publicly proclaimed. A traditional domestic role is, of course, constraining and it is tempting to see the regime's gender policies as a (forced) return to the private sphere, part of the silencing of Spain after 1939.[19] But for loyal adherents of the regime, the opportunities for a public role were greater than ever before.

The Franco regime continued the mobilization of women that had begun under Primo de Rivera, emphasizing national identity and public service. Women's loyalty showed that the force of the *generalísimo*'s rule was not simply that of arms. The 'democracy of the public square' demanded an audience for the dictator, who could then demonstrate his legitimacy through mass spectacle and loyal display. Some notion of a social contract was essential even in an absolute rule. As the regime consolidated, it had to (re)nationalize the masses, but in a way that ensured their docility rather than their mobilization. The *nation* was the ideological mainstay of the regime, not the troubling, politically amorphous 'people'. The Falange was to provide the appearance of a popular dynamic by orchestrating mass expressions of loyalty. Increasingly, it did so through the party's female members: the uncontrollable fascist dynamic was a male one; women, who defined their own role as auxiliary and subservient, seemed easier for the leaders to control. The blue-shirted displays which embellished the early Franco regime saw the women of the Falange's Sección Femenina (SF: Women's Section) present themselves as disciplined comrades, submissive to the Caudillo. Their carefully choreographed demonstrations literally embodied the principles of discipline, order, and hierarchy.

The Franco regime thus relied upon women to an unprecedented extent. The SF provided the regime with a fund of labour, much of it skilled, if not formally trained. This was crucial for, while the Spanish state now had both more vision and a greater capacity, it was still strapped for cash. In 1948 state revenue in Spain amounted to a mere 14.76 per cent of national income, as compared with 21 per cent in Italy and 33 per cent in Britain.[20] A paucity of resources would always trammel the ambitions of the New State but, as the expectation of paid work for women remained low, the state could effectively use the SF as a resource. Its new professional role was to lead by example, providing rudimentary welfare services, educating the rural poor and safeguarding the future of Spain's children.

These tasks took the SF into every pueblo in Spain. Health visitors (*divulgadoras*) taught infant care and hygiene, encouraged breast-feeding, and vaccinated children as part of a drive to reduce infant mortality. The SF claimed that some 3,000 health visitors had carried out over 1,500,000 home visits and administered over 800,000 anti-diphtheria vaccines. Whatever the exact figures, the infant mortality rate fell dramatically—from 109 per 1000 live births in 1935 to 88 in 1945 and 55 in 1955—and maternal death rates fell even more sharply.[21] These campaigns had a real humanitarian impact but they were presented as part of a pronatalist strategy to raise the birth rate and so enhance the greatness of Spain. The legal context was provided by the 1941 abortion law, which outlawed contraception and redefined abortion as a crime against the state.[22] Female behaviour, particularly sexual behaviour, had long been seen as a litmus test for the moral health of the nation. Implicit in the abortion law was a distinction between good and bad women and its repressive effects, particularly for poorer women, were clear to see. This is perhaps why the policy never succeeded in actually increasing the birth rate: life was simply too hard to convince working-class women to have more children. Yet, pronatalist discourse was enthusiastically adopted by the 'good' women of the SF, who looked to strengthen the 'race' both by encouraging sport and physical education for girls and by providing practical training in 'puericulture'.

'Scientific' training, as well as instruction in religion, politics, rural crafts, and literacy, was provided by the *cátedras ambulantes*, which began in 1946 but were eventually funded by the Development Plan of the 1960s.[23] Though the SF would have denied it vociferously, there were clear similarities between the *cátedras ambulantes* and the Republican *brigadas volantes* that had run literacy campaigns during the war. Both were driven by an ideological mission rather than by expertise, used female labour, and offered only rudimentary training. Although there were clear political and ideological differences—for example the SF viewed literacy as a technical rather than an emancipatory skill—both campaigns looked to incorporate citizens in the nation-state. The mass mobilization of women by the Republic during the Civil War had also been determinedly apolitical, based on war-work, aiding the homeless, and campaigns for infant health. The legend of one Republican war poster for children's summer camps—'Fresh air, sun, happiness for the men of tomorrow'—could have served equally well for a Falange *colonia de verano*.[24] Women and children were thus brought into the ambit of the state, not least through education. Co-education was declared illegal, forcing the state to open twenty-two secondary *institutos* for girls.[25] Convent schools still predominated, but the SF provided physical and political education in all girls' schools in Spain. The SF's role within the New State was not simply a benign one of education and charity work. All SF members had a personal file, and access to positions and training places was via recommendation and character reference. Its members penetrated society, furthering the state's knowledge of its least visible citizens, gathered information on behalf of the authorities, as did the purge commissions and other institutions of repression. Health visitors, for instance, would report to the parish priest on the moral and religious health of the families they visited as well as assessing their physical conditions.[26]

The SF's welfare organization, Auxilio Social, had its origins in the war, and was originally modelled on the Nazi's Winterhilfe, providing food and clothing for war orphans.[27] This developed into a system of six months' social service, the equivalent of military service for boys. Both were seen as 'national' service, though that for men was compulsory—and conscientious objectors were severely penalized—while women's was only encouraged. Unmarried women who wanted professional employment, a driving licence, or a passport had to complete social service; others could avoid it. The catchment was thus predominantly middle class, as befitted both the regime's rhetoric of Catholic charity and its assumptions about the nature of women's work. There was also the practical point that only the affluent could afford to dedicate their time to the SF.

There were clear limits to female agency. The hierarchical nature of the state demanded that women, both as individuals and as a sex, remain subordinate to men. The SF was barred from industrial work, military service, and government. Even the national leader, Pilar Primo de Rivera, had no official means of communication with ministers; the *mandos* of the Sección Femenina had to adopt indirect routes such as personal visits, befriending a minister's wife, or dinner invitations. The modes of bourgeois etiquette thus underpinned a political mode of operation that relied on face-to-face contact, personal knowledge, negotiation and persuasion. However, as the SF well knew, some adult women could exert considerable authority over children, domestic staff, employees, and those lower down the social scale. Such women—the *mandos*—could thus mobilize the *female* population along prescribed lines. The SF took women to the heart of the state, albeit in a carefully defined role, and, within that role, it made women representative of that state. The canteens run by Auxilio Social, their work in schools and orphanages, as well as the infant health campaigns in the pueblos—which made explicit the gulf in knowledge, wealth, and status between countrywomen and the Falangists—all fundamentally altered the state's impact on ordinary people's lives. For the first time, welfare provision was presented as a centralized and visible state function. The safety net provided was still rudimentary, but the co-ordinated welfare and social insurance initiatives marked a step change from the multiplicity of devolved responsibilities which characterized welfare provision under the Restoration and, to a lesser extent, the Republic.

The purpose of state-provided welfare was, however, to ameliorate existing conditions rather than eliminate them through the redistribution of wealth. Francoist welfarism should not be confused with the post-war welfare state policies of Scandinavia and Great Britain. Even without the redistributive impetus seen in western Europe, the alleviation of distress meant something different in Spain, both because of the extent of such distress and because so much of it was politically imposed. SF programmes had the paradoxical effect of both relieving and reinforcing the repressive effects of privation. The clearest example lies in food policy. Access to the black market was one of many social realities in postwar Spain that made life easier for those inside the regime, and much harder for those excluded from it. Under rationing—which ended only in 1952—official prices were set for basic commodities, which were then resold at a profit, a process known as the *estraperlo*. This made a few rich and many hungry: in 1947 the civil governor of Valencia pointed out that rationing guaranteed a mere 953 calories a day.[28] Unlike the Falange, the SF had no institutional involvement in the *estraperlo*, and its ethos was well-suited to the parsimonious households of the 1940s where shortages affected all and skills such as needlework and cookery became both technical accomplishments and moral virtues. SF recipes and household hints on 'making do' made it clear that wastage was frivolous, unpatriotic, and even sinful. But most SF activists were only mildly affected by the 'hungry forties': cushioned by the black market, the affluent never suffered like the poor and humble. Even though they ministered to families in desperate need, much of the SF's advice on household economy was directed firmly at the middle classes, publishing recipes which required luxury ingredients and weekly menus with at least three courses per main meal.

The experience of daily life in the postwar period differed markedly according to political history and social class. This was particularly significant for women, as the family home was their 'natural' sphere. Yet, the economic realities of the 1940s and 1950s meant that, for many, the idea of home as an inviolate private space existed only as an aspiration. Even as the repression eased, privation and war damage made home-making impossible for many. Desperation forced some women out of their homes to lead the most public of lives on the street: in 1940s Barcelona the city had 104 licensed brothels and the census showed 20,000 prostitutes in Madrid.[29] 'Official' brothels were legally recognized in Spain until 1956 but many more women resorted to turning tricks occasionally or sent their children out to work, legally or illegally. Poverty was still very real in the 1950s, and the working-class women who struggled to keep their families alive saw domesticity eroded by the physical demands of survival, though it always remained as an aspiration. The distinction between public and private was hard to maintain for a woman who needed to barter and queue, give and receive favours, conceal and steal simply in order to put food on the table. For others, though, life was very different, as the careers of Sección Femenina activists showed. One woman living in Madrid remembered that 'the end of war didn't change my life at all, we found a flat . . . in the barrio Salamanca, very spacious and there I began my married life'.[30]

Secure in its privileged identity, the loyal women of the SF were used to represent the regime to both foreign and domestic audiences, presenting the battered, fractured country of the post-war eva in terms of 'unity' and 'peace'. At the SF's third national congress in 1939, Pilar Primo de Rivera, presented Spain's unity as a project, 'obtained, in large part, by these three things: national syndicalist teaching, music and land'. Each year the annual congress would be held in a different part of Spain, so that all might come to know every part of the Patria.

When Catalans can sing the songs of Castile . . . when flamenco song is understood in all its profundity and all its philosophy and not as cabaret, when the songs of Galicia are known in the Levante; when fifty or sixty thousand voices join in the same song, then we shall have achieved unity among the people and lands of Spain.[31]

Mothers were exhorted to teach children dances from all regions of Spain in order to enhance national unity and, in some ways, to create it. Regionalism became purely aesthetic, cultural pluralism merely folkloric. A display of folk song and dance was included on the programme for the SF's 1939 victory rally, for example, followed by the symbolic presentation of regional produce from every corner of Spain. Members of the Hermandad de la Ciudad y el Campo (founded in 1937) brought up Valencian rice, Andalucian olives, and Castilian wheat. From 1940 they also began collecting regional recipes, traditional costumes, songs, and local dances.

The Spanish right had long dreamt of regenerating Spanish rural life. In the 1920s, General Miguel Primo de Rivera had drawn up some 'well-intentioned but ineffective' plans to improve village life by encouraging rabbit-breeding and introducing poster campaigns to promote 'rules of hygiene'.[32] Such plans finally came to fruition under his daughter. In 1950, the SF set up agricultural schools with the cooperation of the ministry of agriculture, to provide training in animal husbandry and bee-keeping. Handicrafts and artisanal manufacture were encouraged as both 'the inheritance of a glorious past' and 'a type of production divorced from both the capitalist system of mass labour and Marxist gregariousness'.[33] Regional costume was recovered and preserved, partly for aesthetic and sentimental reasons but also to encourage traditional crafts and preserve the specialist female labour that found employment in the rural workshops for lace-making and embroidery established under the auspices of the ministry of labour.

The hymning of traditional, regional Spain reached its apogee under a separate section of the SF, Coros y Danzas, dedicated to folk traditions (Plate 4). The revival of traditional song and dance combined several cultural imperatives for the SF and the regional folk troupes they established proved to be, alongside the cookbooks, their most enduring legacy. A folkloric interest in regional identity characterized commercial culture at the time: radio advertisements sold Valencian rice by rhapsodizing about the local landscape—'Es la tierra Valenciana/ un verdel de poesía./ Con sus flores deoro y grana/ y su luz y su alegría'—while a brand of anis from Asturias claimed to have conquered 'worldwide' fame just as the Pelayo and his warriors reconquered Islamic Spain.[34] Regional identity was part of centralized Spanish unity and, in this context, the SF organized national dance competitions, collected, transcribed, and edited local songs. They thus made regional folk culture available to a national audience: what had been an academic, ethnographic task—severely disrupted if not curtailed by the purges of universities after the Civil War—was rewritten for amateur compliers, a folkloric task at the service of the regime. Spain's cultural heritage, clearly understood as national patrimony, was essentially for display.

The apparently innocuous pastime of folk dancing led to Spain's earliest international rehabilitation when, in 1948, teams from Coros y Danzas competed in the Llangollen international eisteddfod. Tours of South America followed, and the Spaniards became regular competitors in European folk festivals. Political protests accompanied them but, in South America these received less attention than the emotional response of exiled and expatriate Spaniards who, according to the ambassador to Chile, wept, overcome at seeing 'Mother Spain revealing . . . all her happiness and light'.[35] In Valparaiso, the Coros even danced at the Republican Centre, reprising the 'old songs of the pueblo' that united all Spaniards. A film was commissioned: Coros y Danzas would continue to present the eternal Spain, rooted in both the countryside and the past, to audiences at home and abroad. The nation was thus performed, and the truth of this representation was affirmed by those who watched, particularly when, like the exiled Republicans in Valparaiso, they did so with tears in their eyes. 'Red' Spaniards had returned to the fold and the international isolation, which affected Spain until it was accepted into the United Nations in 1955, receded. Crucially, this kind of national representation was neither specifically fascist nor explicitly Catholic, though, in certain respects, it coincided with both. Rather, this essentially secular project owed more to conservative, essentially monarchist, conceptions of the nation.

From the Romantic movement of the nineteenth century, folklore had provided an idea of 'the people' which was 'conceived in a romantic, idealising, aestheticizing and essentialist way'.[36] There was ample evidence of this in the classical music repertoire. With its leading figures, including de Falla and Pau Casals, in exile, and innovative orchestras disbanded, Spanish classical composition reverted to a sentimental *casticismo*, which found a worldwide audience in Rodrigo's *Concierto de Aranjuez*. This cultural insistence on the 'authentic' Spain had a political counterpart in the language of the 'pueblo', preserved most clearly in Carlism. In the former 'Traditionalist communion', the pueblo provided an identity 'above and beyond social and cultural distinctions'. Volunteers from individual pueblos serving together in the Requeté had often refused transfer to safer posts in order to stay with 'their' people.[37] This double meaning, of pueblo as place and as people, was crucial to its rhetorical presence. Traditionalist identities, the *pueblo carlista*, combined community, landscape/territory and political identity.[38] Under Franco, the same understanding was translated into a national idiom. 'Healthy' regionalism, including Carlism, would be represented in an aestheticized way within the greater community of the nation, the *pueblo español*. Carlism was thus deracinated, just as a depoliticized folklore was separated from genuine expressions of regional identity such as the Catalan *sardana*.

Official folklore served an immediate political end, though the careful preservation of local customs also confirmed them as museum pieces. No one considered traditional dress suitable for everyday life: except for folk-dancing displays, the SF presented themselves in the tailored suits favoured by bourgeois ladies. The widely accepted need for women to be attractive had meant that they were always expected to follow fashion. The pages of women's magazines, even those published by the SF, were crowded with fashion features and advertisements for beauty products. These could have a moral gloss: fashion advice often emphasized the advantage of skilful hands in customizing clothes to be flattering and fashionable. But other features, and particularly advertisements, relied on the glamour of Hollywood to sell their products, styling models to look like the stars. The effect was seen in SF members' own self-presentation: uniforms were accessorized with jewellery and court shoes; make-up became an accepted part of grooming; deportment and stance was modelled on Hollywood rather than on traditional modesty. Fashion advice encouraged modern women to make individual choices and so contributed powerfully to the incipient consumerism that characterized 1950s Spain.

The magazines published by the Sección Femenina provided their own counter-text to the official ideology of autarky, sacrifice, and patriotic duty. Women's identity as homemakers was increasingly tied up with their identity as consumers. This made sense in the context of a regime which presented household economy and domestic 'science' as a technical, quasi-professional task: the SF's School of Domestic Service, for example, instructed cooks and maids how to use the new domestic technology, chemical stain-removers as well as 'modern electric utensils'.[39] Technological development, together with changes in commerce and marketing made it possible to purchase a greater variety of goods than ever before. Department stores such as Galerias Preciados—which first opened its doors to customers in 1943 and was much favoured by Franco's wife, Doña Carmen—offered everything the housewife needed under one roof. Household appliances had a particular status: families who owned a fridge in the 1950s and 1960s often placed it in the living-room. Advertising urged women on to competitive standards of hygiene and cleanliness—'Of course my laundry is whiter! I've switched to OMO'—in a newly mechanized world of housework.

The role of the housewife was increasingly to make prudent purchasing choices, safeguarding her domestic economy through sensible shopping and technical know-how. The virtue of thrift was no longer demonstrated simply through darning socks. Other areas of consumption were also burgeoning. The general development of western capitalism, promoted endlessly through the branded, syndicated cultural products of the Hollywood studios, changed how the western world ate, drank, and spent its leisure time. Coca-Cola and Virginia tobacco became fashionable; cosmetics, peroxide, and permanent waves brought Hollywood style within the reach of relatively ordinary women. Americanized consumerism brought with it new aspirational models, which undercut the rhetorical strategies of National-Catholicism and sounded the death knell of economic autarky. The SF proved to be both more adaptable and more malleable than its male counterpart, surviving the main party's political ostracism in the mid-1950s, and keeping the Falange's flame alive during the developmental era of the 1960s. But this adaptability also meant that it had to co-exist with, and even foster, exactly that ideology of liberal western capitalism which fascism had once sought to expunge.

CONSUMING PASSIONS

The grandiloquence of National-Catholicism set the tone for the later Franco regime. Official pronouncements, national holidays, and religious celebrations hymned the glories of 'eternal' Spain in a makeshift ideology maintained, with increasing difficulty, up to the dictator's death in 1975. The envisaged relationship between state and citizens was paternalistic. Until the liberalization of the press laws in 1966—which ended prior censorship though not the state's right to survey and, if necessary, penalize Spanish publications—all newspapers, magazines, books, and broadcasting were subject to state scrutiny. News coverage was rigidly controlled: concern for the nation's 'moral health' led to radio schedules packed with religious broadcasts, and the censors paid close attention to anything that might detract from the 'greatness' of Spain. But as anything 'unpolitical' was, by definition, innocuous, popular culture was exploited by private interests quick to see the links with commerce. Such a state of affairs suited the regime well. Political indifference was testimony to 'the peace of Franco': one Francoist minister, Gonzalo Fernández de la Mora, even claimed that 'political apathy is not a symptom of social disease but of health . . . The health of free states can be measured by the degree of political apathy.'[40] 'Politics' became a dirty word, associated with the disorder and social strife of the Republic: the regime's intention was to 'anaesthetize' the public, which, in the best traditions of paternalism would be docile, and therefore governable.

Women were the ideal recipients of 'anaesthetization', not least because those promoting the new media and its cultural products targeted women as never before. But women were far from being the only consumers, any more than they were the only inhabitants of the domestic sphere. Within Spanish homes, notions of public and private were changing and this was to have a profound affect on the relationship between state and citizen. The growth of radio meant that news, propaganda, and entertainment could now be transmitted into the heart of the family. By the early 1950s, wireless sets occupied a privileged place in the home, alongside 'the Sacred Heart [of Jesus] or the sepia photo of grandfather in the African war'.[41] Radio's penetration of private space allowed the state to address citizens in the privacy of their own living rooms. This could lead to a new intimacy: listening to transmissions helped to cement the paternalist families imagined by the regime. But this very intimacy meant that there was far less control of audience reception than in the public world of rallies and mass addresses. Civic identities were changing: disrespect, dissent, and indifference were all easier to express in private. Convention did not have to be followed scrupulously at home: acts of liturgy were broadcast regardless of whether women had their heads covered; political speeches were heard by people wearing dressing gowns rather than Falangist uniform. Social as well as political etiquette was subverted: Lorenzo Díaz dedicated his history of radio to his mother who 'let me listen to the radio even though we were in mourning'.

There was, of course, considerable state control as to what was broadcast in the first place. Programmes had to appease the censor, hence the melodramatic radio serials centred on the reconciliation of separated families or warring classes, which reached millions during the 1950s. 'Unpolitical' entertainment was provided by advertising-financed commercial radio, which put on music programmes with lively titles such as *La samba, ¡Caramba!*, quizzes, and live football. The schedules of the national channel, Radio Nacional de España (RNE) moved from a stodgy diet of party news, agriculture, and religion in 1941 to a lighter and more varied menu ten years later. This still paid proper obeisance to the thoughts of both the Caudillo and the Pope, but much of the day was now taken up with music, drama, sport, and 'what's on' cultural reviews. Even in 1965, with television reception throughout Spain and a second channel starting, radio programming followed the same successful, undemanding formula.

The retreat into domesticity, leisure, and light entertainment after the ideological paroxysms of the earlier twentieth century has become known as the 'culture of evasion'. Escapism was the key to success, as popular culture allowed Spaniards to escape the political realities of poverty and oppression. Though stigmatized by Raymond Carr and Juan Pablo Fusi as 'false and vulgar',[42] this new mass culture brought a democratic impulse to leisure, which was increasingly driven by the demands of the market rather than the desires of paternalistic elites. Many of the new cultural products had few pretensions to artistic credibility: the gulf between popular writing and literature, for example, remained as wide as ever. But in areas such as graphic design, photography, or film-making, there were significant exchanges between 'high' and 'low' culture, and the best of these products sloughed off all such categorizations. Football—the 'social drug' of Franco's Spain—also had a genuine interclass appeal. The Spanish goal that put England out of the 1950 World Cup was supposedly heard by the entire population.

The depoliticized mass culture of the post-war period was in itself testimony to rapid changes in Spanish life. A sufficiently large and literate audience now had enough disposable income to buy cinema tickets and wireless sets. Even in 1947, Spain had more cinema seats per head of population than any other country except the USA. *¡Hola!*, the most conspicuous commercial success story of Franco's Spain, had a print run of around 1,000,000 during the 1950s while newspaper circulation rose from under 500,000 in 1945 to 2,500,000 in 1967.[43] Such figures reflected a sustained expansion in education: between 1950 and 1967 the number of children enrolled in secondary education increased fourfold. Twenty-three thousand new schools were established after 1957 and, by 1968, official statistics put the illiteracy rate at under 3 per cent of those under sixty years old.[44] While a general overhaul of education had to wait until 1970, schooling—and thus the presence of the state—was clearly expanding in Francoist Spain. Yet, education also altered the expectations of individual citizens. One of its first effects was the growth of consumer demand in the 1960s, and an explosion of comic books, new genres of light fiction, and, eventually, televized soap operas.[45] The process of political 'anaesthetization' thus assumed its own momentum. The social affairs coverage of women's magazines disappeared; the graphic magazines produced for the Falangist children's section, *Flechas y Pelayos*, became comics, their crude political content displaced by strongly drawn cartoons and adventure stories; most conspicuously, the sports supplement, *Marca* overtook its eponymous Falangist daily to become a paper in its own right. The regime took full advantage of this—indeed, a depoliticized mass culture was intrinsic to its political strategy.

Clearly, if political anaesthetization was to succeed, and Spaniards were to remain more or less content with 'evasion', then consumer demand had to be sustained. Such an expansion was inconceivable in the economic conditions of the 1950s: by the end of the decade the regime was staring at bankruptcy. With the policy of autarky revealed as a sham, Franco's government changed in both composition and direction. The 1959 Stabilization Plan revolutionized the regime's foreign policy and brought to prominence a relatively new group of advisers, the 'technocrats' of the Catholic lay organization, Opus Dei. Combining pietism and theological conservatism with professional training and an enthusiasm for business, 'Octopus Dei', as it is termed by some, brought a new modernity to Spanish public life. Convinced that the way of the Lord lay in the world and not apart from it, a syndicate of Opus members took control of one of Spain's leading clearing banks during the 1950s and also built up a substantial publishing empire. The University of Navarre, an Opus foundation, assumed full degree-awarding status in 1960; two years earlier, specialist graduate schools in business and public administration had opened their doors. Rather than eschewing the industrial world, it set forth that Catholics should embrace education and science, using their professional 'vocation' to sanctify modern life.

According to Opus Dei's own *Constitutions*, the 'exercise of public jobs [is] a particular means of apostolate'.[46] Aspiring to public office was part of the organization's rationale: the first Opus cabinet ministers were appointed in 1957 on a specific programme of state-sponsored economic modernization. It would be wrong to see this programme as Francoist in any inspirational sense: by 1959 the regime was ideologically—as well as literally—bankrupt. US aid had amounted to $625m. by 1957 and, as it ran out, reform became inevitable; the only alternative was collapse. The Opus technocrats were a modernizing elite, who came to power 'not because of who they were, but because of what they wanted to do'.[47] They defined the political will to develop Spain, imposing technical (that is, economic) criteria on the political decision-makers, rationalizing the state apparatus in order to give a new primacy to market economics. There was thus a new vision at the centre of the state; one which, if acted upon, would change Spain for ever. And, as the state now had the capacity to introduce and even facilitate such projects of transformative change, the limits were set by how such a modernizing project was defined.

Among the most influential of the *opusdeistas* was Laureano López Rodó, first commissioner of the 1963 development plan. Despite the technocratic emphasis on expertise he was not an economist but a lawyer, whose overriding ambition was to rationalize the Francoist administration. A smoothly functioning modern bureaucracy would exist principally in order to manage the economy: central administrative co-ordination was essential to the technocratic project of economic modernization. The Opus' watchword was dispassionate efficiency and—while this was severely trammelled by a chronic lack of state funds—the 1964 Law on Civil State Officials was the first significant bureaucratic reform since 1918. Appropriately in a civil service that had a very low proportion of regional officials—19 per cent of the total in 1977 as opposed to 27 per cent in France and 57 per cent in Britain—the 1964 legislation introduced central supervision, a uniform organization, and modernized salary structures.[48] The traditional *cuerpos* or specialist corps were retained, inevitably given the accumulation of real power by the Francoist administrative elite. Even so, the 1964 reforms increased the personnel of the state, enhanced their role, and greatly increased efficiency.

López Rodó's reforms also began a process by which the state became—at least potentially—separate from the regime. The absence of political parties gave the administrative elites a genuine presence within the regime: entering a prestigious branch of the civil service—via the system of competitive examinations known as *oposiciones*—was a recognized step to an influential career. Reform also had profound political consequences. For the first time, the executive function of government was separated from the person of the head of state. Discussion of who should succeed Franco was now possible. Eventually, in July 1969, when the Caudillo was 76 years old, a monarchical succession was announced to the Cortes and Prince Juan Carlos became the dictator's heir.

By 1969 Spain had changed profoundly, principally as a result of the Stabilization Plan. The technocratic vision conflated politics with economics and made both issues of management rather than policy. There was a rapid and unexpected rise in industrial production. Motor car manufacture was the most conspicuous success, rising at an annual rate of 22 per cent between 1958 and 1973.[49] The SEAT 600, which went into production in 1957, became emblematic of both the development plan and Spain's modernization. It brought the family car within a relatively modest household budget, transforming daily life for millions of Spaniards and demonstrating how rising standards of living and greater purchasing power were intrinsic to economic 'take-off'. The competitiveness of the 600 went untested: virtually the entire production of the Spanish motor industry was sold on the domestic market. Motor manufacture boosted other industrial sectors, notably steel but also rubber and oil refining. Foreign companies followed SEAT's lead in penetrating the Spanish market, while affluence and the new horizons offered by car ownership made Spaniards more mobile than ever before. Spain was still poor: in the 1960s, the country's Gross Domestic Product (GDP) doubled in real terms rising to 40 per cent that of Italy, though this was still only 23 per cent that of France. Yet, the rate of growth was exponential: between 1959 and 1971, Spain's average annual growth (measured in terms of GDP) was second only to Japan's.[50] Economic growth was remarkable, not least for having been unforeseen. As the name of the 1959 plan indicates, the intention had been to *stabilize* the economy and thereby safeguard the regime, not to embark on an intoxicating and ultimately uncontrollable process of development.

The regime did its best to keep hold of the reins. The development plans opened Spain to foreign investment and encouraged foreign trade, but they did not create a free-market economy. Foreign aid was still crucial, underpinned now by Spain's membership of the International Monetary Fund (IMF). In terms of state planning, there were real continuities from the earlier period of economic autarky. 'Stabilization' was firmly state-led; national planning was key to the very idea. This was hampered by a large and still inefficient public sector—the creation of corrupt Falangist corporatism—and by Franco's stubborn refusal to modernize the fiscal regime, or even address the question of tax reform. The domestic market continued to be highly protected by a protectionist tariff policy while, internally, monopolistic structures stayed intact. Grand public-works schemes continued. For

instance, hydraulic policy—principally the construction of dams and irriga-
tion schemes—went on much as it had done since the government of Primo de
Rivera.

Ever pragmatic, the regime adopted the discourse of peace and development
(*desarrollismo*) and the legend grew that this was a trade-off: prosperity in
return for political compliance. But the actual processes of growth, notably
emigration, urbanization, and the rapid, largely uncontrolled, development
of tourism, had unforeseen effects. Economic development dissolved the
closed space of autarky: in both a rhetorical and a real sense, Spain was now
recognized as part of Europe. As north-west Europe enjoyed the boom years
of 'you've never had it so good', poverty and unemployment were exported
from the poor south. The Stabilization Plan made it easier to leave Spain
in search of work: according to the Instituto Nacional de Emigración, 1.73
million left the country between 1959 and 1973, 700,000 of them never to
return.[51] Migrant workers were absorbed by the burgeoning economies of
northern Europe and the remittances they sent home had a significant effect
on Spain's balance of payments. Emigrants' life experiences—retold on every
journey home—showed how different societies could be. The superiority of
the 'spiritual reserve of the West' seemed far from certain: migrants' children
benefited from free education and health care, acquired second languages and
could expect a very different standard of living from that their parents had
left behind. And the images of affluence did not rely on word of mouth. By
1970, 90 per cent of the nation had access to television, as opposed to the 1
per cent of households that owned a set in 1960. All of Spain could now enjoy
international spectaculars such as the Eurovision Song Contest—which Spain
won in 1968 and hosted the following year—and much of the land could also
receive foreign broadcasting.

'Traditional' rural Spain, the rhetorical heartlands of Francoism, disappeared. Despite the monuments and commemorations, the new public wash
houses erected in inaccessible pueblos—the one in Sedella (Málaga) was
inaugurated on the anniversary of the rising against the Republic—the peasant way of life was being destroyed. An inevitable consequence of economic
development was that agriculture shrank. As agri-business began to penetrate
the peninsula, some farms increased greatly in size while many others disappeared. The Agrarian Census showed around one fifth of all farms disappearing
between 1962 and 1982, as the average size rose from 15.6 to 18.9 hectares.
The cultivation of fruit and vegetables in Valencia, Murcia, and the Canary
Islands thrived but a quarter of all agrarian holdings disappeared in the central
tablelands of Old Castile. These were primarily small wheat-growing farms,
and they fell victim not only to inefficiency but also to changing demand.
During the 1960s, Spain produced too much of the old staple crops of wheat

and rice, but could meet only 62 per cent of the domestic demand for beef.[52] Castile was not suitable for beef or dairy farming and families left in search of work in the cities or the teeming new coastal resorts. The smallest pueblos were abandoned, as were patterns of life that had been handed down from generation to generation.

In 1950, the proportion of Spaniards living in towns of over 100,000 inhabitants stood at 35.7 per cent, rising to 44.1 per cent ten years later, and 51.4 per cent in 1970. Pressure on accommodation was such that shanty towns had sprang up around all major cities in the 1950s. A ministry of housing was established in 1957, following various attempts to sponsor social housing. As so often, the state's response followed a paternalist, but bureaucratic, imperative. The Spanish state continued to be weak but heavy, an increasingly weighty presence in people's lives but without the resources or the political will to resolve—rather than ameliorate—deep-rooted problems. The shortage of affordable urban housing continued even during the construction boom of the 1960s, which offered too many people the opportunity of a quick buck to take account of the needs of the poor. The most lucrative speculative possibilities were found in the new tourist destinations. Obscure villages such as Benidorm, Magaluf, and Torremolinos were parcelled up and concreted over, catering for a package holiday market which brought 34.6 million foreigners to Spain in 1973. Elite destinations also thrived: as the small town of Marbella became a stopping-off point for the international jetset, so its population rose from under 10,000 in 1950 to nearly 75,000 in 1986.[53]

Nowhere in Spain remained unaffected by tourism. Rural depopulation led to profound changes not only in village life but also in old forms of cultural expression. In a general re-creation of communal celebrations, small-scale local fiestas declined and open-air dances were displaced by commercial dance-halls even as new fiestas were created and old ones rediscovered. Fiestas were an important manifestation of Spanishness; being Spanish required communal affirmation, such as that provided by the festive outdoor rituals of processions, picnics, and dancing in the village square. Migrants returned to the pueblo for the harvest-time *ferias*, which continued as affirmations of communal identity while simultaneously acquiring a transient quality. The customs of the village were put on for the occasion by those whose working lives had taken them away from the traditional community. Inevitably, fiestas began to accommodate the tastes and values of a consumerist age. In 1965, the Pamplona bull-running for the feast of San Fermín was officially declared to be 'of great interest to tourists': Spain's fiestas were changing from participatory celebrations for local people into displays to be consumed by outsiders (Plate 12).[54] On occasion, the tensions were obvious—tourists to the *sanfermines* were derided as a 'plague of hippies' and mocked by local lads wearing long wigs—but tourists were now the mainstay of many fiestas. Long-established urban spectaculars such as Valencia's *fallas* or Sevilla's famous *feria* grew both in scale and extravagance, and those who flocked to them were just as likely to be out-of-town Spaniards as foreigners.

Spain itself had become a product to be sold. During the 1960s, the tourist industry enticed visitors with the slogan 'Spain is different'. Images of fiestas and rural pueblos created an impression of unspoilt tradition—the 'difference' of the holiday brochures. The mountain village of Mijas (Málaga) became more whitewashed as it was packaged for day-trippers staying on the Costa del Sol. The local shop began to carry teenage fashions, including hot pants—which the shopkeeper thought unlikely to sell to local girls older than twelve—and visitors in bikini tops no longer attracted comment. By 1971, buses connected the pueblo to the city of Málaga, bringing tourists to buy handicrafts and taking the villagers to work on the coast, while nearly ninety families owned their own car. A mere fourteen years earlier, the village had neither public transport nor private cars and the post came by donkey.[55] Villages depended increasingly on holiday visitors or seasonal returnees, neither of whom lived or worked there. Modernization had blown apart official attempts to save artisanal production. Only the arrival of British, German, and Scandinavian tourists, keen to take home local craft work as souvenirs saved 'peasant' crafts such as ceramics and esparto work.

Mechanization also meant that fewer people were needed to work even those farms that remained. During the 1960s, the proportion of Spain's population involved in farming fell below 50 per cent for the first time. Villages stopped being agrarian communities, bound together by productive relationships stemming from the land; the pueblo became rather an idealized refuge, offering an escape from urban congestion and the stress of daily life. As Lucia Graves remembered from her girlhood in Mallorca, tourism transformed productive farms into 'a landscape to be consumed by tourists—to feed the mind and not the body; and the efforts of men and women, once dedicated to its cultivation, would be channelled into providing new services for the viewers'.[56] For younger generations, who grew up with a knowledge of the pueblo but never belonged to it in the way their parents did, agrarian village life became simply folklore. Issues such as inheritance no longer had the salience that they had done for generations, and those forms of identity carried down through family and community—particularly religious identities—decayed.

The *desarrollo* of the 1960s brought with it a changed understanding of identities and how they are constructed. A new mode of life, particularly among the young, meant less formality, casual attitudes and attire, changes in music, fashion, and sexual mores. In the music they bought, the concerts they went to, the clothes they wore, their manner of smoking a cigarette—or, for girls, that they smoked at all—young Spaniards were subverting or discarding social and political convention. As individuals, these new consumers exerted more autonomy over their choices than the regime cared to admit. Young Spaniards were increasingly likely to attend university, travel abroad, and meet foreigners. This was not simply a 'liberalization' of culture and mores, nor an expansion of those areas (particularly within the economy) that were outside the direct purview of the central state. Rather, in a country which had no deep tradition of individualism—in either a political or an economic sense—the consumer society led to a new understanding of the individual. As consumers, individuals made choices, and those choices both demonstrated and determined their own identities.

The partial liberalization of the economy meant that more choices could now be catered for; identities were expressed that fell far outside the narrow range admitted by the regime. Subaltern identities assumed a new vitality, particularly in those regions, like Cataluña and the Basque Country, where a separate language had long fostered cultural pluralism even in the face of bitter opposition from the centre. The search for a genuine popular cultural expression led to an exploration of folk culture that was imbued with a political content far from that sanctioned by the regime. María del Mar Bonet recorded traditional and new songs in her native *mallorquín*; the *sardana* became the cultural expression of the Catalan nation, danced every Sunday in front of Barcelona cathedral. In gathering to dance, Catalans were recuperating Cataluña's cultural and associational traditions, not bowing in obeisance to the folkloric centralism of the Franco regime.

The Catalan language was the bedrock of Catalan identity and its relationship to other Romance tongues such as Spanish and French made it easy to recuperate, particularly when compared to Basque. Urban infrastructure and a purchasing public—above all in Barcelona—allowed publishing and a modest recording industry to develop.

Despite the watchful eye of the censor, Catalan culture could be marketed, though those who wrote or sang in the language were often subject to banning orders. 1960s Catalan nationalism had a performative quality: the nation would recreate itself through ordinary people using and sharing their native tongue and its cultural artefacts. Live performance allowed for a collective, participative Catalan presence. Instrumental in creating such a presence was Nova Cançó, which combined local political identities, folk music, and the internationalism of left-wing protest songs. From the early 1960s, singers such as Bonet and Joan Manuel Serrat stood alongside their Latin American counterparts—Nueva Canción musicians such as Violeta Parra and Victor Jara—in creating a music of opposition, egalitarianism, and social justice.

The roots of Nova Cançó were as much international as they were Catalan. Throughout the West, traditional music seemed a way for the left to discover its popular origins. The involvement in the anti-Vietnam War campaigns of prominent folk singers such as Pete Seeger and Joan Baez—both of whom had considerable influence over the Nova Cançó singers—made folk-inspired protest music fashionable. Serrat's decision to sing in Castilian as well as Catalan made his music accessible to a mass audience via radio and he was selected to represent Spain in the 1968 Eurovision Song Contest, though he withdrew after being refused permission to sing in his first language. The politics of language was again front-page news. The original Nova Cançó singers were joined by younger artists such as Lluís Llach and listening to their music became an act of political opposition, particularly as concerts were often broken up by police. Spaniards from all regions attended Llach's concerts, often coming together as a choir to sing those songs which Llach had been banned from performing while he stood in silence on the stage. Songs such as 'L'estaca' or 'La gallineta' would be sung by Catalan and Castilian-speaker alike, as an act of protest and participation.

Eventually, Llach was banned from performing in Spain altogether, a prohibition which lasted for five years.[57] Paradoxically, such heavy-handed tactics showed how Nova Cançó had helped to mobilize a profound, bottom-up reassertion of cultural pluralism in Spain. Football rivalries, most notably that between Real Madrid and Barcelona during the 1960s, also helped to establish what Catalans referred to as the *fet diferencial*, or distinctiveness of Cataluña, at a mass level. A new sense of individual choice allowed people to identify themselves in terms of taste, fashion, and choice of football team. This was most noticeable among youth—the main protagonists of the 1960s—but the emerging cultural pluralism affected Spaniards of every age and all social classes. The policy of 'anaethetization' had stagnated: those who went to Nova Cançó concerts were not there simply to enjoy themselves: they went to participate. Even listening to the music could be a response to a call to action. For in the words of Llach's most famous song:[58]

Siset, que no veus l'estaca	Siset, don't you see the stake
a on estem tots lligats?	to which we're all tied?
Si no podem desfer-la	If we don't free ourselves
mai no podrem caminar!	we'll never walk forward.
Si estirem tots ella caurà	If we pull hard, we'll bring it down.
i molt de temps no pot durar	It can't last much longer,
segur que tomba, tomba, tomba,	surely it will fall, fall, fall,
ben corcada deu ser ja.	it must be rotten by now.

Si jo l'estiro fort per aquí	If I pull hard this way
i tu l'estires fort per allà,	and you pull hard that way,
segur que tomba, tomba, tomba,	surely it will fall, fall, fall,
i ens podrem alliberar!	and we can be free.

PACEM IN TERRIS

On 11 April 1963, Pope John XXIII declared human rights to be 'universal and inviolable, and therefore altogether inalienable'. The dignity of the human person meant that man had 'the right to live', 'a natural right to be respected', 'a right to freedom in investigating the truth' and a right 'to take an active part in public life'. *Pacem in Terris* spoke a new language of human equality, insisting that 'a man who has fallen into error does not cease to be a man.' Freedom of conscience, of association and, most significantly, of worship were identified as essential to the common good. 'Man's personal dignity requires . . . that he enjoy freedom and be able to make up his own mind when he acts. . . . There is nothing human about a society that is welded together by force.' The teaching of *Pacem in Terris* was reaffirmed in December 1965, when Pope Paul VI issued *Dignitatis Humanae*, 'On Religious Freedom'—one of the most significant declarations to have emerged from the Second Vatican Council (1962–5)—which declared religious freedom to be intrinsic to 'the very dignity of the human person'. On no account should a man be forced to act 'in a manner contrary to his conscience'.[59]

Vatican II did not come from nowhere, but its impact on Catholicism was such that it permanently separated the conciliar period from all that had gone before. The chronology of the Church became one of before and after the council, in part because of the internal renovation it offered but also because of its repositioning of the Church within the modern world. This process of *aggiornamento* ended the Church's defensive self-image of a fortress besieged by the corruptions of modern life, a view that had enhanced the Church's traditional tendency to look to the protection and privilege offered by the confessional state. In this world view, religious freedom was understood as the freedom to attain salvation; there was no room, legal or otherwise, for 'heresy'. Few national Churches epitomized this position more clearly than the Spanish. But the ecclesiology of Vatican II transformed the universal Church from a 'state-centred to a society-centred institution' or, to use the ecclesiastical language of the times, confirmed 'the presence of the church in the world'.[60] The Church's new self-image was that of the pilgrim, with the community of the faithful collectively and individually seeking after truth.

One has only to compare the definition of social peace elaborated by John XXIII with that given by the Spanish bishops in 1937 to show how far the Church had come. According to the conclusion of *Pacem in Terris*, 'peace is but an empty word if it does not rest upon . . . an order that is founded on truth, built up on justice, nurtured and animated by charity, and brought into effect under the auspices of freedom.' In contrast, the bishops' collective letter 'On the War in Spain' had explicitly defined peace as 'the tranquillity of divine order, national, social, and individual, which assigns a place to everyone and gives him what he is due'.[61] By 1965, Francoism's highly conventional understanding of static hierarchies was already under attack from all sides: the certainties of a social order in which individuals were defined by status and so allocated to a predetermined place were fast being undermined. Under the confessional state, Church and regime had come together to impose Catholic truth on all Spaniards: freedom of religion was expressly denied. As one prelate put it: 'we considered catholicism's triumphalism and social control to be a requirement of faith itself.'[62] Now, by recognizing the right of freedom of conscience, the Church had turned itself into a voluntary, free Church, abandoning confessionalism and renouncing coercion. The legitimacy of the Franco regime was destroyed from within.

Vatican II led to a real examination of conscience within the Spanish Church, a period of soul-searching which not only stood in marked contrast to the Civil War—which had had no such effect—but also led to the abandonment of the premises and ideology of the 'crusade'. This intense process of renewal affected every level of the Spanish Church including, finally, the hierarchy. The realities of social privation had already brought some parish clergy to question the Church's response to the poor, but the hierarchy was still an integral part of the confessional state. Indeed, when Church and State came into conflict in the early Franco regime, the state usually won. The search for official protection was so ingrained as to prevent loud protest even when the regime banned the postwar pastoral letter of the cardinal archbishop of Toledo, 'The Lessons of the War and the Duties of the Peace', disliking its reference to reconciliation. But the bishops who emerged from the conciliar Church were not so supine, while Franco found Pope Paul VI to be far from accommodating. In 1969, Vicente Enrique y Tarancón was appointed to the primatial see of Toledo, only to be moved to the new archbishopric of Madrid in 1971. The translation not only reflected the new urban reality of Spain—Madrid was a centre of power, Toledo was not—but it also gave a truly conciliar churchman authority over the Spanish Church and was accomplished against Franco's wishes.

Under Tarancón, the Spanish hierarchy took a new attitude to workers' rights and social justice, marking a sea change in episcopal attitudes. In the immediate aftermath of Vatican II, the Spanish bishops had seemed intransigent, clamping down on activists in Catholic Action. Established in the early twentieth century as a lay mobilization to sanctify everyday life, Catholic Action brought together various discrete, pious, and charitable groups. From the 1950s, a new kind of activism developed with the foundation of 'specialist' branches among workers and students. The apostolate of the JOC (Juventudes Obreras Cristianas: Young Christian Workers) and HOAC (Hermandades Obreras de Acción Católica: Workers' Brotherhoods of Catholic Action) brought them increasingly into forms of action both the regime and many bishops regarded as 'temporal' and political rather than spiritual and religious. *Pacem in Terris* had opened the way for Catholics to collaborate with Marxists by distinguishing between 'false philosophical teachings' and the social justice campaigns they inspired. Well before this, though, HOAC and JOC activists in the industrial dioceses of northern Spain were working with underground communist unions and co-operating with illegal strikes.[63] In 1964 seven leaders of the underground communist trade union, Comisiones Obreras (CCOO: Workers' Commissions) went on trial (for illegal association) in the Basque province of Vizcaya; six of them were also members of HOAC.

The activism of HOAC and JOC depended on the autonomous action of the, often young, militants. The JOC's 'see-judge-act' methodology, whereby activists would identify a problem or issue, study it in some detail, and then decide on a course of action, meant that participation replaced passivity. Membership required an active commitment while the pastoral agenda was elaborated by the activists themselves rather than their clerical 'superiors'. The militancy of HOAC and JOC showed how the Church was experiencing a spontaneous intensification of associational life but, in the context of a regime that 'encouraged people to see nothing, to have no independent judgement, and to remain isolated and passive' and an episcopate that was the oldest in Europe in 1962, such mobilization was troubling.[64] In 1966, the Spanish bishops made public their reservations about the autonomy of specialist Catholic Action and removed seven chaplains from their posts. At issue was the activists' 'confusion' between the religious and the political. The following year, new statutes reaffirmed episcopal control of Catholic Action, favouring parochial structures over the specialized branches.

In response, a generation of committed Catholic activists voted with their feet. The leaders of the students' group resigned en masse, calling the new statutes 'excessively juridical, excessively concerned with who commands and who has to obey'.[65] The top-down reorganization showed the limits of hierarchical authority: the statutes remained in place but the movement declined. Some had already been moving outside the Church, as pressing human rights issues seemed to require a political rather than a pastoral solution. And, as the crisis showed, the response of the institutional Church was often disappointing. Some activists continued to practise their faith, often in the grassroots 'base communities' then springing up all over Spain, but many left the Church altogether, even though Rome's response to the crisis was to renovate the Spanish hierarchy. In 1968, a mere two years after he had been sacked as JOC chaplain, Ramón Torella i Cascante was consecrated bishop; in 1971, Tarancón became president of the episcopal conference. In 1966, 65 per cent of the Spanish hierarchy were over sixty; by 1973, that proportion had fallen to 40 per cent. The Church moved forward into a new phase, popularly known as *taranconismo*, that the specialized branches of Catholic Action appeared to have anticipated.[66]

The exodus of Catholic Action thus strengthened the democratic opposition. Not only were Catholic militants moving outside the Franco regime, depriving it of legitimacy and enforcing those ranked against it, but a generation of committed activists had been secularized. Many assumed leading roles in the trade unions, neighbourhood associations, and political groups which would eventually help to create the transition to democracy. Ironically, the skills such leaders used to foment political participation and active citizenship—public speaking, organization, running campaigns—had been honed in the bosom of the Francoist Church. The crisis of identity within Catholic Action was thus testimony to a new kind of group activism, which involved both clergy and laity and made the continuation of elite, top-down, episcopally-controlled models hard to envisage. For 'see-judge-act' fed into a new assertion of social movements within Spain and moved the political imperative to the people.

By the early 1960s, the Church touched more of Spain's people than at any other time in the twentieth century. The protection offered by the confessional state, the project of 're-Christianization' posited by the crusade, and, quite possibly, the desire to forge a new moral community after the blood-letting of the Civil War, led to a sustained rise in mass attendance during the 1950s and early 1960s. Rates of religious practice were to fall rapidly from the 1970s, but in 1969 survey evidence showed that 98 per cent of housewives, 83 per cent of students, and 86 per cent of workers and employees defined themselves as Catholic. Ninety-three per cent of all respondents accepted the Christian doctrine of the trinity. The number of religious personnel had risen so that by 1968 the number of diocesan priests stood at 26,190, members of male religious communities at 24,148, and religious sisters at 85,060.[67] Statistics can offer only a crude and approximate indicator of phenomena as emotional and as contradictory as religious belief, but such elevated figures suggest that the Church had a real moral authority in 1960s Spain and, certainly when compared to the 1930s, considerably more reach among the population. The urban working classes were still among the least likely of all social groups to attend mass—a feature of religious practice throughout Europe—but the sharp cleavages of Catholicism and anticlericalism had gone.

During the 1940s and 1950s, the Church had built up parochial and pastoral associations. Many of these were pious or liturgical but, as the specialized branches of Catholic Action showed, others had a social or industrial agenda. Amid 'a society suspicious of itself', the Church provided the space for associational life: priests, workers, and students were just some of those re-articulating a democratic discourse within the social movements which themselves contributed to a re-emerging public sphere.[68] The legal protection offered to the Church meant relative autonomy for its associations and publications and this protected space within the regime served as the core of a re-assertion of civil society. Just as young Catholic Action leaders moved into secular opposition groups, so those active in Catholic student organizations brought participative experiences and democratic values into the professions they entered on graduation. Inevitably, the questions being put to both Church and regime became sharper. The language of charity would no longer suffice to workers clamouring for justice, particularly not once they were organized, and had access to the language both of collective bargaining and of human rights. And that language was often brought to them by the young priests and lay workers who mobilized them through HOAC and JOC.

Among the origins of the sea change undergone by the Spanish Church during the 1950s and 1960s was the increasing disjuncture between pastoral and dogmatic theology. Both culture and practice in the Catholic Church led to the implementation of teaching according to particular circumstances and individual cases. Codes of teaching, both dogma and canon law, were interpreted according to specific instances of pastoral care. But in the difficult social conditions of rapid and unregulated urban expansion, the Church's premises and postulates often seemed inappropriate or irrelevant. And, as Vatican II dramatically showed, the processes of change were not all external to the Church. The state-centred nature of the Spanish Church was not unique but it was unusual. Catholics in England, Scotland, Germany, the Netherlands, or North America had long coexisted with Protestant Churches, secular pluralism and even republican political traditions. State protection was not an option for these Churches, which had been moving in a society-centred direction well before the Second World War. In the 1930s, Catholics across the world had flocked to the aid of a persecuted Spanish Church but, after 1945, with the dangers of the Civil War past, the transnational structures of the universal Church introduced new and more open intellectual currents into Spanish Catholicism.

The rise in the number of religious vocations during the 1940s meant the seminaries were full, and many ordinands went to study abroad, often in Rome but also in cities such as Paris or Innsbruck. The pontifical universities of Salamanca and Comillas developed more open traditions, particularly in theology where the number of translations of foreign academic works rose from 25 per cent in 1950 to 90 per cent by 1965.[69] Religious orders and congregations had strong ties to their communities in other countries, particularly when the mother house lay outside Spain or the order had strong missionary traditions. Many Jesuit priests, for example, travelled the long way from crusade to council, abandoning work in elite boys' boarding schools for pastoral care in slum parishes or the factory floor. The religious offer of the conciliar Church was that of an authentically prophetic voice and, on leaving Spain, many discovered that the national Church and confessional state they had thought to be the Catholic ideal was actually stagnant. Far from leading European Catholicism, the Spanish Church was stuck in a backwater. This only became apparent to many bishops during the Vatican Council itself as they went to Rome full of confidence, to find a worldwide Church they barely recognized. With the conciliar declaration on religious freedom, the discrepancy became apparent to the whole world. The Spanish Church's 'delusions of grandeur' collapsed.[70]

In the wake of this realization, the Church was left divided, both politically and generationally. The hiatus of the 1930s meant that the priesthood was broadly grouped into those over sixty and those under forty and, while they responded in different ways, the searching examination of conscience instigated by Vatican II was discomforting for both groups. Many—though by no means all—of the older generation remained convinced by National-Catholicism, retreating to an ideological bunker defined by the certainties of the Caudillo's confessional state. When Spanish priests were asked in 1970 if it was possible to convert de-Christianized sectors of society without engaging in activities commonly seen as political, 84 per cent of those under 30 answered 'no' as opposed to 41 per cent of those over 60. The lived experience of *aggiornamento*, the rapprochement with secular ideologies and left-wing activists, the emphasis on Christian commitment rather than social deportment and piety—in short, the experience of living in the world rather than apart from it—led many young priests and religious to question their vocation. The same survey showed 51 per cent of priests to feel insecure in their understanding of moral questions, the same proportion that felt their seminary training to have been deficient. Relatively few declared doubts over their faith, but 39 per cent experienced theological uncertainty and 75 per cent felt unprepared to deal with political questions.[71]

The 'prophetic' Church defined 'worldiness' differently from earlier generations, rejecting materialism and 'shallow' consumerism while embracing the
secular life of 'the people of God'. Such a stance distinguished the Church
from the regime that had sponsored and enabled this consumer culture. A
change in moral emphasis meant that the Church now emphasized poverty
over chastity and paid less attention to social conduct and sexual transgres-
sions. Celibacy was often the defining issue for those who left the Church, as
around four hundred Spanish priests did each year between 1966 and 1971
and a third of Spain's Jesuits in the ten years after 1966. The number of
seminarians fell dramatically as Spanish society re-evaluated the role of the
priest. The case of one priest in the Basque coastal village of Itziar was typical.
Like many young Vatican II priests, he introduced new liturgical practices
to his parish, discouraging the 'magic' of traditional peasant religion and
encouraging reflective discussions between priest and people. The effect was
to re-evaluate the sacramental basis of Catholic practice and abandon the
once-sharp distinction between sacred and secular. Working from the basis
that 'one's entire life has to be a sacrament', Fr Mikel Urkola left the priesthood
in 1967, explaining to his former parishioners that he had come to believe in
the priesthood of all believers, a sacramental journey he expounded in a book,
published in Basque in 1968, which 'was decisive in emptying the seminary'.
The number of seminarians in neighbouring Navarrre, fell from 292 in 1968
to 10 in 1970.[72]

The division within the Church was often played out in public, particularly in
areas of high religious practice. Inevitably, these were the regions also affected
by rural depopulation and, in the provincial capitals, the tardy provision
of alternative educational institutions. The days of recruiting priests—who
would travel the villages in regions such as Old Castile and Navarre, arriving
on a moped and leaving with a local boy riding pillion behind him—were
numbered. Most of these boys had never become priests but went to receive
a secondary education in a pious atmosphere. Now they could go often to
the local *instituto* instead. The undisputed moral authority of the Church
was ebbing away. In some pueblos, this was, in part, the result of a close
identification with the Franco regime: the parish priest in Cirauqui (Navarre),
for example, was the incumbent from 1958 to 1978 and came to be seen as, at
best, 'out of step with the times' and, at worst, the representative of repression.
Such priests never adopted lay dress, keeping the traditional soutane both as
emblem of their clerical status and as symbol of their continuing identification
with the political and religious values of the crusade. In marked contrast to
the conciliar Church, they remained resolute in their separation from the
world, a stance which earned them the epithet 'soutanosaurus'. In Cirauqui,
an open letter in 1971 accused the parish priest of treating the laity simply

as an audience and alienating the young. When a young local priest returned from mission work in South America, he became an alternative focus for village religiosity, leading retreats and discussion groups, and taking around 80 per cent of the local youth for an improvised *romería* at a local shrine. Bitter disputes broke out between him and the incumbent, over theology, political involvement, and clerical dress. Open crisis was only averted by the young priest's return to South America.[73]

Vatican II thus destroyed not only the unity and certainty of the Spanish Church but also the sense of hierarchy that underpinned religious, political, and social order in Franco's Spain. The young people of Cirauqui voted with their feet, marching to the local shrine, attending mass outside the village and, for some, eventually leaving the Church altogether. They were no longer controllable. At popular level, the priest's voice still gave authority to dissent, even in the face of episcopal sanction. In Itziar, the sanction and transfer of the parish priest had led to similar protests. As one of 339 priests who petitioned the local bishops in 1960 to protest at the repression of 'the ethnic, linguistic and social characteristics that God gave to the Basques', the local incumbent was banished to a tiny, isolated parish. When he came to celebrate his first Sunday mass there, he found the congregation included all the young people of Itziar. Overcome with emotion, 'he could barely proceed'.[74] Like their priest, these young men and women were making a political as well as an ecclesiastical protest, and they did not feel constrained by the disapproval of their parental or episcopal superiors. The values of deference and hierarchy which had for so long cemented Spanish society were breaking down.

Families became less formal during the 1960s as authoritarian models of paternal authority were rejected, at least by the children. For some, as children became more independent, family relationships grew more affectionate. Others, though, met the end of a time in which 'parents made the law and children submitted' with bewilderment or anger. And few, either in or outside the Church, understood the revolution in sexual mores and social customs which entirely changed how young people—particularly girls—lived their lives, or saw how this undermined all carriers of paternal authority, whether fathers, priests, or Francoist functionaries.

Nowhere were the convulsions of Catholic politics more apparent than in the Basque Country.[75] The suppression of all manifestations of Basque nationalism after the Civil War had led to a disjuncture between the parish clergy and the hierarchy, specifically over the use of Basque in church. Well aware that their congregations were more fluent in Basque, village priests would preach in the vernacular, switching quickly into Spanish if an outsider entered the church. Like its Catalan counterpart, the Basque Church retained that sense of cultural pluralism that had long distinguished it from the Spanish

Church despite a post-Civil War policy of stamping out 'separatism'. Basque sees, for example, were subordinated to Spanish archdioceses—a significant factor in a region where in the mid-1960s, between 79 and 85 per cent of those living in the rural Basque provinces attended Sunday mass.[76] Associational traditions were also strong in the Basque Country. Few pueblos were without a mountaineering society while eating clubs, choirs, and less formal boys' groups were common. Organizing both Basque and Catholic youth movements was thus relatively easy; indeed, it was often hard to see where Basqueness ended and Catholicism began. And, until at least the late 1960s, the natural leaders of such associations came from the parish clergy.

In Itziar, for example, the Catholic Action youth movement, Baserri Gaztedi, heard talks from a French Basque priest, invited by the local incumbent. Connected emotionally and symbolically by their common nationality and language, the young people heard of a very different, active, politics in which being a good Christian meant neither passivity nor authoritarianism. At a small, local level, and aided considerably by the Basque Country's position on the cultural and geographical borders of Spain, the Church was repositioning Spain within the western European mainstream. Basque self-identity was given further impetus by *Pacem in Terris*, which recognized the political and linguistic rights of ethnic minorities. But, as with human rights' discourse more generally, the Christian impetus was only one among several. Postcolonial thought also led directly to the affirmation of the rights of ethnic minorities, as did the more diffuse humanism which linked the various positions, both secular and religious. In Itziar, the Catholic youth group gradually became secularized during the 1960s, expanding their reading to include Freud, Marx, and Mao as well as voguish structuralists such as Althusser, and spending much time discussing sexuality. Eventually, the local priest abandoned the organization because of its Marxist leanings in the early 1970s, the group began to campaign against church-attendance and its ex-seminarian leaders joined clandestine political parties. Basqueness became the defining ideology, with language campaigns and the establishment of a Basque-speaking kindergarten or *ikastola*. Few ordinary members followed their leaders into the underground communist organizations; they identified with the Basque nation rather than the international proletariat, and their loyalties lay with ETA.

Euzkadi Ta Askatasuna (ETA: Basque Homeland and Freedom) came to public attention in 1961 when it attempted to interrupt the annual commemoration of the 18 July rising by derailing trains. The following year, ETA declared itself to be 'a revolutionary Basque organization for national liberation', espousing violence and opposing dictatorship. As the first Basque political organization to declare its aconfessionality, ETA marked a new stage in the secularization of Spain. Yet, as in Itziar, many of its first members came from Catholic youth organizations, trained in the 'see-judge-act' methodology of the JOC. Both in the Basque Country and beyond, the Church acted as a breeding-ground of political consciousness but, as ETA clearly showed, the dynamic that introduced could be uncontrollable. In Itziar, the first ETA militants had all been altar boys in the village church. The local priests, who knew these boys well, found their political trajectory incomprehensible: the fight for justice was a Christian imperative but it was fatally compromised by ETA's decision to kill.

Yet, such questions were rarely clear-cut. Few Basques were actively involved in ETA but many sympathized. In August 1968, for example, an ETA gunman assassinated Melitón Manzanas, a police commissioner in Irún widely believed to be a prison torturer. The military repression unleashed on the Basque Country in reprisal for ETA's actions was instrumental in raising sympathy for the terrorist group. Formal requiems were conducted for *etarras* shot by the Civil Guard while police informers attended mass, reporting on 'subversive' or separatist sermons. Links between ETA and the Church remained even after the uncompromising recourse to violence. Hundreds of arrests followed Manzanas' killing and, in 1970, fifteen defendants went on trial for the murder before a military court in the Castilian city of Burgos. One of the female defendants, who was pregnant at the time of her arrest, was beaten so badly in prison that she miscarried. The only defendant to be acquitted, she was joined in the dock by her husband, another married couple, and eleven other men, two of them priests. All declared themselves to be members of ETA, renounced confessions obtained under torture, and spoke Basque throughout the trial, which was held in public thanks to a campaign by the Basque and Spanish bishops. The bishops also led the successful petition for clemency that followed after five defendants were sentenced to death. But the gaol sentences were harsh and, in the case of the priests, Julen Kalzada and Jon Etxabe, were to be served in the prison the regime had opened for turbulent priests in Zamora.

Opened in 1968 as the only ecclesiastical gaol west of the Iron Curtain, Zamora's first inmate, Albert Gabikagogeaskoa, was Basque and, over the next eight years, a hundred other Basque priests were sent to join him. The gaol was opened with the agreement of the Spanish episcopate and many of its inmates were thorns in the side of their bishops as well as the regime—Julen Kalzada, for example, was arrested in the diocesan offices in Bilbao where he was one of five priests staging a hunger strike in protest at 'the still inadequate voice of the church hierarchy'.[77] But these activist, incarcerated, eloquent men were testimony to just how far the Catholic Church had travelled in a remarkably short space of time. As more priests were prosecuted for public order offences or fined over the content of their sermons and the surveillance of Church activities increased, so a newly invigorated hierarchy found itself less and less prepared to connive with the regime. Protests were raised at the civil prosecution of priests, and impediments found to the legal process. After 1972, the Basque bishops refused to consent to the prosecution of their priests. In 1973, 352 Basque priests wrote an open letter on gaol conditions and the treatment of political prisoners to the Vatican and the bishops of Basque dioceses in Spain and France. 'A prisoner is someone deprived by society of his liberty,' the letter stated, 'he should not be someone who has completely disappeared, whose fate is unknown, whose situation people know nothing about.'[78] The Zamora gaol, seen by the regime as the symbol of the cooperation of Church and State, became for the Church a cause of shame.

The year after the Burgos trial, with the Basque Country seething with revolt, Spain's episcopal conference issued a statement, asking pardon for not having acted as true ministers of reconciliation during the Civil War. In 1973, it supplemented this with a careful and lengthy letter 'On the Church and the Political Community' which declared its respect for political pluralism and set out the need to separate Church and State. The Church's withdrawal from the Franco regime could not have been more clear, particularly as the bishops voted in favour of the document by 59 to 20. Yet, despite the conference's condemnation of prelates holding political office, it could not force a recalcitrant bishop such as Guerra Campos to give up his seat in Franco's Cortes nor prevent him from hymning the virtues of crusade and Caudillo on public television.[79] The divisions in the Church remained, and the bishops' pronouncements came at a time when reconciliation seemed as remote as ever. But the process of renewal within the hierarchy had transformed the Spanish Church, which was now clearly looking beyond the Franco regime. Whatever political role the Church played in the twilight of the dictatorship, it would be very different from any it had ever played before.

6

Joining Europe, 1973–2002

THE AGONY OF THE GENERAL

By 1973, the death knell was sounding for Francoist Spain. *España, una grande, libre* continued to reverberate through the official insignia of the regime, but much of Spain shared the opinion of the traveller in the jungle who swam unharmed through a crocodile-infested river, chanting 'Spain, One, Great, and Free'—a claim the crocodiles couldn't possibly swallow. This loss of legitimacy was manifested in the growth of public opposition and was also apparent in the regime's increasing recourse to force. States of emergency and martial law were again used to depict opposition as sedition and political protest as a simple problem of public order. Strikes were illegal, criminalizing those who took part in them, and in 1968 the Supreme Court declared the semi-public trade unions, the Comisiones Obreras to be illegal and subversive. Neither measure could stop the agitation, though repression did temporarily fragment the CCOO. Nevertheless, in 1970, Spain experienced 1,595 strikes and, after a brief lull, the figure rose to 2,290 in 1974 and 3,156 in 1975. In the year Franco died, over 14.5 million working hours were lost, 2.5 million of them in Barcelona.[1] 'Public order' disturbances on this scale could not be dealt with simply by police measures; yet, by the 1970s, the regime had no other solutions to offer.

The relationship between military force and public order was never more visible than during the crisis of the regime from 1973 to 1977. 'Official violence' had always been at the disposition of the government, essentially on a discretionary basis, and the militarized structures of emergency powers subordinated juridical and police powers to the army.[2] In 1974, around 6,000 Spaniards were awaiting trial on political charges, equivalent to the total number of Italian political prisoners under Mussolini between 1927 and 1939.[3] Spiralling dissent led to further crackdowns. Courts-martial were used more frequently and torture was systematically applied to those in prisons and police cells. People taken into custody disappeared from sight; lawyers were impeded from seeing their clients and courts refused to hear evidence of torture but accepted uncorroborated confessions. A lawyer defending a student tortured during the 1971 state of exception was charged with 'insults to the Spanish nation', as well as contempt, for refusing to be silenced about his client's suffering.[4]

Official rhetoric persisted in simply denying the undeniable. According to the government, the state of exception declared in Guipúzcoa and Vizcaya in April 1975 led to 189 detentions. Unofficial estimates, broadly verified by Amnesty International, put the real figure at over 2,000: legal guarantees were ignored and the police acted as an executive force in its own right. Right-wing vigilante groups acted with apparent impunity, protected by the security forces, who beat and tortured at will: 'I was arrested . . . by 10 or 12 police who came to my house in the early hours of the morning. I was taken to the police station where they hit me in the stomach and kicked me in the testicles and face . . . They beat me so badly that I don't know with what or how or how long because one hour seemed like five . . . They said that an accident could happen to one of my relatives. They said that nothing mattered to them, not even Franco . . .'[5]

The renewed use of the death penalty was stark evidence of the reversion to naked force. In November 1971, the 1947 Law of Banditry and Terrorism was incorporated into the code of military justice, returning to prominence the crime of 'military rebellion' and making it punishable by death. In 1974, a young Catalan anarchist, Salvador Puig Antich, was garrotted in Barcelona in the first execution in Spain since that of the communist Julián Grimau in 1963. On 22 August 1975, in a legal move which seemed explicitly to link the repression of the 1940s with that of the 1970s, the death sentence became mandatory for those who, like Puig Antich, were convicted of killing a member of the security forces.[6] Five people were executed in October, just one month before Franco died. The terms of the new law created a national state of exception—habeas corpus was suspended and police allowed to search premises at will—which underlined the fact that, in the absence of political answers, the regime would resort to military ones.

Widespread political dissent had forced the regime to show the iron hand, so long concealed by a consumerist glove. But in the 1970s repression created noise rather than silence: brutality and censorship made protest more widespread and the opposition more visible. In 1974, Bishop Añoveros of Bilbao was placed under house arrest after authorizing a sermon defending the rights of ethnic minorities. The government ordered him out of the country; supported by the Vatican, he refused to go. Despite its growing moral stature among the opposition, the Church's influence was weakening—as one student activist put it, Catholicism had 'cracked up'—but this in itself contributed to student radicalism, which grew apace. Authority—parental, priestly, or professorial—was to be resisted; sexual mores and bourgeois convention were as much forces of oppression as was the lack of political freedom. In the case of university students, who came overwhelmingly from relatively comfortable middle-class backgrounds, this meant a conscious separation from the political and social values of their parents. Between 1968 and 1970, three states of emergency were declared on university campuses and the faculties taken by force. By 1973, every university campus in Spain was in permanent crisis. A generation was locked in 'an oedipal revolution aimed at the symbolic death of the parents'.[7]

Together with Catalan, and above all Basque, Nationalists, workers and students became synonymous with dissent. Regional Nationalists and organized labour had opposed the regime from the Civil War, but the opposition of middle-class, university-educated youth was a betrayal. As with the conciliar Church, this was a 'treason of the clerks' that hollowed out the regime from within, even as social peace crumbled under the impact of economic recession and spiralling discontent. In the 1970s, political and social cleavages were being played out between strikers and secret policemen, students and Civil Guardsmen in every major city in Spain. The street—that long-established locus of national life, the place where Spaniards ate, strolled, socialized, and forged a communal life—was no longer governed by the regime. The disjuncture between rulers and ruled could not have been sharper.

Such a disjuncture has been seen as a function of the regime's 'immobilism'. Economic development had introduced new pressures and dynamics into Spain, which now seemed increasingly out of step with a political apparatus that neither could nor would adapt to them. The use of repression in the 1970s was thus not a crisis measure determined by the circumstances of the decade, but the inevitable response of a regime that had not changed since the 1940s. Economic development and 'stabilization' were if not accidental then determined by international factors far outside the purview of the Spanish government.[8] The logic followed by the 'immobilism' argument is that of economic determinism: affluence and development had breached the dam of authoritarianism and, as political structures changed to reflect economic and demographic realities, dictatorship would give way to democracy. In such an analysis, political freedom becomes a kind of collective bargaining, and democracy a function of market capitalism. And in any case, the Franco regime was not static.[9] To suggest that it could have survived from 1939 with no serious challenge to its authority without adapting or changing is inherently implausible. The use of repression as a political policy changed during the 1940s and, more positively, economic 'stabilization' would not have been possible without the directive and coordinating power of the state.

Economic development was a *political* strategy and so by definition reformist. Its architects, the technocratic ministers of Opus Dei, made much more convincing politicians than they did economists, despite their emphasis on professional expertise. The reformist effects of development were also encouraged by other strategic changes, notably the relaxation of censorship in 1966 and the acceptance of some de facto rights of association, labour representation, and collective bargaining. Limited and contingent as they were, these were nevertheless civil rights, which may have broken down during the crisis years of the 1970s but were entirely absent in the 1940s. The differences between the two decades were very marked in several respects. The legal reconfigurations of the 1960s had helped to encourage the development of a public sphere that, as the regime found, was hard to curtail. Even the brutality unleashed after 1973 failed to crush the anti-Francoist opposition. The relationship between the state and its citizens had changed for ever. Though in organizational terms, the opposition was weak and fragmented, its public prominence helped to confirm the democratic culture that now existed among broad swathes of the Spanish population. Protest made such a culture visible, while those who protested were both example and symbol of resistance.

According to Víctor Pérez-Díaz, Spain's civil society 'had become to a large extent liberal democratic'.[10] But the state had also changed, not least as a result of the state-sponsored process of technocratic development. In terms of both capacity and vision—the abstract ability to 'see like a state'—Spain had come a long way down the road to modernity. Significantly, this had little to do with the dictator himself. A man of limited vision, Franco had to be convinced of the need for reform, which was implemented by technocratic ministers and functionaries who thereby took their reformist project inside the machinery of the state and gave the bureaucratic elite a real role in how the state was ordered. The *cuerpos* were active participants in the administration, and could also act in defence of their own interests. This tendency towards corporatism was eventually curbed by democratic governments, but the bureaucracy that administered the Franco regime was the same as that which implemented the transition to democracy after the dictator's death.[11] The bureaucrat Adolfo Suárez, for example, was appointed by King Juan Carlos as prime minister of what was still the Francoist state and went on to serve, in an apparently seamless transition, as prime minister of democratic Spain. The reformist, Christian Democrat *Tácito* group—which was to have considerable influence in elite circles during the construction of democracy—had its power base within the state bureaucracy. This liberal group, founded in 1973, was convinced that Francoism had become an impediment to further development, not least because it precluded closer relations with the European Union. Virtually all leading *Táctios* were civil servants, either in the *cuerpos* or the diplomatic corps, but few held political office.[12] As the case of *Tácito* suggested, the civil service's acquisition of power as well as expertise, together with its involvement in the project of rational capitalist development in Spain, allowed a separation the regime and state. In the final years of Francoism, the bureaucracy put some distance between itself and the dictatorship, constructing a state rather than a personal rule.

This process was an unforeseen result of the Opus Dei technocratic project begun in 1959.[13] For the technocratic vision of subordinating economic policy and development to the rationality of the market had broken the Falange's earlier dominance of the bureaucracy, together with its insistence on the primacy of political rationales in decision-making and, by implication, the complete identification between state and regime. When the technocrats were abruptly removed from government in 1973 the distance that already existed between state and regime became a gulf. The sacking of technocratic ministers, which so starkly revealed this central weakness, preceded its body blow, ETA's dramatic assassination of Franco's prime minister, Admiral Luis Carrero Blanco, on 20 December 1973.

This audacious act of terrorism changed the immediate course of Spanish history. A Madrid-based *etarra* commando placed a bomb under a manhole on the Calle Claudio Cuello, detonating it just as the PM's chauffeur-driven limousine drove back from daily mass, and sending the car to land several storeys up on a neighbouring building. Any hopes of a Francoist succession went with it. For Carrero Blanco was not only the general's prime minister but also his political heir, and the regime was now in its death-throes. Carrero Blanco seemed irreplaceable and his eventual successor, Arias Navarro, had neither political stature nor much support. The government was bereft of political options, and those on whom it had for so long relied were looking for the continuity of the state, but not necessarily the survival of the regime.

The post-1973 crisis was thus the crisis of Francoism, not of the Spanish state. Increasingly frail, the dictator was entering his eighties, the 'arthritic grip' of his dictatorship apparently mirroring his physical condition.[14] The final agony of the Franco regime was marked by a new international isolation (particularly marked after 1974) which saw the regime ostracized even as it tried to clamp down on the 'public order' problems caused by an increasingly restless society. Reverting to the brutal methods of the 1940s could not disguise the changed international context. The Second World War left Spain invisible during the 1940s but now it was a conspicuous exception to the western European norm, particularly after a neighbouring authoritarian regime was toppled in the Portuguese revolution of 1974. As a member of the United Nations, Spain was scrutinized by both governments and non-governmental organizations. Amnesty

International sent missions, the Minority Rights Group issued reports, the Vatican added its voice to appeals for clemency for those condemned to death, and Spanish embassies abroad were regularly targeted by demonstrators. After the five death sentences carried out on 27 September 1975, four embassies were set alight by protestors—that in Lisbon was sacked—while, at state level, thirteen ambassadors were withdrawn from Madrid, including those of all European Community (EC) countries except Ireland.[15]

Spain had become a *cause célèbre* among European human rights activists, which added to the government's difficulties. The political elites were divided, the Church estranged. Nor could Franco look to his original supporters; the political coalition which had brought him to power long ago during the civil war had disappeared. Demoted to a secondary role in the regime long before their usurpation by the Opus, the Falange had fragmented into various splinter groups. Though each one claimed a role as keeper of the true fascist flame, they were effectively reduced to an ungainly jostling for the very limited support that remained on the far right of the political spectrum. Here, they were joined by the remnants of the Traditionalist Communion but this was now only a minor part of the Carlist movement. Carlism had not only fractured but most of its adherents had also changed sides.

Long eclipsed by the Falange, Carlism had been reduced to a walk-on part in Franco's Spain, permitted a folkloric presence—most conspicuously during the annual commemoration of its 'martyrs' on Montejurra hill—but no high-level power. Carlism had never had a credible or defined political programme, achieving most success, as during the 1930s, as a vehicle for generalized reaction. After 1939, many were content with the terms offered by the Francoist victory but others—particularly those loyal to the principles of either dynastic monarchism or regional autonomy—became disenchanted with the regime. Carlist dissent developed even before Vatican II threw its most cherished identity into disarray. As defenders of true religion, the Carlists had made up in spiritual fervour what they lacked in political coherence, and the old certainties of Catholic 'tradition' came to an end with Rome's declaration on religious liberty. Carlism's inchoate creed was best understood emotionally, and, taking a lead from the new pretender, Carlos-Hugo, and his sisters, the 'red' princesses, a new generation transformed the identity they had as a birthright. The movement became a political party, which spoke of socialism and 'self-development', and declared itself among the opposition. In response, diehard traditionalists accused it of treason and betrayal while the regime closed Carlist papers, banned rallies, and excluded the 'royal' family from Spain.[16]

Carlism's reinvention was dramatic and exciting but it could not disguise the ebbing-away of support. The rediscovery of populism—which lay at the heart of Carlos-Hugo's new direction—was not enough in itself to bring the people back, particularly after internal divisions resulted in violent confrontations at Montejurra in 1976. Carlos-Hugo's faint hopes of succession became even less plausible after 1969 when Juan Carlos was confirmed as Franco's heir. But the regime's frigid reaction to the evolution of Carlism showed again the poverty of its situation. Challenges to authority multiplied during the 1970s, and the government's response was always repressive. This came from desperation: the outmoded institutions of an ailing dictator had no political solution (and probably no real political option) to offer and, despite the soldiers on the streets, the weakness of the regime was obvious. The reversion to brute force and 'disciplining' had profound consequences even among Franco's erstwhile adherents. For in behaving once again as an army of occupation, the military regime abandoned the discourses and strategies of legitimacy built up around social peace, economic prosperity, and political paternalism. This destruction of Francoism's fragile and contingent legitimacy did not come entirely from within. ETA's assassination of Carrero Blanco destroyed the regime's myth of invulnerability and, in the same year, the oil crisis cracked its reputation for sound economic management. While the dictatorship could hardly be blamed for the OPEC price rises, the sudden hike in the cost of oil damaged both the experience and the expectation of affluence. The peace of Franco was at an end.

Those dismayed by the prospect of street-fighting and determined to avoid political and social cleavage were increasingly convinced that dictatorship had no future. The legacy of Franco was becoming the preserve of far-right ultras and armed guerrilla bands, as international indifference to the dictator's death demonstrated. The general died during the night of 19 November 1975, after a prolonged deathbed agony. The dictator's faith may have lain with the holy relic—St Teresa's arm—that accompanied him in his final hours but it was the medical technology to which he was wired up that kept him alive. He was laid to rest in the Valle de los Caídos, the mausoleum built by Republican prisoners after the Civil War, in a requiem conspicuous for both its grandiloquent ceremony and the absence of foreign dignitaries. The massed crowds, mounted ceremonial guard, and solemn Catholic liturgies were observed by the vice president of the United States, but otherwise only by General Pinochet of Chile and Imelda Marcos. In contrast, King Juan Carlos' coronation was attended four days later by the presidents of France and Germany, the German prime minister, Britain's Lord Privy Seal and the Duke of Edinburgh. Neither Pinochet nor Marcos were invited, though the USA was, once again, represented by Nelson Rockefeller.[17]

On a visit to Madrid in 1970, Henry Kissinger had remarked that Spain was 'as if suspended, waiting for a life to end so that it could rejoin European history'.[18] But, as the contrasting spectacles of funeral and coronation showed, this was less the case for Spaniards than for those outside. The 1970s saw more political activity in Spain than any decade since the 1930s and the situation was fragile. Underground opposition alliances multiplied after Carrero Blanco's assassination, as did semi-legal democratic platforms, such as the Communist-inspired Junta Democrática or the socialist alternative, Plataforma de Convergencia Democrática. Franco's death led to little immediate—and less apparent—change. As one CCOO organizer in Barcelona put it: 'everyone waited for something to happen and nothing happened.'[19] Juan Carlos was now head of state but, as Franco's protégé and appointed heir, only those in his innermost circle were confident of his reformist ambitions. A hundred thousand Falangists still had the right to carry arms and, for all the progress that had been made towards a modern state administration, the military remained, segmented within the state, as a powerful constraint on any rapid or revolutionary change. The prime minister, Arias Navarro, stayed in post, despite the king's mistrust, ETA went on killing and, in response, police torturers and ultra-right-wing guerrillas acted with apparent impunity.

For many, things got worse, not better. This was certainly true in the Basque Country but in Cataluña too—where the number of new Catalan-language publications in 1976 finally equalled that of 1936—quasi-fascist groups carried out violent attacks on bookshops and publishing houses. In 1977, after the end of censorship, the renowned theatre group Els Joglars staged a work, *La torna*—a satire about torture and a tribute to the executed anarchist, Puig Antich—which led to some performers being imprisoned and others exiled.[20] Nor were reprisals confined to the nationalist periphery. On 24 January 1977 a small group of gunmen entered the offices run by a group of left-wing lawyers in the calle Atocha in Madrid. They lined up those inside against the wall and opened fire: five died, three of them instantly. The remaining three lawyers survived their wounds, though the only woman, Dolores González Ruíz, lost both her husband and her unborn child in what became known as the 'Atocha massacre'.

Radical lawyers' offices were vital to the left-wing struggle, essentially because the paternalist nature of Francoist labour legislation allowed for arbitration and some representation of workers' interests. The complexity of the regulation created numerous opportunities for legal involvement and, as the number of industrial disputes rose exponentially from the late 1960s, so did the number of law suits, which could act as showcases for the opposition. Radical law practices not only offered some kind of protected space for those working at the margins of the law, they also often helped to articulate the formal demands of those on strike. The leading radical lawyers in Barcelona represented as many as 100,000 workers between 1960 and 1975, their offices serving as an unofficial meeting place for those on strike. Law firms established local networks of inter-class solidarity, bringing together left-wing, but middle-class, professionals with men from the factory floor. As with neighbourhood associations and Church organizations, these 'horizontal' axes of communication contributed in no small way to the active and oppositional reconstruction of citizenship during the final years of the Franco regime.

The opposition's efforts to mobilize and represent industrial workers formed a crucial backdrop to the transition to democracy. As labour representation developed from the 1960s, so the unions looked to improve working conditions, including wages. With the crackdown on CCOO after 1968—the national coordinating committee was arrested in 1972—the struggle was also to establish free conditions of negotiation and representation, that is legal trade unions. There were local differences: more workplace leaders were involved in the opposition in Madrid, but those in Barcelona were more likely to take strike action. As the CCOO's 1972 decision to move to Barcelona showed, state surveillance was tight in Madrid and there was less support from the wider community. In contrast, Barcelona had stronger, more generalized anti-regime feeling than anywhere outside the Basque Country. The city had ninety neighbourhood associations (*asociaciones de vecinos*) by 1974, campaigning on local issues to do with urban infrastructure, housing, or welfare. Communist party militants were often active in setting up these associations, precisely so that they could mobilize discontent among the less politically committed. Neighbourhood associations were also legal, which suited the Communists' tactics of working through official channels where possible and of mobilizing the wider community. Residents' organizations encouraged women to mobilize, in marked contrast to both organized industrial labour and the clandestine Communist Party. In a far cry from the women's demonstrations orchestrated by the Sección Femenina, young women from the high-rise estates marched in protest at local conditions while 'grandmothers kept watch for the police armed with tin whistles'.[21] The separation between the regime and wider society was being enacted on the streets of Barcelona for all to witness.

The semi-legal nature of the union struggle—the entryist tactics and search for legal recourse and protected space—meant that, on the factory floor, there was often no clear-cut division between opposition and regime figures. CCOO's long-established strategy of standing for election in the regime syndicates meant that the same people often held office in both sets of unions. Labour militants were also adept at public protest: the streets of Barcelona were regularly filled with strikers and demonstrators, reclaiming public space for the workers rather than the regime. In July 1974, the area of Baix Llobregat was brought to a standstill by a three-day general strike after a specific industrial dispute was made into a community affair by petitions, sit-ins, and street collections. Unlike most strikes—which often resulted in punitive dismissals and stoppages—Baix Llobregat was a conspicuous success, mobilizing both labour and the community. But it had originally been called by the *official* syndicate representatives, not, apparently, by the opposition at all.[22]

The workplace elections held during 1975 left the division between those within the regime and those outside it even less distinct. To contest the elections, the CCOO instigated a united slate (CUD: Cadidaturas Unitarias y Democráticas or United Democratic Candidature), which won a clear victory in all the major Catalan factories and took most of the posts in the local branches of the official syndicates. Just as the CCOO had first emerged from within the Francoist trade unions in Madrid in 1964, so it now dominated their grass roots, agitating for free representation from a legal space defined by the regime. Such a strategy showed not only a pragmatism honed by years of clandestine activity in the underground Communist Party but also, at a wider level, a tacit acceptance of the structures and principles of market capitalism. In the 1970s, free collective bargaining, often with a strongly unionized workforce, was the norm throughout western Europe. Playing by the rules of the capitalist game also characterized the other side of the fence; Arias Navarro's first, hardline cabinet, for example, contained a former president of the *Telefónica* as vice-president and, at under-secretary level, several members of *Tácito*.

It was this parallel process of divergence and convergence, both within the state and without, that laid ground for the transition to democracy. There was, on the one hand, an obvious disjuncture between an authoritarian state and increasingly democratic society, within which there was, however, some convergence. For example, employers and unions spoke a common language of collective bargaining, ignoring the supposedly official framework of state arbitration. On the other hand, cracks were appearing *within* the regime as it became clear that many were looking for state stability, but saw no necessary relationship between that and the continuation of either Francoism or the government of the day. The ban on free trade unions was rescinded in April 1977, some time after they had already been re-established in practice. Indeed, with democratic elections scheduled for June, some unions had already opened offices and distributed membership cards,[23] repeating a wider pattern of de facto change followed by de jure ratification. It would take a determined act of political will on the part of those governing Spain if they were to control the process of transition to democracy.

DEMOCRATS

The fracturing of Francoism created the space, both real and metaphorical, for an antagonistic and highly visible occupation of the public sphere. Strikes, demonstrations, riots, and the mass public funerals held for the lawyers killed in Atocha and, much more regularly, fallen *etarras* in the Basque Country testified to the end of Francoism. What would replace it, though, was neither clear nor certain. Such an open-ended process of regime transition threw into question not only the nature of the state but also the definition of citizenship and, as a consequence, the relationship individual citizens had both to the state and to each other. This was a fluid, fragile process, which was not dominated by the organized anti-Franco opposition, despite its apparent monopoly of public space.

The strength of organized labour was more apparent than real. Militants were a minority even during exciting times and the level of strikes and stoppages made many fear for a prosperous future, which was after all what most working families, as well as economic policy makers, aspired to. Police brutality or a fear that violence was being condoned by the state led to mass protest: tens of thousands accompanied the cortege for the murdered Atocha lawyers, their respectful and disciplined behaviour pointing the contrast between democratic protest and illegitimate violence. Here, the opposition read the public mood. Popular revulsion was instrumental in ensuring that the ultra gunmen responsible for the massacre were brought to justice, in a trial which highlighted their links to the Falange and the neo-fascist party, Fuerza Nueva.[24] Public interventions occurred at the key points of the transition process, making the 'people' a protagonist in the transition. Spain's largest ever wave of strikes took place in early 1976 confirming the political need for democratization and affecting the course that this would take.[25] Profound discontent with the slow pace of reform was instrumental in forcing Arias Navarro's resignation.

Popular sovereignty lay at the heart of democratization, but a public mood does not make 'the people' into a political actor. Many groups spoke in their name—among them the trade unions, neighbourhood associations, and a myriad of political parties—but none could claim truly to represent them. The everyday business of the genuine grassroots organizations was essentially parochial, though this was often disguised, particularly in the labour movement, by the common ground between their grievances and anti-Francoist political aspirations.

In Madrid, for example, the *vecinos* associations gave every appearance of a concerted, inter-class social movement, though the city's high degree of social segregation meant that local associations were often dominated by a single class and always depended on the keen commitment of a few activists.[26] There was a close correlation between *vecinos* militants and membership of either the Communist Party Or the Maoist Organización Revolucionaria de Trabajadores (ORT: Workers' Revolutionary Organization), which was insignificant at national level. Locally, their success came thorough mobilizing on single issues. Campaigns, such as that to prevent the development of La Vaguada, an area of undeveloped land amidst the high-rise housing of El Pilar, attracted a very broad base of support, including anarchists, ecologists, Maoists, Socialists, Communists, the parish priest, and local residents. The political parties negotiated a solution with the developers whereby they provided community facilities and open spaces in return for controlled building. This was an attainable solution that suited the electoral strategies of the Socialists and Communists. For while the neighbourhood associations' strong territorial identity allowed them potentially to offer an alternative form of popular representation, in fact the groups they represented simply became constituencies. Political parties became the instinctive channel of communication between people and government.

The left-wing parties needed links with the grass roots, not to encourage alternative models of democracy but to show how the parties represented the people and responded to their demands. During the 1970s, both Communists and Socialists were avowedly class-based, Marxist parties, a radical stance that encouraged the association with local activists. In the higher echelons of the Socialist Party, though, an oedipal revolt at the beginning of the 1970s brought young men to prominence, among them Felipe González, Alfonso Guerra, and Javier Solana. In contrast to this visible process of generational change, the Communists were still led by the Civil War veteran Santiago Carrillo. The strict, even brutal, discipline of democratic centralism that had served the Communist Party so well in clandestinity now began to count against it, particularly once the party was legal and there were no longer penalties for political activity. Party boundaries were becoming much more fluid. There was, for example, an influx of Christian Democrats into the Socialist Party, among them the prominent Catholic lawyer Gregorio Peces-Barba, defence counsel in the Burgos trials.[27]

Such collaboration was crucial to the successful repositioning of the Socialist Party after 1975. The latent but keenly felt threat of popular mobilization helped bring Socialism back to prominence during the transition. Like the Communists, Socialists could act as representatives of the grass-roots opposition. The fear of uncontrollable unrest led a new and able generation of Socialist leaders to believe that *ruptura* (breaking with the past) could most easily be achieved in collaboration with progressive *aperturista* elements inside the regime. Such a realistic appraisal of the political imperatives of transition allowed the Socialists to wrest the initiative from the Communist Party. For Spain's dictatorial regime was not destroyed but dismantled, the result of complex, and often precarious, negotiations between progressives within the regime and those outside it.

Despite Franco's death, the law of the land was that of the dictatorship. The corporate, elite nature of the Francoist political system meant that opposition leaders were brought within the loop—there were even rumours of Carrillo being smuggled in the boot of a car to see Juan Carlos—but the dispersed nature of the opposition helped to keep the mechanisms of transition within the governing elites. Those who implemented democratization in Spain acted within a political culture established during the final years of Francoism. Indeed, the most remarkable fact about the Spanish transition to democracy is that it represented an act of political will on the part of those who governed. There was no obvious *ruptura*, but a state-sponsored process of legal transition, achieved under Arias Navarro's successor. Adolfo Suárez persuaded the left to abandon any clear break with the past, and the right, including the army, to accept legal reforms.[28] As a career bureaucrat and former minister and secretary-general of Franco's *Movimiento*, Suárez's new position emphasized the technocratic character of the Spanish state and the separation between that state and the Franco regime. For Suárez would devise, or 'translate', new political rules in such a way as to satisfy most of those within the old regime and most of those who actively opposed it.

The delicacy of this balancing act emphasized the fragility of the transition: if either part faltered than the entire process would be thrown into doubt. However, the rewards were high, for those constructing democracy were claiming a double legitimacy: that of the people and that of the law. The first was inevitable. If the decisions made by the governors failed to resonate among the governed, they would fail, which would not necessarily prevent democracy in Spain but would ensure that it came about in a messy and uncontrolled way. The paradoxical strategy of acting within the law was, though, not simply a tactic to appease the right. Legitimation is intrinsic to the act of ruling; those in power have to convince themselves, as well as their subjects, of their fitness to govern. Acting within legality offered a powerful legitimation to those elites who had once identified with Francoism and also resonated outside those reduced circles, particularly among those who were neither active within the regime nor actively opposed to it. Such people had no particular voice during the transition, but they still needed to be convinced. Civil society is heterogeneous and cannot be identified with any one political option. But it is from within society that the rules and assumptions governing everyday behaviour come—how things should work, how people should behave—and it is these rules and assumptions which in turn determine whether or not political rule is legitimate.[29]

In this sense, Adolfo Suárez was the lynchpin of the transition. Once appointed as premier in July 1976, Suárez was able, with the full support of the king, to engineer a speedy and apparently smooth process of legal democratization. The dismantling of the Francoist regime began almost immediately. While Suárez held regular meetings with opposition leaders—confirming Felipe González in his belief that a freely negotiated democratic constitution would be the *ruptura* the opposition was seeking—a law of political reform was elaborated, carefully and privately negotiated and, in September, approved by the council of ministers. Scrupulous adherence to legality required that the law then be ratified by the national council of the single party, or *Movimiento*, and then passed by a two-thirds majority in the Cortes. This was achieved: on 18 November, 425 Cortes delegates voted the reform into existence and themselves out of it. Only 59 deputies voted against this spectacular act of political harakiri, with 34 either abstaining or absent.[30] On 15 December, a national referendum also accepted the turn of events with 94 per cent of a 77 per cent turnout voting in favour of the political reform law. Despite the opposition's unconvincing call for abstentions, the referendum conferred, and was immediately seen as conferring, considerable legitimacy on the transition process. In an incipient democracy, the people's voice could not be ignored.

The law of political reform established in broad terms the constitutional groundwork for democracy, delineating a bicameral Cortes and providing for free elections, to be held under the auspices of the existing government. The executive thus retained considerable power over the transition process: forty seats in the senate were reserved for royal appointees and elections were eventually called, for 14 June 1977, by royal decree. In order to fight the election, old political parties were legalized—the Communists on 9 April, a mere two days before the elections were convened—and new ones created. Former minister Manuel Fraga attempted to mobilize 'sociological Francoism', establishing a conservative party, Alianza Popular (AP: Popular Alliance), that clearly looked to capture the legacy of the dictatorship. More significant was the group which coalesced around Suárez, the Unión de Centro Democrático (UCD: Union of the Democratic Centre). The backbone of this highly contingent political grouping was former members of the Francoist bureaucracy who shared a common culture of face-to-face negotiations, horse-trading, and political favours. *Tácito* reformers thus rubbed shoulders with lower level provincial bureaucrats who had come up through the ranks of the *Movimiento*. The Church's refusal to endorse any particular political option also benefited the UCD as it provided a home for several small Christian Democrat groupings. Cardinal Tarancón was adamant that, in terms of party politics, the Church had to be neutral, a decision that had profound ramifications for the nature of democratic politics in Spain. Practising Catholics were found in all political parties, from Blas Piñar's ultra-rightist Fuerza Nueva to the Communists, and in the UCD they lined up alongside some small liberal and social democrat factions as well as the erstwhile apparatchiks.

Aided by their access to the governmental machinery, the UCD emerged from the 1977 polls as the overall victors. The continuity of the state amid the ruins of the regime seemed assured, particularly as the same year also saw Spain's most significant fiscal reform since the 1840s. The country finally had an income tax, and the basic building block for strengthening and modernizing the edifice of the state was now in place. The UCD's margin of victory on 15 June was narrow, however; Suárez's coalition won 34.3 per cent of the vote but the Socialists had taken 28.5 per cent. The Socialist success came as a surprise to many: commentators throughout Europe had expected the Communists to emerge with an Italian-style hegemony on the left. But all those towards the far ends of the political spectrum polled poorly: the Communists gained 9.3 per cent of the vote and Alianza Popular (AP) 8.4 per cent. Anti-system, ultra-right parties fared far worse: Fuerza Nueva, for example, won just over 5,000 votes, a derisory 0.03 per cent, while the vote for all neo-fascist factions combined did not amount to 2 per cent of the total.[31]

The 1977 election results did show a broad left–right division[32] that appeared to reflect Spain's historic divide: there was a correlation between CEDA votes in 1936 and UCD votes in 1977 and an even stronger correlation between Popular Front votes in 1936 and left-wing votes in 1977. Even after the long years of dictatorship, those born into republican families voted overwhelmingly for the socialist left. Conversely, only 14 per cent of those from Francoist families voted Socialist as opposed to 40 per cent of them who supported the UCD.[33] Despite these resilient republican identities, the similarities with the 1930s were more apparent than real. For the UCD, aided by its apparent separation from the old regime and certainly unencumbered by any association with the diehard Francoist bunker, had eclipsed both AP and the non-democratic right by emphasizing its occupation of the centre ground. Its principal campaigning slogan was 'The centre is democracy', elaborated in some posters to include 'Because it impedes confrontation and establishes dialogue.'[34] Centrism was presented as the key strategy for avoiding the conflicts of the past, and the electorate responded to Suárez's calls to 'dedramaticize' Spanish politics. The UCD's majority was a resounding endorsement for his strategy of legal reform and the 1977 elections established the transition upon the centre ground.

A widespread fear of the consequences of derailing democratization conditioned both elite decisions and the popular mood, creating a new discourse of consensus.[35] The spectre of civil conflict thus stalked the transition, brought to the fore by every violent demonstration or terrorist outrage and sharpened by the real possibility of military intervention. The fragility of the transition was often palpable, and the development of a shared public rhetoric of negotiation and consensus emphasized stability over the volatility of the streets. The symbolic universe of democracy began with a break from the past. At Juan Carlos' investiture, Cardinal Tarancón had asked that he be 'king of all Spaniards'—a phrase used by the monarch on every possible occasion thereafter—and that his reign be one 'of justice for all . . . with everyone subjected to the rule of law and with the law always at the service of the community'[36]. The transition developed its own symbolic language—that of harmony, dialogue, and above all of *convivencia* (living together). Tarancón's sentiments were echoed in Juan Carlos' announcement of Suárez's appointment, which spoke of 'a new generation' that could 'through the work of all Spaniards . . . make possible the clear and peaceful participation of all citizens in . . . our political future.'[37]

The acceptance of democratization, as both discourse and event, was reflected in the voters' rejection of Fraga and Carrillo for Suárez and González. The contrast went beyond party leaders. Thirteen of AP's sixteen elected deputies had also sat in Franco's Cortes and their average age in 1977 was 54; in contrast, three-quarters of the UCD's deputies were aged under 50, as were nearly 80 per cent of the Socialists. The Socialists and Communists may not have abandoned Marxism but they had jettisoned republicanism, accepting constitutional monarchy and the national flag. In contrast AP still spoke the language of Francoism, framing their manifesto around social peace, national unity, and opposing 'the legalization of communist, terrorist, and separatist groups'. This failure to accept political pluralism and civil rights, or even to understand the political ground that was now being contested, prevented the AP from becoming a significant political force during the transition. Similarly, the Communists were never able to shake off their association with the violence of the Civil War. Both the memory of the war and the rhetorical tropes of Francoism reminded Spaniards of a time of political immaturity, when they were told of their inability to govern themselves. Now, though, the enemy had become an adversary, one with whom dialogue and negotiation were possible. The transition was an act of political maturity, its terms far removed from the paternalistic infantilization of Spaniards that had held sway under Franco.

Moderation, rational discussion, and control were thus fundamental not only to the transition but also to how most Spaniards wanted that transition to be. The praxis of consensual politics became both the symbol of democracy and a moral good in its own right. Evidence of this was found in the Socialist Party's congress in May 1979 when González resigned in order to force the party to abandon its self-definition as Marxist. Its 'Bad Godsburg' was presented as a milestone on the road to modernization, a journey that had also been travelled by the German Socialist Party, the SPD, and would be by the British Labour Party. It is also commonly referred to as a transition within a transition, a conceit that reinforces the connection between politics and executive control. The electorate may have rejected any Francoist salvage operation but they still valued 'order and peace', accepted as essential by 80 per cent of survey respondents in 1975.[38]

As economic recession threatened to destabilize Spain, social peace was a sensitive issue. The political imperatives of democratization meant that no coherent economic policy was elaborated even in a recession and, by the summer of 1977, inflation was running at 29 per cent, the balance of payments deficit was worsening rapidly, and the peseta had just been devalued. In response to the crisis, the government negotiated an austerity package with the Socialist and Communist parties, which pegged wage rises at 22 per cent and introduced monetarist measures in an effort to bring down inflation. Organized labour was not directly involved in this agreement, known as the Moncloa pact, but the unions recommended that their members accept the wage ceiling, both to contain unemployment and to protect the democratic settlement. Paradoxically, the Moncloa pacts thus reaffirmed the political imperatives of the transition, the stabilization of politics and the redefinition and revaloration of citizenship. Though far from being a solution to Spain's economic difficulties, the pacts demonstrated the left's commitment to negotiation. The rather ambiguous role of the unions in the austerity measures in one sense confirmed the elite nature of transition politics but in another showed that the people could not be left outside the process, even if they were not shaping it. For citizenship is both conferred by law and created through civic activity and discourse. There was thus a sense in which democratic citizenship came into being through the 1978 constitution, which aimed to 'guarantee democratic co-existence [*convivencia*]' and so established equality before the law regardless of 'birth, race, sex, religion, opinion, or any other personal or social circumstance or condition whatsoever'. The age of majority was set at eighteen, and no Spaniard might be deprived of his or her nationality.[39] In practice, however, such an understanding of citizenship was already in operation, not least in the referenda that approved, first the law of political reform and then, on 6 December 1978, the constitution itself.

The constitution was the fundamental step towards normalizing Spanish politics and both the document and its elaboration testified to the resolution of several historic cleavages.[40] Popular campaigns for political amnesty—supported by many parliamentarians—insisted that Spaniards should not be imprisoned or deprived of voting rights for political crimes or, as others might see them, active acts of citizenship. Such a law was passed in 1977, making proclaiming the rule of law much simpler. By now, there was no longer a religious question: the constitution acknowledged 'the religious beliefs of Spanish society' and committed the public power to 'relations of co-operation with the Catholic Church and other denominations', but privileged no confession over any other. The Church's supposed 'neutrality' was a key element in the consensual process, but any belief in its 'apoliticism' was soon shown to be naive. The Church continued to expect a public role, lobbying on particular areas of interest, notably education, family life, and reproductive policy. The search for state protection was, however, over: reconciled to democratic pluralism, the Church now campaigned on policy issues, acting essentially as a pressure group.[41] The other burning question of the 1930s—land reform—was also effectively resolved before the transition took place. The constitution alluded to social justice but there was no pressing rural need to satisfy. Old divisions over land ownership had been made redundant by economic development; the price of oil was now far more important than the right to cultivation.

The parameters of the new democracy were in many ways already established by the 1970s—equal citizenship, rule of law, freedom of association, freedom of worship, private property. Without such common ground, consensus would have been impossible, and it was far from being automatic in any case. Emphasizing the consensual nature of the constitutional process testifies to its considerable achievement. Yet, such an emphasis also reinforces the perception of democratization as a high political affair, carried out by governmental elites. Who else, after all, could negotiate, broker pacts, and arrange compromises? But though the constitutional process marginalized non-parliamentary interest groups, the definition of who were to be citizens of the new Spain was still relatively fluid. Ideas of participative democracy continued to inform other areas of governance, notably local administration, as the *vecinos* associations campaigned for local participation in municipal government and planning. Municipal elections were held in April 1979, leading to a clear Socialist–Communist victory in Madrid. As a result, neighbourhood councils were established, on which political parties were represented alongside *vecinos* committees, sports clubs, cultural groups and other civic associations. This was the citizens' movement's greatest victory, but it proved unable to retain an autonomous identity. Some activists moved into politics; others returned to community work or private life. The proud claims of participative democracy dissipated, in part because they could be met through more conventional, parliamentary channels. Significantly, in the general elections held in March 1979 the centre and right had won a majority of Madrid votes.[42]

In a similar way, 60 per cent of those who voted for the UCD in 1977 were female, yet women received almost no specific attention during the transition, despite the historic problem of female citizenship.[43] Women's associations—notably the housewives' associations that had done much to foster an active civic engagement among women during the 1960s and

1970s—failed to achieve even the limited presence attained by trade unions and neighbourhood groups. As consumer groups, the housewives' associations could have been incorporated into mainstream political discourse just as the responsible, patriotic home-maker had been wooed by other centre-right European governments at times of national reconstruction. The consistent prioritizing of parliamentary goals over economic ones during the transition did nothing to help the idea of the consumer-citizen, which suffered from the Franco regime's promotion of the consumer-housewife and, quite possibly, from the left's general discomfort with 'materialism'. The housewives' associations also remained determinedly non-political in a party sense, though they adopted the language of democracy and *convivencia*, campaigning for work within the home to be given the same status as paid employment.

Such campaigns fell on deaf ears. Though no one ever seriously suggested that adult women should not be full citizens in the sense of nationality or enfranchisement, those who governed—rather than simply voted—were gendered male. This notion of active citizenship extended down to the 'breadwinner' or head of family, even within the citizens' movement. One neighbourhood association in Madrid typically voted in favour of a husband attending meetings rather than his wife as his contribution was more important.[44] To the centre-right, housewives were irrelevant, to the left they were reactionary, a view apparently confirmed by the existence of parallel, feminist women's organizations, many of them led by Communist Party activists, for whom gender equality would only be found outside the home, in the public world of work. Given the impossibility of creating a single constituency out of such a disparate group as 'women', the left's assumptions held sway. Even though in the mid-1970s only 30 per cent of Spanish women were in the workforce, it was widely assumed by those interested in such matters that both citizenship and emancipation required education, paid employment, and fewer domestic responsibilities.

During the turbulent 1970s, many younger people participated in citizens' movements and experimented with social and communal housing, Christian base communities, labour agitation, and other forms of radical urban living. The belief that the personal was political profoundly affected a generation of activists but the effect it had on the wider population was hard to discern. Twentieth-century Europe had, for example, seen various experiments with radical feminism, from women-only political parties in Weimar Germany to separatist lesbian communes in 1980s London, but all had floundered. Modern European women identified themselves in many ways and only rarely did gender identification take precedence over all others. 'Women' remained a mythical political category: the 'women's vote', like the Catholic one, was spread across the political spectrum.

The greatest danger for democracy came from much more tightly defined and coherent groups, notably those non-Spanish Spaniards in Cataluña and the Basque Country. Years of discrimination and, in particular, the ferocious repression unleashed on the Basque Country meant that communal identities were too strong to be dissipated by the generic egalitarian guarantees of the 1978 constitution. And the fact that these rights and liberties were being conferred by a central, elite, Spanish authority was a problem for many. ETA did not abandon its violent fight against the Spanish state after Franco's death, and, indeed, killed more people per year during the transition to democracy than it had done under the dictatorship.[45] The effects of blanket repression in the Basque Country were such as to rewrite historical memory. It was generally believed that, from 1937, when the Basque Country fell during the Civil War, the Franco regime had treated the area punitively. Yet, this punishment for being Basque—which was indeed meted out after 1968—did not substantially affect the post-Civil War Basques, who fared better than many of their fellow Republicans, protected as they were by Catholicism.[46] By the time democracy returned to Spain, however, those earlier times had been overlaid by more recent experiences of repression and a powerful nationalist myth. A belief in the 'occupation' of the Basque Country meant that more people voted 'no' in the referendum on the 1978 constitution here than anywhere else in Spain: in some provinces only a minority voted yes. 51.1 per cent of the Basque electors abstained—as they had been advised to do by the PNV which had not been included in the constitutional *ponencia*—and, of those who voted, 23.5 per cent said no.[47]

Despite the Basques, the 1978 constitution passed into law approved by 88 per cent of those who expressed an opinion, though a national abstention rate of nearly 33 per cent brought that figure down to 59 per cent of the electorate as a whole. Even without Basque recidivism, the question of regional minorities was the most difficult for the framers of the constitution, faced with, on the one hand, ETA violence and, on the other, an intransigent and discontented military determined to defend the national integrity of Spain. As many *etarras* acted in hope of provoking a coup d'état, and as ETA still attracted little condemnation in the Basque Country, the cost of error was potentially very high. Forty years of Francoism had left an indelible association between centralizing nationalism and authoritarian dictatorship. Retaining a unitary state was both impossible and undesirable but federalism would not be countenanced by either the right or the army. The constitutional solution was asymmetric devolution. Article 2 declared the constitution to be 'based on the indissoluble unity of the Spanish Nation, common and indivisible *patria* of all Spaniards, and recognizes and guarantees the right to autonomy of the nationalities and regions of which it is comprised . . .'.

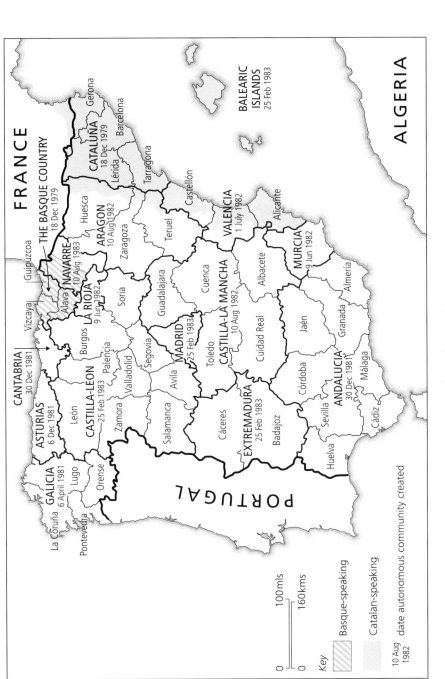

FRANCE

THE BASQUE COUNTRY
18 Dec 1979

CATALUÑA
18 Dec 1979

Gerona

Barcelona

Lérida

Tarragona

Castellón

Huesca

ARAGON
10 Aug 1982

Zaragoza

Teruel

VALENCIA
1 July 1982

Alicante

BALEARIC
ISLANDS
25 Feb 1983

ALGERIA

Guipúzcoa

Vizcaya

NAVARRE
10 Aug 1983

Álava

LA RIOJA
9 Jun 1982

Soria

Guadalajara

Cuenca

MURCIA
9 Jun 1982

Almería

Granada

Albacete

CASTILLA-LA MANCHA
10 Aug 1982

Cuidad Real

Jaén

Málaga

CANTABRIA
30 Dec 1981

Burgos

Palencia

Valladolid

Segovia

MADRID
25 Feb 1983

Toledo

Ávila

ASTURIAS
6 Dec 1981

CASTILLA-LEÓN
25 Feb 1983

León

Zamora

Salamanca

Cáceres

EXTREMADURA
25 Feb 1983

Badajoz

Córdoba

Sevilla

ANDALUCIA
30 Dec 1981

Cádiz

Huelva

GALICIA
6 April 1981

Lugo

Orense

Pontevedra

La Coruña

PORTUGAL

Democratic Spain, 1978–2002

100mls

160kms

0

0

Key

Basque-speaking

Catalan-speaking

10 Aug
1982   date autonomous community created

This 'extraordinary', and certainly paradoxical, article seemed 'both to rule out regional autonomy . . . and also specifically to rule it in'.[48] The profound ambiguity was reinforced in article 8, which gave the armed forces the duty of defending Spain's territorial integrity even though the state—which was itself far from clearly defined—was given exclusive competence over the military (article 149.1.4). Compromise was an inevitable result of consensual praxis; the aim had been to elaborate an acceptable founding document rather than a precise charter for government. The discrediting of centralist solutions had also led to an uncertainty as to what the nation actually was. Constitutional compromise was thus a function of the competing ideas of Spain that existed in the minds of many Spaniards.[49] Understandings of nationhood are never precise, and identities overlap, often inchoately, for both individuals and communities. But once the 1978 constitution had passed into law, the questions changed from ones of principle to those of politics. The constitution set the legal—and in many ways the imaginative—foundations for the future development of centre–periphery relations in Spain.

The new constitutional arrangements guaranteed an open-ended process of asymmetric devolution. The 'historic' regions—Galicia, Cataluña, and the Basque Country—proceeded swiftly to autonomy, the right to which was clearly granted in the constitution. There was, though, no *definition* of autonomy, which had to be painstakingly negotiated, particularly as the principle of asymmetric devolution meant that its terms differed in each case. The Basque Country, whose statute was negotiated by the PNV, despite its ambivalence towards the constitution, gained direct tax-raising powers in recognition of its historic foral rights; Cataluña, in contrast, had most of its revenue as grants from the central state. Their respective statutes were approved—first by parliament and then in regional referenda—in 1979 and autonomous elections were held in March 1980. Abstention rates were high—40.6 per cent in the Basque region and 37.9 per cent in Cataluña—but the results were clear. The PNV, with 38.8 per cent of the vote, won a solid majority against the Socialists, though the only successful anti-system party in Spain, Herri Batasuna, took 16.4 per cent of the votes. Cataluña had no terrorist problem and the centrist Convergència i Unió (CiU: Convergence and Union) won a narrow majority in the Generalitat, providing its first elected post-Civil War president, Jordi Pujol.[50]

These first statutes led to an outbreak of 'autonomy fever' as all the remaining regions applied for autonomy, as they were obliged to do so. The process—and, indeed, the very idea of the *estado de las autonomías*— was a powerful reassertion of the regional basis of Spanish identity. Valen-cia, Navarre, and the Canaries—what might be called the 'semi-historic' regions—were allowed an intermediate status and proceeded faster than the other incipient *autonomías*. Such regions undoubtedly had distinct cultural personalities, but even in Catalan-speaking Valencia, struggles over the relationship between regionalism, centralism, and nationalism were by no means all one way. The famous *fallas* became the site of one such struggle as right-wing anti-catalanist regionalists fought with left-wing Valencian nationalists for control of this quintessentially Valencian fiesta.[51] Non-nationalist regional movements developed in many parts of Spain, often, as in the Valencian case, in response to more clamorous local nationalisms, but always reworking Spanish national identity.[52] For while autonomy irrevocably changed Spain's territorial identities, it did not destroy the claims of the centre, or the place this held in the identity of Spaniards. The region's new-found prominence in the guise of *autonomía* did not make the category unproblematic. Just as national identities are often less visible at regional level, so regional identities may be far less apparent at municipal or parish level. Even in the case of the Basques, Catalans, and *galegos*, regional autonomy was not the result of a primordial or long-lasting sense of the nation but the concrete experience of repression and a reaction to state power.

Autonomy introduced a new dynamic into the relationship between nationalism and regionalism in Spain. Those regions with separate languages and historical institutions reasserted them: the *ikurriña* flew again in the Basque Country and 'Els Segadors' was sung throughout Cataluña. The flags and anthems of the non-historic regions were generally decided through competitions. If the region as *autonomía* was to survive, then it had to be invented. Regional and municipal governments financed cultural events and exhibitions; savings banks and universities funded local research projects; regional-studies titles flooded the bookshops. In those areas where regional identities were strongest, the result was an increasingly emphatic cultural and political identity. The *Diada*, or Catalan national day, became a noted festival—the 1977 one had seen over a million people demonstrate in Barcelona for the return of the Generalitat—and the Catalan language not only recuperated its former strength but soon surpassed it. And in both Cataluña and the Basque Country, general as well as regional election results consistently supported devolution.

Devolution was the trickiest and potentially least consensual question facing those looking to construct democracy in Spain. The constitutional compromise and the subsequent autonomy statutes could not have been seen by anyone as an end to the problem but they did suggest the beginning of a solution. This in itself, however, was difficult for those diehard, centralizing Castilian nationalists for whom the unity of Spain was still couched in Francoist terms. And the highest concentration of such nationalists were to be found in the military, which remained an unresolved question for democracy in Spain. For, despite the enhanced strength of the Spanish state, it still could not be assumed that the military was its servant, at the orders of whichever legitimate government happened to be in power. The Franco regime had made the army subservient to the dictator—succeeding, for example, in implementing the kind of professional reform that had eluded previous governments—but only by pandering to its vanity. The armed forces were, supposedly, the guardians of Spain's future; the 'defence' of Spain lay in eternal vigilance against internal enemies. The ideological nature of this threat perception was given material form in the deployment of troops, which were stationed around major cities, in effect as security cordons.[53]

Already aggrieved by the legalization of the Communist Party announced over an Easter weekend when high-ranking officers were out of town, military sensibilities were further inflamed by the rapid moves towards devolution. The Francoist state's repressive response to the terrorist problem had deliberately conflated ETA and the Basque people: by granting autonomy, the democratic regime seemed to be rewarding the internal enemy. ETA's policy of targeting military personnel exacerbated these feelings: 171 military and police officers were killed between 1979 and 1980. Despite this dangerous counterpoint, the fundamental problem was the inability of large sections of the military to accept political and cultural pluralism in Spain. Without such pluralism, democracy could not exist but democracy played little part in military culture. In 1981, an estimated 25 per cent of recruits to Spain's foremost military academy were from families who supported 'ultra' parties, mostly Fuerza Nueva. Pérez Galdós' claim in the 1880s that 'military men consider themselves to be a class apart, like a state within a state' still seemed to hold true. Internal recruitment was a major factor in determining the character of the armed forces: in the period 1978–81, 60 per cent of army officers had fathers who had pursued a military career and the same was true for 74.5 per cent of naval officers and 44.3 per cent of those in the air force. That these figures represented a decline from previous decades simply showed how engrained the problem was.[54]

Coming from predominantly Castilian military families, educated in military schools and academies, often married to officers' daughters, it is hardly surprising that the upper echelons of the armed forces remained ideologically separated from most of society during the transition. As they were also unreconciled to the new regime, the potential for some kind of military intervention was very great. However, when a coup finally came, it owed much to the vacillations of the UCD government which had come to be perceived as directionless. Suárez was increasingly uncomfortable in the position of premier and, despite a second general election victory, he resigned in 1981. The UCD had attempted some reform of the military—notably the rationalization of the command structure through a single defence ministry—but had done little either to woo the armed forces or to deal firmly with those plotting a *golpe* or coup d'état. Thus, when Lieutenant-Colonel Antonio Tejero of the Civil Guard marched into the Cortes on 23 February 1981—just as the deputies were preparing to vote on Suárez's successor—he was already known to the authorities as a *golpista*. Tejero's intention was to hold the political class prisoner (and hostage) and so disarticulate constitutional government. As he entered the chamber, gun drawn, virtually all the deputies sensibly dived for cover. Among those who did not were Santiago Carrillo, who can have been under no illusion as to the danger he was in, and the career officer, General Gutiérrez Mellado who marched to the front—where he was joined by Adolfo Suárez—and ordered Tejero to remember his oath of loyalty and obey a superior officer. The political histories of these three men could hardly have been more different but their responses showed very similar understandings of dignity and personal courage.

As Tejero stormed the chamber, the veteran General Milans del Bosch brought tanks on the streets of Valencia and General Alfonso Armada began a duplicitous game aimed at implicating the king. The political aims of the plotters remained confused: Tejero aspired to a Latin-American style junta, Milans del Bosch to a Primo de Rivera style dictatorship, and the less conspicuous but more dangerous Armada to a Gaullist-style national government. There was a rather Ruritanian theatricality to the turn of events but, as everyone in Spain knew, this was democracy's most dangerous moment. With the government held prisoner, the political initiative fell to the king whose role as commander-in-chief was in any case crucial. Armada failed in his bid to become the king's intermediary with the rebels. Rather, the king began an urgent round of telephone diplomacy with commanding officers and military governors across the land. Educated at the Zaragoza military academy, with stints in the naval and air force academies as well, Juan Carlos was a trained soldier, who used his personal and professional contacts to the full. At 1.15 a.m., the king addressed the nation on television. The crown would not tolerate attempts to interrupt the 'democratic process determined by the constitution and approved by the Spanish people'. The king repeatedly ordered soldiers and officers to return to their barracks, and made it clear to Milans del Bosch that he would neither abdicate nor support the coup. If the rebels were to prevail, they would have to shoot the king.[55]

The king's actions were decisive, but so were the swift actions of the police who cordoned off the Cortes, and the under-secretaries and civil servants who set up an interim government. A significant role was also played by the captain-general of Madrid, Guillermo Quintana Lacaci, an unrepentant Francoist who simply obeyed the monarch: 'the king ordered me to stop the coup on 23 February. If he had ordered me to assault the Cortes, I would have done so.'[56] The paradoxes and peculiarities of the Spanish transition to democracy were brought out clearly in the aftermath of the attempted coup. Quintana Lacaci—the anti-democrat who had helped save democracy—was murdered by ETA in 1984, proving the connection between *etarras* and *golpistas*, despite their sworn enmity. Juan Carlos, an unelected, army-educated head of state, chosen by Franco as his heir, had worked tirelessly against the coup, proving instrumental to its failure. And, on 27 February, three million people took to the streets of Spain's cities in the largest public demonstration even seen in a European democracy. The crowds in Madrid—one and half million strong—cheered deputies from all political parties, prompting Manuel Fraga to exclaim 'I think that one should never use the clenched fist salute, but if it is done while shouting "Long live the king" then it is acceptable.'[57]

In several respects, the resolution of the 1981 coup attempt followed an established pattern of political events during the transition: executive action followed by popular ratification. Yet, the sense that there had been many possible outcomes of the night of 23–24 February, and very few of them were good, helped to renew the democratic process. Suárez's successor, Leopoldo Calvo-Sotelo, was confirmed in post and measures were at last taken to bring the army to heel, notably by taking Spain into NATO in May 1982. A new impetus was not enough, however, to keep the UCD together. As a bridge between the Francoist and democratic regimes it had functioned successfully enough but it had always operated as an appendage of government rather than a political party.[58] The UCD's historical moment proved to be the transition and the party did not survive beyond it. The UCD imploded in the general elections held in October 1982, which saw Felipe González's Socialist Party win a resounding victory.

The election of Spain's first Socialist government since the 1930s marked the end of the transition to democracy. A peaceful handover of power is the litmus test of any democracy and though military plotters were again scheming against democracy—and this time against the king as well—the putative coup was disarticulated on the eve of the elections before the soliders left their barracks. González's highly televisual campaign was fought on the slogan 'Por el cambio'—'For change'—and offered the promise of democratic consolidation. Considerable change had already taken place: only 19.1 per cent of the Socialist vote had come from manual workers. Class was not the only indeterminant: over 50 per cent of practising Catholics had voted for the Socialists rather than any of the centre or right-wing options on offer. A new fluidity of identities and alliances characterized democratic Spain: the socialists had won an overwhelming victory but it did not rest on any one particular class, regional, or even ideological base.

EUROPEANS

The Socialist Party was to remain in power for fourteen years and, while the final years of government were messy and compromised, it enjoyed nearly a decade of hegemony. This period saw a fundamental consolidation of democracy in Spain, a process that undoubtedly benefited from the Socialists' clear electoral majority and unambiguous authority. The dominance of the Socialist government owed much to the implosion of the UCD, whose collapse left AP as the main opposition, although it only took 26 per cent of the vote in 1982 as against the socialists' 48 per cent.[59] As the heterogeneity of the Socialists' electoral support showed, Spain was largely convinced of the left's centrism, but Fraga's party was still viewed with suspicion by many. During the 1980s, AP consolidated its core vote but consistently failed to break through an electoral ceiling of c. 25 per cent. Only when José María Aznar became leader in 1990 did the party put its internal difficulties behind it, reinventing itself along less ambivalent Christian Democratic lines as the Partido Popular (PP: People's Party).[60]

During the 1980s, the Socialists dominated national politics, although the configuration of the Spanish state introduced a new, and not always predictable, regional dynamic in political life. The positions of the regional nationalist parties, particularly the PNV and CiU were already mapped out, but that of non-nationalist regional figures was evolving fast. Aznar first came to prominence, for example, as president of the autonomous government of Castilla-León, a position he held from 1985. Other centre-right politicians travelled in the other direction, impelled by the collapse of the UCD, to front regional parties in the emerging *autonomías*. Devolution offered relatively open territory for new political options, particularly perhaps for those trained in a political culture of face-to-face dealings. As a normal mode of political operation *enchufismo* survived much longer at local level, a factor which no doubt attracted those interested in preferment. More significant figures also realized the career possibilities offered by regional politics. Manuel Fraga, for example, achieved great prominence as president of Galicia and thereby did much to reconcile the right to the cause of regionalism. The Galician PP became the first branch of the party to accept the term 'historic nationality' in regard to the regions.[61]

Although the issues around devolution were still far from settled—the uncertainty over the demarcation lines between national and regional government led to duplication in the state machinery and huge bureaucratic inefficiencies—other areas of state reform were dealt with systematically.

Felipe González—the first elected Socialist premier Spain had ever had—was genuinely popular: he remained the party's greatest electoral asset even after 1992, when it was increasingly mired in scandal. His popularity—and increasingly presidential style—enhanced the weight of the executive in Spain. The constitution had deliberately given the executive, and particularly the president of the government, extensive powers, even over parliament where, technically, sovereignty resided.[62] A leader with a stable government and a commanding majority was thus in a very strong position indeed, and it is no surprise that it was the Socialist administration, and not its more fragile UCD predecessor, that tackled the most intractable issues of state reform.

Foremost among these was reform of the military, but there had also been no reform—let alone purging—of the civil service. Such profound continuities are often explained in terms of a *pacto del olvido* or 'agreement to forget', whereby the past was set aside, the transition regarded as a new beginning, and no one had to account for what they had done either under Franco or during the Civil War.[63] Yet, the nature of the 1978 constitution itself, couched as it was in generalities, also necessitated further reform. This had to be a legislative process: for all its complexities the constitution had clearly established the sovereignty of law. The urgent need for reform was also becoming more and more obvious. A new territorial framework had been established for Spain but with no clarity as to the division of powers between centre and region. The resulting fluidity was politically beneficial but an administrative disaster, particularly given the overlapping competencies which already existed in Spanish law, which recognized organic, ordinary, basic and fundamental laws even without the new jurisdiction of the *autonomías*. Problems of a different kind of competence existed within the legislature itself, as Cortes deputies had little in the way of technical support, even though such support was essential for drafting robust, and usually complex, legislation.[64]

The technical bureaucratic support needed by a modern state cannot simply be willed into existence. The 1984 reform of the civil service was essentially a starting point: further legislation followed in 1987, with a new ministry of public administration created the previous year. The 1984 reform had looked to curb the corporatist tendencies of the civil service, removing barriers between different strata of public administration and so downgrading the traditional, *cuerpo*-based, structure. Functionaries could now be transferred between central government and the *autonomías*, which should have allowed for streamlining. However, between 1982 and 1991, the number of functionaries in the autonomous governments multiplied by twelve while the number of those working for central government fell by only 23 per cent; similarly, over 20 per cent of the national budget was transferred to the regions in 1988 as was 25 per cent in the mid-1990s.[65] A legalistic, bureaucratic culture with a profound tendency towards corporatism proved highly resilient, even under a stable democracy.

A similar culture existed in the military; though here far-reaching reform was achieved, in part because of the clear need to subjugate the generals to the state. Entrenched military hostility towards 'Reds' meant that the Socialist administration had to tread carefully but there was no lack of resolution. Under Narcís Serra, defence minister from 1982 to 1991, the government modernized the armed forces by increasing military budgets for new equipment and training, redeployed them using defence rather than public-order criteria, and fundamentally altered military career structures, terms of service, and education. The requirements of NATO membership helped the government build up the navy and the air force at the expense of the army, which was reduced in size and made less dependent on national servicemen. The aim was clearly to produce an efficient, highly trained, professional defence force, a move symbolized in the abolition of military governorships in the 1990s.[66] On the diplomatic stage, such reforms made Spain a much more convincing international player; domestically, they finally reduced the distance between military and civilian society.

In international terms, successive Socialist governments confirmed Spain in a broadly Atlanticist stance, albeit with some qualifications. Most dramatically, González's first government, having fought the election on a ticket opposed to NATO membership, campaigned even more vigorously in favour of remaining in the Western Alliance before a referendum in March 1986.[67] The government won the day: 52.5 per cent of the votes cast were in favour of Spain staying in NATO, though with the guarantee of remaining non-nuclear. As a quid pro quo, US military bases on the Spanish mainland were to be reduced. The Socialists' volte-face on NATO was undoubtedly pragmatic rather than ideological, conditioned in large part by international relations. Membership of NATO would further professionalize the Spanish military, give it access to the latest in technology and strategic thinking, and bring its commanding officers into regular contact with other members of the Atlantic club. Democratic values—most notable that of disinterested service to successive elected governments—were thereby reinforced within Spain's most recalcitrant institution.

Membership of NATO was also to bring Spain a prominence on the international stage it had not had for two hundred years. Although Spanish ambivalence towards NATO—which persisted, particularly at popular level, even after the referendum—meant that the country did not join the integrated military structure until November 1996, this was finally achieved under a Spanish secretary-general, Javier Solana. Born in Madrid in 1942, Solana had been involved in student dissent in the early 1960s and travelled to the USA on a Fulbright scholarship to complete a doctorate in physics. He taught at Madrid University, joined the Socialist Party when it was still illegal and was elected to the Cortes in 1977. In 1982, he joined González's first cabinet, and served as foreign minister between 1992 and 1995, when he went to NATO. As secretary-general, Solana became the first Spaniard ever to occupy a major post in the international arena, testimony both to Spain's new visibility and to the durability of the Atlanticist alliance.[68] Yet, Solana's personal history was also paradigmatic of the generation that achieved democracy in Spain, particularly in his experience abroad; the determination to situate Spain on the world stage, to end the isolation and cultural poverty of the past was a key determinant in the process of democratization.

A strategy of 'joining Europe' had underpinned Spanish aspirations throughout democratization. Juan Carlos' first speech to the Cortes as king of Spain proclaimed that '[t]he idea of Europe would not be complete without reference to the presence of Spain . . . we the Spaniards are European.'[69] Europe was the key to a new international presence as well as to democratic reform. The breadth of the consensus behind Europe meant that as early as the 1977 elections, both main political parties spoke the magic language of Europeanization: 'The key to Europe is in your hands. Vote PSOE' proclaimed the Socialists; 'Vote centre. The ideologies that make possible a democratic Europe' claimed the UCD.[70] In 1977, as in 1898, 'Europeanization' meant everything and nothing: it was simply an aspiration for change. By the late twentieth century, however, the existence of supranational European institutions meant that such aspirations acquired content. 'Europeanization' quickly became defined as membership of the European Community (EC).

Economic modernization had initially propelled Spain towards an integrated Europe: the first, unrealistic application to the Common Market had come in 1962. When the UCD government formally applied for EC membership in July 1977, however, the agenda had broadened from membership of an economic club to strengthening democracy and rehabilitating Spain on the world stage. The prospect of EC membership was still a panacea for all Spain's ills—particularly among the public—but the nebulous historic discourse of 'Europeanization' had been translated into a series of specific political goals and Spain became the twentieth member of the Council of Europe in 1979.[71] The panacea effect was reflected in unanimous parliamentary approval for the resolution to seek EC membership: no parliamentary party dissented from the strategy of Europeanization, which was rapidly incorporated into the wider consensus on democratization.

There were, of course, economic arguments for membership. As Spain was already dependent on European markets in both trade and finance, closer integration offered a powerful prospect of economic development while isolation suggested the opposite. Negotiations over accession began in 1978 and were often difficult, trapped by internal EC disagreements or mired in practicalities, both of which reflected the strains imposed by the entry not just of Spain but also of Portugal and Greece, all of them relatively poor.[72] Spain's negotiating process continued until 1985 but was boosted by the NATO referendum, which forged a connection between Spain's membership of the alliance and that of the community. Indeed, convincing the public of this connection was crucial to González's victory in the referendum, and the strategy also proved to be an essential bargaining chip at the EC negotiating table. Support for Spanish entry was confirmed, Spain and Portugal joined the EC in January 1986, and the NATO referendum was held in March. With membership of all the major supra-national institutions ratified, Spain was a fully paid-up member, not just of the European club, but of the Western one.

There is no doubt that the European Union (EU) has a supportive and, indeed, a normative effect on democracy. This was manifest in EC responses to the Franco regime well before the transition to democracy and the accession of the former southern dictatorships served as a powerful symbol of a new European direction. But while often bracketed with Portugal and Greece, Spain was much larger, and the size of its economy much greater. There were echoes of this during the 1986 referendum, with robust responses to the suggestion that Spain might play a similar role to Ireland, staying in the EC but rejecting NATO. For Spain clearly had the potential to become a major rather than a minor player and, for many Spaniards, 1986 marked a re-entry onto the world stage, and a reassertion of Spain's rightful place.

Such perceptions—together with the real correlation between 'Europeaniz-ation' and democratization—help to explain why Spaniards remained among the most pro-EU of all Europeans. Certainly, Spain did well out of the EU, benefiting dramatically from the greater availability of structural funding after 1988. 'Cohesion' funds were established to bring less developed member states—Spain, Portugal, Greece, and Ireland—to the level needed for economic and monetary union (EMU). By the beginning of the 1990s, Spain was the greatest beneficiary of all the fifteen member states, receiving a greater net amount—though not necessarily more per capita—than the other cohesion countries. Indeed, the cumulative effect of EU funds was estimated to have raised Spain's GDP by 4 per cent between 1986 and 1999. As funds were direc-ted towards structural improvements, particularly in communications and the environment, they had a significant effect on public infrastructure and thence the wider economy. The combination of a historically-impoverished state and difficult topography had left Spain with a grossly inadequate transport system that was only substantially improved with EU funding. Now, the development of high-speed rail links between Madrid and Barcelona connected networks between Seville and Paris, increasing regional, as well as national and European cohesion.[73] As redistribution between regions was also an effect of EU funding, tangible evidence of 'European' improvements thus came into existence all over Spain, providing both a symbol of modernization and, in an entirely literal sense, a route towards it.

A communications infrastructure appropriate for the age of motorways and air travel made explicit the connections between nation and region as well as those between nation and continent. Spaniards could now move easily between one place and another, experiencing almost effortlessly those passages between city and countryside, coast and mountain, north and south that make up a national journey of self-discovery. The voyage of national identity became an everyday occurrence. With good roads into France and Portugal, and flights all around the world, the contrasts offered extended to those between what was Spanish and what was not. Europe thus both enabled and defined this contemporary journey of national self-discovery: the EU had become Spain's 'national project'. On the tenth anniversary of Spanish accession, one of the leading papers, the left-leaning *El País*, talked of 'the fixing of Spain's destiny firmly with that of the rest of Europe' and declared that '[t]here can be no serious Spanish national project outside Europe.'[74]

Although Spain was a latecomer to the EU, the decision to join was a clear act of political will, made by a national government on behalf of a nation state. Just as the original six member-states had voluntarily surrendered some national sovereignty to a supranational organization in 1957 as part of the postwar reassertion of the nation-state, so Spain enthusiastically ceded greater, though still carefully defined, areas of sovereignty to Brussels. Neither in 1957 nor in 1986 was this a position of weakness; rather the process of integration was intrinsic to the contemporary development of the European nation-state.[75] In the Spanish case, entering the EU was a means to strengthen a national presence, both domestically and on the international stage. Membership of the EU became an essential component of modern Spanish identities, and not simply because Spain's prominence within Europe is seen as a national achievement. Between 1996 and 2002, the number of people who saw themselves as both Spanish and European increased, though barely 6 per cent put the European identity before the national one. In this, the Spanish experience mirrors that of Europeans more generally: the growing tendency to identify with Europe implies no lessening in national feeling. Those who saw themselves as only Spanish, however, declined over this period, to around 30 per cent between 2000 and 2002.

The question of regional identity is complex. Those who identified themselves as having both a regional and a national identity, as being, for example, equally Aragonese and Spanish, seemed to have little difficulty in adding 'European' to their multivalent list of identities. However, those who identified exclusively with a region, who saw themselves as simply Basque, for example, were less likely to see themselves as European, even compared to those who claimed to be exclusively Spanish.[76] The underlying trend towards Europe is positive, though 'Eurosceptic' feeling is easily provoked. There was, for example, strong reaction to newspaper reports that Brussels was about to remove the ñ from the Spanish alphabet—the equivalent to Britain's periodic 'Eurosausage' scandals. Pro-European feeling also faltered quite seriously in 2001, as Spain prepared to join the Euro and abandon the peseta. Emotional reactions to perceived threats to what are—as are both the ñ and the peseta—potent symbols and constituents of that everyday national identity that defines Spanishness are unsurprising. The negative attitudes towards Europe found among some regional groups proved more resilient. Antipathy towards Europe in Galicia, for example, seemed to result from specific circumstances such as the negative effects of EU entry on *galego* fishing and dairy-farming. Similarly, declining sectors such as the heavy industry that characterized Asturias and the Basque Country experienced little 'European' prosperity.

Spaniards' identity as Europeans is thus to some extent pragmatic, just as it is throughout the EU. However, unlike in some other peripheral countries—notably Britain and Scandinavia—European integration is perceived positively rather than antagonistically and so has been incorporated relatively easily into national and (some) regional identities, particularly given the conflation of 'Europe' and democracy. As King Juan Carlos put it in his 1992 Christmas address, '[t]he fact of belonging to Europe enriches our national identity.'[77] At the regional level, this would seem to be true for many Catalans. Jordi Pujol—elected president of the Catalan Generalitat between 1980 and 2003—made Europe an integral part of his nationalist strategy of *fer país* or 'making a country'.[78] As president, Pujol established the Patronat Català Pro Europa, taking Cataluña to the heart of Brussels (and vice versa), and so giving an institutional expression to Catalan nationalists' long-held belief that their nation was more European than Spanish. Such a contrast was in part a reference to Catalan modernity as against Spanish backwardness, and economic prosperity and business-friendly initiatives were key to Pujol's moderate nationalist stance. A 'Europe of the regions' would enable progressive sectors such as Catalan business and finance to bypass national state structures which a globalized economy was, in any case, making increasingly redundant. A European identity had become constitutive of Catalan identity, which was thus firmly established as an inclusive, pluralist, 'civic' nationalism, available to all those who lived in or identified with the Catalan lands.[79]

European integration has afforded new possibilities for stateless nations, not least through the emergence of a multilayered European order. For Pujol's CiU, the EU offered the prospect of an additional political arena, an alternative model of non-state based sovereignty and authority, and a discourse that allowed a minority language and culture to be presented in a non-parochial way. The desire to promote a regional agenda within the EU is shared by Galicia and the Basque Country, who cooperate with other western coastal regions in the 'Atlantic Arc'. These inter-regional *fora* provide an added dimension to non-state identities within Europe, but there is no easy correlation between pro-European and anti-national identities. While the dominant Catalan position was that EU membership would strengthen the region against the Spanish state, many Basque nationalists saw the EU as an impediment to independence, as European treaties define and limit the regional autonomy within the member state, which is, after all, the constituent body.

Basque political culture has been profoundly marked by terrorism. ETA killed over 800 people between 1968 and 2001 and survey evidence from the 1990s suggested that most local people viewed active political participation with fear and mistrust.[80] Although the number of people defining themselves as non-nationalist—at least to researchers—had risen to 54 per cent in 2000 as against 44 per cent in 1991, the dominant cultural and political discourse was still separatist. And in this discourse, the Basque presence in the EU, the Basque statute of autonomy, and the greatest degree of autonomy that the region has ever had, have been reworked into *impediments* to self-government rather than an acknowledgement of it. For many Basques, the experience of European democracy has been ambivalent, an ambivalence that was reinforced during the early 1990s by revelations over the Grupo Antiterrorista de Liberación (GAL: Antiterrorist Liberation Group).[81] The GAL's 'dirty war' against ETA was conducted mainly in France, apparently with the aim of forcing the French government towards extraditing *etarras*. Its actions were brutal and indiscriminate but the real GAL scandal lay in the strong presumption of government authorization. No direct order or link to González was ever shown, but his former minister of the interior, José Barrionuevo, was gaoled for kidnap on a split verdict in 1998. His quick pardon by the Conservative government of José María Aznar, who succeeded González in 1996, did nothing to help the corrosive effect the scandal had on Basque views of Spanish democracy.

Though there was clearly no one single relationship between region, nation, and Europe, the end of the twentieth century did see a widespread belief that the nation-state was changing. This was common currency in Cataluña, but in the Basque Country too commentators point to changing understandings of sovereignty, which should be 'unpacked' to enable its distribution around the most appropriate levels of decision-making.[82] In European terms, such ideas are commonly bracketed together as 'subsidiarity' and provide a response, not simply to the challenge of regionalism but to that of globalization. For while the nation-state exerts more power—at least in terms of knowledge and control of its own citizens—than ever before, the policy-making capacity of national governments have become increasingly curtailed. The nation-state may have been rescued by European integration, but that process has itself profoundly changed the nature of the nation-state.[83]

By the introduction of the Euro in 2002, Spaniards, like all other Europeans, negotiated a range of identities, whether described as 'nested', 'multilevel', or complementary. For most, this was an effortless, almost an unthinking process, which had been naturalized into a way of 'being Spanish'. For others, many of them Basque, the process was more antagonistic, and could be conflictual, particularly in terms of the relationship between region and central state. But such identities were not only political: the self-conscious 'I' of the twentieth-century individual fits easily into a range of settings, as a sexed being, a family member, a neighbour, a citizen, a consumer, a friend, a parishioner, a voluntary worker, or a supporter of a football team. All are identities, yet few, if any, are subject to the intense scrutiny that regional feelings attract. And these everyday identities, these ordinary, unremarkable ways of being Spanish did not stand still during the final years of the twentieth century. For, in identifying themselves as Europeans, Spaniards were also staking a claim to modernity and affluence, democracy and cultural pluralism.

In 1992—Spain's *annus mirabilis*—these identities were put on display to the world. During the quincentenary of Columbus' voyage to the Americas, Seville became the site of the twentieth century's last universal exposition and the city of Barcelona hosted the Olympic Games. Nation and region were thus on display simultaneously, sometimes with surprising results. The king of Spain's first words at the Olympic opening ceremony were in Catalan, and the symbols of Cataluña—language, flag, and anthem—were given equal prominence with those of Spain. Given the tensions that had arisen over this issue—both in the press and in public opinion—it was not remarkable that King Juan Carlos' words were greeted with great applause. More surprising was the tumultuous reception given to his son, the prince of Asturias, a member of the yachting team, as he carried the national flag into the stadium, and the extraordinary number of Spanish flags flying alongside Catalan ones during the football final, contested by the Spanish team on the hallowed turf of Barcelona FC's Nou Camp stadium.[84]

The Olympics became emblematic of Spanish achievement, demonstrating not only sporting prowess—the country's athletes won more medals than ever before—but also organizational capacity. All levels of government benefited from the games, national, regional, and municipal, while the city of Barcelona was transformed. Pujol's Generalitat made much of Cataluña's European outlook, its historic connections with Europe, and Catalans' capacity for hard work. Bringing the games to Barcelona, was seen as a local triumph, although their success emphasized Spanish as well as Catalan achievement, presenting an image of integrative nationalism played out on the world's television screens every time a Catalan athlete stood for the national anthem or Spanish and Catalan flags flew together in a stadium.

The same image of integrative nationalism was presented during Expo92 in Seville. The 'universal' status and commemorative theme—the 're-encounter' with America—meant that Latin American countries were given prominent billing. Yet, a document drawn up for local schoolchildren claimed that Expo was also to bring 'the attention of the international community to Spain's integration in Europe'.[85] Visitors wandered between national, sub- and supra-national pavilions, tracing the relationship between Spain, its autonomous communities, its former colonies, and its European partners. Expo thus showcased Spain's new sense of itself. The Spanish pavilion stood at the head of the 'Avenue of Europe' and also dominated one side of the 'Lake of Spain', with the pavilions of the *autonomías* clustered together in a horseshoe on the opposite side.[86] The use of space was reminiscent of the Plaza de España created for Seville's 1929 exhibition but rather than symbolically holding the regions captive in a single defined space, visitors were now invited to wander through the different pavilions, following a trajectory that was entirely their own, sampling the exhibits that appealed to them, participating in the experience of Expo.[87] As was obvious to any visitor, participation was only made possible by corporate sponsorship, which further highlighted the complex position of the nation-state in the contemporary world, despite the survival of highly traditional forms of representation, such as the inevitable cultural performances and folkloric displays.

Expo92 provided a model of Spain in the world: most visitors were Spanish, and they were invited to visit, experience, and consume the idealized landscape before them. They could collect stamps on an Expo 'passport' or survey the 'world' around them from various vantage points. The EC pavilion was a tower decorated with the national flags of the member states, its central position in the 'Avenue of Europe' offering the kind of panoptic view that the Spanish pavilion had over the 'Lake of Spain'. What could not be included on the Expo site—most notably natural landscape—could be conveyed cinematically. The big hit of the Spanish pavilion was its Moviemax cinema, which took viewers through the Spanish landscape, strapped into seats that moved in synchrony with the images, jolting the audience through a camel ride on the Canaries, inviting an imaginative inscription into the national landscape in front of them as well as enjoyment of the technological spectacle. Regional pavilions recreated nature in the same way, that of the dairy-farming region of Asturias, for example, even presenting virtual cows in lieu of the real thing. Again, such techniques, while they made no disguise of their artificiality, invited the observer to situate him/herself imaginatively in the landscape that was being recreated. The Asturias pavilion is now part of the region's ethnographic museum in Gijón.

The emphasis on communications technology made a virtue of European modernity. Corporate sponsors for Expo92 included Siemens, Fuijitsu, and Rank Xerox, so advertising Spain and, by implication, Europe as an investment opportunity. The relationship between multinational corporations, nation-states, and the EC reflected not only the dynamics of globalization but also the new relationship between citizens and governments. The freedom of choice offered by Expo—certainly when compared to earlier exhibitions held on Spanish soil—suggested that visitors came to Seville as citizens rather than subjects. There was an equivalence and a modernity to the exhibits, which was highlighted by their juxtaposition to the historic experience of 1492, commodified in the pavilions of the discovery and the fifteenth century. Those passing through Expo did so as individual consumer-citizens entrusted with rational choices, not as members of social hierarchies or even local communities. For the architectural kitsch that had so distinguished early twentieth-century exhibitions had, with a very few, largely eastern European, exceptions, disappeared.

Modernism was the hegemonic architectural idiom of Expo92, uniting the Spanish pavilion with those of the autonomous communities and linking together the EC member states. Steel, glass, and uncompromising cubes—in for example the pavilions of Spain and Castilla la Mancha—spoke self-consciously and deliberately of new identities rather than of traditional ones (Plate 8). Expo was thus a showcase of nationalism (in various guises), internationalism, and modernity. One of the most spectacular pavilions was the work of a leading Spanish architect, Santiago Calatrava. His graceful and innovative structure made full use of his characteristic curves, with a set of hydraulic ribs that could be opened up from the platform or closed into it, creating either a protected or an open space.[88] The mastery of engineering technology made its own statement. Yet, this quintessentially contemporary commission did not represent Spain but Kuwait. Calatrava, who spoke five languages and worked from Geneva, worked in an international market, and his work on the Kuwaiti pavilion was eloquent testimony to the fluid identities of contemporary Spain.

The year 1992, which saw the creation of a single market within the EU, marked Spain's entry into the alliance of Western nations. The material legacy of the *annus mirabilis* was both symbolic and infrastructural—Calatrava's Montjuic telecommunications tower in Barcelona, the Andalusian architects Cruz and Ortiz's railway station in Seville, highspeed rail links, bridges over the Guadalquivir, and the redevelopment of urban space. In 1999, the Royal Institute of British Architects awarded its gold medal to the city of Barcelona for its commitment to urbanism. Spain was now a leader as well as a follower, an example to the rest of Europe rather than simply a recipient of structural funding. The gap between Spain and 'developed' Europe narrowed still further, impelled in economic terms by the demands of convergence before the introduction of the Euro but also reflecting the profound social and cultural change that took place in Spain during the last decades of the twentieth century.

Like every other European country, Spain has a strong and distinct national culture. To the incomprehension of millions of tourists, Spaniards still have lunch at three and dinner towards midnight. There may be some local varia-tion—Catalans are generally more temperate in their approach to mealtimes than are Andalucíans—but every neighbourhood still has dozens of small shops which shut for two hours at lunchtime and close on Saturday afternoon. This traditional pace of life cannot be observed by all—those who work with international financial markets, for example, have no prospect of a two-hour break in the middle of the day—but it survives. The evening *paseo* continues, above all in provincial towns, but also in urban neighbourhoods where parents take their children to the park in the early evening, running a few errands, and often stopping for a drink or a chat. Family as well as social life takes place on the street; Spaniards still live much of their life in the open air. Public space—the park and the *plaza*, cafés with pavement tables—is thus hugely important, though it is notable how much of this is actually used for private social and family discourse. For the family remains the strongest institution in Spain, its durability reflected in one of Europe's lowest divorce rates. In 1990, 0.6 Spaniards in every thousand were divorced, as compared to 1.9 Germans; by 2001 the Spanish figure had risen to 1.0, the German to 2.4. Although the birth rate has fallen sharply in Spain, reflecting in part the much greater prominence of women in both higher education and the workforce, households are still comparatively large, containing an average of 3.2 people in 1998, the largest in the EU.[89]

The resilience of family structures, and the continuing importance of the home, cannot disguise the fact that the birth rate has dropped below replacement levels and Spain's population is ageing. The problems facing Spain in the early twenty-first century are those facing every other European state. Sustained affluence has brought its own problems, notably the crisis in pensions and the increasing difficulty of funding universal welfare policies.

The funding conundrum facing the welfare state, is as intractable a problem for Spain as it is for Britain or Germany. There is no longer an indigenous supply of cheap labour and, for the first time in its modern history, Spain attracts economic immigrants. Labourers from Morocco leave their homes to harvest vegetables in Almería just as Spanish labourers once travelled to pick grapes in France. Women from the Philippines or eastern Europe are employed as maids and nannies in middle-class homes, replacing the village girls who used to be a regular source of domestic labour. In contrast to northern Europe, with its established immigrant communities, multiculturalism is a new phenomenon in Spain and the tensions of assimilation are not always offset by the economic need for migrant labour, as the race riots that broke out in Almería in 2000 showed.

Impediments to multiculturalism are no longer religious. Indeed, a shared desire to see more respect for faith groups has lead to the Catholic Church making common cause with other religions. For Spain has become a secular society. Catholicism may still have a cultural prominence—above all in public commemorations such as saints' days and Holy Week—but religious faith is seen as a matter of private conscience. The number of practising Catholics fell from 37 per cent in 1979 to 17 per cent in 1995 and although the number of atheists remained very low—5 per cent of the 19 per cent who defined themselves as 'non-religious' in 1995—the proportion of non-believers was higher among young people.[90] The move from confessional state to secular society has been rapid—the numbers leaving the Church in the 1980s were greatest in regions such as Navarre and the Basque Country that had historically been most Catholic—and many Spaniards still have little direct experience of cultures other than their own. The numbers of immigrants to Spain is low in European terms, but the country's geographical position creates an impression of vulnerability. The distance between Spain and Africa is the narrowest north/south border in the world and from being a peripheral European power, Spain has become a pivot on a north/south trajectory that is a growing preoccupation of Western politicians.

Migration—legal and otherwise—is simply one of the forces creating a globalized world. It is determined by forces outside the purview of the nation state and the problems raised are often too far-reaching to be adequately addressed by individual governments. One response to globalization is, of course supranational governance. The EU can, for example, formulate European policy with regard not only to the movement of people but also to the economic power wielded by multinational corporations and the policy positions of national governments. The question of the role of the nation-state at the beginning of the twenty-first century is thus not one that has a quick or easy answer. European integration has begun a new phase in the development of the European nation-state, which is marked by a new openness to region-alism and national identity but trammelled by the increasing political weight of institutions above, beyond, and outside that nation-state.

For Spain, there may be an irony in that the country achieved a modern nation-state at precisely the time that the accelerating processes of European integration changed that state for ever. There are many questions over the nature of government and state power in Spain but all of them echo problems also found elsewhere. The corruption scandals of the 1990s raised fears of a 'democratic deficit' as some political scientists argued that the process of state formation—in particular its crystallization around the caciques—had damaged the capacity for functioning democracy and transparent government. Such a deficit was, however, seen as a southern rather than a Spanish phenomenon. And while the lurking question of the 'quality' of Spanish democracy remains, any club that has Italy as a member cannot see corruption as a specifically Spanish problem.

The same is true of the 'nationalities' question. The future trajectory of the territorial Spanish state was not resolved by either the 1978 constitution or European integration. Open questions as to the status of the regions, the role they played in Europe, and the extent of devolved powers remained live issues in 2002. But, again, these questions have as much salience in Belgium as in Spain and also find some resonance in Britain. The challenges faced by the nation-state are far from over: a global age may pose sharper questions even than those put during the twentieth century. Yet, if Spain is in no better position to answer these challenges than her European neighbours, it is, for the first time in its modern history, in no worse a position either. The problems of the twenty-first century are unforeseeable and may conceivably lead to some major reconfiguration of the modern state. But the story of Spain between 1833 and 2002 is of the creation of that state and of the establishment of legitimate government within it.

Afterword: Escaping the Past

When, in 1983, I first began travelling regularly to Madrid, there was a certain moment at Barajas airport when I knew I had arrived in Spain. As passengers got off the airport bus that took them from the aeroplane to the terminal and pushed through the double doors to passport control, their senses were assaulted by the smell of Madrid airport—a mixture of heat, black tobacco, and marble floor tiles. Over the decades that smell faded—the result primarily of greater observance of no-smoking regulations—but it never disappeared. A weak but omnipresent state had long since created a heavily ruled society in which few obeyed the rules. But, as the decline of tobacco fumes around Barajas showed, these habits were changing. By the twenty-first century, the Barajas terminal buildings, opened by the *generalísimo* in the mid-1960s, seemed both as self-consciously modern and as quaintly useless as a redundant typewriter.

When I flew into Madrid in 2006, I landed at the new terminal four, winner of that year's Sterling Prize for architecture. Designed jointly by Britain's Richard Rogers Partnership and Spain's Estudio Lamela, this gargantuan building dwarfs the people within it, who move between escalator, monorail, and eventually aeroplane. The scale seems inhuman: the building processes travellers and luggage, moving them along the conveyor belts demanded by the timetable of international travel. For the terminal is disassociated from its Spanish surroundings; it is not a gateway but a hub, an interchange for passengers on flights between Europe and South America. A global concern with energy conservation has led the architects to make much use of natural light: huge windows provide vistas of the surrounding hills, though these are now defined by runways and hangars. The landscape is a backdrop for passengers protected from the heat and smell of Spain. The terminal's much-admired wavy ceiling is made of bamboo—a material with more cultural references to Manila than to Madrid—and the only Spanish products to be seen are the ironic reworkings of folkloric or artistic motifs found in the souvenir shops.

In an age when a national airline was a potent symbol of a nation-state—just as public buildings, cities, or shipping had been in earlier periods—an airport needed a clear local identity: the old Barajas brought the visitor to Spain. Now the new terminal offers internet cafés and mobile phone coverage, allowing visitors to situate themselves in whichever social and cultural communities they choose. For just as the development of supra-national governance and multinational corporations has 'hollowed' out the political life of the state, so the development of truly global communications is changing the fundamental relationship a state has with its territory.

Cyberspace—a multilingual, democratic, informative, unreliable, and sometimes dangerous place—now exists within all nation-states as well as outside them. Internet access allows information to spread widely, quickly and, to an extent, uncontrollably. Government is no longer territorially bounded in the way it once was: not only is its sphere of action more constrained by multi- and supra-national organizations but its citizens' activities potentially have a much wider reach. One effect of this is a new valorization of the individual, around whom political and social life is increasingly structured. The virtual communities created through the internet are often transient, and individuals may move between them with great ease, aided by the multiple identities some people assume in cyberspace. Yet this very ease of communication enables the creation of campaigning groups, who define themselves in terms of a political programme as well as or instead of in terms of social intercourse.

One example is the campaigns that have emerged in Spain around the issue of 'historical memory'. These look to recover the 'memory' of the Civil War by locating the often still unmarked graves of victims of the Francoist repression and commemorating their fate.[1] The Asociación para la Recuperación de la Memoria Histórica (ARMH: Association for the Recovery of Historical Memory) began by exhuming one such grave in 2000. Its ongoing campaigns have attracted much attention—2006, the seventieth anniversary of the Civil War, was deemed the 'year of historical memory'—and this unquiet past has become a matter of public debate as well as of public history. Scientists have worked, often on a voluntary basis, alongside members of the public in forensic excavations all over Spain. Their work has been publicized through the ARMH, numerous websites, newspaper articles, and television documentaries. Historical memory is an excellent source of media stories, in part because it is a matter of genuine public interest.

What is less clear, though, is what this interest in historical memory means in the context of twenty-first-century Spain. The initial impetus for the excavations was often personal: individuals and families who wished, finally, to bring an old and painful story to a close. But the narratives around the excavations are profoundly informed by a contemporary understanding of human rights, a particular narrative of the transition to democracy and, importantly, the experiences of other former dictatorships, particularly those in Latin America. The ARMH, for example, uses the same form of words, '*recuperación de la memoria histórica*', as a similar project in Guatemala, where the violence of civil war was both more recent and more extensive. Similarly, the role of the Spanish judge, Baltasar Garzón, in apprehending General Pinochet in London in 1998 drew attention to the fact that there had still been little public debate—and less official recognition—of the post-Civil War repression in Spain. The contrast between Spain and its sister new democracies in South America seemed sharp.

The current concern with historical memory in Spain is *not* about democracy. There is no serious suggestion that these issues represent a flaw in the fabric of Spanish democracy; rather it has become commonplace to assert that, as only now has it become possible to address the question of the repression, so historical memory actually attests to the robustness of consolidated democracy. The inference is clearly that the Spanish state now has the kind of legitimacy that allows its citizens to pursue difficult issues and controversial—even divisive—debates. For, while the concern with historical memory does raise questions about the relationship left-and particularly right-wing political parties have with Spain's recent past, there is no fear of debate leading to open conflict. It is rather a question of extending the limits of dialogue. And that profound, if obvious, historical fact shows that Spain has escaped the past in a much deeper way than discussion of historical memory often suggests.

The debates set in train by the ARMH also offer an example of a political agenda set from below and outside the established channels of citizen participation. The original initiative was informed by a particular understanding of both human rights and human psychology: the search for 'closure' has become characteristic of a psychoanalytic age which prioritizes the individual to an extent unique in human history. These individuals have access to unprecedented levels of information and communication, and in consumerist democracies they make choices in almost every area of their lives.

Individual identities thus have a new political salience. They are never fixed: people define themselves in response both to what they know and to what they do not know. And, in this context, the relationship between state, nation, region, and locality is ever changing, as is that between individual, family, and community, albeit at a different speed. Like other Europeans, Spaniards have little difficulty in assuming multiple identities: it is these identities themselves that are changing. This happens in response to both changing constitutional arrangements—the even greater devolution of power to the regions for example—and the implementation of European human rights legislation in the EU member states. Expansion of the EU has brought a new understanding of who Europeans are, which is itself challenged by the

the debates over Turkish entry. Coexistence with new migrant communities has also led to shifts and redefinitions in identity for Spaniards as has, most spectacularly, the emergence of a new terrorist threat.

The emergence of separatist terrorist groups in 1970s Europe—and the way in which nation-states responded to that challenge—changed regional and national identities in shifting and complex ways. This was as true in Spain as in Britain and Ireland, and when on 11 March 2004 a series of bombs went off on commuter trains in Madrid, some immediately assumed ETA responsibility. Yet, the Madrid bombings were a global incident, a direct consequence of the attacks of 11 September 2001 carried out by terrorists widely assumed to have a connection with al-Qaeda. This assumption is in itself sufficient for millions of Europeans—not all of them in Spain—to renegotiate their identities around understandings of Islam. More directly, in response to the attacks, European states have assumed even greater powers of interrogation, detention, and, above all, surveillance. Individuals in the West have more legally defined rights than ever before and may move more freely and quickly around the globe, but they are routinely and repeatedly stopped for document and security checks. Surveillance has become a part of daily life: we expect it and submit to it with little, if any, fuss. But such routines change the way we think about ourselves, our governments, and those from whom the threat appears to come. This is as true in Cataluña as in Andalucía or Castile: indeed national and regional boundaries are irrelevant; the security concerns posed by air travel are the same throughout the world.

We do not know how the world will change, but we can be sure both that it is changing and that the way in which it is changing will profoundly affect both people and state. In Spain as elsewhere, the sense of what it is legitimate for governments to do has altered even since 2002. There are new and greater challenges to the power of the nation-state and these are both internal—as in the continuing negotiations as to the boundaries of authority and competence between regional, national, and supra-national government—and external. The emergence of a genuinely globalized world will affect both state legitimacy and how we understand that legitimacy. But, as the choice of Madrid as a terrorist target showed, Spain is now a fully fledged Western state and, as the aftermath of that attack has shown, the legitimacy of that state is not, for the moment, in doubt.

Endnotes

NOTES TO INTRODUCTION

1. Cited Juan Pablo Fusi, *España: La evolución de la identidad nacional* (Madrid, 2000), 163–4.
2. But see the work of Juan Pablo Fusi (e.g., ibid. and 'Centralismo y localismo: la formación del estado español' in Guillermo Gortázar (ed.), *Nación y estado en la España liberal* (Madrid, 1994), 77–90) and Eduardo González Calleja (esp. *El razón de la fuerza: orden pública, subversión y violencia política en la España de la Restauración, 1875–1917* (Madrid, 1998) and *El mauser y el sufragio: orden pública, subversión y violencia política en la crisis de la Restauración, 1817–31* (Madrid, 1999)).
3. The classic statement is Borja de Riquer i Permanyer's trenchant article, 'La débil nacionalización española del siglo XIX', *Historia Social* 20 (1994), 97–114.
4. See, e.g., José Alvarez Junco, *Mater Dolorosa: la idea de España en el siglo XIX* (Madrid, 2001).
5. Eugen Weber, *Peasants into Frenchmen* (Stanford, Calif., 1976).
6. James C. Scott, *Seeing Like a State* (New Haven and London, 1998).
7. See, e.g., David Ringrose, *Spain, Europe and the 'Spanish Miracle', 1700–1900* (Cambridge, 1996).
8. This notion of crystallization comes from Michael Mann, who has strongly influenced my understanding of state power. See *The Sources of Social Power* published as *A History of Power from the Beginning to AD 1760* (Cambridge, 1986) and *The Rise of Classes and Nation-States, 1760–1914* (Cambridge, 1993).
9. José Varela Ortega, *Los amigos politicos: partidos, elecciones y caciquismo en la Restauración, 1875–1900* (Madrid, 2001) and José Varela Ortega, *El poder de la influencia: geografía del caciquismo en España, 1875–1923* (Madrid, 2001).
10. See, e.g., Helen Graham, *The Spanish Republic at War, 1936–9* (Cambridge, 2003).
11. Víctor Pérez-Díaz, *The Return of Civil Society to Spain: the Emergence of Democratic Spain* (Cambridge, Mass., 1993).

NOTES TO CHAPTER 1

1. Richard Herr, in Raymond Carr (ed.), *Spain: An Illustrated History* (Oxford, 2000), 203.
2. Quoted Isabel Burdiel, 'Myths of Failure, Myths of Success: New Perspectives on Nineteenth-Century Spanish Liberalism', *Journal of Modern History* 70 (1998), 902.

3. José Alvarez Junco, 'La difícil nacionalización de la derecha española en la primera mitad del siglo XX', *Hispania* 209 (2001), 831–58 and his *Mater Dolorosa*.

4. Pere Anguera, 'La subversió carlina: entre la guerra i el bandidatge. Notes per a una discussió' in Josep María Solé i Sabaté (ed.), *El carlisme com a conflicte* (Barcelona, 1993), 71–95.

5. Jordi Canal *El carlismo* (Madrid, 2000), 9–27.

6. María Rosa Saurín de la Iglesia, 'Poder económico y represión ideológico en Galicia, 1827–41', *Hispania* 41 (1981), 7.

7. Raymond Carr, *Spain, 1808–1975* (Oxford, 1982), 157–65.

8. Jesús Millán and María Cruz Romeo, 'Was the Liberal Revolution Important to Modern Spain? Political Cultures and Citizenship in Spanish History', *Social History* 29/3 (2004), 286–92.

9. Isabel Burdiel and María Cruz Romeo, 'Old and New Liberalism: The Making of the Liberal Revolution, 1808–1844', *Bulletin of Hispanic Studies* (Glasgow) 75/5 (1998), 65–80.

10. Burdiel, 'Myths of Failure', 900.

11. Juan Pablo Fusi and Jordi Palafox, *España, 1808–1996: El desafío de la modernidad* (Madrid, 1997), 41–51.

12. Quoted Burdiel, 'Myths of Failure', 905.

13. Jesús Cruz, 'An Ambivalent Revolution: the Public and the Private in the Construction of Liberal Spain', *Journal of Social History* 30 (1996), 17–18.

14. See, e.g., Jesús Millán, 'The Liberal Revolution and the Reshaping of Valencian Society', *Bulletin of Hispanic Studies* (Glasgow) 75/5 (1998), 39–63.

15. Jesús Cruz, *Gentlemen, Bourgeois and Revolutionaries: Political Change and Cultural Persistence among Spanish Dominant Groups, 1750–1870* (Cambridge, 1996), 159–60.

16. Mann, *The Rise of Classes and Nation-States*, esp. ch. 3.

17. Where this can be traced, José Manuel Cuenca Toribio and Soledad Miranda García, 'Nobleza y poder ejecutivo', *Historia Contemporánea: El estado en España*, 17 (1998), 162.

18. Mann, *The Rise of Classes and Nation-States*, 67.

19. Gracia Gómez Urdáñez, 'The Bourgeois Family in Nienteenth-Century Spain: Private Lives, Gender Roles and a New Socioeconomic Model', *Journal of Social History* 30/1 (2005), 66–85 at 75.

20. Adrian Shubert, *A Social History of Modern Spain* (London, 1990), 60; see also the argument laid out 1–6.

21. Quoted Gabriel Tortella, *El desarrollo de la España contemporánea* (Madrid, 1994), 47.

22. Ibid. 51; Richard Herr, *Rural Change and Royal Finances in Spain at the End of the Old Regime* (Berkeley and Los Angeles: University of California Press, 1989), 717–18; Juan Pablo Fusi (ed.), *España: Autonomías* (Madrid, 1989), 664.

23. Shubert, *Social History of Modern Spain*, 76–7.

24. Gómez Urdáñez, 'Bourgeois Family'.

25. 'An Ambivalent Revolution', 7.
26. Tortella, *El desarrollo*, 162.
27. Eventually the courts simply substituted 'rent' for *pecha*, Alfredo Floristán Imízcoz, 'Un largo enfrentamiento social: pechas y pecheros en Navarra', *Hispania* 44 (1984), 19–47.
28. Saurín de la Iglesia, 'Poder económico y represión ideológico', 9–21.
29. Francisco Comín Comín, *Hacienda y economía en la España contemporánea: El afianzamiento de la hacienda liberal 1800–74* (Madrid, 1988), 38–43, 412–25.
30. Gianfranco Poggi, *The State: its Nature, Development and Prospects* (Cambridge, 1990), 29; see also his *The Development of the Modern State* (London, 1978), 101–7.
31. Tortella, *El desarrollo*, 163.
32. Quoted Alejandro Nieto, *La retribución de los funcionarios en España: historia y actualidad* (Madrid, 1967), 128.
33. Only in 1869 were all men over 25 given the vote in local elections (Teror).
34. Alvarez Junco, *Mater Dolorosa*, 366–81.
35. Julio Aróstegui, 'El estado español contemporáneo: centralismo, inarticulación y nacionalismo', *Historia Contemporánea* 17 (1998), 31–57.
36. Mann, *A History of Power*, 1–33.
37. Juan Pro Ruíz, *Estado, geometría y propiedad: los orígenes del catastro en España, 1715–1941* (Madrid, 1992).
38. Ibid., 91.
39. See also Tortella, *El desarrollo*, 158.
40. Roger J. P. Kain and Elizabeth Baigent, *The Cadastral Map at the Service of the State* (Chicago, 1992).
41. J. B. Harley, 'Maps, Knowledge and Power' in Denis Cosgrove and Stephen Daniels (eds.), *The Iconography of Landscape* (Cambridge, 1988), 277–312; Geoffrey Cubitt 'Introduction' to Cubitt (ed.), *Imagining Nations* (Manchester, 1998) 10–11.
42. Scott, *Seeing Like a State*, 11–83. esp. 76–83.
43. Max Weber, 'Politics as a Vocation' in *From Max Weber: Essays in Sociology*, ed. H. M. Gerth and C. Wright Mills (London, 1991), 77–128; Poggi, *The State*, 4–6.
44. Richard Pennell, 'State Power in a Chronically Weak State: Spanish Coastguards as Pirates, 1814–50', *European History Quarterly* 25/3 (1995), 353–79.
45. Diego López Garrido, *La Guardia Civil y los orígenes del Estado centralista* (Barcelona, 1982), 23–84.
46. Manuel Balbé, *Orden público y militarismo en la España constitucional, 1812–83* (Madrid, 1985), 141–54.
47. Quoted Clive Emsley, *Gendarmes and the State in Nineteenth-Century Europe* (Oxford, 1999), 264 fn. 32.
48. Quoted López Garrido, *La Guardia Civil*, 146.
49. See e.g. ibid.

50. Gabriel Cardona, *El problema militar en España* (Madrid: Historia 16, 1990), 58–61 at 59.

51. Ibid., 44–74; Miguel Alonso Baquer, 'The Age of Pronunciamientos' in Rafael Bañón Martínez and Thomas M. Barker (eds.), *The Armed Forces and Society in Spain* (Boulder, Colo., 1988).

52. Quoted Stanley Payne, *Politics and the Military in Modern Spain* (Stanford, Calif., 1967), 25.

53. Eric Christiansen, *The Origins of Military Power in Spain, 1800–54* (Oxford, 1967), 108.

54. Payne, *Politics and the Military*, 10.

55. Samuel Finer, *The Man on Horseback: The Role of the Military in Politics* (London, 1962), 40.

56. Mann, *Rise of Classes and Nation-Sates*, 402–40 esp. 438–40; Poggi, *Development of the Modern State*, 92–5

57. Mann, *A History of Power*, 26.

58. Javier Alvarado Planas, 'La codificación del derecho militar en el siglo XIX' in Alvarado Planas and Regina Mª Pérez Marcos (eds.), *Estudios sobre ejército, política y derecho en España* (Madrid, 1996), 279–300.

59. Quoted Carolyn Boyd, 'The Military and Politics, 1808–1874' in José Alvarez Junco and Adrian Shubert, *Spanish History since 1808* (New York, 2000), 37–8.

60. Quoted Christiansen, *Origins of Military Power*, 110.

61. Demetrio Castro Alfín, 'Unidos en la adversidad, unidos en la discordia: el Partido Demócrat, 1849–68' in Nigel Townson (ed.), *El republicanismo en España, 1830–1877* (Madrid, 1994), 59–85.

62. José María Jover Zamora ' "Era isabelina" y "Sexenio Democrático": La continuidad del proceso', cvi–cxviii in Jover Zamora (ed.), *La era isabelina y el sexenio democrático, 1834–1874* (Madrid, 1981).

63. Pi y Margall, later president of the First Republic in 1873.

64. Raymond Carr, 'Spain: Rule by Generals' in Michael Howard (ed.), *Soldiers and Government* (London, 1957), 139.

65. Miguel Angel Esteban Navarro, 'De la esperanza a la frustración, 1868–73' in Townson (ed.), *Republicanismo*, 87–112; Antoni Jutglar i Bernaus, 'La revolución de septiembre, el gobierno provisional y el reinado de Amadeo I' in Jover Zamora (ed.), *La era isabelina*, 645–99.

66. Tortella, *El desarrollo*, 164.

67. For federalism, see José A. Piqueras Arenas, 'Detrás de la política: República y federación en el proceso revolucionario español' in José Piquera and Manuel Chuste (eds.), *Republicanos y repúblicas en España* (Madrid, 1996), 1–44.

68. Quoted C. A. M. Hennessey, *The Federal Republic in Spain* (Oxford, 1962), 173.

69. Antonio María Calero, 'Los cantons de Málaga y Granada' in Manuel Tuñón de Lara (ed.), *Sociedad, política y cultura en la España de los siglos XIX y XX* (Madrid, 1973), 81–90.

70. Antoni Jutglar, *Ideologías y clases en la España contemporánea* (Madrid, 1973), 313.

71. Quoted José María Jover Zamora, 'Federalismo en España' in Guillermo Gortázar (ed.), *Nación y estado en la España liberal* (Madrid, 1994), 148.

72. Juan Díaz del Moral, *Historia de las agitaciones campesinas andaluzas* (Madrid, 1973: 1st publ. 1928), 78–92.

73. Carr, *Spain*, 334.

NOTES TO CHAPTER 2

1. Luis Núñez Astrain, *The Basques: Their Struggle for Independence* ([Cardiff] Wales, 1997), 12.

2. Quoted John Hooper, *The Spaniards* (1987), 225.

3. Fernán Caballero, *La gaviota*, (Leipzig, 1881; 1st publ. 1849), 113.

4. All statistics from Adrian Shubert, *Death and Money in the Afternoon: a History of the Spanish Bullfight* (Oxford, 1999).

5. Valeriano Bozal, *Pintura y escultura española del s.XX, 1900–39* (Madrid, 1992), 19–21, 56, 551.

6. Nicholas Green, *The Spectacle of Nature: Landscape and Bourgeois Culture in Nineteenth-Century France* (Manchester, 1990).

7. Rafael Altamira, *A History of Spain* (Toronto, 1949), 629.

8. Cubitt, 'Introduction', 13.

9. Roland Barthes, 'The Discourse of History' trans. Stephen Bann, *Comparative Criticism* 3 (1981), 19.

10. Quoted Carolyn Boyd, *Historia Patria: Politics, History and National Identity in Spain, 1875–1975* (Princeton, 1997), 68.

11. Beth S. Wright, *Painting and History during the French Restoration: Abandoned by the Past* (Cambridge, 1997).

12. José García (1866), quoted Carlos Reyero, *La pintura de historia en España* (Madrid, 1989), 35.

13. Quoted ibid., 36.

14. Stephen Bann (ed.), *The Image of History*, Special Issue of *Word and Image* 16 (2000).

15. Carolyn Boyd, 'The Second Battle of Covadonga' in Ranaan Rein (ed.), *Spanish Memories: Images of a Contested Past*, Special Issue of *History and Memory* 14 (2002), 37–64.

16. *Politics without Democracy: Great Britain, 1815–1914* (London, 1984).

17. Shubert, *Social History of Modern Spain*, 115.

18. José Varela Ortega, 'Sobre la naturaleza del sistema político de la Restauración' in Guillermo Gortázar (ed.), *Nacion y estado en la España liberal* (Madrid, 1994), 175.

19. Francisco Villacorta Baños, 'Estructura y funcionamiento de la nueva administración' in Manuel Espadas Burgos (ed.), *La epoca de la Restauración, 1875–1902 Estado, política e islas de ultramar* (Madrid, 2000), 151.

20. Ibid., 187–8.
21. Boyd, *Historia Patria*, 4–12; Alvarez Junco, *Mater Dolorosa*, 546–50; Francisco Villacorta Baños, *Profesionales y burócratas: Estado y poder corporativo en la España del siglo XX, 1890–1923* (Madrid, 1989), 77–97.
22. Figures given Clara Eugenia Nuñez, *La fuente de la riqueza: educación y desarrollo económico en la España contemporánea* (Madrid, 1992), 203, 308.
23. Varela, 'Sobre la naturaleza del sistema político', 178.
24. 'Estructura y funcionamiento', 169; Alicia Fiestas Loza, 'Codificación procesal y estado de la Administración de Justicia, 1875–1915' in José Luis García Delgado (ed.), *La España de la Restauración: Política, economía, legislación y cultura* (Madrid, 1985), 413–36 at 417.
25. Tortella, *El desarrollo*, 139; Marcia Pointon, 'Money and Nationalism' in Cubitt (ed.), *Imagining Nations*, 229–54, quote at 229.
26. Paul Heywood, *The Government and Politics of Spain* (London, 1995), 16–17.
27. Alvarez Junco, *Mater Dolorosa*, 542–3, 557–60; on Madrid's economic role, see Ringrose, *'Spanish Miracle'*, 249–90.
28. Santos Juliá, David Ringrose, Cristina Segura, *Madrid: Historia de una capital* (Madrid, 1994); Santos Juliá, 'En los orígenes del gran Madrid' in José Luis García Delgado (ed.), *Las ciudades en la modernización de España* (Madrid, 1992), 415–29.
29. Clementina Díez de Baldeón, *Arquitectura y clases sociales en el Madrid del s.XIX* (Madrid, 1986), 133–4.
30. Ibid., 139–63.
31. Galdós, 'Some observations on the contemporary novel in Spain' (1870) quoted Jo Labanyi (ed.), *Galdós* (London, 1993), 33.
32. Quoted Oscar E. Vázquez, 'Defining *Hispanidad*: Allegories, genealogies and cultural politics in the Madrid Academy's competition of 1893', *Art History* 20 (1997), 111.
33. Ibid., 100–23.
34. *Fortunata and Jacinta* tran. Agnes Moncy Gullón (London, 1988), 435.
35. Manuel Tuñón de Lara (ed.), *Historia del socialismo español* vol. 1 (by Santiago Castillo) (Barcelona, 1989), 78–9 and illustration facing p. 241.
36. Frances Lannon, *Privilege, Persecution, and Prophecy: the Catholic Church in Spain, 1875–1975* (Oxford, 1987), 59–88.
37. *Fortunata and Jacinta*, 17, 14.
38. Juan Pablo Fusi, *Un siglo de España: la cultura* (Madrid, 1999), 29.
39. Cubitt, 'Introduction', 12.
40. Carmelo Lisón Tolosana, 'Un gran encuesta de 1901–2: Notas para la Historia de la Antropología en España' in *Antropología Social en España* (Madrid, 1971), 91–172, quote at 146.
41. Orvar Löfgren, 'The Nationalisation of Culture', *Ethnologia Europea* 19 (1989).
42. Canal, *El carlismo*, 211–72.

43. Xosé-Manoel Núñez, 'The Region as Essence of the Fatherland: Regionalist Variants of Spanish Nationalism, 1840–1936', *European History Quarterly* 31/4 (2001), 483–518.
44. Boyd, *Historia Patria*, 5.
45. Frances Lannon, 'The Socio-Political Role of the Spanish Church: A Case Study', *Journal of Contemporary History* 14 (1979), 193–210.
46. Castillo, *Historia del socialismo*, 263–9.
47. Angel Pestaña, *Trayectoria sindicalista* (Madrid, 1974), 79–87.
48. Doloren Ibarruri, *They Shall Not Pass* (London, 1966), 62–3.
49. Pepe Pareja (José Rodriguéz Quirós) to Jerome Minz, *The Anarchists of Casas Viejas* (Chicago, 1982), 85.
50. Paul Heywood, *Marxism and the Failure of Organised Socialism in Spain, 1879–1936* (Cambridge, 1990), 13–15.
51. Temma Kaplan, *Anarchists of Andalucía, 1868–1903* (Princeton, 1977), 88.
52. Anselmo Lorenzo, *El Proletariado militante* (Madrid, 1974), 236–7.
53. Cited José Alvarez Junco, La *ideología política del anarquismo español, 1868–1910* (Mexico, 1991), 21.
54. Minz, *Casas Viejas* 60–1.
55. George Esenwein, *Anarchist Ideology and the Working-Class Movement in Spain, 1868–1898* (Berkeley and Los Angeles, 1989), 146–52 esp. 146–8.
56. Amaro del Rosal, *Historia de la UGT en España, 1901–1939* (Barcelona, 1977); Paloma Biglino, *El socialismo español y la cuestón agraria, 1890–1936* (Madrid, 1986).
57. Shubert, *Social History of Modern Spain*, 184; Mann, *The Rise of Classes and Nation-States*, 63.
58. Varela, 'La naturaleza' and *Los amigos políticos*.
59. Alicia Yanini Murcia in Varela Ortega (ed.), *El poder de la influencia*, 426–8, quote at 428.
60. María Antonia Peña Guerrero and María Sierra, 'Andalucía' in ibid., 17–43.
61. Temma Kaplan, 'Redressing the Balance: Gendered Acts of Justice around the Mining Community of the Río Tinto' in Victoria Enders and Pamela Beth Radcliff (eds.), *Constructing Spanish Womanhood: Female Identity in Modern Spain* (New York, 1999), 287–8.
62. Emsley, *Gendarmes and the State*, 207.
63. *The Spanish Labyrinth* (Cambridge, 1943), 156.
64. Borja de Riquer i Permanyer, 'El surgimiento de las nuevas identidades contemporáneas' in Ana María García Rovira (ed.), *España ¿Nación de naciones? Ayer* 36 (Madrid, 1999).
65. Varela, 'La naturaleza'.

NOTES TO CHAPTER 3

1. Alvarez Junco, *Mater Dolorosa*, 568–71.
2. Oscar Vázquez, 'Translating 1492: Mexico and Spain's First National Celebration of the "Discovery" of the Americas', *Art Journal* 51 (1992).

3. 'The Book of the Fair', 71, available at *http://columbus.gl.iit.edu/*. The pictures in question were José Garnelo, *Columbus Honoured in the New World* (1892) and Leandro Izaguirre, *The Torture of Cuauhtémoc* (1893).
4. Borja de Riquer, 'El surgimiento de las nuevas identidades', 46.
5. *The Nationalization of the Masses: Political Symbolism and Mass Movements in Germany* (New York, 1975).
6. Sebastian Balfour, *The End of the Spanish Empire, 1898–1923* (Oxford, 1997).
7. Balfour, ' "The Lion and the Pig": Nationalism and National Identity in *Fin-de-Siècle* Spain' in Clare Mar-Molinero and Angel Smith (eds.), *Nationalism and the Nation in the Iberian Peninsula* (Oxford, 1996), 111, 107, 109.
8. José Alvarez Junco, ' "Los amantes de la libertad": la cultura republicana española a principios del siglo XX' in Townson, *El republicanismo*, 285.
9. Emile Verhaeren, *España Negra* tran. and ill. by Darío de Regoyos (Madrid, 1963; 1st publ. 1909).
10. José Gutiérrez-Solana, *La España Negra* (Barcelona, 1972); Bozal, *Pintura y escultura españolas*, 51–5, 138–9, 535.
11. Arturo Barea, *The Forge* (London, 1984; 1st publ. 1943), 68, 66.
12. Ramón Ruíz Alonso SJ, *El patriotismo* (Madrid, 1910), 81–2.
13. Ibid., 16.
14. Quoted Shubert, *Death and Money*, 2.
15. Quoted Donald L. Shaw, *The Generation of 1898 in Spain* (London, 1975) 10; see also Alvarez Junco, *Mater Dolorosa*, 584–93.
16. José Alvarez Junco, *El Emperador del Paralelo: Lerroux y la demagogia populista* (Madrid, 1990); there is a shorter English version, *The Emergence of Mass Politics in Spain: Populist Demagoguery and Republican Culture, 1890–1910* (Brighton, 2002).
17. Comín Comín, *Hacienda y economía*, 47–53.
18. Eric Storm, 'The Rise of the Intellectual around 1900: Spain and France', *European History Quarterly*, 32/2 (2002), 150–3.
19. See, e.g., by Alvarez Junco, *Mater Dolorosa*, 590–1.
20. Jesús Millán and Mª Cruz Romero, 'Was the Liberal Revolution Important to Modern Spain? Political Cultures and Citizenship in Spanish History', *Social History*, 29/3 (2004), 292–9.
21. *Marxism and the Failure of Organised Socialism*, 21.
22. *Quod Multum*, 1886; *Divini Illius Magistri*, 1929; *Militantis Ecclesiae*, 1897.
23. 1888–9 prospectus, cited Lannon, *Privilege, Persecution and Prophecy*, 69.
24. For the ILE, see Boyd, *Historia Patria*, 30–6, and Vicente Cacho Viu, *La institución libre de enseñanza* (Madrid, 1962); on the ACNP, see José Manuel Ordovas, *Historia de la Asociación Católica Nacional de Propagandistas (1923–1936)* (Pamplona, 19993), 19–82.
25. María Jesús González, ' "Neither God nor Monster": Antonio Maura and the Failure of Conservative Reformism in Restoration Spain (1893–1923)', *European History Quarterly* 32/3(2002), 307–34; Mercedes Cabrera, 'El conservadurismo

maurista en la Restauración: Los límites de la revolución desde arriba', in García Delgado, *La España de la Restauración*, 55–70; Balfour, *End of the Spanish Empire*, 188–210.

26. Quoted González, 'Neither God nor Monster', 312.

27. Quoted Ramiro Reig, 'El caso valenciano: un proceso de modernización involutivo' in José Luis García Delgado (ed.), *Las Ciudades en la modernización de España* (Madrid, 1992), 224.

28. Pamela Beth Radcliff, 'Política y cultura republicana en Gijón de fin de siglo' and Ramiro Reig, 'Entre la realidad y la illusion: el fenómeno blasquista en Valencia, 1898–1936' in Townson (ed.), *El republicanismo*, 373–423.

29. Borja de Riquer, 'Los límites de la movilización política', 21–3.

30. Alvarez Junco, *Emergence of Mass Politics*, 68.

31. Robert Hughes, *Barcelona* (London, 1992).

32. Quoted Ludger Mees, *Nationalism, Violence and Democracy: The Basque Clash of Identities* (London, 2003), 12.

33. Borja de Riquer, *Lliga Regionalista: la burgesia catalana i el nacionalisme* (Barcelona, 1977); Juan Pablo Fusi, *El País Vasco: pluralismo y nacionalidad* (Madrid, 1984).

34. Marianne Heiberg, *The Making of the Basque Nation* (Cambridge, 1989), 235–7.

35. Quoted ibid., 61.

36. Figs. from Fusi, *País Vasco*, 45–8; of 13, 000 miners in Vizcaya in 1910, only c. 3,000 were Basque by birth.

37. Balfour, *End of the Spanish Empire*, 109.

38. Smith, 'The Rise of Labour', 24–5; strike figs. from Tortella, *El desarrollo*, 203.

39. Ibarruri, *They Shall Not Pass*, 26–7.

40. Pamela Beth Radcliff, 'Women's Politics: Consumer Riots in Twentieth-Century Spain' in Radcliff and Enders (eds.), *Constructing Spanish Womanhood*; Balfour, *End of the Spanish Empire*, 106–12.

41. González Calleja, *La razón de la fuerza*; Joaquín Romero Maura, *La 'rosa del fuego': el obrerismo barcelonés de 1988 a 1909* (Madrid, 1989).

42. Joaquín Romero Maura, *La romana del diablo: Ensayos sobre la violencia política en España* (Madrid, 2000), 110–42.

43. Museu Nacional d'Art de Catalunya at http://www.mnac.es/cat/dinou/s17.htm

44. Scott, *Seeing like a State*, 58–63.

45. Ibarruri, *They Shall Not Pass*, 30–3; Radcliff, *From Mobilisation to Civil War*, 208–9.

46. Julio de la Cueva, 'Movilización política e identidad anticlerical, 1898–1910' in Rafael Cruz (ed.), *El anticlericalismo* and 'Católicos en la calle: la movilización de los católicos españoles, 1899–1923', *Historia y Política* 3 (2000/1), 55–79.

47. Quoted Reig, 'El caso valenciano', 224.

48. González Calleja, *La razón de la fuerza*, 332–40.

49. Quoted Joan Connelly Ullman, *The Tragic Week: A Study of Anticlericalism in Spain, 1875–1912* (Cambridge, Mass., 1968), 138.
50. Outlined programmatically in Tortella, *El desarrollo*, 203–4.
51. *La razón de la fuerza*, 447–53 esp. 449.
52. Romero Maura, *La 'rosa del fuego'*, 511–12.
53. Gerald Meaker, 'A Civil War of Words: The Ideological Impact of the First World War on Spain, 1914–18', in Hans A. Schmitt (ed.), *Neutral Europe between War and Revolution, 1917–23* (Charlottesville, Va., 1988), 4.
54. Gerald Meaker, *The Revolutionary Left in Spain, 1914–23* (Stanford, Calif., 1974), 109, 103.
55. Carolyn Boyd, *Praetorian Politics in Liberal Spain* (Chapel Hill, NC, 1979).
56. Meaker, 'A Civil War of Words', 43.
57. del Moral, *Historia de las agitaciones campesinas*, 265–76.
58. Finer, *Man on Horseback*, 117.
59. Leader of Juventud Maurista, Valladolid, quoted Jesús María Palomares Ibáñez, *La dictadura de Primo de Rivera en Valladolid* (Valladolid, 1993), 13.
60. Shlomo Ben-Ami, *Fascism from Above: the Dictatorship of Primo de Rivera in Spain, 1923–1930*, (Oxford, 1983), 19–33.
61. Quoted ibid., 64.
62. Varela Ortega, 'Sobre la naturaleza', 188–9.
63. Eduardo González Calleja, *La España de Primo de Rivera: La modernización autoritaria 1923–1930* (Madrid, 2005), 83–94; Boyd, *Historia Patria*, 169–93; Clara Eugenia Núñez, *La fuente de la riqueza*, 291, 301–18.
64. Quoted Boyd, *Historia Patria*, 171; González Calleja, *La España de Primo*, 87–8.
65. *La Razón*, 9 March 1928, quoted Joseph M. Roig Rosich, *La dictadura de Primo de Rivera a Catalunya* (Montserrat, 1992), 35.
66. See, e.g., Julio de la Cueva, 'Inventing Catholic Identities in Twentieth-Century Spain: the Virgin Bien-Aparecida, 1904–1910', *Catholic Historical Review* 87 (2001), 624–42.
67. María Teresa González Calbet, *La dictadura de Primo de Rivera: El Directorio Militar* (Madrid, 1987), 318.
68. Boyd, *Historia Patria*, 186–93.
69. González Calleja, *El Máuser y el sufragio*, 275.
70. Quoted ibid., 293–4.
71. Brenan, after Madariaga, *Spanish Labyrinth*, 75.
72. González Calleja, 'La defensa armada del "orden social" durante al dictadura de Primo de Rivera' in García Delgado (ed.), *España entre dos siglos, 1887–1931* (Madrid, 1991), 61–108; *El Máuser y el sufragio*, 255–302.
73. Quoted Mary Vincent, 'Spain' in Kevin Passmore (ed.), *Women, Gender and Fascism in Europe, 1918–45* (Manchester, 2003), 190–8 at 195.
74. Elections were either local or plebiscitary.
75. Mercedes Ugalde Solano, *Mujeres y Nacionalismo Vasco: Génesis y desarrollo de Emakume Abertzale Batza, 1906–1936* (Bilbao, 1993), 180–1, 184, 185–6.

76. Heywood, *Marxism and the Failure of Organised Socialism*, 93–4; José Luis Gómez-Navarro, *El regimen de Primo de Rivera*, (Madrid, 1991). 204–5.

77. Quoted William J. Calllahan, *The Catholic Church in Spain 1875–1998* (Washington, 2000), 167.

NOTES TO CHAPTER 4

1. Dámaso Berenguer, *De la Dictadura a la República*, (Madrid, 1975), 327.

2. Ibid., 332; Carr, *Spain*, 602.

3. *Madrid, 1931–1934: De la fiesta popular a la lucha de clases* (Madrid, 1984), 7–21 at 17.

4. Shlomo Ben-Ami, 'The Republican "Take-Over": Prelude to Inevitable Catastrophe?' in Paul Preston (ed.), *Revolution and War in Spain 1931–9* (London, 1984), 29.

5. Quoted Federica Montseny, *Mis primeros cuarenta años* (Barcelona, 1987), 62.

6. 'Caciquismo y democracia', *Obras completas* I (Mexico, 1966), 471–2.

7. Evelyne Ricci, 'La célébration de la Seconde République à Malaga: les modèles de la fête' in J. R. Aymes and S. Salaün (eds.), *Le métissage culturel en Espagne* (Paris, 2001), 288–9.

8. Quoted González, 'Neither God nor Monster', 317.

9. Manuel Suárez Cortina, 'Viejo y nuevo republicanismo en la España del siglo XX' in Antonio Morales Moya (ed.), *Ideologías y movimientos políticos* (Madrid, 2001), 113.

10. Fernando de los Ríos speaking during the debates on the religious causes of the constitution, *Diario de Sesiones de las Cortes Constituyentes* (Madrid, 1931–3; henceforth *DSCC*), 1527.

11. Quoted Manuel Revuelta González, 'La recuperación eclesiástica y el rechazo anticlerical en el cambio del siglo' in *España entre dos siglos*, 213–34.

12. Quoted Martínez, Laguna et al. in Jorge Uría (ed.), *La cultura popular en la España contemporánea* (Madrid, 2003), 163.

13. Figs. from Núñez, *La fuente de la riqueza*, 301–18; Mariano Pérez Gálan, *La enseñanza en la Segunda República* (Madrid, 1975), 329–49.

14. Sandie Holguín, *Creating Spaniards: Culture and National Identity in Republican Spain* (Madison, Wis., 2002), 47–78, 90–114, 124–34; Eugenio Otero Urtaza, *Las misiones pedagógicas: una experiencia de educación popular* (Coruña, 1982).

15. Maura, *Así cayó Alfonso XIII* (Mexico, 1962), 265–9.

16. Suárez Cortina, 'Viejo y nuevo republicanismo', 117–18, 119–20.

17. See, e.g., Nigel Townson, *The Crisis of Democracy in Spain: Centrist Politics under the Second Republic, 1931–6* (Brighton, 2000), esp. 41–6.

18. *DSCC*, 1527.

19. Azaña, *Memorias*, I, 469–70; entry for 20 May 1932.

20. Julián Casanova, 'La cara oscura del anarquismo' in Santos Juliá (ed.), *Violencia política en la España del siglo XX* (Madrid, 2000), 96.
21. Christopher Ealham, 'Anarchism and Illegality in Barcelona, 1931–7', *Contemporary European History* 4 (1995), 144.
22. José Antonio Primo de Rivera, *Selected Writings*, ed. Hugh Thomas (London, 1972), 56.
23. David Jato, *La rebelion de los estudiantes: Apuntes para la historia del alegre SEU* (Madrid, 1953), 93.
24. José María Gil Robles, *No fue posible la paz* (Barcelona, 1968), 100.
25. José Monge y Bernal, *Acción Popular: Estudios de Biología Política* (Madrid: 1936), 145.
26. Gil Robles, *No fue posible la paz*, 616.
27. Adrian Shubert, *The Road to Revolution in Spain: The Coal Miners of Asturias, 1860–1934* (Urbana and Chicago, 1987), 150–1.
28. Quoted Julio Gil Pecharromán, *Historia de la Segunda República Española* (Madrid, 2002), 213.
29. Quoted Antonio Mª Calero, 'Octubre visto por la derecha', in Germán Ojeda (ed.), *Octubre 1934* (Madrid, 1985), 162–3.
30. Quoted ibid., 168.
31. Santos Juliá, 'The Origins of the Spanish Popular Front' in Martin Alexander and Helen Graham (eds.), *The French and Spanish Popular Fronts: Comparative Perspectives* (Cambridge, 1989).
32. Mary Vincent, *Catholicism in the Second Spanish Republic: Religion and Politics in Salamanca, 1930–6* (Oxford, 1996), 241; Luis Garrido González, *Colectividades agrarias en Andalucía: Jaén, 1931–9* (Jaén, 2003), 21–6.
33. Reproduced in Cipriano de Rivas Cherif, *Retrato de un desconocido: vida de Manuel Azaña* (Barcelona, 1979), 665–6.
34. Urbano Orad de la Torre in Ronald Fraser, *Blood of Spain: The Experience of Civil War, 1936–9* (London, 1979), 53.
35. Helen Graham, *The Spanish Republic at War, 1936–9* (Cambridge, 2003), 94 n.
36. José Luis Ledesma, *Las días de llamas de la revolución: Violencia y política en la retaguardia republicana de Zaragoza durante la guerra civil* (Zaragoza, 2003), 106–27.
37. Gerald Brenan, *Personal Record, 1920–1975* (New York, 1975), 307–8.
38. Antonio Montero Moreno, *Historia de la persecución religiosa en España 1936–1939* (Madrid, 1961), 606–7.
39. Julio de la Cueva, 'Religious Persecution, Anticlerical Tradition and Revolution: On Atrocities against the Clergy during the Spanish Civil War', *Journal of Contemporary History* 33/3 (1998), 355–69; Mary Vincent, '"The Keys of the Kingdom": Religious Violence in the Spanish Civil War, July–August 1936' in Chris Ealham and Michael Richards (eds.), *The Splintering of Spain: New Historical Perspectives on the Spanish Civil War* (Cambridge, 2005), 68–89.
40. *Confederación* (Murcia) 5 Feb. 1937.

41. 'Statues of the Workers' Free collective of Tamarite de Litera' reproduced Gaston Leval, *Collectives in the Spanish Revolution* (London, 1975), 215–18 at 217.

42. Graham, *The Spanish Republic at War*, 233.

43. Julián Casanova (ed.), *El sueño igualitario* (Zaragoza, 1988).

44. Quoted Julián Casanova, *Anarquismo y revolución en la sociedad rural aragonesa, 1936–8* (Madrid, 1985), 133, 136. See also Michael Seidman, *Republic of Egos: A Social History of the Spanish Civil War* (Madison, Wis., 2002), 124–45.

45. Francisco Cobo Romero, *La Guerra Civil y la repression franquista en la provincia de Jaén, 1936–50* (Jaén, 1993), 18–19.

46. Quoted Rafael Quirosa-Cheyrouzy y Muñoz, *Política y Guerra Civil en Almería* (Almería: Cajal, 1986), 134.

47. Montero Moreno, *Historia de la persecución religiosa*, 390–5, 414–15.

48. Jennifer Milliken and Keith Krause, 'State Failure, State Collapse and State Reconstruction: Concepts, Lessons and Strategies' in Jennifer Milliken (ed.), *State Failure, Collapse and Reconstruction* (Oxford: Blackwell, 2003), 2.

49. Aurora Bosch Sánchez, *Ugetistas y liberarios: Guerra Civil y revolución en el País Valenciano, 1936–9* (Valencia, 1983), 40–2. The orange was Spain's major foreign currency earner.

50. Quoted Casanova, *Anarquismo y revolución*, 106 and Burnett Bolloten, *The Spanish Civil War: Revolution and Counterrevolution* (New York and London, 1991), 201.

51. José Alvarez del Vayo, *Freedom's Battle* (London, 1940), 207–8.

52. Quoted Bolloten, *The Spanish Civil War*, 202.

53. Graham, *Spanish Republic at War*, 232.

54. Quoted Casanova, *Anarquismo y revolución*, 136.

55. Aurora Bosch, 'Collectivisations: The Spanish Revolution Revisited, 1936–39', *International Journal of Iberian Studies* 14 (2001), 4–16.

56. Julián Casanova, *Caspe, 1936–8: conflictos politicos y transformaciones sociales durante la Guerra Civil* (Zaragoza, 1984), 87–8.

57. Quoted Holguín, *Creating Spaniards*, 173–4.

58. Martha Gellhorn, 'The Beseiged City' in *The Face of War* (London, 1993).

59. Francisco Cobo Romero, *Guerra Civil y la repression franquista*, 453–8; c. 10% of Cataluña's population was made up of refugees by 1937.

60. Francisco Espinosa, *La columna de la muerte* (Barcelona, 2003); examples at 17–19, 154–8, 242.

61. 'Massacre in Badajoz', *Chicago Tribune*, 30 Aug. 1936.

62. Quoted Paul Preston, *Franco: a Biography* (London, 1993), 166.

63. Quoted Ignacio Martín Jiménez, *La Guerra Civil en Valladolid, 1936–9: amaneceres ensangrentados* (Valladolid, 2000), 147.

64. Ramón J. Sender, *The War in Spain* (London, 1947), 302–6 at 306; Ramón Sender Badayón, *A Death in Zamora* (Albuquerque, N. Mex., 1989).

65. Gerald Brenan, *The Face of Spain* (London, 1950), 122–48; quotes at 139, 140, 145; Ian Gibson, *The Assassination of Federico García Lorca* (London, 1979).
66. Gibson, *Assassination*, 108–9; Brenan, *Face of Spain*, 129–31.
67. Julios Ruiz, *Franco's Justice: Repression in Madrid after the Spanish Civil War* (Oxford, 2005), 79–81.
68. Manuel Risques Corbella, 'Disciplinados en 1936, ejecutados en 1939. Proceso sumarísimo a la Guardia Civil de Barcelona' in Conxita Mir Curcó (ed.), *La represión bajo Franco, Ayer* 43 (2001).
69. Sheelagh Ellwood, 'Falange Española and the Creation of the Francoist "New State"', *European History Quarterly* 20 (1990), 215.
70. *The Red Domination in Spain: The General Cause* (Madrid, 1953), 7.
71. Isidro Sánchez, Manuel Ortiz and David Ruiz (eds.), *España Franquista: Causa General y actitudes sociales ante la Dictadura* (Cuidad Real, 1993).
72. *Oscuro Heroismo* (Sevilla, 1939), 27.
73. Michael Richards, *A Time of Silence: Civil War and the Culture of Repression in Franco's Spain, 1936–1945* (Cambridge, 1998), 79.
74. Quoted Emilio Silva and Santiago Macías, *Las fosas de Franco: Los republicanos que el dictador dejó en las cunetas* (Madrid, 2003), 131.
75. C. Molinero, M. Sala, and J. Sobrequés (eds.), *Una inmensa prisión: los campos de concentración y las prisiones durante la guerra civil y el Franquismo* (Barcelona, 2003).
76. Julián Casanova (ed.), *Morir, matar, sobrevivir: La violencia en la dictadura de Franco* (Barcelona, 2002), 8; Julius Ruiz, 'A Spanish Genocide?: Reflections on the Francoist Repression after the Spanish Civil War', *Contemporary European History* 14 (2005), 178.
77. Manuel Azaña, *Vigil in Benicarló* trans. Paul and Josephine Stewart (London and Toronto, 1982), 76–7.
78. Ruiz, *Franco's Justice*, 85–130.
79. Conxita Mir Curcó, *Vivir es sobrevivir: justicia, orden y marginación en la Cataluña rural de la posguerra* (Lleida, 2000) and 'Violencia política, coacción legal y oposición interior' in Glicerio Sánchez Recio (ed.), *El primer franquismo, 1936–59 Ayer* (Madrid, 1999), 115–46.
80. Jane Caplan and John Torpey, *Documenting Individual Identities: The Development of State Practices in the Modern World* (Princeton, 2001), 1–12.
81. Brenan, *Face of Spain*, 123.
82. Ronald Fraser, *In Hiding* (London, 1972); Jesús Torbado and Manuel Leguineche, *The Moles* (London, 1981).

NOTES TO CHAPTER 5

1. Stanley Payne, *The Franco Regime, 1936–75* (Madison, Wis., 1987), 245.
2. Franciso Moreno Gómez, *Córdoba en el posguerra: la represión y la guerrilla, 1939–50* (Córdoba, 1987), esp. 460–514.

3. Secudino Serrano, *Maquis: Historia de la guerrilla antifranquista* (Madrid, 2001), 374.

4. For an indication of the range and complexity of feelings towards the early Franco regime, see Ismael Saz Campos, *Fascismo y franquismo* (Valencia, 2004), 184–96, quotes at 195, 190.

5. Quoted Mª Encarna Nicolás Marín, 'Los poderes locales y la consolidación de la dictadura franquista' in Sánchez Recio (ed.), *El primer franquismo*, 78.

6. This argument goes against that put forward by Antonio Cazorla-Sánchez, *Las políticas de la Victoria: La consolidación del Nuevo Estado franquista, 1938–1953* (Madrid, 2000), 43–60, though it draws upon his evidence.

7. Angela Cenarro, 'Elite, Party Church: Pillars of the Francoist "New State" in Aragon, 1936–45', *European History Quarterly* 28/4 (1998),461–86, quote at 465.

8. Cazorla-Sánchez, *Políticas de la victoria*, 57.

9. Boyd, *Historia Patria*, 242–6.

10. *Palabras del Caudillo* (n.p. but Madrid, 1939), 289.

11. Paul Preston, *Franco: A Biography* (London, 1993), 189, 346, 642.

12. Richard Wright, *Pagan Spain* (London, 1957), 86–7.

13. Quoted Juan Pablo Fusi, *Franco: A Biography* (London, 1987), 49.

14. Richards, *A Time of Silence*, 67–88, at 69.

15. Scott, *Seeing Like a State*, 87–102, 147–80, 223–61; quote from Proudhon, 183.

16. Spanish bishops, quoted Pilar Folguera, 'El franquismo. El retorno a la esfera privada (1939–75)' in Elisa Gerrido (ed.), *Historia de las mujeres en España* (Madrid, 1997), 530.

17. *Casti Connubii* §26–7.

18. Saz, *Fascismo y franquismo*, 190, 194.

19. Folguera, 'El retorno a la esfera privada', 527–48; Carme Molinero, 'Mujer, franquismo, fascismo: la clausura forzada en un "mundo pequeño"', *Historia Social* 30 (1998), 97–117.

20. Payne, *Franco Regime*, 389.

21. Pilar Primo de Rivera, *Recuerdos de una vida* (Madrid, 1983), 267; Payne, *Franco Regime*, 391.

22. Mary Nash, 'Pronatalism and Motherhood in Franco's Spain' in Gisela Bock and Pat Thane (eds.), *Maternity and Gender Politics* (London, 1991), 160–77.

23. Primo de Rivera, *Recuerdos*, 224–42.

24. Cart. 1/245, 'Art i Propaganda. Cartells de la Universitat de València' at www.uv.es/cultura/v/docs/expartipropaganda.htm

25. Boyd, *Historia Patria*, 241.

26. Kathleen Richmond, *Women and Spanish Fascism: the Women's Section of the Falange, 1934–59* (London, 2003), 79–80; Carme Molinero, *La captación de las masas: Política social y propaganda en el regimen franquista* (Madrid, 2005), 158–85.

27. Mónica Orduña Prada, *El Auxilio Social 1936–1940: La etapa fundacional y los primeros años* (Madrid, 1996).

28. Payne, *Franco Regime*, 389.
29. Mirta Núñez Díaz-Balart, *Mujeres Caídas: prostitutes legales y clandestinas en el franquismo* (Madrid, 2003).
30. Quoted Folguera, 'El retorno a la esfera privada', 533.
31. Pilar Primo de Rivera, *Cuatro discursos* (n.p. but Madrid, 1939), 22.
32. Javier Tusell, 'La descomposición del sistema caciquil', *Revista de Occidente* 127 (1973), 85.
33. 'Fuero del Trabajo', *Fundamental Laws of the State* (Madrid, 1967) article 4, 43–56.
34. Lorenzo Díaz, *La radio en España, 1923–97* (Madrid, 1997), 204–5.
35. Luis Suárez Fernández, *Crónica de la Sección Femenina y su tiempo* (Madrid, 1993), 221, 237. See also Carmen Ortiz, 'The Uses of Folklore by the Franco Regime', *The Journal of American Folklore* 112 (1999), 491–3.
36. Ortiz, 'Uses of Folklore', 480.
37. Javier Ugarte Tellería, *La nueva Covadonga insurgente* (Madrid, 1998), 371–84 at 377.
38. Jeremy MacClancy, *The Decline of Carlism* (Reno and Las Vegas, 2000), 112.
39. Aurora Morcillo, *True Catholic Womanhood: Gender Ideology in Franco's Spain* (DeKalb, Ill., 2000), 46–76.
40. Quoted Raymond Carr and Juan Pablo Fusi, *Spain: Dictatorship to Democracy* (London, 1979), 47.
41. Díaz, *La radio en España*, 232.
42. *Spain*, 118.
43. Ibid., 119; Payne, *The Franco Regime*, 512.
44. Boyd, *Historia Patria*, 276, 278–9.
45. Marie Franco, 'La prensa popular: tebeos, mundo rosa y crímenes, los placers de una sociedad' in Uría (ed.), *La cultura popular*.
46. Joan Estruch, *Saints and Schemers: Opus Dei and its Paradoxes* (New York and Oxford, 1995), 224.
47. José V. Casanova, 'The Opus Dei Ethic, the Technocrats and the Modernization of Spain', *Social Science Information* 22/1 (1983), 27–50 at 46.
48. Heywood, *Government and Politics of Spain*, 123, 126, 128–9.
49. Tortella, *El desarrollo*, 284.
50. Keith Salmon, *The Modern Spanish Economy* (London and New York, 1991), 4–5.
51. Joseph Harrison, *The Spanish Economy in the Twentieth Century* (London, 1985), 145.
52. Ibid., 158–9 and Joseph Harrison, *The Spanish Economy from the Civil War to the European Community* (London, 1993), 38–9.
53. Salmon, *Modern Spanish Economy*, 167–8.
54. Javier Escalera Reyes, 'El franquismo y la fiesta: Régimen político, transformaciones sociales y sociabilidad festiva en la España de Franco', in Uría (ed.), *La cultura popular*, 253–61, esp. 258–9; Clotilde Puertolas, 'Masculinity versus Femininity: The *Sanfermines*, 1938–78' in Enders and Radcliff (eds.), *Contesting Spanish Womanhood*, 95–122, esp. 97, 107, 108.

55. Ronald Fraser, *The Pueblo: A Mountain Village on the Costa del Sol* (Newton Abbot, 1974), 152, 182–3.

56. Lucia Graves, *A Woman Unknown: Voices from a Spanish Life* (Washington DC, 1999), 45.

57. Catherine Boyle, 'The Politics of Popular Music: On the Dynamics of New Song' in Helen Graham and Jo Labanyi (eds.), *Spanish Cultural Studies: An Introduction* (Oxford, 1995), 291–4.

58. Lluís Llach, L'estaca (1968) at http://www.lluisllach.com.htm © Copyright 1968 by Lluís Llach Grande, Barcelona (España). Edición autorizada en exclusiva para todos los países a EDICIONES QUIROGA, Alcalá, 70, 28009 Madrid (España). Copyright cedido en 1985 a SEEM, S. A., Alcalá, 70, 28009 Madrid (España).

59. *Pacem in Terrris* (1963) at http://www.vatican.va/holy_father/john_xxiii/encyclic als/index.htm; *Dignitatis Humanae* (1965) at http://www.vatican.va/archive/hist _councils/ii_vatican_council/

60. José Casanova, *Public Religions in the Modern World* (Chicago, 1994), 70–4 at 71; Estruch, *Saints and Schemers*, 189–90.

61. Jesús Iribarren (ed.), *Documentos colectivos del episcopado español, 1870–1974* (Madrid, 1974), 235–6.

62. Vicente Enrique y Tarancón, *Recuerdos de juventud* (Barcelona, 1984), 348.

63. José Castaño Colomer, *La JOC en España, 1946–70* (Salamanca, 1978), 49–117; Feliciano Montero García, *La Acción Católica en el Franquismo: Auge y crisis de la Acción Católica especializada* (Madrid, 2000).

64. Lannon, *Privilege, Persecution, and Prophecy*, 232–48 at 234.

65. Reproduced Montero García, *Acción Católica*, 278–9.

66. Ibid., 244–5; Casanova, *Public Religión*, 85.

67. Guy Hermet, *Los católicos en la España Franquista*, Vol. 1 (Madrid, 1985), 72, 29.

68. Víctor Pérez-Díaz, *The Return of Civil Society: the Emergence of Democratic Spain* (Cambridge, Mass., 1993) at 142–3.

69. Juan María Laboa, 'La Iglesia española en los últimos treinta años' in Olegario González de Cardedal (ed.), *La Iglesia en España, 1950–2000* (Madrid, 1999), 117–18; Lannon, *Privilege, Persecution, and Prophecy*, 47.

70. Pérez-Díaz, *Return of Civil Society*, 163.

71. José María Martín Patino, 'La iglesia en la sociedad española' in Juan Linz et al., *España: un presente para el futuro*, vol. 1 (Madrid, 1984), 160–2.

72. For Itziar, see Joseba Zulaika, *Basque Violence: Metaphor and Sacrament* (Reno, 1988), 36–73.

73. For Cirauqui, see MacClancy, *Decline of Carlism*, 206–8; 211–14.

74. Zulaika, *Basque Violence*, 44–5.

75. Lannon, *Privilege, Persecution and Prophecy*, 107–13, 251–2; Anabella Barroso Arahuetes, 'Iglesia vasca, una Iglesia de vencedores y vencidos. La represión del clero vasco durante el franquismo', *Ayer* 43 (Madrid, 2001), 87–109.

76. Rogelio Duocastella, Jesús A. Marcos, José María Díaz Mózaz (eds.), *Análisis sociológico del catolicismo español* (Barcelona, 1967), 44–5.

77. Lannon, *Privilege, Persecution and Prophecy*, 111–12; for ETA, Robert P. Clark, *The Basque Insurgents: ETA, 1952–1980* (Madison, Wis., 1984).

78. Amnesty International, *Political Imprisonment in Spain* (London, 1973), appendix 3.

79. Frances Lannon, 'An Elite of Grace: the Spanish Bishops in the Twentieth Century' in Lannon and Preston (eds.), *Elites and Power*, 20.

NOTES TO CHAPTER 6

1. José María Maravall, *Dictatorship and Political Dissent* (London, 1978), 33; Carme Molinero and Pere Ysàs, 'Workers and Dictatorship' in Smith (ed.), *Red Barcelona*, 200.

2. Mir, 'Violencia política, coacción legal', 129, 131.

3. Saz, *Fascismo y franquismo*, 179–80.

4. Amnesty International, *Political Imprisonment in Spain* (London, 1973) and *Report on Torture* (London, 1973), 165–8.

5. *Report of an Amnesty International Mission to Spain* (London, 1975), quotes at 18–20; Kenneth Medhurst, *The Basques and Catalans* (Minority Rights Group Report 9; London, 1982).

6. *Mission to Spain*, appendix C.

7. Pérez-Díaz, *Return of Civil Society*, 157; Maravall, *Dictatorship and Political Dissent*, chs. 5 and 6.

8. See, e.g., Borja de Riquer i Permanyer, 'Social and Economic Change in a Climate of Political Immobilism' in Graham and Labanyi (eds.), *Spanish Cultural Studies*, 259–71.

9. Pérez-Díaz, *Return of Civil Society*, 154–5.

10. Ibid., 35.

11. Julián Alvarez Alvarez, *Burocracia y poder político en el régimen franquista* (Madrid, 1984), 116–18; José Casanova, 'Modernization and Democratization: Reflections on Spain's Transition to Democracy', *Social Research* 50 (1983), 960–3.

12. Charles T. Powell, 'The "Táctio" Group and the Transition to Democracy, 1973–7' in Lannon and Preston (eds.), *Elites and Power*, 249–68; Cristina Palomares, *The Quest for Survival after Franco: Moderate Francoism and the Slow Journey to the Polls, 1964–77* (Brighton, 2004), 124–30.

13. Casanova, 'Modernization and Democratization', 966–72.

14. Borja de Riquer, 'Social and Economic Change', 259.

15. Paul Preston, *The Triumph of Democracy in Spain* (London, 1986), 74.

16. Canal, *El carlismo*, 366–82; Francisco Javier Caspistegui, *El naufragio de los ortodoxias* (Pamplona, 1997).

17. Charles Powell, *Juan Carlos of Spain* (London, 1996), 82–4.

18. Quoted Preston, *Franco*, 752.

19. Sebastian Balfour, *Dictatorship, Workers and the City: Labour in Greater Barcelona since 1939* (Oxford, 1989), 191–235 at 219.

20. Balcells, *Catalan Nationalism*, 147–8; Eamonn Rodgers (ed.), *Encyclopedia of Contemporary Spanish Culture* (London, 1999), 277–8.
21. Balfour, *Dictatorship, Workers and the City*, 196; Robert Fishman, *Working-Class Organization and the Return to Democracy in Spain* (Ithaca, NY, 1990), 105.
22. Balfour, *Dictatorship, Workers and the City*, 205–18; Maravall, *Dictatorship and Political Dissent*,
23. Fishman, *Working-Class Organization*, 87.
24. Santos Juliá, Javier Pradera, Joaquín Prieto (eds.), *Memoria de la transición* (Madrid, 1996), 185–92.
25. Pérez-Díaz, *Return of Civil Society*, 34, 39.
26. Manuel Castells, *The City and the Grassroots* (London, 1983), 213–88.
27. Paul Heywood, 'Mirror-Images: the PCE and the PSOE in the Transition to Democracy in Spain', *West European Politics* 10/2 (1987), 193–210 at 203; Abdón Mateos, *El PSOE contra Franco: continuidad y renovación del socialismo español, 1953–74* (Madrid, 1993), 456–65.
28. José Casanova, 'Las enseñanzas de la transición democrática en España' in Manuel Redero San Román (ed.), *La transición a la democracia en España*, *Ayer* 15 (Madrid, 1994), 15–54 esp. 38–9). For Suárez, see Preston, *Triumph of Democracy*, 91–160.
29. This is to use another term for the process described in Pérez-Díaz, *Return of Civil Society*, 28–9.
30. 85.5% of the Cortes voted for the law. Alvaro Soto Carmona, 'De las Cortes orgánicas a las Cortes democráticas' in Redero San Román (ed.), *La transición a la democracia en España*, 109–34.
31. http://en.wikipedia.org/wiki/Elections_in_Spain
32. Overall, the right won 45% of the popular vote and the left 44% though under the d'Hondt system of proportional representation, the right gained more seats.
33. José María Maravall, *The Transition to Democracy in Spain* (London and New York, 1982), 23–9.
34. Laura Edles, *Symbol and Ritual in the New Spain* (Cambridge, 1998), 51, 53, 54.
35. Paloma Aguilar, *Memoria y olvido de la Guerra Civil española* (Madrid, 1996), 209–354.
36. Quoted Paul Preston, *Juan Carlos: A People's King* (London, 2004), 325.
37. Edles, *Symbol and Ritual*, 41–80 at 65.
38. Quoted Aguilar, *Memoria y olvido*, 352.
39. http://www.constitucion.es/
40. Ramón Cotarelo, 'La Constitución de 1978' in José Féliz Tezanos, Ramón Cotarelo, Andrés de Blas (eds.), *La transición democrática española* (Madrid, 1989), 317–45 at 318. See also Gregorio Peces-Barba, *La elaboración de la Constitución de 1978* (Madrid, 1988); Heywood, *Government and Politics of Spain*, 37–56.
41. William Callahan, *The Catholic Church in Spain 1875–1998* (Washington DC, 2000), 565–73; Casanova, *Public Religions*, 87–91.
42. Castells, *City and the Grassroots*, 236, 273–4.

43. Pamela Beth Radcliff, 'Citizens and Housewives: The Problem of Female Citizenship in Spain's Transition to Democracy', *Journal of Social History* 36/1 (2002), 77–100 and 'Imagining Female Citizenship in the "New Spain": Gendering the Democratic Transition, 1975–8', *Gender and History* 15/3 (2001), 498–523; voting figures in Preston, *Triumph of Democracy*, 119.
44. Radcliff, 'Citizens and Housewives', 91–2; Castells, *City and the Grassroots*, 246.
45. Fernando Reinares, 'Democratización y terrorismo en el caso español' in Tezanos et al., *La transición democrática española*, 611–44.
46. Paloma Aguilar, 'The Memory of the Civil War in the Transition to Democracy: The Peculiarity of the Basque Case' in Paul Heywood (ed.), *Politics and Policy in Democratic Spain: No Longer Different?* (London, 1999), 5–25.
47. Heywood, *Government and Politics of Spain*, 45; Jorge de Esteban,. 'El proceso constituyente español, 1977–8' in Tezanos et al., *La transición democrática*, 294–8.
48. Heywood, *Government and Politics*, 52; see also Xosé Manoel Núñez-Seixas, 'Nacionalismos y regionalismos ante la formación y consolidación del Estado autonómico español (1975–95)' in Tusell et al., *Historia de la transición y consolidación democrática*, vol. 1, 427–56.
49. Pere Ysàs, 'Democracia y autonomía en la transición española' in Rodero San Román (ed.), *La transición a la democracia*, 99–102.
50. Ibid., 102–3; Heywood, *Government and Politics*, 142–64.
51. Gil Manuel Hernández i Martí, 'Valencianismo fallero, franquismo y transición en Valencia' in Tussel et al. (eds.), *Historia de la transición y consolidación democrática*, vol. 2, 567–78.
52. Núñez-Seixas, 'Nacionalismos y regionalismos', 432.
53. Rafael Bañón Martínez, 'The Spanish Armed Forces during the Period of Political Transition, 1975–85' in Bánón Martínez and Barker (eds.), *Armed Forces and Society*, 311–53; Heywood, *Government and Politics*, 58–68.
54. Julio Busquets, *El militar de carrera en España*, 3rd edn (Barcelona, 1984), 140–86, figs. at 154.
55. Preston, *Triumph of Democracy in Spain*, 147–9, 195–202; Powell, *Juan Carlos*, 169–75.
56. Quoted Preston, *Juan Carlos*, 485.
57. quoted ibid., 487.
58. Jonathan Hopkins, *Party Formation and Democratic Transition in Spain: The Creation and Collapse of the Democratic Centre* (London, 1999), 189–215.
59. http://en.wikipedia.org/wiki/Spanish_general_election%2C_1982 The UCD won under 7% of votes and a mere 11 seats.
60. Sebastian Balfour, 'The Reinvention of Spanish Conservatism: the Popular Party since 1989' in Sebastian Balfour (ed.), *The Politics of Contemporary Spain* (London and New York, 2005), 146–68.
61. Xosé-Manoel Núñez Seixas, 'Conservative Spanish Nationalism since the early 1990s' in Balfour (ed.), *Politics of Contemporary Spain*, 128–9.

62. Paul Heywood, 'Governing a New Democracy: the Power of the Prime Minster in Spain', *West European Politics* 14/2 (1991), 97–115.

63. Aguilar, *Memoria y olvido*.

64. Alejando Nieto, *La organización del desgobierno* (Barcelona, 1984), 140–4.

65. Heywood, *Government and Politics*, 129–4; Santos Juliá, 'The socialist era, 1982–1996', in Alvarez Junco and Shubert (eds.), *Spanish History since 1808*, 335.

66. Heywood, *Government and Politics*, 62–6; Carlos Navajas Zubeldía, 'La política de defensa durante la transición y consolidación democráticas' in Tusell et al. (eds.), *Historia de la transición y consolidación democrática*, vol. 1, 186–92; Rafael Bañón Martínez, 'The Spanish Armed Forces during the Period of Political Transition, 1975–85' in Barrer and Bañón Martínez (eds.), *Armed Forces and Society*, 311–53.

67. Angel Viñas, *En las garras del águila: Los pactos con Estados Unidos de Francisco Franco a Felipe González, 1945–95* (Barcelona, 2003), 471–510; Heywood, *Government and Politics*, 265–70.

68. Viñas, *En las garras del águila*, 508–9; for Solana see *http://www.nato.int/cv/secgen/solana.htm*

69. Quoted Julio Crespo MacLennan, *Spain and the Process of European Integration, 1957–85* (Basingstoke, 2000), 121.

70. Edles, *Symbol and Ritual*, 57.

71. Carlos Closa and Paul M. Heywood, *Spain and the European Union* (London, 2004), 13–30.

72. Crespo MacLennan, *Spain and the Process of European Integration*, 150–79.

73. Mary Farrell, *Spain in the EU* (London, 2001), 119–20.

74. Closa and Heywood, *Spain and the European Union*, 240–5, at 245.

75. Alan Milward, *The European Rescue of the Nation-State* (2nd ed.: London, 2000), 2–19.

76. Closa and Heywood, *Spain and the European Union*, 31–5; Juan Díez Medrano and Paula Gutiérrez, 'Nested Identities: National and European Identity in Spain', *Ethnic and Racial Studies* 24/5 (2001), 753–78.

77. Quoted Díez Medrano and Gutiérrez, 'Nested Identities', 768.

78. http://www.jordipujol.com/pre_jordi_pujol.asp. More generally, see Andrew Downing, 'Convergència i Unió, Catalonia and the new Catalanism' in Balfour (ed.), *Politics of Contemporary Spain*, 106–20.

79. Michael Keating, 'European Integration and the Nationalities Question', *Politics and Society* 32/3 (2004), 367–88.

80. Ludger Mees, *Nationalism, Violence and Democracy: The Basque Clash of Identities* (London, 2003) and 'Between Votes and Bullets: Conflicting Ethnic Identities in the Basque Country', *Ethnic and Racial Studies* 24/5 (2001), 798–827; José Manuel Mata, 'Terrorism and Nationalist Conflict: the Weakness of Democracy in the Basque Country', in Balfour (ed.), *Politics of Contemporary Spain*, 81–105.

81. Paddy Woodworth, *Dirty War, Clean Hands: ETA, the GAL and Spanish Democracy* (Cork, 2001).

82. Mees, *Nationalism, Violence and Democracy*, 187.
83. Keating, 'European Integration', 343; Montserrat Guibernau, *Catalan Nationalism: Francoism, Transition and Democracy* (London, 2004), 152–65.
84. John Hargreaves and Manuel García Ferrando 'Public Opinion, National Integration and National Identity in Spain: the Case of the Barcelona Olympic Games', *Nations and Nationalism* 3/1 (1997), 65–87; Núñez-Seixas, 'Nacionalismos y regionalismos', 454.
85. Quoted Penelope Harvey, *Hybrids of Modernity: Anthropology, the Nation State and the Universal Exhibition* (London, 1996) at 61.
86. *Guía oficial Expo'92* (Seville, 1992).
87. Harvey, *Hybrids of Modernity*.
88. Luca Molinari, *Santiago Calatrava* (Milan, 1999); Dennis Sharp (ed.), *Calatrava* (London, 1994).
89. Statistics on social trends may be found at http://www.unece.org/stats/trend/contents.htm and http://www.msc.es/estadEstudios/estadisticas/inforRecopilaciones/generales.htm
90. Juan González-Anleo, 'La religiosidad española: presente y futuro' in González de Cardedal (ed.), *La Iglesia en España*, 11–57; Fundación Santa María, *La sociedad española de los 90 y sus nuevos valores* (Madrid, 1992); Carlos Alonso Zaldivár and Manuel Castells, *Spain beyond Myths* (Madrid, 1992), 21–68.

NOTES TO AFTERWORD

1. Silva and Macías, *Las fosas de Franco* and the website of the ARMH: http://www.memoriahistorica.org/; Georgina Blakeley, 'Digging Up Spain's Past: Consequences of Truth and Reconciliation', *Democratization* 12 (2005), 44–59; Madeleine Davis, 'Is Spain Recovering its Memory? Breaking the *Pacto del Olvido*', *Human Rights Quarterly* 27 (2005), 858–80.

Glossary of Spanish Terms

alcaldes	mayors
autonomías	post-1978 devolved regions or 'autonomous communities'
ayuntamientos	town councils/town halls
beata	pious woman, usually elderly
bienio	biennium, period of two years
blasquistas	followers of Blasco Ibáñez
braceros	day-labourers
caciques	local patrons/political bosses
caciquismo	political clientelism, especially electoral fixing
casa del pueblo	Socialist Party centres (lit. 'house of the people')
cenetista	member of the CNT
comarca	sub-provincial territorial division
consumos	tax on certain purchased goods
convivencia	peaceful co-existence
Cortes	Spanish parliament
corrida	bullfight
costumbrismo	genre literature and painting depicting local customs
cuerpos	specialist corps within the civil service
denuncia	denunciation; information passed to the authorities
desamortización	disentail; sale of entailed lands
desarrollo	development
diputaciones	provincial govering councils
dueño	landlord, boss
enchufismo	nepotism, favouring those known to you (lit. 'pluggism')
espadón	military champion of a political party
etarra	member of ETA
fallas	Valencia fiesta
feria	fair, local fiesta
fueros	traditional laws and privileges of the Basque Country and Navarre
fuerzas vivas	local elites or bigwigs
galego	Galician
golpe	military coup
golpista	person plotting a coup
instituto	secondary school

jefe	boss, chief
justicia al revés	reversed or 'back to front' justice
latifundio	consolidated landed estate of over 250 hectares
madrileños	inhabitants of Madrid
merienda	snack
modernisme	Barecelona's Art Nouveau style
neo-mudéjar	architectural style inspired by Islamic building
oposiciones	competitive examinations for entry to public employment
orgullo	pride
paseo	evening stroll
patria chica	home town, native area
plaza de toros	bullring
pronunciamiento	coup d'état
romería	village celebration, usually for the feast of a patron saint
ruptura	break with the past
sardana	Catalan dance, emblematic of Catalan identity
Somatén	citizens' militia
tertulia	cafe discussion group, usually all-male
turno pacífico	governmental system whereby parties alternated in power
upetista	member of Primo de Rivera's Unión Patriótica (UP)
vecinos	neighbours
zarzuela	Spanish operetta

Further Reading

This guide to further reading simply top-slices an extensive literature. More specific bibliography is given in the references.

Among numerous **single-volume histories**, Raymond Carr's *Spain, 1808–1975* (Oxford, 1982) and *Modern Spain, 1875–1980* (Oxford 1980) still hold their own. Adrian Shubert, *A Social History of Modern Spain* (London, 1990) and Gabriel Tortella, *El desarrollo de la España contemporánea* (Madrid, 1994) provide satisfying narratives of social and economic change. For cultural history, Helen Graham and Jo Labanyi (eds.), *Spanish Cultural Studies: An Introduction* (Oxford, 1995) covers the later period.

The starting point for this book was the relationship between the Spanish state and its citizens. The question of **state power** received early attention in Juan Linz, 'Early State-Building and Later Peripheral Nationalisms against the State: the Case of Spain' in S. N. Eisenstadt and Stein Rokkan (eds.), *Building States and Nations: Analyses by Region* Vol. 2 (Beverley Hills, Calif., and London, 1973) and has since been taken up sporadically by Spanish historians (for example, Juan Pablo Fusi 'Centralismo y localismo: la formación del estado español' in Guillermo Gortázar (ed.), *Nación y estado en la España liberal* (Madrid, 1994) and Julio Aróstegui, 'El estado español contemporáneo: centralismo, inarticulación y nacionalismo', *Historia conemporánea* 17 (1998)), but there has been little sustained investigation, despite an extensive comparative literature. See further, Gianfranco Poggi, *The State: its Nature, Development and Prospects* (Cambridge, 1990); Michael Mann, *The Sources of Social Power* published as *A History of Power from the Beginning to AD 1760* (Cambridge, 1986) and *The Rise of Classes and Nation-States, 1760–1914* (Cambridge, 1993); James C. Scott, *Seeing Like a State* (New Haven and London, 1998); Jane Caplan and John Torpey (eds.), *Documenting Individual Identities: The Development of State Practices in the Modern World* (Princeton, 2001); and Jennifer Milliken (ed.), *State Failure, Collapse and Reconstruction* (Oxford, 2003).

In contrast, studies of **nationalism** abound. For the nineteenth century, see José Alvarez Junco, *Mater Dolorosa: la idea de España en el siglo XIX* (Madrid, 2001) and 'La difícil nacionalización de la derecha española en la primera mitad del siglo XX', *Hispania* 209 (2001); Carlos Serrano, *El nacimiento de Carmen: símbolos, mitos, nación* (Madrid, 1999); Borja de Riquer i Permanyer, 'La débil nacionalización española del siglo XIX', *Historia Social* 20 (1994); and, more generally, Ana María García Rovira (ed.), *España ¿Nación de naciones? Ayer* 36 (Madrid, 1999) and Clare Mar-Molinero and Angel Smith (eds.), *Nationalism and the Nation in the Iberian Peninsula* (Oxford and Washington DC, 1996). On the 'ordinariness' of national feeling and the inter-relatedness of local and national identities, see Geoffrey Cubitt (ed.), *Imagining Nations* (Manchester, 1998); Tim Edensor, *National Identity, Popular Culture and Everyday Life* (Oxford,

2002; and Xosé-Manoel Núñez, 'The Region as Essence of the Fatherland: Regionalist Variants of Spanish Nationalism, 1840–1936', *European History Quarterly* 31/4 (2001).

The only feature of **state power** in the nineteenth century to have received much attention is that of policing and the army. Samuel Finer's classic study *The Man on Horseback: The Role of the Military in Politics* (London, 1962) remains illuminating, not least on segmented authority within the state. See also Gabriel Cardona, *El problema militar en España* (Madrid, 1990) and Rafael Bañón Martínez and Thomas M. Barker (eds.), *Armed Forces and Society in Spain: Past and Present* (New York, 1988). On the Civil Guard, Manuel Balbé, *Orden público y militarismo en la España constitucional, 1812–83* (Madrid, 1985) and Diego López Garrido, *La Guardia Civil y los orígenes del Estado centralista* (Barcelona, 1982). For other aspects of state power, see Francisco Comín Comín, *Hacienda y economía en la España contemporánea: El afianzamiento de la hacienda liberal 1800–74* (Madrid, 1988) and Juan Pro Ruíz, *Estado, geometría y propiedad: los orígenes del catastro en España, 1715–1941* (Madrid, 1992).

Political history is much better covered, even in English. For the main debates, see Isabel Burdiel, 'Myths of Failure, Myths of Success: New Perspectives on Nineteenth-Century Spanish Liberalism', *Journal of Modern History* 70 (1998) and, with María Cruz Romeo, 'Old and New Liberalism: The Making of the Liberal Revolution, 1808–1844', *Bulletin of Hispanic Studies* (Glasgow) 75/5 (1998); Jesús Cruz, 'An Ambivalent Revolution: the Public and the Private in the Construction of Liberal Spain', *Journal of Social History* 30 (1996) and *Los notables de Madrid: los bases sociales de la revolución liberal española* (Madrid, 2000); José María Jover Zamora (ed.), *La era isabelina y el sexenio democrático, 1834–1874* (Madrid, 1981); and Jesús Millán Cruz Romeo, 'Was the Liberal Revolution Important to Modern Spain? Political Cultures and Citizenship in Spanish History', *Social History* 29/3 (2004). On the opposite poles of radicalism and reaction, see Nigel Townson (ed.), *El republicanismo en España, 1830–1877* (Madrid, 1994) and Jordi Canal, *El carlismo* (Madrid, 2000).

For the **Restoration state**, see José Varela Ortega, *Los amigos políticos: partidos, elecciones y caciquismo en la Restauración, 1875–1900* (Madrid, 2001) and (ed.) *El poder de la influencia: geografía del caciciquismo en España, 1875–1923* (Madrid, 2001). On the growth of the state apparatus, see Francisco Villacorta Baños, *Profesionales y burócratas: Estado y poder corporativo en la España del siglo XX, 1890–1923* (Madrid, 1989) and his 'Estructura y funcionamiento de la nueva administración' in Manuel Espadas Burgos, *La época de la Restauración, 1875–1902: Estado, Política e islas de ultramar* (Madrid, 2000) On **education**, see Carolyn Boyd, *Historia Patria: Politics, History and National Identity in Spain, 1875–1975* (Princeton, 1997) and Clara Eugenia Nuñez, *La fuente de la riqueza: educación y desarrollo económico en la España contemporánea* (Madrid, 1992). The **Church** is well covered by Frances Lannon, *Privilege, Persecution, and Prophecy: the Catholic Chruch in Spain, 1875–1975* (Oxford, 1987) and William J. Calllahan, *The Catholic Church in Spain 1875–1998*, (Washington DC, 2000).

On **political violence**, see Eduardo González Calleja, *La razón de la fuerza: orden público, subversión y violencia política en la España de la Restauraración* (Madrid, 1998) and *El Mauser y el sufragio: orden pública, subversión y violencia política en* *la crisis de la Restauración, 1817–31* (Madrid, 1999) and Joaquín Romero Maura, *La romana del diablo: Ensayos sobre la violencia política en España* (Madrid, 2000). On the **rise of mass politics**, see José Alvarez Junco, *El Emperador del Paralelo: Lerroux y la demagogia populista* (Madrid, 1990) and *The Emergence of Mass Politics in Spain: Populist Demagoguery and Republican Culture, 1890–1910* (Brighton, 2002). For **Barcelona's working-class movements**, see Chris Ealham, *Class, Culture and Conflict in Barcelona 1898–1937* (London, 2005); Angel Smith (ed.), *Red Barcelona: Social Protest and Labour Mobilization in the Twentieth Century* (London, 2002); and Joaquín Romero Maura, *La 'rosa del fuego': el obrerismo barcelonés de 1988 a 1909* (Madrid, 1989).

On **urban centres** more generally, see José Luis Garcá Delgado (ed.), *Las ciudades en la modernización de España: los decenios interseculares* (Madrid, 1993); Santos Juliá, David Ringrose, and Cristina Segura, *Madrid: Historia de una capital* (Madrid, 1994); Deborah L. Parsons, *A Cultural History of Madrid: Modernism and the Urban Spectacle* (Oxford, 2003); and Robert Hughes, *Barcelona* (London, 1992).

The **post-1898 crisis** is considered in Sebastian Balfour, *The End of the Spanish Empire, 1898-1923* (Oxford, 1997); Juan Pablo Fusi and Antonio Nino (eds.), *Vísperas del 98: orígenes y antecedente de la crisis del 98* (Madrid, 1997); and Juan Pan-Montojo (ed.), *Más se perdió en Cuba: España, 1889 y la crisis de fin del siglo* (Madrid, 1998). For the **Maurist regeneration**, see María Jesús González, *Ciudadania y acción: el conservadurismo maurista 1907–23* (Madrid, 1990) and ' "Neither God nor Monster": Antonio Maura and the Failure of Conservative Reformism in Restoration Spain, (1893–1923)', *European History Quarterly* 32/3 (2002). On **1914–18**, see Gerald Meaker, 'A Civil War of Words: The Ideological Impact of the First World War on Spain, 1914–1918' in Hans A. Schmitt (ed.), *Neutral Europe between War and Revolution* (Charlottesville, Va., 1988) and Francisco J. Romero Salvadó, *Spain 1914–1918: Between War and Revolution* (London, 1999). For the **Primo de Rivera regime**, see Eduardo González Calleja, *La España de Primo de Rivera: La modernización autoritaria 1923–1930* (Madrid, 2005) and Shlomo Ben-Ami, *Fascism from Above: the Dictatorship of Primo de Rivera in Spain, 1923–1930* (Oxford, 1983).

On the **Second Republic**, see Julio Gil Pecharromán, *Historia de la Segunda República Española* (Madrid, 2002) and Paul Preston (ed.), *Revolution and War in Spain 1931–9* (London, 1984). Much of the literature debates the question of responsibility for the Civil War, for example, the contrasting works of Paul Preston, *The Coming of the Spanish Civil War* (London, 1994; 1st edn. 1978); Stanley Payne, *Spain's First Democracy: The Second Republic, 1931–6* (Madison, Wis., 1993). Nigel Townson, in *The Crisis of Democracy in Spain: Centrist Politics under the Second Republic, 1931–6* (Brighton, 2000), takes a different angle on the question. Mary Vincent, *Catholicism in the Second Spanish Republic: Religion and Politics in Salamanca, 1930–6* (Oxford, 1996) and Pamela Beth Radcliff, *From Mobilization to Civil War: The Politics of Polarization in the Spanish City of Gijón* (Cambridge, 1996) offer local studies of very different areas. Sandie Holguín, *Creating Spaniards: Culture and National Identity in Republican Spain* (Madison, Wis., 2002) examines educational policy and national feeling.

The problem of political violence—put into context in Santos Juliá (ed.), *Violencia política en la España del siglo XX* (Madrid, 2000)—was thrown into relief by the outbreak of **the Civil War**. See Stathis N. Kalyvas, *The Logic of Violence in Civil War* (Cambridge and New York, 1996). Among the classic histories of the Civil War, Ronald Fraser's, *Blood of Spain: The Experience of Civil War, 1936–9* (London, 1979), stands out. Michael Seidman, *Republic of Egos: A Social History of the Spanish Civil War* (Wis., 2002) also focuses on the lived experience of war and revolution, while the revolution itself is examined in Julián Casanova (ed.), *El sueño igualitario* (Zaragoza, 1988), Aurora Bosch, 'Collectivisations: The Spanish Revolution Revisited, 1936–39', *International Journal of Iberian Studies* 14 (2001), and Julio de la Cueva, 'Religious Persecution, Anticlerical Tradition and Revolution: on Atrocities against the Clergy during the Spanish Civil War', *Journal of Contemporary History* 33/3 (1998). Helen Graham's monographic study, *The Spanish Republic at War, 1936–9* (Cambridge, 2003) informs her *The Spanish Civil War: A Very Short Introduction* (Oxford, 2005). See also Chris Ealham and Michael Richards (eds.), *The Splintering of Spain: New Historical Perspectives on the Spanish Civil War* (Cambridge, 2005).

On **Franco's army** see Sebastian Balfour, *Deadly Embrace: Morocco and the Road to the Spanish Civil War* (Oxford, 2002), Gabriel Cardona, *El gigante descalzo: el ejército de Franco* (Madrid, 2003), and Paul Preston, *The Politics of Revenge: Fascism and the Military in Twentieth-Century Spain* (London, 1995). On mobilization in an area of high support for the rising, see Javier Ugarte Tellería, *La nueva Covadonga insurgente* (Madrid 1998). Much attention has been paid to the **Francoist repression**: see Michael Richards, *A Time of Silence: Civil War and the Culture of Repression in Franco's Spain, 1936-1945* (Cambridge, 1998); Conxita Mir Curcó, *Vivir es sobrevivir: justicia, orden y marginación en la Cataluña rural de la posguerra* (Lleida, 2000); Julián Casanova (ed.), *Morir, matar, sobrevivir: La violencia en la dictadura de Franco* (Barcelona, 2002); C. Molinero, M. Sala, and J. Sobrequés (eds.), *Una inmensa prisión: los campos de concentración y las prisiones durante la guerra civil y el Franquismo* (Barcelona, 2003) and Julius Ruiz, *Franco's Justice: Repression in Madrid after the Spanish Civil War* (Oxford, 2005).

The relationship between **fascism and Francoism** has been long debated. See Stanley Payne, *Fascism in Spain, 1923–1977* (Madison, Wis., 1999); Ismael Saz Campos, *Fascismo y franquismo* (Valencia, 2004) and 'Fascism, fascitization and developmentalism in Franco's dictatorship', *Social History* 29/3 (2004) and, on the dictator himself, Paul Preston's *Franco: A Biography* (London, 1993). Less work has been done on the **consolidation of the Francoist regime**, but see Antonio Cazorla-Sánchez, *Las políticas de la Victoria: La consolidación del Nuevo Estado franquista, 1938–1953* (Madrid, 2000) and 'Beyond "They Shall Not Pass": How the Experience of Violence Reshaped Political Values in Franco's Spain', *Journal of Contemporary History* 40/3 (2005); and Angela Cenarro, 'Elite, Party Church: Pillars of the Francoist "New State" in Aragon, 1936–45', *European History Quarterly* 28/4 (1998) and *La sonrisa de Falange: Auxilio Social en la guerra civil y en la posguerra* (Barcelona, 2006).

Stanley Payne, *The Franco Regime, 1936–75* (Madison, Wis., 1987) covers the entire regime while José V. Casanova, 'The Opus Dei Ethic, the Technocrats and the Modernization of Spain', *Social Science Information* 22/1 (1983) looks at Spain's development. Cultural history may be approached through Luis de Llera Esteban (ed.), *La modernización cultural de España, 1898-1975* (Madrid, 2000) and Jorge Uría (ed.), *La cultura popular en la España contemporánea* (Madrid, 2003). Changing patterns of consumption are considered in Aurora Morcillo, *True Catholic Womanhood: Gender Ideology in Franco's Spain* (DeKalb, Ill., 2000). For **rural Spain**, see Julian Pitt-Rivers, *The People of the Sierra* (London, 1954); Carmelo Lisón Tolosana, *Belmonte de los Caballeros* (Oxford, 1966); and Ronald Fraser, *The Pueblo: A Mountain Village on the Costa del Sol* (Newton Abbot, 1974).

The growing divergence between people and state is examined in Víctor Pérez-Díaz, *The Return of Civil Society: The Emergence of Democratic Spain* (Cambridge, Mass. 1993). Studies of the **anti-Francoist opposition** include José María Maravall, *Dictatorship and Political Dissent* (London, 1978) and Sebastian Balfour, *Dictatorship, Workers and the City: Labour in Greater Barcelona since 1939* (Oxford, 1989). For the Church, see Feliciano Montero García, *La Acción Católica en el Franquismo: Auge y crisis de la Acción Católica especializada* (Madrid, 2000); Olegario González de Cardedal (ed.), *La Iglesia en España, 1950-2000* (Madrid, 1999); and Lannon, *Privilege, Persecution, and Prophecy*. For ETA, see Robert P. Clark, *The Basque Insurgents: ETA, 1952–1980* (Madison, Wis., 1984); Joseba Zulaika, *Basque Violence: Metaphor and Sacrament* (Reno, Nev., 1988); Marianne Heiberg, *The Making of the Basque Nation* (Cambridge, 1989); and Ludger Mees, *Nationalism, Violence and Democracy: The Basque Clash of Identities* (London, 2003).

There is an extensive comparative political science literature on **transitions to democracy**: see Juan J. Linz and Alfred Stepan, *Problems of Democratic Transition and Consolidation* (London and Baltimore, 1996) and Richard Gunther, Nikiforos Diamandouros, and Hans-Jürgen Puhle, *Politics of Democratic Consolidation* (Baltimore, 1995). Studies of the Spanish transition include José María Maravall, *The Transition to Democracy in Spain* (London and New York, 1982); Paul Preston, *The Triumph of Democracy in Spain* (London, 1986); José Féliz Tezanos, Ramón Cotarelo, and Andrés de Blas (eds.), *La transición democrática española* (Madrid, 1989); and Manuel Redero San Román (ed.), *La transición a la democracia en España, Ayer* 15 (Madrid, 1994). The focus on elite political actors that dominates many of these studies is countered in Santos Juliá, Javier Pradera, and Joaquín Prieto (eds.), *Memoria de la transición* (Madrid, 1996). See also José Casanova, 'Modernization and Democratization: Reflections on Spain's Transition to Democracy', *Social Research* 50 (1983); and, on the regional question, Montserrat Guibernau, *Catalan Nationalism: Francoism, Transition and Democracy* (London, 2004) and Mees, *Nationalism, Violence and Democracy*.

Much historical attention is currently being paid to the **memory of the Civil War**: see Paloma Aguilar, *Memory and Amnesia: the Memory of the Spanish Civil War in the Transition to Democracy* Oxford, 2003) and Santos Juliá (ed.), *Memoria de la guerra y del franquimso* (Madrid, 2006). Many sources are available for the study of **contemporary Spain**, but the following remain excellent starting points: Sebastian Balfour (ed.), *The Politics of Contemporary Spain* (London and New York, 2005); Carlos Closa and Paul M. Heywood, *Spain and the European Union* (London, 2004); and Paul Heywood, *The Government and Politics of Spain* (London, 1995).

Index